科技法学论丛
Science and Technology Law Series

《科技法学论丛》编辑委员会

主　　任 王家福

编辑委员会成员（按姓氏拼音顺序排列）

　　　　　段瑞春　范建得　冯震宇　刘江彬

　　　　　刘尚志　罗玉中　王家福　吴汉东

　　　　　杨立范　易继明　张新宝　郑成思

　　　　　郑中人　周汉华　朱苏力

论丛主编 易继明

The Development and Reformation of Electronic Contract under the Knowledge Economy Era

知识经济下电子合同之发展与变革

林瑞珠 ◎著

北京大学出版社
PEKING UNIVERSITY PRESS

图书在版编目(CIP)数据

知识经济下电子合同之发展与变革/林瑞珠著.—北京:北京大学出版社,2005.11
(科学法学论丛)
ISBN 978 – 7 – 301 – 09528 – 7

Ⅰ.知… Ⅱ.林… Ⅲ.电子商务 – 合同法 – 研究 – 中国
Ⅳ.D923.64

中国版本图书馆 CIP 数据核字(2005)第 094354 号

书　　　名：知识经济下电子合同之发展与变革
著作责任者：林瑞珠　著
责 任 编 辑：邹记东
标 准 书 号：ISBN 978 – 7 – 301 – 09528 – 7/D·1271
出 版 发 行：北京大学出版社
地　　　址：北京市海淀区成府路 205 号　100871
网　　　址：http://www.pup.cn
电　　　话：邮购部 62752015　发行部 62750672　编辑部 62752027
　　　　　　出版部 62754962
电 子 邮 箱：law@ pup.pku.edu.cn
印　 刷 　者：三河新世纪印务有限公司
经 销 　者：新华书店
　　　　　　650 毫米×980 毫米　16 开本　21.5 印张　367 千字
　　　　　　2005 年 11 月第 1 版　2007 年 7 月第 2 次印刷
定　　　价：33.00 元

未经许可,不得以任何方式复制或抄袭本书之部分或全部内容。
版权所有,侵权必究
举报电话:010 – 62752024　电子邮箱:fd@ pup.pku.edu.cn

目　　录

1 绪论 …………………………………………………………………… (1)
　1.1　动机与目的 ………………………………………………………… (1)
　1.2　研究方法 …………………………………………………………… (4)
　1.3　研究之理念与重点 ………………………………………………… (6)

2 当前两岸有关电子商务议题的发展与适应 ………………………… (19)
　2.1　大陆电子商务发展现况与调整 …………………………………… (19)
　2.2　台湾地区电子商务发展现况与调整 ……………………………… (39)

3 以电子数据交换法制为基础的电子贸易 …………………………… (57)
　3.1　无纸化交易环境的形成 …………………………………………… (57)
　3.2　电子数据交换的产生背景及发展 ………………………………… (58)
　3.3　使用电子数据交换的主要法律问题 ……………………………… (72)
　3.4　通过电子数据交换缔结合同所生的主要问题 …………………… (88)
　3.5　应用电子数据交换的解决方案 …………………………………… (94)

4 电子合同的成立与生效 ……………………………………………… (102)
　4.1　电子化交易环境的形成 …………………………………………… (102)
　4.2　传统国际贸易合同的法源 ………………………………………… (105)
　4.3　合同电子化的相关问题 …………………………………………… (122)

5 论电子交易的管辖 …………………………………………………… (150)
　前言 ……………………………………………………………………… (150)
　5.1　概说传统管辖权 …………………………………………………… (150)
　5.2　电子交易中管辖权问题的缘起与冲击 …………………………… (152)
　5.3　国际立法与美国实务的发展 ……………………………………… (154)
　5.4　解决网络管辖权冲突问题的寻思 ………………………………… (172)
　5.5　结语 ………………………………………………………………… (180)

6 电子合同之因应与建议 ································· (182)
6.1 电子合同之法理新思维 ··························· (182)
6.2 电子合同法制化之建议 ··························· (189)

致谢 ··· (196)

参考文献 ··· (198)

附录
1. 两岸电子商务合同法制对照表 ···················· (209)
2. A/CN.9/WG.IV/WP.108 ···························· (211)
3. UNIDROIT PRINCIPLES OF INTERNATIONAL
   COMMERCIAL CONTRACTS 2004 ···················· (232)
4. PRELIMINARY DRAFT CONVENTION ON
   EXCLUSIVE CHOICE OF COURT AGREEMENTS ············ (270)

1 绪 论

1.1 动机与目的

回顾电子商务的发展历程,先是网络科技带给人类前所未有的希望,这是一种弹指间神游世界的梦想。然而快速但不切实际的资本市场操作,却让网络科技在具体孕育出网络产业前将网络的商务应用推入泡沫化的危机,在历经去芜存菁的演变过程后,我们很欣慰地看到各个方面的发展渐趋成熟。首先,我们看到网络应用科技已逐渐协助企业迈入 E 化的环境,而电子交易的选择也日趋多元,尤其在政府本身 E 化速度加快以及网络金流问题逐渐获得解决后,电子商务已然不再只是一种会幻灭的梦想,而是真实存在于你我之间的交易类型。面对这种发展,我们看到电子商务的发展也随经济理论由信息经济进一步延伸为知识经济或新经济,日益成熟。此时社会的需求已不再仅是概念式的诠释电子商务的概念,相对地,大家必须很清楚地了解他们在谈论的电子商务是怎样的交易? 如何界定交易? 如何厘清交易内容? 如何保护消费者? 依经济理论来说,交易的信息不明将导致交易双方无法期待从而无从形成供需体制。准此,在社会需求已然形成而整体社会体制仍未臻成熟之际,除了期待政府协力外,如何借助既有之商业惯例更是重要。这也是早期贸易领域中之电子数据交换(Electronic Data Interchange, EDI)为国际间电子商务实务所重视,并借重其自律机制发展电子交易国际规范之因。发展至今,虽然许多电子交易的规范均已成型,然则在涉及交易标的电子信息化时,其本身有别于传统商品及服务的特性,不断衍生出许多原有民商法律无法涵盖的问题,尤其在电子交易之标的为信息之本身时,其牵涉的基本适用法律已不再限于民商法,更及于知识产权法。这也是为何美国在电子商务初始的 1997 年即积极在电子商务政策纲领,及之后的千禧年著作权法案与 WIPO 修法中,推动著作权保护领域之扩大及于网络接取权(public access right)等的原因所在。整体言之,知识经济必须始于对知识属性交易标的之保护与权利界定,而这也是在交易发生之初就必须具备者。然则一旦新类型的交易标的(信息或知识)在知识产权架构下获得保障,则民法的交易法规必然面对其交易属性无法为原有法制所涵盖的尴尬处境,从而民法的修改或调整无法避免,此可证之于联合国贸易法律委员会之立法趋势、美国的计算机信息交易法与中国的合同法。本书之撰写即在于对应知识交易环境之发展,侧重于整体电子交易应有之调适部分,然将范围局限在国际贸易惯例所及之合同领域,而以电子合同为研究重点。

面对电子商务之发展,知识经济的兴起逐渐将传统的交易环境推向全球化、科技化与多元化个性化的方向,这对于用来规范并促进变迁中交易行为之法制而言,是一大挑战。此带给合同法制之冲击,主要呈现在对原有的信任基础、法律的基本原则与交易惯例产生的根本性之质疑,此亦系牵动电子合同法制兴革方向的重要因素。基本上,交易当事人得不利用纸与笔来完成其交易时,传统书面形式和签章都将被计算机网络中传输之数位资讯所取代时,此亦隐含书面形式与签章之概念需重新加以界定。最早的合同电子化发展系以电子数据交换模式来呈现,以实务运作经验言,虽被认为是无纸化交易发展过程中的重要里程碑,惟其于发展过程中亦遭遇难以突破之法律问题,如:(1) 书面形式之问题;(2) 签章之问题;(3) 证据法上之问题。如何解决传统法律所要求之文书形式与无纸交易特性之兼容性问题,便成为电子交易法制化之发展重点。而为因应电子交易法制化发展之需求,联合国及国际商会等组织快速投入电子交易法律之建构,在可预见的未来电子交易法制将呈现出从国际到国内的统一化趋势,应如何配合全球化的法制发展趋势,以利新世纪交易之进行,已成为两岸中国人所不可忽视之法律研究课题。基此,本书特以既有国际贸易规范出发并就联合国国际贸易法律委员会(UNCITRAL)于2001年起着手研议《藉数据电文缔结或证明之(国际)合同公约草案初稿》(Preliminary Draft Convention on [International] Contracts Concluded or Evidenced by Data Messages)[①]发展趋势,加以评析以为借鉴。

---

① 本草案系根据联合国国际贸易法律委员会电子商务工作小组第38届会议决议而来,工作小组近期将于2004年10月11—22日假维也纳第43届会议中提出公约草案初稿,并送交国际贸易法律委员会会议审议, United Nations Commission on International Trade Law Working Group on Electronic Commerce, Forty-third session, A/CN.9/WG.IV/WP.108.(2004)。

随着国际规范内国化之发展历程,电子合同的问题①,亦从早期的假设性探讨及侧重电子交易合同之研究,进入内国法制定后之具体适用问题。以台湾地区之发展经验而言,虽电子签章法已正式颁行,但该法尚无法完全解决电子交易所须面临的民事问题,故电子合同的探讨,除电子签章法之规定外,亦应就其与现有民事法规之关联性与兼容性加以涵盖:例如,在当事人身份之确认问题上,有关电子签章与传统签章观念之差异性②;在自动化计算机系统与电子代理之应用问题上,有关民法代理规定之适用可能性;在数字商品为交易标的之问题上,有关民法中权利客体概念之适用;在非对话意思表示之生效时点问题上,有关生效时点认定与意思表示撤回之可能性等,均其着例。此外,究应如何判断电子合同缔结过程中,电子讯息的出处或归属?如何评价"再确认"机制之法律性质?均有待吾人加以探究。对此,本书拟以民事合同之基本规范为基础,遵循网络规范之发展模式,自国际而内国的角度来检视当前台湾地区电子合同法制所面临之挑战;其中将纳入电子签章法颁行后所涉之问题,及其与国际规范或其他国家相关法律制度发展方向之歧异,进而回归到基础民事法相关规定之探讨,以作为两岸后续法规调适之参考。

继前述民商法相关的基础性探讨,纠纷之处理乃研究电子合同法制不可或缺的一环,而电子化环境的冲击,也确未错过此部分。以电子合同之民事管辖课题言,于传统电子数据交换交易中,当事人间往往透过前置协议来决定双方之通讯设备与网域或网址名称,从而形成以协议来取得管辖基础之做法,此虽较无争议,唯于涉外管辖中自律安排应否加以承认则成问题。再者,随网络交易机制之发展,运用自动化交易系统与数字商品交易时,合同成立、生效时点之认定,成为影响管辖决定因素之重要课题。目前,虽已有论者开始就这类问题加以着墨,但如何自既有相关理论出发,掌握信息社会之特殊性,进而提出可能解决方向的全面性思考,仍有努力之空间,就此本文拟针对涉外电子合同之民事管辖课题之缘起及其可能之解决方案为探讨。

最后,本书将在结论中,具体对于相关法制建设之课题与应有努力方

---

① 本文所称电子合同,系指狭义之电子合同而言。盖广义的电子合同,是指以数据电文形式订立的合同,其方式包括但不限于电子数据交换、电子邮件、电报、电传与传真等方式;从狭义而言,电子合同系指以电子数据交换、电子邮件等电子信息的形式,通过计算机互联网缔结之商品或服务交易合同。赵金龙、任学婧:《论电子合同》,载《当代法学》2003年第8期,第43页。

② Mohammad Nsour, "Articlefundamental Facets of the United States-Jordan Free Trade Agreement: E-commerce, Dispute Resolution, and Beyond", *Wash. U. J. L. & Pol'y* 2004 (27): 742.

向提出建议。以中国大陆而言,现代化或工业化是改革开放后的首要任务,随网络环境之蓬勃发展,信息化社会之建设已成为平行于工业化之另一要务,这其中电子交易之重要性或其法律制度之建设,都成为政府当局所重视之课题,甚至成为其"十五"计划之重要主题。究竟这些发展涵括了哪些重点,与国际间当前之发展趋势是否相契合,都是值得观察之重点。毕竟中国之现代化步伐方兴,市场机制之经验尚在累积,如何自其发展过程中重要课题之掌握,对照国际规范与台湾地区法规之发展经验,以勾画出当前电子交易环境对合同法制之影响,均为本书探讨之重点。

1.2 研究方法

从华人的角度来观察世界法律的发展脉络,虽不难理解其动态与内容,然以大陆当前在国际社会所受重视程度,以及其在国际社会中之各种参与经验,其法制自社会主义、社会主义市场经济到现今接近一般的市场经济,整个过程乃同时植基于现代化与信息化双轨并进的轨道上,这种经验是世界上少有的。值此之际,如何在全球相关法制发展的愿景中,以台湾地区既有且较能衔接资本市场观点的法律研究为基础,进行与大陆现行充分与国际接轨之发展原则的科技法制加以比较研究,进而厘清两岸未来研究大陆电子合同法制度时之诠释理念,并将此种观点发展成为具国际学术研究价值的课题,在研究方法的运用上,随研究进度与内容的需求,至少会使用到下列不同的方法:

一、资料之搜集

在研究初期,会先进行相关资料之搜集,除传统的数据搜集方式外,将大量使用计算机辅助检索工具,如 West-Law 与 Lexis-Nexis 等。惟,鉴于电子数据之过度引用足以减损论文之学术价值与可信度,故此所有检索成果仍将以直接使用原件为主。此外,原始资料(primary authority)之使用亦将为本研究处理资料过程中的基本原则,以求立论基础之真确。

二、归纳分析方法

针对搜集到之资料,将采行归纳分析方法配合研究提纲加以汇整,以凸现相关问题之核心及其成因,此外,此方面之分析成果,也将被据以作为建构研究大纲之基础与立论凭据。

三、演绎法

除上述之归纳方法外,同时并将针对搜集到的数据,按所谓之演绎法加以分析处理,冀能自其中发现与研究提纲所需论证相关之观点,以为研究立论之用;研究成果之撰写将同时强调"法律现象"——"法制检讨"——"问题之提出"——"解决方式"之逻辑思考,希望以事实的掌握来印证法制之不足,进而呈现问题之所在,以为进一步探求解决方式之依据。

四、比较法学

比较法学方法之使用早已在法界蔚然成风,本研究除延用此方法外,更将强调比较法学探求法律体制之基本差异的精神,在完成初步资料整理分析工作后,以两岸之特殊需求为核心,来从事不同国家间的法制异同研究,使外国法例之引用不致流于概念化之堆砌,而能自外国法律之基本原则与考量出发,具体反映出在参考援引时所容有之本土化思考。

五、历史方法

为落实前述各种方法之使用,完整掌握各种法律之源起、变革与发展趋势均成为必须,而这也正是本研究使用历史方法之价值;是以,在前述基础上,本研究将特别针对援用参考之国内外法例从事历史方法之研究,以知其规定之所以然。

六、经济分析法学

对于科技相关法律之研究言,经济分析方法之使用容有其特殊价值,故此,在前述研究基础上,本研究将援用经济分析之方法来探求应有法制之理性基础,就研究方向言,基于法制化过程中的发展充满了不确定性,不论是涉及民商法或自治理念的电子商务交易法制,抑或就管理与推动相关发展所须的公法上规范体制言,经济分析就如何降低交易成本与促进交易之发展以发挥法制之效益(efficiency),均有积极之贡献。故此,虽然本研究并不认为经济分析的结果能当然取代法律的判断,然则经济分析能提供法学研究一个更具体而有说服力的方向,则确系本文采用此种方法的重要理由与期待。

七、政策分析法学

所谓政策分析法学系指由政策导向（Policy-oriented）法学者就法律与公共秩序（public orders）之关系加以探究（inquiry）时采行的方法。其主要步骤为：（1）界定目标（思考之目标）；（2）检视过往的发展趋势（passed trend）；（3）分析可能之变量（此属科学思维）；（4）预拟未来之可能发展；及（5）替代政策之探讨与评估。本研究之最终目的仍在于对于国家社会之需求提出建言，故而政策分析法学之运用亦同具重要性。本书之研究将参考此研究方法，希望让研究成果亦能供做未来立法及决策上之参考。

1.3 研究之理念与重点

本书的撰写，意在对电子合同法制部分加以说明，以国际组织与各主要工业国家的发展为借鉴，作为探讨主题；以下谨针对"研究的滥觞"、"电子商务的发展对合同法制的影响"与"电子合同的发展及其变革"分述本书的研究理念与重点如下：

一、研究的滥觞

近年来因特网[①]（Internet）自被普遍地使用在商业上以来，各国无不对之投以相当的关注。伴随着整个社会环境的信息化，数字化环境下电子商务[②]的发展已全面冲击到世界上的每一个角落，这种冲击甚至被誉为自工业革命以来的另一次工业革命。至 1998 年，全球网络人口已突破 2 亿万人，网络主机则超过 2000 万台。美国著名的研究公司 Forrester Research 也指出，1998 年是电子商务真正萌芽并茁壮成长的一年，该年度网上交易额已高达 510 亿美元，其中企业对企业部分为 430 亿美元，企业对

[①] Internet 为没有中央控管、全球性的计算机和网络的集合，过去仅供美国国家实验室及高科技界从事学术交流。1980 年代末期开放使用后，网际网络串联了全球一百多个国家的计算机网络，遍布各地的学术界、政府机构与工商界的数千万计算机使用者都能借着这个网络，跨越国界交流信息。Nicholas Negroponte：《数位革命》，齐若兰译，台北：天下出版社 1995 年版，第 315—316 页。

[②] 所谓电子商务，是指物理性的交换或不通过直接的物理性接触，而由当事人不拘形式通过电子通讯进行商业性交易。电子商务可以从"特定企业间的交易（闭锁式的电子资料交换）；即 Electronic Data Interchange，简称 EDI），亦即公司与公司间的连结"；"利用网络，企业与个人（消费者）间发生的商业交易"；"不特定企业间的交流，亦即利用网际网络与他企业间联系、进行电子商业交易"等三种方向来加以诠释。牧野和夫：《电子商务取引法（EC LAW）之现状》，载《国际商事法务》1988 年第 7 期，第 738 页。

一般终端用户部分则为80亿美元①;按照这个发展趋势,美国Jupiter Communication研究单位更预测至2005年时,美国B2B市场将有超过6兆美元的产值,此一数字将占美国B2B非服务支出(non-service spending)项目总额的42%②,从而也使电子商务成为从事商业交易、行销及广告等商业行为所不可避免的重要工具及媒介;换而言之,就其将提供给全球消费者、制造者、销售者及企业经营者的功能或机会而言,网际网络上的电子商务将发展出一个潜力无穷的市场机会,各国无不积极展开对于这些机会的把握。

美国1997年春天在WTO提出的电子商务政策纲领,就是为配合全球贸易电子化的发展及贸易版图的重新分配所提出的游戏规范蓝图。在其政策宣示中,美国提出所谓的五大基本原则及九大议题③,一时间,美国俨然成为主导国际贸易电子化过程的主要力量。近来,美国更是将这种意图反映在亚太经合会议(APEC)的议题上,并于1998年新加坡召开的会议中强力运作,促使APEC通过了几项与电子商务发展密切相关的原则,这些充分体现了美国主导这方面发展的企图。其他诸如欧洲1998年提出的有关电子商务交易的相关指令④;日本自1996年开始推动电子认证等相关制度⑤,并于2001年4月1日开始实施电子签名及认证业务相关法律;新加坡1998年伴随电子交易法的通过产生的发展,以及台湾地

---

① 果芸:《企业如何运用电子商务赚钱》,载《信息与计算机》1999年第4期,第738页。
② http://www.find.org.tw/news_disp.asp?news_id=870(visited 2004/7/19)。
③ 有关美国所提出的政策纲领,请参见:《电子商务概述》,国际贸易局1997年版,台北:"经济部"国际贸易局,第28页;另请参阅网址http://www.whitehouse.gov/WH/New/Commerce/summary-plan.html(visited 1998/2/21);其纲要如下:
(一)五大基本原则:1.私人企业应居领导地位;2.政府应避免对电子商务为不必要的限制;3.政府参与的目的支持及实施一个可预测的、最小化的、持续的、及简单的商业法律环境;4.政府应肯认网际网络的独特性质;5.网际网络上电子商务的推动应以全球为基础。
(二)九大议题:1.财务方面:(1)关务与税捐的课征;(2)电子付款系统的建立。2.法律方面:(1)统一商法典的制定;(2)知识产权的保护;(3)隐私权的保障;(4)网际网络的安全机制。3.市场方面:(1)对电信基础架构与信息科技的建构;(2)对网络内容及广告的管制;(3)对技术标准的决定。
④ 有关欧洲的发展,严格来说欧洲目前还没有统一的电子商务法规,但为了避免各会员国间因法规不同造成电子商务发展的障碍,欧联刻正建构一共同法律架构,其中与电子商务议题直接有关的,包括远距合约、电子商务、电子签章及数据保护等。详请参阅欧联内部电子商务法律指令草案,详见"经济部"国贸局贸(八八)三发字第〇九六八一号函及"经济部"贸易局编,"台湾地区参与国际经贸事务项目小组电子商务工作分组"1988年度第二次会议议程(1999.09.03)。
⑤ 有关日本的发展,请参见:《电子取引法制に关す研究会(制度关系小委员会)报告书ヅュリスト》(特集·电子取引法制のあり方),1998(7):14—32。

区"行政院"于 1999 年 7 月 1 日积极推动的产业自动化与电子化方案[①],均透露出各国家、地区积极介入这方面发展的意图。基本上,电子商务的发展已被认为至少将加速国际贸易的发展速度达 6 倍以上,按联合国贸易与发展组织(UNCTAD)发布的《电子商务与发展报告》表明,截至 2002 年底,全球互联网用户数目约有 5.91 亿人口,年增长率 20%[②]。此外,甚至有估计,到 2006 年,全球电子商务交易额将占到全球贸易总额的 18% 左右[③],从而彻底改变贸易分配的版图。

随着网际网络时代的来临,EDI 在 1990 年左右开始被进一步的运用,并通过网络缩短了与现实世界的距离,不属于传统贸易类型的诸多网络交易模式也随之诞生,这其中包括了所谓的 B to B(商人对商人)、B to C(商人对消费者)、C to C(消费者对消费者)等类型,也影响到了传统民商法的分野。其次,网络交易所涉及的相关交易主体的出现,也冲击到了原有的民商法体系,这其中有人及人的意志延伸的问题,更有电子代理(electronic agent)与虚拟(virtual)主体的影响,从而对于以合同自由及当事人真意的探讨为基础的传统法制而言,如何重新建构出能一并适用于各种交易主体的合同法原则至为重要。再者,由于技术本身的发展性,以及交易发生的欠缺地域或法域限制性,主权的概念与管制的可能都会受到稀释,从而使得合同本身的执行力或拘束力也同样的受到影响。因此,如何诠释合同的成立、生效,又如何来履行合同,这些都牵涉到法律对同时存在于虚拟环境与实体社会中的合同行为的认知与诠释,而这也将是对于整体执法体系的一大考验。

电子合同的出现,已经对传统的民商法造成了相当的冲击,而在探讨其相关的问题时,首先应当回到对于早期 EDI 交易经验的把握,透过 EDI 的发展,我们可以看出人们如何对于无纸化的电子交易建立信心,如何在虚拟与实体之间来运作;此外,伴随电子商务发展而来的诸多问题,显然不如传统 EDI 那样单纯,因为在欠缺预设协议的基础上,网络上的当事人往往是以几无时间差的方式,在互不认识的情形下交易。如何去探求一个能一并适用于各种合同类型的法律原则,确实是不容易。如果 EDI 的实施经验得以被使用来作为探讨无纸化电子交易法制的基础,那么 EDI

---

① 台湾地区"经济部"此方面的努力请参阅其网站资料,请查阅台湾地区"经济部"商业司,网址为 http://www.moea.gov.tw(visited 2004/7/30)。
② 其中,欧洲互联网用户占全球用户的 31.5%,亚太地区占 30.9%,北美地区占 30.1%,拉丁美洲占 5.5%,非洲和中东各占 1%。参 http://www.unctad.org(visited 2004/7/30)。
③ 中国电子商务协会,参见 http://www.ec.org.cn(visited 2004/7/30)。

发展至今所遇到的主要问题,自然也应被作为探讨的课题。其中比较重要的基础性问题有:(1) 书面形式的问题;(2) 签章的问题;(3) 证据法上的问题。如何解决传统法律所要求的文书形式与 EDI 贸易中无纸特性的兼容性问题,正是我们在探讨贸易电子化的问题时首先面对的法律课题。因此,这部分的探讨应是本文所要强调的最主要课题。

实际上,国际贸易中所使用的电子数据交换应是最早的电子商务类型,只不过原先所采用的封闭式系统,以及限于商人对商人(贸易伙伴)间的交易模式,远不如当前电子商务下合同类型的多元化;而随着近来加值网络(Value Added Network)与信息服务提供者(Information Service Provider)的日益盛行,原本国际贸易合同所使用的 EDI,已经逐渐走向开放式,而且随着电子商务的发展而提供跨国即时交易的机会,不论是将信息类型商品直接传输,还是以邮递方式交付,新的支付工具及具较高安全性的安全付款机制,如 SSL 或 SET 等,都已将国际贸易的战场,由商人与商人之间拉近到商人与最终商品使用者之间,从而也导致国际贸易的概念愈来愈接近电子商务。究其根源,应在于传统贸易商以对信息的掌握来争取提供服务机会的优势已经丧失,在全球信息架构将逐渐建构完成个人虚拟网络(private virtual network)的今天,贸易过程的基本行为,如招商、下单、押汇、汇兑、保险、运送、交付等都会随着电子商务基本架构的规划完成,而被纳入电子交易的环境中;是以,未来贸易商所必须处理的,除了不可避免的实物交付外,可能都可以通过电子环境或电子工具、媒介来完成;换言之,除了必要的物流外,讯息流、金流与其他物流都将能通过电子交易模式来完成。面对电子商务发展的压力,国际贸易领域中的 EDI 也在国际商会(ICC)与联合国的主导下,展开了新一轮的规划。

以目前的法律研究来说,对于法律现象的掌握往往是零碎而片面的,或以介绍 EDI 为主,或以介绍国家信息基础建设(National Information Infrastructure)所涉及的问题为内容,少有以法律现象为基础,从对法律关系的把握切入权利义务内容,进而具体掌握法制方面应有的思考的。换而言之,我们可以很容易地从外国的发展经验中感到自己的不足,但是法律的建构或调整却不能是片断而无体系的,这一点在思考传统国际贸易的问题时更为突出。由于国际贸易的本质具有国际性,除了国际条约外,国际惯例在规范其交易关系上都具有重要的地位,此外,由于国际贸易合同的本质通常属于买卖,所以各国民商法对此也都有不同的规范,从而必须通过国际私法来调整其管辖与法律适用问题。

然而,在从事电子交易的相关研究时,我们必须了解,由于电子交易所涉及的问题多具有国际性,所以以比较法的方式来探讨很有必要,但是我们应该注意英美法系与大陆法系之间的理念差异,国内相关法制的特殊性也都应该适当地被纳入考量,以免有指鹿为马或东施效颦之误。至于属民商合一的制度下的台湾地区,对于合同关系的诠释,较接近大陆法系的概念,所以在援引英美法系的文献时,应对法系间体系上的差异有所了解。例如在合同的效力问题上,英美法系的"约因"(consideration)一向有关键地位,然而相对的这个合同要素并不存在于大陆法系的合同法制中,而且也不等同于对价观念,因此在使用英美文献时应有所注意。这方面的问题还存在于诸如"发信主义"或"到达主义"的适用上的差异,对于证据法则的规定等不一而足,但却都与法律关系的界定密切相关。尤其在美国统一计算机信息交易法(Uniform Computer Information Transaction Act;U.C.I.T.A.)中纳入新的交易标的——信息(information),并以信息交易(information transaction)合同来界定这种类型的"买卖"(sales)后,如何以这种商品的交易为核心,重新掌握其交易的法律关系,更是大陆法系国家在思考如何调整对电子交易的规范时所必须特别重视的内容。以上这些尝试融合不同法系与国际间规范发展趋势的努力,则是本文自诩对电子合同法制的发展有所贡献之所在。

二、电子商务的发展对合同法制的影响

正如大家所知,随着当今电子科技、通讯技术的不断进展,以及家庭中个人计算机的普及、参与网际网络人口的遽增,网际网络上电子交易也将倍增。此时,鉴于电子交易的交易环境虚拟化,导致传统以书面性为前提的法规范环境将有所不足;所以,思考如何重新建构电子交易当事人间的法律上的权利义务,十分必要,从而也引发了所谓"虚拟(cyber)合同法"、"虚拟电子商务法"或"虚拟民法"等新法律分野的探讨。因为如果从交易的交涉、成立或履行等实务来看,既然是通过计算机网络或网际网络来完成,那么在探讨其对传统合同法制的影响时,应该可以就下列三种交易形态来看[①]:第一种,是指特定企业间交易以使用所谓"电子数据交换(Electronic Data Interchange,EDI)"的方法完成的,这是特定企业间(集团公司内或相关公司间等)的电子数据交换;第二种,是利用网际网络来进行的企业与个人(消费者)间的电子商业交易,例如消费者在网际网络中

---

① 牧野和夫:《电子商取引法(EC LAW)の现状について(1)—总论および电子契约法〔上〕》,《国际商事法务》,1988,26(7):738—739。

所谓"虚拟（cyber）商场"购物的情形；第三种，是克服电子数据交换中无法与不特定企业交流的封闭特性，以交换电子数据的方式利用相关公司间的网络（公开的网络），与其他集团企业进行电子商业交易的情形。原则上，这三种交易形态都属于电子交易的类型。①

而在电子商务交易中，合同的要约、承诺、成立以及该合同的债务履行或完成，全在计算机网络或网际网络上进行。例如：在"虚拟（cyber）商场"中购物，利用该网络进行下订单、接受订货、交货等都属于新类型的法律行为，也是当前各国必须调整现有法规以与其适应的重点。以发展最快的美国来说，由于其传统合同法制至今仍以书面交易为前提，导致现有法规范及其延伸的规定都无法适应这种情况，从而导致统一商法典（Uniform Commercial Code, U.C.C.）面临自1951年U.C.C.制定以来的最大规模的修改。② 而日本，其国内也已经开始探讨电子化社会的法制对应之道，例如，在1996年7月，其法务部就确认，以书面为前提的现行法制已无法面对急速扩展的电子商务，从而决定招揽各方专业人士，组成研究会，着手研拟相关的法律规范。近来，日本又提出了应该从数字签章立法着手，并先确立完善认证机制（Certificate Authority，简称CA）的政策。③

而以实务观点来看，网际间的商务，已不仅是计算机间资料交换的问题，甚至更直接地影响了公司的营销策略及市场力；因此，随着这不断扩大的领域，我们在策划公司的各种活动时，都必须重新纳入电子商务的配合，而其中涉及信息和服务交换的安排，将是最不可缺少的一环。这也正足以解释前文美国推动U.C.C第2B条（现为计算机信息交易法）的立法缘由。基本上，本书相信，电子商务在各种层次领域会发展出更新的技术，使得成本下降、效率增加；换而言之，电子商务创造了一个开放的市场空间，使整个价值链中人们自发的互动、提供人际关系的管理平台，以及赋予消费者在购买过程中更强的决定能力，这都是过去EDI所未及的。此外，电子商务的发展也提供了一个买卖商品的途径，但如果我们只把网际商务当作是另一个复制的买卖关系，可能它所带来的利润并不会使人

---

① 管知之：《电子商取引に関おる诸问题》（特集 グローバルネットワークの法的课题）（第21回法とコソピュータ学会研究报告），法とコソピュータ，1997，（15）：77—78。

② Committee On The Uniform Commercial Code, An Appraisal Of The March 1, 1990, Preliminary Report Of The Uniform Commercial Code Article 2 Study Group. , Prepared By A Task Force Of The A. B. A. Subcommittee On General Provisions, Sales, Bulk Transfers, And Documents Of Title, Delaware Law School of Widener University, *Inc. Del. J. Corp. L.* 1991 (16): 981.

③ 参见 Tomaszewski, John P., "The Pandora's Box of Cyberspace: State Regulation of Digital Signatures and the Dormant Commerce Clause", *Gonz. L. Rev.* 1997/1998 (33): 436.

太满意,唯一不同的是,电子商务所提供的交易商品,可能不同于传统商品或劳务,例如信息商品即是。另外,在交易过程中,还会有新的要素被放入,例如成为交易媒介的电子代理(electronic agent)的产生,都是促成新形态的贸易、服务和数字化市场发生的因素。

综上,EDI 发展至今,已不断被加入新的附加价值,过去 EDI 在中小企业中的普及率并不高,主要是因为成本太高,而且太过复杂,而现在网络技术明显地提供了克服困难的机会,从而使 EDI 也逐渐以更便宜、更便利和更开放的架构来呈现,这也将更加扩大贸易市场的规模。基本上,网络的发展所带来的商业化,可以从四个层面来探讨:即沟通、网络应用、多媒体与电子商务,本书的重点则在最后一项,然而如果我们要比较传统国际贸易所运用的 EDI 与当前电子商务的差异,则后者带来的互动性、自发性、广泛性以及市场的建立模式应是重点。基本上,面对电子商务的发展,传统合同法制应将它纳入并为特别考量,针对这些特性会对我们与消费者、供货商及其他交易环境带来的影响加以评估;也就是借这个领域中新技术的不断发展,来探讨对传统交易的价值应如何调整,整体价值体系应如何新建;进而具体了解网际网络上的商业实务的现况与发展,包括电子商务与传统交易制度及 EDI 的异同、市场的评估等,这些都是本书所要强调的,以作为思考电子合同的法律建制的参考。

三、电子合同的发展及其变革

当国际贸易合同的缔造是通过 EDI 或电子合同形式来完成时,是以包括硬件、软件在内的计算机技术、通讯技术为基础,基于该技术的限制或发展的可能性,其在计算机或网络上传输、储存数据的方式也有异于传统的书面交易所采用的书面信息储存方式,所以,在探讨合同电子化的法律制度时,仍须对其与传统交易或合同间的差异作充分讨论。此时,有关电子交易合同的讨论,首先应注意到有关电子交易的以下两大特性:

第一,为公司内外交易系统网络化的特性。对于公司内部系统的联机部分,已经很少有通过非网络化的独立系统来处理交易信息的交换,而大多必须与 EOS(补充发单系统)等存货管理系统或会计系统互动,并与自动处理的特性相辅相成,以达成经营效率化的目的。对于公司外部系统的联机部分,也必须实施与价金支付银行、运输公司、仓库公司等物流系统的联机。第二,信息自动处理特性。最单纯的自动处理事例为格式转换的处理,也就是在多数下、接单的信息交换的场合,收到下单者的下单信息,可以不通过他人,将其转换为接单信息、出货指示信息,或转换为支付信息,作为会计上使用。

以这些特性为前提,有关电子交易在法律实务上最重要的事项,自然关系到确保电子交易的可信赖性、安全性。例如,下、接单信息交换系统发生障碍,可能导致价金支付迟延或价金支付金额错误的情形;另外,价金支付不足时,还可能使相对人资金支付产生影响,从而遭到银行交易停止处分等不利益。基本上,接单信息处理上有错误时,受该错误影响的,并不仅限于接单人,其他如流通业也可能受到影响,而商品信息的错误,也可能造成相对人缺货、停产,甚至发生人、物的损害。因此,在合同电子化的过程中,确保交易安全性、信赖性的相关事项,可以说是电子交易中最重要的课题。为了防止电子交易发生这类不测,目前各方都在研究各种技术性措施,然而主要从技术层面来探讨而已,未能从立法层面来进行。以法律的立场看来,针对个别交易的疑点、风险,如何通过采用具安全性、信赖性的技术来适应,而且法律应对于合同就该技术手段的安排赋予怎样的法律效果,在我们调和电子合同法制的过程中,应该是首要课题。

基本上,电子签章技术的运用,属于用科技来解决安全性问题的对策,然而究竟我们应如何来看待电子签章的运用,却值得我们进一步的深思。原则上,签章的重要性,应在其通过签署的文字所传递的讯息,而不在其文字本身。由于签章(signature)通常被要求用来表彰认证的真正(authenticity),我们可以因此推定该签章的出处,所以在探讨传统文字基础的签章相关问题时,通常焦点会被放在签章的真正与否上。因此,当我们将问题转向电子签章的探讨时,自然的也就将电子签章的真正与其出处的归属(attribution)问题列为重点。然而不同于传统签章的在于,电子签章的归属很难全然以交易当事人的意志为唯一对象[1],因为在使用电子设施从事交易的安排过程中,合同成立与生效的相关认定,已倾向于依据数据传输电子设施的选用方式来处理,因而相关安全性的考量就逐渐超越了一般人的经验,使不具电子文书处理经验的人,因本身无法充分了解交易过程,而产生对于运用科技从事交易的不信任;这种不信任尤其在 B to C 的交易结构中最为明显,从而也导致消费者保护课题,发展为电子商务的重要议题。[2]

---

[1] Rubin, Edward L., "Consumer Protection And The Uniform Commercial Code: The Code, The Consumer, And The Institutional Structure Of The Common Law", *Wash. U. L. Q.* 1997 (75): 11.

[2] 有关网络上的安全问题,请参阅 Shaw, Paul D., *Managing Legal and Security Risks in Computing and Communications*, Oxford: Butterworth-Heinemann. 1998。

综上,数字世界的动态可塑性毕竟与人类的真实生活不完全一样,创造一个可以提供类似邮局的存证信函、户政事务所的印鉴证明、法院的公证的电子社会,实在是不容易。① 然而建立安全及可信赖的网络环境,确保信息在网络传输过程中不易遭到伪造、窜改或窃取,并能鉴别交易双方的身份,防止事后否认有进行交易的事实,是电子商务得以全面普及的关键。整体而言,目前涉及安全性的问题很多,然而其中最为各方所关注的仍然是电子签章所涉及的问题,因为传统公私领域的通信及交易行为,是以书面文件(如合同书)及签名、盖章来确定相关的法律责任,电子商务则须依赖电磁纪录及电子签章作为通信及交易的基础,但大陆现有法令并没有明确规范电磁纪录及电子签章的法律地位,必须配合今后信息化及网络化社会的发展,建立电磁纪录及电子签章的法制。② 其他国家为建立安全及可信赖的电子通信及交易环境,普及电子商务的应用,亦有规划电子签章法的相关立法。例如,英国(2000 年)、法国(2000 年 3 月)、德国(1997 年 8 月)、马来西亚(1997 年)、意大利(1997 年 3 月)、新加坡(1998 年 6 月)、韩国(1998 年 12 月立法,1999 年 7 月生效)、日本(2000 年 5 月)、美国联邦(2000 年 6 月)以及各州(已有 40 余州完成立法)。

然而,如果我们要进一步探讨电子合同法制的发展,则美国修改统一商法典(U.C.C.)的经验特别值得重视。早在 1996 年 7 月间,美国法学会在配合电子合同的发展修正 U.C.C. 第 2 条(Article 2)时,就已经针对 EDI 所涉合同成立问题加以审慎思考,并寻求解决方案。例如,在当时所

---

① 有人认为,应该先深入了解国际标准组织已颁布的金钥鉴别架构标准、开放系统连接安全架构与存证标准等,将它应用在信息社会及电子化政府的各个作业中,以建立适合我们使用的存证证据的电子文件交换作业安全协议及公证作业,见樊国桢:《型式认证在台湾地区社会可信赖的信息使用环境中所面临的问题与挑战》,载《信息法务透析》1998 年第 5 期,第 41 页。

② 为配合国家信息通信基本建设的推展,台湾地区在 1986 年由"经济部"委托资策会科法中心进行数字签章法的研究,并建议政府应尽速研订电子签章法,以律定电子签章及电磁纪录的法律地位,建立电子凭证机构的管理制度,界定凭证机构(Certificate Authority, CA)与使用者的权责,建立跨国认证的机制,以解决现有法令规范不足或不确定之处。当时,为建立安全及可信赖的电子交易环境,裨益电子商务的发展,"行政院"研究发展考核委员会依据"行政院"国家信息通信基本建设小组的决议,于 1987 年 1 月会同"行政院"法规会、"法务部"、"财政部"、"经济部"、"交通部"、工研院电通所、财团法人信息工策进会科技法律中心及有关学者专家组成"数字签章法研拟小组",负责草案研拟工作。研拟小组于 1987 年 1 月成立,经参酌主要国家的立法经验,以及联合国及欧盟等国际组织订定的电子签章立法原则,研订电子签章法草案,详见参考资料《台湾地区电子签章法草案》。

提的草案第 2-208 条(a)项中,除废除所谓的信箱原则(The "Mailbox" Rule)①外,还将"书面"的观念,扩大到如今所有的技术发展。此外,起草人也开始注意到计算机在无人(行为)介入自动进行交易的情形,这就是所谓的"电子代理"(electronic agent)②,而这也是整个新的合同法律架构与传统架构最重大不同之处。由于电子代理与传统以人类行为为客体的代理原则不同,所以草案第 2-102 条第(19)项中特别针对"电子代理"下一定义:"'电子代理'是指一方当事人,为能在非经个人审视的过程下发出或响应电子讯息或表现,所设计、选用的计算机程序。当电子代理的表现(performance)与利用电子代理的当事人意欲具备的功能一致时,该电子代理的行为即应属代理权限范围内的行为"。③

这个定义是十分重要的一项发展,也是影响新的电子合同法制的关键因素。在传统的代理原则下,判断的依据着重于对于人类行为及其真意的探讨④,然而在 EDI 的运作下,电子讯息的传输,却是在交易各方预设的条件下,交由电子软硬件来自动传输。因此,就个案而言,交易双方实际上没有再针对个别交易标的作意思表示的交换。就此草案而言,将目标着眼于当事人对于电子设施的选择以及其对设施功能的理解来判断电子代理与交易当事人间的关系,确实具有重大意义。然而究竟电子代理与传统代理之间有何异同,而且这种代理的定义对于电子合同的成立或生效的影响如何,也值得研究。基本上,运用代理的相关规定,将计算机

---

① 该原则主要是指,承诺应于被要约人的承诺已离开其控制的范围时发生效力(once acceptance has been placed out of the offeree's possession, the acceptance is effective),然而在电子缔约的场合,由于要约与承诺的讯息互换至为迅速,原信箱原则的发生背景,如生效与撤回等问题,是否仍有必要加以探讨,是否原则有调整的必要,都值得加以研究。参见 Kent D. Stuckey, *Internet and Online Law* §1.02 [4][c] (1998),以及后文的探讨。

② 参阅 U.C.C. §2-102 (19)。另于新修正的 U.C.I.T.A. 亦有相似的规定 SECTION 102. DEFINITIONS. TRANSACTIONS ACT (27) "Electronic agent" means a computer program, or electronic or other automated means, used by a person to initiate an action, or to respond to electronic messages or performances, on the person's behalf without review or action by an individual at the time of the action or response to the message or performance。

③ 按电子代理的概念而言,虽然起草人采取限制性的方法,限于电子代理的行为与当事人利用电子代理所欲达成的功能相一致时,才认为其行为是在代理权的范围内,但这仍容易造成法院认为电子代理是在所有方面与人为代理相同。而且到目前为止,起草人对电子代理的限制,并没有对实际进行商业交易的人产生助益,因为律师及法官多认为,既然法律允许 EDI 技术来实现其效益时,起草人似乎应扩大电子代理的观念到所有电子合同条款,而不应直接加以限制。

④ 以表见代理的认定为例,必须取决于行为外围情况来认定当事人的真意。如今,如果以电子代理的原则来取代,则势必面临如何通过电子设施的表现来判断当事人真意的困难。因为在计算机软件通常是由使用者以外的第三人所设计,而电子讯息的发送收受通常又是由电子设施在自动操作的条件下来进行时,如何将电子代理与当事人的真意联系起来实有相当困难。

视为当事人的代理人,应该是一项不错的选择。这样看来,当电子合同的交易当事人是在无人为介入或同意的情形下来缔约时,合同条款的效力,仍应与一般通过代理所签署①的合同效力相同。换而言之,当行为人按使用其他工具的态度,通过计算机来缔约或履约时,原则上,法律应该将计算机与其他工具一视同仁。因此,当一方当事人选择通过计算机作为传送讯息给他人的媒介时,计算机的功能与传真机或信件无异。但是即使如此,我们仍不可否认,应该只有在该当事人是采用与传统使用代理人相同的方式来利用计算机时,法律才有赋予其与代理人相同地位的必要。美国 U.C.C. 新修条文纳入所谓"无人介入"(no human input,简称"NHI")合同的概念,不论对于商业交易当事人、律师或法官来说,都极具意义,也极具挑战。首先,正如同有些通过电子数据传送的讯息,在品质上已被认为具备与书面文书交易合同相同的拘束力及真实性;同理,计算机在 NHI 合同交易下所提供的相似功能,也应该被同等对待,而被认为通过其缔结的合同,应与通过人类代理行为所缔结的具有相同的法律效果。反之,如果我们仍拘泥于按传统法律架构或模式,将原有法律原则适用到新科技所产生的困扰,可能会使交易当事人及法院面临更大的风险。

综上,当前美国 U.C.C. 修法过程中所发展的新代理模式概念,确实是值得我们借鉴。然而在意图援引电子代理的理论作为电子合同交易的法律基础时,究竟其理论的周密性如何?与传统代理原则的异同如何?有何限制?都值得更进一步的探讨。基本上,U.C.C. 的修法方向是纳入了所谓验证的机制,并以适当的验证作为判断讯息归属的依据,而且以此作为取代人类代理人有无从事行为的判断标准。实际上,只要我们排除伪造(forged)的讯息或骇客(hacker)所为破坏行为的当然归责,以验证机制来处理责任归属问题应更为可靠。因为电子讯息在传输过程中所留下的纪录,是远比人的记忆或主观认知更为精确的,这就是所谓的交易不可否认性。所以,我们认为,只要提供给本人适当的机会去发现或检视记录,则计算机可以成功地扮演本人的代理的角色,而且其缔结的合同应与(人类)代理人有相同的效果。这样看来,应足以适用到所有验证的方法,其中也应该包括 NHI 合同的计算机验证,换而言之,当计算机依照当事人的指示去验证记录时,人们可以说是该方当事人已拥有该计算机"现有的

---

① 原美国统一商法典对签署的定义为:"包括任何有现存意思认证某文书的当事人所作成或采用的任何符号。"中兴大学法律研究所译:《美国统一商法典及其译注》(上册),台北:台湾地区银行经济研究室编印,1986 年版,第 14 页。

意图"去验证该记录。而适用代理模式到电子合同后,"签名"将意味着任何被当事人以"现有真意"来验证记录所使用或采用的方法;因而,凡经选用作为验证记录的电子代理可以推论其是在执行本人的意思。

然而这种代理模式将面临两个质疑,即:1. 是否可以满足以"同意"为创设本人——代理人间的关系的要件;2. 是否可以将计算机视同为法律上的"人"。就第一个质疑而言,在采用电子代理的模式时,我们必须了解到,在传统的代理法则下,必须要通过双方当事人间的同意,才足以创造出一个"本人与代理人"的关系。而现在,由于计算机之本身并不具备传统人类所熟悉的"同意"能力,因而当我们试图建构出"本人——计算机"间的代理关系时,就必须慎重考虑到因计算机本身条件的限制所可能引发的理论上问题。解释上,除非科技或人工智能已发展到可以自为同意,否则,通过法律的推定或拟制来加以诠释,是很有必要的。再就第二个质疑而言,计算机是否可以视同为法律上的"人"? 这涉及更重要的哲理问题,因为我们即使能就这种法律上的拟制赋予条件,然而人工智能的存在与运作,与人类的知觉和自治是有显著的差异的,因此,就传统出自人本主义的法律基础来看,人类的自尊很难让人同意将人的定义扩大到计算机,因为这种扩张被认为会导致对人类定义的贬损。[①] 准此,本文所提的建议并非本诸于传统以电子代理为人的法则,而是将电子代理以本人之物或代理来看待。换而言之,将代理原则适用于计算机模式,仅限于在计算机主体是执行本人的意志时,也就是只限于将计算机的身份视为代理人时(deal with agents as agents)。在美国提出的修正条文中,并没有把传统代理法则中的本人(deal with agents as persons)纳入,也就是并没有特别就传统代理法制下,代理人与本人之间的权利义务关系加以规定。这样看来,现在所采用的代理模式,法律所侧重的是代理人的功能性意义,而唯一真正重要的人,则是指导"电子代理"行事的本人。正由于这种代理模式从不认为计算机也可以成为本人,所以在理论上,将基本代理原则扩大到计算机,应该不会导致发生无法解决的哲理困扰。

综上,信息时代的来临,使得全球产业发展趋势迈入后工业时代,此际,除地球村的成员正在重新分工,形成新的世界秩序外,随之而起的信息科技产业更将全面性的颠覆传统的经济社会态样,进而彻底影响人类的生活模式与生存空间;值此世纪交替之际,我们所应关心者,除全球化

---

① Fischer, John P., "Computers As Agent: A Proposed Approach to Revised U. C. C. Article 2", *Ind. L. J.* 1997 (72): 569—570.

之冲击外，两岸之互动乃我们这一代，乃至21世纪之华人所必须共同关注之焦点。以大陆积极推动的信息化社会而言，电子商务与信息产业之发展均被列为重点，故在全球网络产业一片低迷声中，大陆的网络工程及贸易电子化却仍在蓬勃的发展；这其中，相关法律及其制度的建立更是成为时任中国国家主席江泽民口中的重点工作。基本上，电子商务之发展在技术上具有全球共通性，故国际社会对于大陆电子商务的技术与商业并不陌生，然对于必须植根于民族特性之法律制度，则难以掌握。以大陆导入资本主义市场经验并追求现代化的过程中，在政策上形成了直接迈入信息化社会之筹划的强烈企图，这种追求现代化（工业化）之过程中同时追求讯息化（信息化）的设计，一方面有其在全球化发展过程中之重大意义，另一方面则提供给我们一个透过新兴信息化社会及其规范本身之全球属性，来思索两岸之异同，进而超越单纯以国家主权领域为范围，追求在规范建制上提升共识可能之机会，应是吾等责无旁贷之任务。

2 当前两岸有关电子商务议题的发展与适应

2.1 大陆电子商务发展现况与调整

一、前言

近年来,中国网络信息化(信息化)蓬勃发展,电子商务也随之兴起,麦肯锡公司提出的研究报告中曾指出,大陆加入WTO后,网际网络和电子商务将为国内外企业开启与国际接轨的大门,如果能顺利解决物流与金流的障碍,并建立完善的电子商务法规,则可以预言大陆电子商务的前景将无可限量。① 面对这个商机以及两岸日渐密切的互动,我们不得不对这已逐渐成形的大陆电子商务法制发展状况加以把握。就大陆电子商务的发展而言,是随着网际网络的发展而逐渐蓬勃的,大约可分为二个阶段:第一阶段,自1987至1993年,科研部门开展了联网的课题与科技合作工作,实现了电子邮件转发系统的连接,为一些重点院校、研究所提供了国际网络电子邮件的服务②。第二阶段,从1994年开始,在这个阶段实现了和网络的传输控制/网络通讯协议(Transmission Control Protocol;TCP/Internet Protocol,IP)连接,开通了网际网络的功能服务。整体而言,大陆

---

① 参阅网上法,《中国大陆电子商务现况及发展趋势》,http://www.ipeclaw.com.tw/issue_member/china/china_ec_main.php(visited 2004/7/30)。

② 最早使用互联网的机构,集中在少数研究单位和高等学府如中科院、清华大学、北京大学、上海复旦大学等。

网络开通虽然较晚,但发展却极为迅速①,而四大互联网的相继开通,更使网际网络在大陆得以迅速的发展。②

面对网际网络的快速发展,中国政府积极展开一系列的配套措施,主要有:第八届人大会议上通过的《中华人民共和国经济和社会发展"九五"计划和二〇一〇年远景目标纲要》,该纲要中明确揭示了"加快国民经济信息化过程,促进信息产业发展"的任务;在这个基础上,为强化网络基础设施建设的工作,特成立了国务院信息化工作领导小组,全面负责信息化发展工作③;而中央为落实这项重点工作,又制定了中国信息化"统筹规划、国家主导、统一标准、联合建设、互联互通、资源共享"的24字方针,为全面发展大陆信息化建设和电子商务开启了重要的指导作用④,这也对电子商务的发展起了推波助澜的作用。于是在1996年成立了"中国国际电子商务中心"⑤,奠定了电子商务发展的基础;1997年,国务院电子信息系统推广办公室联合八个部委建立了"中国电子数据交换技术委员会",为电子商务的发展开启了新页;因而,电子商务在1998年掀起一阵热潮,中

---

① 2004年4月1日,国务院信息化工作办公室在京举行新闻发布会,向社会各界发布《2003年中国互联网络信息资源数量调查报告》。截至2003年12月31日,全国域名数为1187380个,比去年同期增长了26.3%。网站数为595550个,比去年同期增长了60.3%。从网站性质与服务内容来看,企业网站数的比例最大,占整个网站总数的70.9%;其次为商业网站,占8.2%;政府网站比去年同期增长了1.5个百分点达到3.2%。网页总数为311864590个,平均每个网站的网页数为523.7个。在线数据库数为169867个,与2002年同期相比增长了104.8%。http://tech.sina.com.cn (visited 2004/7/30)。

此外,根据中国互联网络信息中心(CNNIC)第13次《中国互联网络发展状况统计报告》的数据,截至2003年12月31日,中国大陆上网计算机总数已达3089万台,和2002年底相比增长了48.3%;中国大陆互联网站点数为595550个,与2002年底相比增长了60.3%。http://www.cnnic.com.cn (visited 2004/7/30)。

② 即中国国家公用经济信息通信网(CHINAGBNET)、中国教育和科研计算机网(CERNET)、中国科学技术网(CSTNet)、中国国家公用经济信息通信网(CHINAGBNET)。参阅陈敏:《电子商务在大陆的现状和发展》(上), http://www.ecpress.com.tw/ECinchinese3.htm, (visited 2001/3/16)。

③ 其推行"金桥、金卡、金关"一系列三金工程,以激活"21世纪中小企业信息化建设培训示范项目",并推进国民经济信息化。

④ 参阅王冠玺:《中国大陆电子合同法律问题简析》,资策会科技法律中心, http://stlc.iii.org.tw/articles/Netlaw/200009w.htm (visited 2004/7/30)。

⑤ 由中国政府投资设立的中国国际电子商务中心,就针对中国经贸问题提供一连串的解决方案。该中心副主任张大明在11月1日由e21corp于美国硅谷圣塔克拉拉会议中心举办的"中国数字化论坛"上指出,该中心从1996年开始,就着手进行一连串推动政府经贸相关单位业务电子化的金关、金卡、金桥及金税等计划,即所谓的"四金工程", http://www.e21times.com/ei/e21fd.asp?rtid=3416&sid=34 (visited 2004/7/30)。

国大陆称为"电子商务年"①;从 1999 年起,中国大陆电子商务进入应用发展阶段,首套自行研发的电子商务 CA 安全认证系统已通过国家技术鉴定,并在扩大实施中。② 其后,有鉴于电子商务发展之需求,为规范电子签名行为,维护各方的合法权益,于 2004 年年 8 月通过《电子签名法》,至此,中国电子商务的发展框架已逐步成形。

二、大陆电子商务法制环境概况

电子商务的发展是商品交易与先进计算机技术相结合的交易模式,已经冲击到传统的各个部门,就立法层面而言,因为具有无时差、无国界、迅速的特点,很难靠传统的思维模式与规制方法加以规范,而如何适应这个新生事物的特点,将使法律规范更显困难。而且电子商务是一个全球运作、极其复杂的国际社会系统工程,其法制建设所涉问题既广泛又庞杂。③ 所以,大陆目前还没有对这方面的专门立法。如何架构一套完善的电子商务交易的法规范环境,是现阶段的首要任务。

关于规范电子商务的立法方式,学者间有两种不同立场,有认为应由国务院协调各相关主管部门,制定单一的《网络法》或《电子商务法》④;还有的认为,应该由相关主管部门针对各自掌管的业务制定专法或修正现

---

① 1998 年被称为"电子商务年"。在这一年,大陆电子商务得到空前的发展。从 IBM 的"电子商务大都会"、HP 的"电子化世界"到各种名目的电子商务研讨会,从外经贸部的"中国商品交易市场"、首都电子商务工程到以电子贸易为主要内容的"金贸工程",有关电子商务的活动和项目大量涌现,令人目不暇接。从 IT 业界到流通、金融业界,从媒体、学者到政府机构,再到江泽民主席在亚太经合组织会议上关于"电子商务代表着未来贸易方式的发展方向"的讲话,在社会各界的共同努力下,中国电子商务经过前两三年的酝酿和准备,在 1998 年出现了前所未有的兴旺局面。http://www.5ipda.com/big5/viewbook.php3? bookid =511(visited 2004/7/30)。

② 据统计 1999 年中国大陆 1000 多个电子商务网站的购物金额达 1 亿 8 千万人民币。参阅王冠玺:《中国大陆电子合同法律问题简析》,资策会科技法律中心,http://stlc.iii.org.tw/articles/Netlaw/200009w.htm(visited 2004/7/30)。

③ 主要的有:1. 电子商务交易中基础法律关系的确立问题;2. CA 认证机构的建置、职责、地位、权限、标准等问题;3. 电子商务企业的设置、名称、行业范围及经营活动必要的规范建立等问题;4. 电子支付与网站银行的基础法律关系的确认问题;5. 网络检查及网络犯罪的法律问题;6. 网上内容的审查与管理问题;7. 电子商务企业的税收问题;8. 电子商务中消费者权益保护的问题;9. 网站危机的保护问题;10. 电子商务业筹资过程中的一些政策法律问题;11. 网络经营者及 ISP 等法律责任问题;12. 电子商务交易中相关知识产权问题;13. 网上广告的相关法律问题;14. 网上法律问题的签转问题;15. 电子商务交易过程中的损失赔偿问题等。

④ 参阅网上法,《中国大陆电子商务现况及发展趋势》,http://www.ipeclaw.com.tw/issue_member/china/china_ec_main.php(visited 2004/7/30)。

行法障碍之处,针对网际网络的特性与行为规范制定一套规范架构。① 对此,于大陆相关法规范中,早有部分为适应电子商务交易的特点而加以调整的②,而相关主管部门及法学专家亦积极针对电子商务所引发的交易安全、知识产权保护、电子支付、交易课税、隐私权保障,及网络犯罪等相关问题进行探讨③,而随着大陆 2004 年 8 月电子签名法的通过,可见似朝向后者之发展趋势。

三、大陆电子商务相关法规的立法现况

在这里试着就大陆电子商务相关法规的立法状况,简析如下:
(一)有关网络安全部分

大陆为保障电子商务交易的安全,相关部门已经着手建立完善电子商务的工程系统。2000 年初,计划由外经贸部中国国际电子商务中心开发的"商业电子信息安全认证系统"④,成为中国大陆电子商务和网上应用的安全平台,这可以说是技术面上的重大突破。鉴于原有的法律制度难以规范信息化建设所形成的新法律关系,在立法层面上,大陆为了维护信息流通安全、保密、防止病毒散播,首先针对计算机软件、信息系统安全和国际联网行为加以规范。分别颁布了《计算机软件保护条例》、《计算机信息系统安全保护条例》和《计算机信息网络国际联网管理暂行规定》、《计算机信息系统国际联网保密管理规定》、《计算机信息网络国际联网安全保护管理办法》等法令。另外,大陆的《刑法》与《商用密码管理条例》也设有相关的规定,在这里就主要的说明如下⑤:

1.《中华人民共和国计算机信息网络国际联网管理暂行规定》的相

---

① 并强调即便是号称制定世界第一部网络单一法(即多元媒体法)的德国,严格说来,并非单一的电子商务法,而是对因特网应用与行为规范提出单一的法律架构。参阅网上法,《中国大陆电子商务现况及发展趋势》, http://www. ipeclaw. com. tw/issue_member/china/china_ec_main. php(visited 2004/7/30)。

② 如《合同法》中,对于采用数据电文形式订立合同(即合同)已有规范。

③ 也有论者主张应订立专法加以规范,以求周妥。参阅网上法,《中国大陆电子商务现况及发展趋势》,请参 http://www. ipeclaw. com. tw/issue_member/china/china_ec_main. php(visited 2004/7/30)。

④ 已经科技部和国家密码管理委员会的科技成果鉴定,亦通过公安部计算机信息系统安全产品质量监督检查机关的认可。参阅王冠玺:《中国大陆电子合同法律问题简析》,资策会科技法律中心, http://stlc. iii. org. tw/articles/Netlaw/200009w. htm(visited 2004/7/30)。

⑤ 参阅北京君思电子商务研究发展中心/Beijing Juns E-Commerce R&D Center,《国内主要网络管理法规简介》,君思电子商务世界, http://www. juns. com. cn/,(visited 2001/3/16);网上法,《计算机信息安全保护的相关规定》, http://www. ipeclaw. com. tw/issue_member/china/china_ec_main. php? serial = 1 - 5 - 1(visited 2004/7/30)。

关规定①

这是大陆目前有关计算机互联网络管理方面最重要的法律规范,其主要内容包括:成立国务院信息化工作领导小组(国务院信息办),以负责协调、解决有关国际联网中的重大问题,并制定具体管理办法;任何单位和个人都必须使用邮电部国家公用电信网提供的国际出入口进行国际联网;现有的中国金桥信息网、中国教育科研网和中国科学技术网等互联网络,分别由电子工业部、国家教育委员会和中国科学院负责管理;对拟从事国际联网经营活动和非经营活动的相关单位,分别实行国际联网经营许可证制度和审批制度。

2.《中国公用计算机互联网国际联网管理办法》的相关规定②

此管理办法规定了接入中国公用互联网的接入单位应具备的条件及应办理的程序;要求接入单位需负责对用户加以管理,并按规定与用户签订协议,确立双方的权利和义务;另外,接入单位和用户应遵守国家法规,对其提供的信息内容负责。

3.《中华人民共和国计算机信息系统安全保护条例》的相关规定③

大陆为保护计算机信息系统的安全,国务院特制定此条例,有如下要点:

(1)由公安部主管全国计算机信息系统安全的保护工作(第6条)。

(2)任何组织或个人,不得利用计算机信息系统从事危害国家利益、集体利益和公民合法利益的活动,亦不得危害计算机信息系统的安全(第7条)。

(3)进行国际联网的计算机信息系统,使用单位应报省级以上人民政府公安机关备案(第11条)。

(4)由公安部负责管理对计算机病毒和危害社会公共安全的防治研究工作(第15条)。

(5)对国家计算机信息系统安全专用产品的销售采行许可证制度。④

---

① 国务院1996年2月1日颁布,1997年5月20日修正实施。参阅君思电子商务世界,《国内主要网络管理法规简介》,http://www.juns.com.cn/,(visited 2001/3/16)。

② 原邮电部1996年4月3日颁布,参阅君思电子商务世界,《国内主要网络管理法规简介》,http://www.juns.com.cn/,(visited 2001/3/16)。

③ 参阅网上法,《计算机信息安全保护的相关规定》,http://www.ipeclaw.com.tw/issue_member/china/china_ec_main.php?serial=1-5-1(visited 2004/7/30)。

④ 至于具体办法由公安部会同有关部门制定(第16条),公安部乃据此制定《计算机信息系统安全专用产品检测和销售许可证管理办法》。

(6) 有关罚责的规定。①

4.《计算机信息网络国际联网安全保护管理办法》的相关规定②

为公安部所制定,要点如下:

(1) 任何单位和个人不得利用国际联网危害国家、泄露国家秘密,不得侵犯国家、社会、集体的利益和公民的合法权益,亦不得从事违法犯罪活动(第4条)。

(2) 任何单位和个人不得利用国际联网制作、复制、查阅和传播淫秽、色情、赌博、暴力、教唆犯罪、公然侮辱他人、捏造事实诽谤他人、及违反宪法、法律和行政法规的信息(第5条)。③

(3) 任何单位和个人不得从事危害计算机信息网络安全之活动(第6条)。④

(4) 用户的通信自由和通信秘密受到法律保护(第7条)。⑤

(5) 规范使用计算机信息网络国际联网的法人和其他组织之备案程序。⑥

(6) 与香港、澳门及台湾地区联网的计算机信息网络的安全保护管理,亦参照本办法执行(第24条)。

5.《刑法》的相关规定⑦

大陆针对网络犯罪的问题,特修正现行刑法的规定,以作为规范。其

---

① 故意输入计算机病毒以及其他有害数据危害计算机信息系统安全;或者未经许可出售计算机信息系统安全专用产品者,由公安机关处以警告或罚款;有违法所得者,除予以没收外,可处以违法所得1至3倍的罚款(第23条)。

② 参阅网上法,《计算机信息安全保护的相关规定》,http://www.ipeclaw.com.tw/issue_member/china/china_ec_main.php? serial = 1 − 5 − 1 (visited 2004/7/30);参阅君思电子商务世界,"国内主要网络管理法规简介",http://www.juns.com.cn/, (visited 2001/3/16)。

③ 违反的,由公安机关给予警告;有违法所得的,予以没收;可并处罚款;情节严重的,可并处6个月以内停止联网、停机整顿的处罚,必要时可建议原发证、审批机构吊销经营许可证或取消联网资格;构成违反治安管理行为的,依治安管理处罚条例处罚;构成犯罪的,依法追究刑事责任(第20条)。

④ 未经允许,进入计算机信息网络或者使用计算机信息网络资源;未经允许,对进入计算机信息网络功能进行删除、修改或者增加;未经允许,对计算机信息网络中存储、处理或者传输的数据和应用程序进行删除、修改或者增加;故意制作、传播计算机病毒等破坏性程序;其他危害计算机信息网络安全的活动。

⑤ 任何单位和个人不得违反法律规定,利用国际联网侵犯用户的通信自由和通信秘密。

⑥ 应自网络正式联通之日起30日内,到所在地的省、自治区、直辖市人民政府公安机关指定的受理机关办理备案手续。违反者,由公安机关给予警告或者停机整顿不超过6个月的处罚(第12条、第23条)。

⑦ 参阅网上法,《计算机信息安全保护的相关规定》,http://www.ipeclaw.com.tw/issue_member/china/china_ec_main.php? serial = 1 − 5 − 1 (visited 2004/7/30)。

主要特点有四点:即确立计算机信息系统安全秩序视为公共秩序中的独立对象;依行为人与计算机系统功能、程序和数据发生关系的行为方式来区分此罪与彼罪的原则;明确规定以计算机为犯罪工具或手段进行的犯罪行为的处理原则;根据计算机犯罪的发生特质与危害特点,规定相应的罚责。① 在此举主要的说明如下:

(1)违反国家规定,侵入国家事务、国防建设、尖端科学技术领域的计算机信息系统的,处3年以下有期徒刑或者拘役(第285条)。

(2)违反国家规定,对计算机信息系统功能进行删除、修改、增加、干扰,造成计算机信息系统不能正常运行者,应处以有期徒刑或者拘役(第286条)。②

(3)利用计算机实施金融诈骗、盗窃、贪污、挪用公款、窃取国家秘密或者其他犯罪的,依照本法有关规定,定罪处罚(第287条)。

(4)违反国家规定,擅自设置、使用无线电台(站),或者擅自占用频率,经责令停止使用后拒不停止使用,干扰无线电通讯正常进行,造成严重后果的,处3年以下有期徒刑、拘役或者管制,并处或者单处罚金;单位犯前款罪的,对单位判处罚金,并对其直接负责的主管人员和其他直接责任人员,依照前款的规定处罚(第288条)。

6.《商用密码管理条例》的相关规定③

为了加强商用密码管理,大陆国务院特制定此条例作为规范,在此试说明其要点如下:

(1)商用密码技术属于国家机密。对国家商用密码产品的科研、生产、销售和使用实行专控管理(第3条)。

(2)由国家密码管理委员会及其办公室,主管全国商用密码管理工作(第4条)。

(3)商用密码产品,必须经国家密码管理机构指定的产品质量检测机构检测合格(第9条)。

(4)任何单位或个人只能使用经国家密码管理机构认可的商用密码

---

① 周忠海:《电子商务导论》,北京邮电大学出版社2000年版,第308—310页。
② 违反国家规定,对计算机信息系统功能进行删除、修改、增加、干扰,造成计算机信息系统不能正常运行,后果严重的,处5年以下有期徒刑或者拘役;后果特别严重的,处5年以上有期徒刑;违反国家规定,对计算机信息系统中存储、处理或者传输的资料和应用程序进行删除、修改、增加的操作,后果严重的,依照前款的规定处罚;故意制作、传播计算机病毒等破坏性程序,影响计算机系统正常运行,后果严重的,依照第1款的规定处罚(第286条)。
③ 参阅君思电子商务世界,《国内主要网络管理法规简介》,http://www.juns.com.cn/zlk/(0911).htm,(visited 2001/3/16)。

产品,不得使用自行研制或境外生产的密码产品(第14条)。①

(5)除外国驻华外交代表机构、领事机构外,境外组织或个人在中国大陆境内使用密码产品或者含有密码技术的设备,必须报经国家密码管理机构批准(第15条)。②

综合上述,可见大陆就有关网络安全问题在立法上所作的努力。此外,全国人大常委会还通过"维护互联网安全"决定,打击网络犯罪并取缔网络上的异议言论。③

(二)有关网络交易部分

电子合同的签订,是确认电子商务交易当事人间权利义务关系的关键要素,基于互联网的全球性和电子商务的跨国性特点,使得电子合同的缔结与现行法律兼容性,产生了一些问题。所以,大陆在修正合同法之际,纳入部分电子合同的概念,修订现行法以与之适应,在此试举其要点说明如下④:

1. 合同签章的问题

按照大陆合同法的规定,需经双方当事人签字或盖章,合同才成立。然而在网际网络上交易时,无法传递当事人的亲笔签名,因此必须通过电子签章等加密技术解决这个难题,同时,在利用电子签章时,如何避免网络通信被人截获、窜改,以确保电子合同文本的真实性,都尚存在问题。有鉴于此,大陆于2004年8月通过《电子签名法》,藉以规范利用电子签名时所面临的法律适用疑义。

关于大陆《电子签名法》之规范架构,约可分为五个部分:(1)总则;(2)数据电文;(3)电子签名与认证;(4)法律责任;(5)附则。兹分别介绍如下:

---

① 违反者,国家密码管理机构根据不同状况分别会同公安、国家安全机关没收其密码产品(第21条)。

② 违反者,由国家密码管理机构会同公安机关给予警告,责令改正,可以没收其密码产品或者含有密码技术的设备(第15条、第24条)。

③ 于第9届全国人大常委会第19次会议中通过"维护互联网安全"的法律,根据新华社的报道,这项法律主要规定了骇客行为与言论自由的部分。为吓阻骇客,该法中规定"对侵入国家事务、国防建设、尖端科学技术领域的计算机信息系统,故意制作、传播计算机病毒造成损害者",还有,对"利用互联网煽动颠覆国家政权或分裂国家、破坏统一,以及从事其他违法犯罪活动者,有触犯刑法的将依法追究刑事责任,构成民事侵权的将依法承担民事责任"。将在网络上的侵权行为与言论管制的部分都做出明确的规范;参阅网上法,《中国新网络安全法通过》,http://www.ipeclaw.com.tw/news_net.php?serial=316(visited 2004/7/30)。

④ 参阅王冠玺:《中国大陆电子合同法律问题简析》,资策会科技法律中心,http://stlc.iii.org.tw/articles/Netlaw/200009w.htm(visited 2004/7/30)。

(1) 总则

总则部分,除就《电子签名法》之立法目的、电子签名与数据电文加以说明外,大陆对于《电子签名法》之运用,仍以私法自治原则为其基本精神,此可证诸该法第3条规定,民事活动中的合同或者其他文件、单证等文书,当事人可以约定使用或不使用电子签名、数据电文,不难得知。

在私法自治的精神下,除基于纷争预防抑或事件特殊性之需要外,立法者原则上并不会对于法律形式、要件加以规定,因此,由第3条之规定即可得知,当事人既已约定使用电子签名、数据电文之文书,则不得仅因为其采用电子签名、数据电文的形式而否定其法律效力。此条文即明白宣示,当事人间一般的要约、承诺等行为,只要非属法定要式行为,法律本来就不会介入规范当事人必须以电子文件抑或须以书面来作成,所以绝大部分以电子文件完成的在线交易行为,将更得确定其法律效力,而不容其他人之任意否认,准此,于将来电子商务之各种场合中,任何人更不能单纯仅因其属电子记录存在形式而拒绝其提出适用。① 此外,立法者亦于第7条中明文规定数据电文不得因其存在形式而被拒绝做为证据使用,此等立法明文之保障,可避免电子签名、数据电文之法律效力将来处于不明确地位。

然而,值得注意者,在于私法中强制规定之适用问题,于法定要式行为之情形,如立法者要求契约之订立应以书面作成并应签名时,许多采取电子签名、数据电文传输行为,因为无法符合现有法律规定"书面、签名盖章"要件,而面临窒碍难行之情形,为消除这种适用上之障碍,于第4条特规定,数据电文能够有形地表现所载内容,并可以随时调取查用,视为符合法律、法规要求的书面形式。即以数据电文取代书面文件,必须要满足两项条件,一是数据电文能够有形地完整呈现书面文件的内容;一是在日后能够随时调取查用。只要能够符合上述两项要件,使数据电文符合与书面文件相同功能性之要求,使赋予其与书面文件相同之法律效力。此即联合国 UNCITRAL 所谓"功能相等"原则,其思考点并非使电子文件直接等同于书面纸本,而是考量现实法律中之所以规定"书面"其要求为何,归纳出必要功能要件,而使具有这些特性之电子文件得以符合所谓"书面"之法律要求。信息科技固然为人类带来莫大的便利与福祉,唯正如同其他科技一样,以密码学为基础的电子签名技术,亦有其潜在的安全风

---

① 李科逸:《电子签章法重要法律议题之探讨及初议》,载《律师杂志》第256期,2001年1月,第31页。

险。尽管可透过技术、作业及管理的措施以降低风险,但为确保民众免于因疏失造成重要权益受损,而采循序渐进原则,于第 3 条后段规定,将与涉及身份法益、重大财产权益等事项明文排除不适用电子签名、数据电文的形式。

(2) 数据电文

针对电子商务实务之运作,书面形式、证据要求及收发时点之认定,向为发展电子商务之关键所在。其中,关于书面形式、原件认定暨相关保存要求,大陆《电子签名法》系以功能等同之方法为基本立法架构,换言之,如该数据电文具有(1) 有效表达之功能及(2) 可供随时调查取用者,即"视为"满足法律、法规规定之要件。① 此外,证据向为定纷止争之判断依据,于电子交易之情况下,因电子证据形式之特殊性,当事人往往否认其证据能力而导致不必要之纷争产生,为杜绝此一适用之疑义并达到纷争解决之一次性与迅速性,大陆《电子签名法》第 7 条明定,数据电文不得仅因其为电子、光学或类似手段生成、发送等而拒绝其做为证据使用。至于数据电文之收发主体与收发时间之认定,因涉及当事人主体之认定及意思表示是否生效、是否拘束当事人之问题,大陆《电子签名法》第 9 条至第 12 条皆设有相关规定。

值得一提者,数据电文章共设有 9 条规定,其中"视为"之规定共有 6 条并使用达 8 次,"视为"之法律意义有二,一为本质之歧异性;一为不可推翻性,申言之,因本质之歧异,故而未能涵盖于现行法之规范范围之中,而以法律的拟制"视为"而赋予与相同之法律效果。准此,似可推知大陆关于数据电文之立法态度,应系为赋予非书面而与书面同等法律效果,此一立法态度相较于台湾地区《电子签章法》之规定,并不相同。②

(3) 电子签名与认证

所谓电子签名,依《电子签名法》第 2 条之规定,指数据电文中以电子形式所含、所附用识别签名人身份并表明签名人认可其中内容的数据。依同法第 14 条之规定,"可靠"的电子签名,具有与手写签名或盖章同等效力。准此,大陆于电子签名之判断上,需注重者在于该电子签名是否"可靠"。

可靠与否,依《电子签名法》之规定,大别有二:(1) 约定可靠;(2) 视

---

① 参《电子签名法》第 4 条至第 6 条。
② 由台湾地区《电子签章法》第 4 条可知,电子文件于符合一定要件后应属书面,而非将其认定为非书面而以"视为"之方式赋予其法律效果。

为可靠。依第13条第2款之规定,约定可靠者,系指依当事人约定的可靠条件所为之电子签名;至于"视为可靠",则是指符合第13条第1款之电子签名。关于"视为可靠"之判断,因其基础构成要件已由法律明文规定,适用上固无疑义。唯就约定可靠者,因欠缺明文规定而流于一个模糊的不确定法律概念[①],适用上不免滋生疑义,虽电子签名法设有认证机制及认证机构之规定,唯该法并无明文规定经认证机构认证者,为可靠之电子签名,基此,约定可靠似与认证机构与机制无关。然为求法规适用之完整性与周延性,如当事人约定需经认证机构认证者,因认证机构之设立除需申请并获许可外,更需向信息产业主管部备案,亦需符合电子签名法之相关规范,准此,或可将之认为电子签名经认证者,应得推定为可靠条件之一种;当然,如当事人约定认证以外之其他可靠之条件时,基于私法自治的原理,亦可肯认其效力无疑,唯仍须由法院视具体个案而定。

(4)法律责任

按不法程度之高低,法律责任者有民事责任、刑事责任及行政责任之分。于电子商务交易环境中,依行为之不同,自应有不同之责任形态。准此,《电子签名法》第32条即界定民事责任及刑事责任之分;另,第29条及第30条亦规定行政责任之规范依据。然而,这些规范除具有明确规定责任形态与依据内容之功能外,值得注意者,应在即使于无纸化之电子交易环境之中,其法律责任形态亦应与传统法律交易环境下之责任形态无异,差别应仅在于构成要件认定上之困难。诸如:收、发文时点之认定等。然而,这并非意味着,电子商务法律问题与传统法律问题无异。举例而言,为确保电子交易之安全性,往往透过认证机构为电子签名之认证机关,藉由认证制度以强化电子签名之真确性,然而,法律主体之增加,其权利义务、责任形态亦将因此而有所变更。从而《电子签名法》第28条即规定了电子认证服务提供者之推定过错责任。申言之,此时大陆之立法态度即在于以传统法思维为起点,针对电子商务之特性所为之配套措施,值得赞同。唯就第28条之立法,适用上不免滋生疑义,依第28条之规定:"电子签名人或者电子签名依赖方因依据电子认证提供者提供的电子签名认证服务从事民事活动遭受损失,电子认证服务提供者不能证明自己没有过错者,承担赔偿责任。"准此,似容易产生凡运用认证制度之电子交

[①] 就《电子签名法》第3条及第13条第2款之规定分别以观,当事人虽得约定使用电子签名、数据电文,然就可靠与否,仍须另为判断,非仅系诸当事人依第3条所为之约定;当然,吾人亦不排除当事人于约定使用电子签章、数据电文时,同时约定可靠之条件,此亦为私法自治落实之必然结果。

易所生之损失,皆应由电子认证服务提供者先证其无过错后,始毋庸负担赔偿责任之法评价依据。然而,吾人以为,就第 28 条之文义以观,或有此一解释之可能,唯就该条之意涵言,应不能涵盖诸如债务不履行等民事责任,解释上应将第 28 条之责任范围限于与认证服务提供相关之行为责任。或有论者以为,电子认证服务提供者既可透过证明其无过错而毋庸负担赔偿责任,故无须对文义有所限缩;然吾人以为,电子认证服务提供者诉讼成本之降低与避免,应系电子认证服务提供者加入市场之重要诱因之一,为促进电子商务之发展、使电子认证服务提供者乐于提供服务,应采如上之解释而认为第 28 条之规范内涵应仅限于与认证服务提供相关之行为责任。

此外,值得研究者,在于第 32 条行为态样是否仅以伪造、冒用、盗用为限?即第 32 条系属列举规定抑或例示规定?吾人以为,伪造、冒用或盗用固为电子商务中所关切之重要问题,然法律规范上应不仅止于此而应认为此一规范属例示规范为宜。再者,由第 32 条"依法追究"一词亦可得知,立法者所着重者,应在于法律规范之态样为何,从而针对该行为予以规范,而非仅限于伪造、冒用或盗用。

(5) 附则

为求规范定义之明确化,附则特别针对电子签名人、电子签名依赖方、电子签名认证证书、电子签名制作数据、电子签名验证数据之定义予以明文化之规定,值得赞同。

2. 电子合同的要约与承诺问题

一般说来,合同是经由当事人一方发出要约,他方作出承诺而成立。然而电子合同的缔结,是通过网际网络来完成,可能会发生一方发出的要约和他方所作的承诺,不能充分反映双方当事人的真意,而且双方有时会察觉不到错误的发生[①];所以,如何认定要约与承诺的效力,是个问题。

另外,有关电子合同的生效时间问题,就电子合同的缔结,多数是非对话的意思表示,究竟以承诺的发出还是到达之时为合同的成立时间,对

---

① 例如:"张岩诉金贸网拍公司网上拍卖纠纷案 1999 年 10 月",原告张岩在中国商品交易拍卖市场网站举办的"海星计算机卖场拍卖会""主办者是国安五龙拍卖公司,承办者是金贸网拍公司"上参与竞购,并对 3 台计算机打出当时的最高价位,从而在网站公布的拍卖结果中被确认成交。但其后该网站称拍卖结果的出现是系统故障所致,对竞拍结果不予承认。今年 3 月,法院判决北京金贸网拍公司和国安五龙拍卖公司应退还竞标人张岩购物款 10275.5 元及利息,并承担诉讼费 400 元,但却驳回张岩要求给付计算机的请求。参阅王冠玺:《中国大陆电子合同法律问题简析》,资策会科技法律中心, http://stlc.iii.org.tw/articles/Netlaw/200009w.htm (visited 2004/7/30)。

于纠纷发生时责任的认定,更具有相当重要的意义。在这一点上,大陆《合同法》是采取到达生效主义①,而英美法系的国家对电子合同的成立,则采取"发出生效主义",因此不同的法律体系下,设有不同的标准,一旦产生跨国的商务纠纷时,如何协调,也很值得探讨。

3. 电子合同(文件)的证据法问题

电子签章技术及认证机制,既能确保电子合同在网络上传输过程中,避免遭窃取、删改或假冒,又能避免真正发文者为逃避法律责任而否认自己的发送。因此,在立法上除应认可电子签章的效力,也应认可经电子签章的电子合同(文件)在证据法的有效性。早期,随着电子商务发展的迫切需要,在新合同法中已承认了电子合同的书面性问题,而赋予其法律上等同书面的效力②,唯于证据法上,则无相关之规定,迄至2004年电子签名法通过,该法第7条规定,数据电文不得仅因为其是以电子、光学、磁或者类似手段生成、发送、接收或者储存的而被拒绝作为证据使用。即为透过电子签章以确认电子合同于证据法上之有效性依据。

除了上述合同法在立法层面上的努力外,大陆在技术面上还通过中国金融认证中心的建设③,希望达到保证互联网上电子交易的安全性,并防范交易及支付过程中的诈欺行为。具体而言,除了在信息传输过程中采用更强的加密算法等措施外,还需要通过网上认证机制的建立;所以,在大陆信息产业部研订的电子商务发展总体框架中特别强调,统筹规划认证体系的建设,由政府有关主管部门实行授权管理,建置权威性、可信赖性及公正性的第三方认证机构,是实现电子商务重要的关键。④

---

① 《合同法》第26条规定:"承诺通知到达要约人时生效"。关于到达时间的确定,《合同法》第16条第2款规定:"采用数据电文形式订立合同,收件人指定特定系统接受数据电文的,该数据电文进入该特定系统的时间,视为到达时间;未指定特定系统的,该数据电文进入收件人的任何系统的首次时间,视为到达时间。"

② 《合同法》第11条规定:"书面形式是指合同书、信件和数据电文(包括电报、电传、传真、电子数据和电子邮件)等可以有形地表现所载内容的形式"。

③ 由中国人民银行发起,联合中国工商银行、中国农业银行、中国银行、中国建设银行、交通银行、招商银行、中信实业银行、华夏银行、广东发展银行、深圳发展银行、光大银行、民生银行等12家商业银行,共同建设了中国金融认证中心(China Financial Certificate Authority,简称CFCA)。中国金融认证中心为一权威的、可信赖的、公正的第三方信任机构,为参与电子商务各方的各种认证需求提供证书服务,建立彼此的信任机制,为中国大陆的电子商务及网上银行等网上支付业务提供多种模式的认证服务,在不远的将来实现与国外CA的交叉认证。http://tech.taiwan.com/column/e21times/20010521/01.htm(visited 2004/7/30)。

④ 参阅新华社,《我国网上安全支付基础建设取得突破进展》,人民网 http://www.people.com.cn/GB/channel5/28/20000704/129717.html(visited 2004/7/30)。

按照这个理念,中国金融认证中心在通过国家有关部门的审查后①,于 2000 年正式对外提供服务,其采用 PKI(Public Key Infrastructure)技术,对电子商务环境中各个交易实体颁发电子证书,以证明各交易实体身份的真实性。② 在实务运作上,电子证书是各交易实体在网上进行商务活动的身份证明,因为在电子交易的各个环节中,交易当事人都需要验证对方电子证书的有效性,而该中心即专门负责为金融业的各种认证需求提供证书服务,为参与网上交易的各方提供安全基础,建立彼此信任的机制。③ 认证中心的成立与运行,将可奠定网上安全支付的基础,从而也象征着大陆电子商务已进入可提供跨银行安全支付的新阶段。④

(三)有关知识产权保护部分

1. 著作权与专利权的相关规定

早期,大陆关于网络知识产权的保护较为薄弱,为保护中外著作权人的权益,遂根据 2001 年 10 月 27 日第九届全国人民代表大会常务委员会第二十四次会议《关于修改〈中华人民共和国著作权法〉的决定》,修正大陆的著作权法的修正内容,其中即包括网络环境的著作权保护等议题。

2. 网域名称的相关规定

(1)网域名称与商标法的相关规定

随着网际网络的快速成长与日益商业化,容易辨识网站的网域名称,如同好听易记的电话号码一样,也成为工商业争逐的目标,因此,网域名称的争议就相当的多。就网域名称的属性而言,其基本方向是认定网域

---

① 这个项目的建设自 1999 年 2 月 26 日正式启动,它采用了世界上最先进的安全认证技术及公安部认可的 ISS 产品,同时按照国家有关规定,对系统中的密码产品模块进行了本地化,经过 9 个月的努力,中国金融认证中心已经完成从网络到业务系统的全面建设。参阅新华社,《我国网上安全支付基础建设取得突破进展》,人民网 http://www.people.com.cn/GB/channel5/28/20000704/129717.html(visited 2004/7/30)。

② 参阅新华社,《我国网上安全支付基础建设取得突破进展》,人民网 http://www.people.com.cn/GB/channel5/28/20000704/129717.html(visited 2004/7/30)。

③ 认证中心的业务应用范围,目前可支持 B to C;B to B 以及 B to G(Government)的模式。在 B to B 及 B to C 的模式目前可发放 SET(安全电子交易)证书和 NON-SET PKI 证书。SET 证书用于支持以信用卡、借记卡支付的 SET 交易(B to C);PKI 证书可用于 B to B 和 B to C 交易,支持网上银行、网上证券交易、网上购物以及安全电子文件传递等应用。参阅网上法,《电子商务付款》,http://www.ipeclaw.com.tw/issue_member/china/china_ec_main.php?page=2&serial=1-4-6(visited 2004/7/30);参阅新华社,《我国网上安全支付基础建设取得突破进展》,人民网 http://www.people.com.cn/GB/channel5/28/20000704/129717.html(visited 2004/7/30)。

④ 认证中心建设初期还属于试点工程,虽然规模不大,但功能齐全,近期预计每年发放 15 万张 NON-SET 证书及 10 万张 SET 证书。参阅网上法,《电子商务付款》,http://www.ipeclaw.com.tw/issue_member/china/china_ec_main.php?page=2&serial=1-4-6(visited 2004/7/30)。

名称具有商标的性质,所以,使用相同或近似他人注册商标名称作为网域名称,并在网站促销与他人同一或类似商品,则可能构成商标侵害[①];然而如果商品与该他人商标所指定商品不属于同一或类似,则不构成商标侵害。此外,并针对商标"使用"的定义加以修正,试图界定"无体形态的网络是否也属于商标的使用"的问题。

(2)《中国互联网络域名管理办法》的相关规定

关于网域名称的管理,虽在大陆允许不同类别的商品使用相同的商标,但在网络上域名却只有一个。由于域名的"唯一性"异于商标的相对"不唯一性",加上为获取商业利益,使域名与商标或企业名称相冲突的可能性增加,如域名中包含他人的注册商标、域名恶意抢先注册、域名与其他企业名称相同等等。

为避免域名注册的纠纷,大陆先是以《中国互联网络域名注册暂行管理办法》加以规定[②],该办法第17条即规定,申请人必须对自己选择的域名负责,并保证其选定的域名注册不侵害任何第三方的利益,且非为违法的目的。其后于2002年时,则是通过《中国互联网络域名管理办法》,藉以调整《中国互联网络域名注册暂行管理办法》之规定。[③] 该办法第22条规定域名注册完成后,域名注册申请者即成为其注册域名的持有者。因持有或使用域名而侵害他人合法权益的,责任由域名持有者承担。

至于域名纠纷的处理,《中国互联网络域名注册暂行管理办法》第23

---

① 故以相同或近似他人网站名称作为商标注册,就网站名称的独创性、知名度、商品的关联程度等事项斟酌,商标注册有致公众误信之虞者,网站所有人得申请评定商标注册无效。

② 该办法规定由中国互联网络信息中心(CNNIC)工作委员会,负责管理和运行中国顶级域名CN。大陆互联网络的二级域名分为"类别域名"和"行政区域名"两类。按照"先申请先注册"的原则受理域名注册,不受理域名预留。在大陆,公民个人不能申请域名,域名注册申请人必须是依法登记并且能够独立承担民事责任的组织。且申请人应当保证其申请文件的真实性,并在其了解的范围内,保证其选定的域名的注册不侵害任何第三方的利益。同时为防止他人透过抢注域名谋利,该管理办法还规定了注册域名可以变更或者注销,但禁止转让或者买卖。在大陆用户注册域名时通常有两种选择,一为注册在美国管理的国际通用顶级域名,或者注册中国CN域名,此两种域名均可在全球使用,且都是顶级域名。其间的差别为:CN标志可容易使人了解是来自大陆的企业,并受大陆法律的保障与规范,在外国注册的域名,则受外国法令规范,是否能真正保障中国企业较有疑义。参阅网上法,《中国大陆网络域名注册程序》,http://www.ipe-claw.com.tw/issue_member/china/china_ec_main.php?serial=1-2-1 (visited 2004/7/30)。

③ 根据CNNIC在2000年初对注册商、注册代理以及注册用户的调查,各方反映的热点问题集中在注册手续繁琐、限制条件过于苛刻、收费过高等方面。暂行办法对域名注册的限制较为苛刻,需先行审批,规定CN域名注册申请人必须是依法登记并且能够独立承担民事责任的组织。这就将众多欲申请注册CN域名的个人排除在CN域名之外,致使中国个人只能注册国际域名。在域名注册费方面,现在CN域名的年注册费为人民币300元,这与国际域名不到100元人民币的年费标准差距不小。这也是造成大量中国机构和个人注册国际域名的重要原因之一。http://www.sipo.gov.cn/sipo/zscqb/zonghe/t20020822_7752.htm (visited 2004/7/30)。

条订定了下列三项原则:1.申请人自理纠纷,政府部门不介入;2.若未提出异议,则域名持有方可以继续使用其域名。3.若权益对方异议时,则暂保30日使用权。① 举例而言,大陆曾发生都拥有Panda(熊猫)注册商标的熊猫电子集团公司与北京日化二厂间域名注册冲突。按照该办法规定,两家公司都有权以panda为域名申请注册,但panda.com.cn却只能有一个,由于北京日化二厂先提出此域名注册申请,中国互联网络信息中心按"先来先注册"原则批准了其注册申请;事后,熊猫电子集团公司就无法再获得同一域名注册,只能申请注册pandagroup.com.cn及nanjingpanda.com.cn。因此,一旦域名被他人先行合法注册,将难以回复。② 相对于此,《中国互联网络域名管理办法》则增定域名争议一章,明订域名注册管理机构可以指定中立的域名争议解决机构解决域名争议,唯该域名争议解决机构之裁决仍须服从于人民法院或者仲裁机构发生法律效力的裁判。此外,大陆并设有中国互联网络信息中心域名争议解决办法与中国互联网络信息中心域名争议解决办法程序规则,藉以解决互联网络域名争议与保证域名争议解决程序的公正性、方便性及快捷性。

(四)有关征税问题部分

传统的税收制度是建立在税务登记、查账征收和定额征收的基础上的;所以,税务机关通过对纳税人营业场所、经营品种、经营数量及经营行为等指针,并对各种票证和账簿的审核来确定应缴纳的税种和税率。然而这种面对面的操作模式在电子商务时代,显然不能适应实际的需要,电子商务的虚拟化、无形化、随意化、隐匿化给税收征管带来了前所未有的困难。

当电子商务通过无纸化进行,各种销售凭证都以电子数据的形式存在,税收征管监控失去了最直接的实物对象;同时,电子商务的快捷性、直接性、隐匿性、保密性等特质,使依法课税变得非常困难。新兴的电子商

---

① 具体而言,1.申请人自理纠纷,官方不介入:各级域名管理单位不负责向国家工商行政管理部门及商标管理部门查询用户域名是否与注册商标或者企业名称相冲突,是否侵害第三者的权益。任何因这类冲突引起的纠纷,由申请人自己负责处理并承担法律责任。2.若权益对方未异议,可继续使用域名:当某个三级域名与中国大陆境内注册的商标或者企业名称相同,并且注册域名不为注册商标或者企业名称持有方拥有时,注册商标或者企业名称持有方若未提出异议,则域名持有方可以继续使用其域名。3.若权益对方异议,可暂保留30日使用权:若注册商标或者企业名称持有方提出异议,在确认其拥有注册商标或者企业名称之日起,各级域名管理单位为域名持有方保留30日域名服务,30日后域名服务自动停止,其间一切法律责任和经济纠纷与各级域名管理单位无关。

② 参阅网上法,《中国大陆网络域名纠纷处理》,http://www.ipeclaw.com.tw/issue_member/china/china_ec_main.php? serial=1-2-1(visited 2004/7/30)。

务是否收税、如何收税等问题,一直是财税部门研究的重要课题①,所以,大陆国家税务总局除已成立了电子商务税收对策研究小组,加紧研究具体税收框架外②,更设有《2002—2006年中国税收征收管理战略规划纲要》,除仍强调电子商务改变传统的贸易和结算方式而具有无国界、数字化等特点外,更因电子商务加大了税收征管的难度,产生了较大的税款流失风险和税款转移的可能。因此认为必须在传统的税收征管体系之外,建立一套依托于因特网的电子税收征管体系,对电子商务进行比较有效的监管,维护国家的利益。③ 然而,如何落实与建构相关措施,是一个值得研究的问题所在。

(五) 有关基础电信业务部分

1.《中国公众多媒体通信管理办法》的相关规定④

所谓公众多媒体通信业务是指,通过中国公众多媒体通信网,向最终用户提供的公众多媒体通信与信息服务。⑤ 如多媒体信息检索、多媒体数据处理、声像点播、远程医疗、远程教育、电子商务等。就其业务经营者,可分公众多媒体通信接入服务经营者与公众多媒体信息源提供者两种⑥;按照该管理办法第5条的规定,大陆对公众多媒体通信业务采取不同的管理制度,就公众多媒体通信接入服务经营者,是采取经营许可制度;而对公众多媒体信息源提供者,则采取申报核准制度。由邮电部及各省、自

---

① 根据Gartner顾问公司调查,1998年大陆电子交易总额为1.7亿美元,预估2004年将达820亿美元。1998年亚太地区的电子交易额为25亿美元,至2004年将成长至9,030亿美元。http://be1.udnnews.com/2001/2/16/NEWS/FINANCE/EC/164758.shtml,(visited 2001/7/10)。

② 参阅北京晨报,《国家态度谨慎具体框架待定,电子商务暂时免税》,人民网,http://www.people.com.cn/GB/channel5/30/20000804/173357.html(visited 2004/7/30)。国家税务总局局长金人庆在接受中国日报采访时表示,为保护税制的权威与公正性,中国大陆不会像部分发达国家那样对电子商务免税。税收中立性原则表明税制不应因不同类型的贸易而变化,电子商务的电子形式并不改变其贸易的特性。http://202.130.245.40/chinese/2281.htm,(visited 2001/7/10)。

③ 《关于2002—2006年中国税收征收管理战略规划纲要》,请参国家税务总局,http://www.chinatax.gov.cn(visited 2004/7/30)。

④ 参阅君思电子商务世界,《国内主要网络管理法规简介》,http://www.juns.com.cn/,(visited 2001/3/16);网上法,"公众多媒体通信业务范围": http://www.ipeclaw.com.tw/issue_member/china/china_ec_main.php?serial=1-3-3(visited 2004/7/30)。

⑤ 根据《中国公众多媒体通信管理办法》第2条规定:公众多媒体通信的定义,是指向公众提供的,集声音、文字、图像、数据等多种通信媒介为一体的,具有集成性、同步性与交互性的通信方式。

⑥ 具体而言,(1)公众多媒体通信接入服务经营者:指租用或建立必要的接入设施或接入能力,与中国邮电电信总局签订协议,或受其委托,为用户接入中国公众多媒体通信网提供服务的单位。(2)公众多媒体信息源提供者:指采集、加工、存储多媒体信息,并通过公众多媒体通信网向用户提供公众多媒体的单位。

治区、直辖市邮电管理局按管理权限负责审批与核准;未经批准,不得经营前开业务(第8条)。①

2.《中华人民共和国电信条例》的相关规定②

按照该条例的定义,所谓"电信",是指利用有线、无线的电磁系统或者光电系统,传送、发射或者接收语音、文字、数据、图像以及其他任何形式信息的活动,都包括在其中。至于"增值电信业务",是指利用公共网络基础设施提供的电信与信息服务的业务。③ 经营增值电信业务者,依本条例第13条规定,应具备下列条件:(1)经营者为依法设立的公司;(2)有与开展经营活动相适应的资金和专业人员;(3)有为用户提供长期服务的信誉或者能力;(4)国家规定的其他要件。另,依第9条规定,业务覆盖范围在两个以上省、自治区、直辖市者,须经国务院信息产业主管部门审查批准,取得跨地区增值电信业务经营许可;未跨区者,须经省、自治区、直辖市电信管理机构审查批准,取得增值电信业务经营许可。

对于外国、香港、澳门及台湾地区的组织或个人在中国大陆投资与经营电信业务者,依该条例第80条规定,由国务院另行制定规定,以作为规范。④

(六)有关互联网信息服务管理及内容监督部分

1.《中国公众多媒体通信管理办法》的相关规定⑤

该办法是首次以法律规范的形式,确立接入服务经营者和信息源提供者的概念,并对前者采取经营许可证制度,对后者则采取申报核准制度。该管理办法中有关信息内容的法律责任的规定,尤其应加以注意,其规定信息源提供者应对其向中国公众多媒体通信网所提供信息的合法性与真实性承担主要责任,但同时网络经营者和接入服务经营者也要承担

---

① 违反者,通信主管部门予以警告;情节严重者,由公安机关依法处罚;构成犯罪者,提请司法机关追究刑责(第16条)。
② 参阅网上法,《互联网信息服务增值电信业务经营范围》,http://www.ipeclaw.com.tw/issue_member/china/china_ec_main.php? serial = 1 - 3 - 1 (visited 2004/7/30)。
③ 依分类目录包含下列九种:(1)电子邮件;(2)语音信箱;(3)在线信息库存和检索;(4)电子数据交换;(5)在线数据处理与交易处理;(6)增值传真;(7)互联网接入服务;(8)互联网信息服务;(9)可视电话会议服务。
④ 所以,依邮电部1993年制定的《从事开放经营电信业务审批管理暂行办法》第6条第2项规定,境外组织和个人以及在中国大陆境内的外商独资、中外合资和合作企业,不得投资、经营或者参与经营电信业务。关于《从事开放经营电信业务审批管理暂行办法》,请参照 http://www.ctiforum.com/resource/law/law0410.htm (visited 2004/7/30)。
⑤ 参阅君思电子商务世界,《国内主要网络管理法规简介》,http://www.juns.com.cn/, (visited 2001/3/26);网上法,"公众多媒体通信业务范围",http://www.ipeclaw.com.tw/issue_member/china/china_ec_main.php? serial = 1 - 3 - 3 (visited 2004/7/30)。

相应的责任。

2.《互联网信息服务管理办法》的相关规定①

按照该办法的定义,所谓经营性互联网信息服务,是指通过互联网向上网用户有偿提供信息或者网页制作等服务活动。于第 7 条中规定,除应当向省、自治区、直辖市电信管理机构或者国务院信息产业主管部门申请办理"互联网信息服务增值电信业务经营许可证"外,严格管制网络信息提供者不得散布违反中国大陆宪法的基本原则。②

3.《互联网医疗卫生信息服务管理办法》③

按照该办法的规定,医疗信息网站在申请办理经营许可证前,应先经中国卫生行政部门的审核同意,并且所有的医疗卫生网站,只能提供医疗卫生咨询服务,不得从事网上诊断和治疗活动。该办法还规定,利用互联网开展远程医疗会诊服务,属医疗行为,只能在具有医疗机构职业许可证的医疗机构间进行。本办法特别强调,"医疗卫生网站登载的信息必须科学准确,注明信息来源,登载或转载卫生政策、疫情、重大卫生事件等信息必须遵守有关的法律、法规。"④

(七)有关网络广告及电子邮件部分

1. 有关网络广告的相关规定

据统计,1999 年大陆的网络广告营业额已经接近 1 亿元人民币,2002 年时则约有 4.9 亿元人民币,而根据市场调查公司 AC 尼尔森的评估⑤,2003 年大陆网络广告收入约增加到 7.8 亿元,比 2002 年增加 2.9 亿元,增幅达 59%,同时,在未来 3 年的时间里,将会以每年 38% 左右的幅度增长,并且在 2005 年达到 15.5 亿元。准此,网络广告成为新兴的产业,不难预料,然而有关网络广告的管理规范则显得滞后。大陆对网络广告的监

---

① 参阅网上法,《互联网信息服务增值电信业务经营范围》,http://www.ipeclaw.com.tw/issue_member/china/china_ec_main.php? serial=1-3-1(visited 2004/7/30);"中国网络管理方针出炉严格控制网络内容",http://www.ipeclaw.com.tw/news_net.php? category=net&serial=20(visited 2004/7/30)。

② 另外,针对新闻、出版等特别行业特别要求得经主管机关的审查同意。开办电子布告栏需要提出专项申请。互联网信息服务提供者应在其网站主页的显著位置标明其经营许可证编号,违反者,由电信管理机构责令改正,处 5 千元以上 5 万元以下人民币罚锾(办法第 12 条、第 22 条)。

③ 参阅网上法,《中国卫生部公布〈互联网医疗卫生信息服务管理办法〉》,http://www.ipeclaw.com.tw/news_net.php? serial=380(visited 2004/7/30)。

④ 信息服务分为经营性和非经营性两类,经营性服务是指向网上用户有偿提供信息或网页制作等服务活动;非经营性服务是指向网上用户无偿提供具有公开性、共享性信息,http://202.84.17.11/big5/wjxw/123859594.htm(visited 2004/7/30)。

⑤ http://www.new54.com/article/A02031124.php(visited 2004/7/30)。

管,是由国家工商局广告监管司负责,目前正积极建构互联网广告的有效监管方式,为制定互联网广告法规作准备,其将制订一系列规范以有效地规范中国互联网广告市场,使互联网行业逐步走向规范化和法制化。① 值得注意的,北京市已于2001年4月10日依据《中华人民共和国广告法》及《中华人民共和国广告管理条例》有关规定,制订《北京市网络广告管理暂行办法》,藉以规范网络广告内容和广告活动,保护经营者和消费者的合法权益。

2. 有关电子邮件的相关规定

随着网络运用日趋普及,出现有人使用电子邮件大量发送商业广告,造成垃圾邮件泛滥的现象,减损了电子信箱使用资源,降低了网络正常传递信息的功能。为保障广大网络用户的合法通信权益,确保电信网络的正常运行,中国电信集团公司于是制定《垃圾邮件处理暂行办法》,同时,中国电信集团公司也已为用户提供受理垃圾邮件投诉的信箱,而且在受理用户业务时,也将在业务登记表或相关协议中增加有关垃圾邮件的规定,以约束用户的行为。② 然而,根据大陆互联网协会的统计数据显示,2003年,国内的邮件服务器共收到1500亿封垃圾邮件,尽管其中60%到80%被服务器过滤掉,但至少有470亿封最终流入用户的信箱。鉴于垃圾邮件泛滥日益加剧的趋势,于中国互联网协会主办的"2004中国反垃圾邮件高峰论坛"上,中国信息产业部表示,针对垃圾邮件问题之改善与消除,计划设置《电子邮件服务管理办法》,藉以管制电子垃圾邮件的泛滥趋势。③

四、结束语

许多人认为,大陆的电子商务与全球市场一样面临着重大的危机,却不知道对于大陆这个初历市场经济的地区而言,以工业革命为本的现代化与迎合全球经济发展需求的信息化是同等重要的,尤其是2001年初,江泽民在公开讲话中正式称许电子商务的价值并要求各单位健全相关法制后,电子商务已成为中国大陆的重点基础建设事项,这其中,法律课题的重要性尤其值得我们重视。本书的撰写正在于掌握大陆相关法制的发

---

① 参阅,《我国将出台互联网广告法规》,载《市场报》2000/06/22 第5版,人民网 http://www.people.com.cn/GB/channel5/28/20000622/113790.html(visited 2004/7/30)。

② 参阅网上法,《电子商务广告管理——垃圾邮件处理》,http://www.ipeclaw.com.tw/issue_member/china/china_ec_main.php?serial=1-4-3(visited 2004/7/30)。

③ http://it.sohu.com/2004/04/27/25/article219962524.shtml(visited 2004/7/30)。

展,并希望通过系统的分析整理提供两岸相关研究的参考。

2.2 台湾地区电子商务发展现况与调整

从全球网际网络的扩张速度来看,网络的应用与发展对每一个国家或社会在信息文明的未来竞争,势必有决定性的影响。目前国际间电子商务的发展已是如火如荼,身为地球村的一员,当需积极掌握国际趋势,并调整现行的法制规范,以保障当事人权益,促进社会整体的福利,更用以避免乱象丛生而无法可用的窘境,因此如何创设一个适当且符合电子商务的法律环境便成为当务之急。

一、台湾地区电子商务政策纲领的提出

(一) 缘起

继美国于 1997 年 7 月发布全球电子商务纲要(A Framework For Global Electronic Commerce)后,为了抢得网际网络上的商机及确保各国商品与服务在国际贸易上的竞争力,并消除网际网络发展环境的许多不确定因素,国际间相继发表电子商务政策蓝图。[①] 台湾地区也于 1998 年 11 月在吉隆坡举行的亚太经合会(APEC)经济领袖会议中[②]公布了电子商务政策纲领(Policy Guidelines for Electronic Commerce in Chinese Taipei),向国际说明台湾地区未来电子商务发展蓝图;通过电子商务的应用,希望将台湾地区建设成为 21 世纪亚太地区的商务中心。整体而言,其发展目标,是为了使台湾地区成为具备便利、效率、亲和、先进与网络化等特点的商务中心,积极服务 APEC 区域内各会员体及国际社会;提升台湾地区产业总体竞争力,确保下一世纪竞争优势;并借助专业人力资源及计算机高科

---

① 主要的有:于 1997 年 7 月 8 日在波昂由德国与欧洲联盟(European Union)等 29 个国家共同主导的"全球信息网络—实现潜能"(Global Information Networks-Realizing the Potential)会议中,由部长级会议所发表的波昂宣言(Bonn Declaration),达成对全球信息网络的发展的 69 项共识;全球商业联盟(The Alliance for Global Business)又于 1999 年 10 月提出"全球电子商务行动方案"(A Global Action Plan for Electronic Commerce),详见台湾地区"经济部"商业司编:《1999 中华台北电子商务年鉴》,台北:"经济部"2000 年版,第 15 页。

② 1998 年 11 月于吉隆坡举行的亚太经合会(APEC)经济领袖会议,公布领袖宣言明确支持由部长级会议所研拟的 APEC 电子商务行动蓝图(APEC Blueprint For Action On Electronic Commerce)。APEC 部长级会议根据各成员不同的经济发展程度、社会文化、管制架构规划出电子商务行动蓝图,以强化 APEC 各经济体从事电子商务的能力,促使各经济体进行技术与经济的合作,而能从中获取经济利益。

技外围产业的支持,使台湾地区在电子商务的应用上取得领先地位。①

（二）台湾地区电子商务发展的策略

台湾地区电子商务发展的策略是依电子商务的本质,以民间为主导力量,从当局做起带动电子商务应用风气,并积极参与国际各项合作,并确保中小企业公平参与的机会。举主要的说明如下②:

1. 政策上将由民间部门主导电子商务的发展,当局则积极协助建构良好的发展环境,并主动提供产业发展电子商务所需要的协助与信息。

2. 当局以身作则,带动电子商务应用风气,逐步推动电子公文、电子采购、线上数据库与网络报税等措施,有效利用社会资源提高全民网络应用水准。

3. 积极参与国际合作,电子商务为全球性活动,无法由单一区域或经济体推动,台湾地区身为地球村的一员,愿意积极参与任何国际社会间的电子商务合作计划。

4. 确保中小企业公平参与的机会。在推动电子商务的过程中,当局必须建立公平参与的环境,确保中小企业于公平的基础上参与竞争。

（三）台湾地区电子商务政策纲领的立场

就台湾地区电子商务政策纲领的立场言,可约略归类成为十大议题,试分述其要点如下③:

1. 在法律机制方面

（1）建构电子商务法律机制的基本原则

健全法制环境是电子商务发展不可或缺的一环,法律应给予电子商务与其他形式商业活动平等的待遇,法律规范与制度必须遵守功能性平等(Achieving Functional Equivalence)与科技中立原则(The Related Principle of Ensuring Technology Neutrality),应该优先让市场机制与技术本身解决电子商务的问题,政府的介入或相关法规的调整应为最后的手段。

（2）寻求电子商务法规与国际规范的协调

电子商务发展属于全球性的活动,所以应注重电子商务法律架构与

---

① 中华台北电子商务政策纲领,详参 http://wwwdoc.trade.gov.tw/BOFT/web/report_detail.jsp?data_base_id=DB008&category_id=CAT367&report_id=469（visited 2004/7/30）。

② 台湾地区"经济部"商业司编:《1999中华台北电子商务年鉴》,台北:"经济部"2000年版,第17页。

③ 中华台北电子商务政策纲领,http://wwwdoc.trade.gov.tw/BOFT/web/report_detail.jsp?data_base_id=DB008&category_id=CAT367&report_id=469（visited 2004/7/30）。

各经济体法律规范的协调①,以避免因法律冲突、不协调产生新的法律障碍。

(3) 建置电子商务法律规范的目标

建置电子商务法规的目标,应朝向网络电子商务应用、解决现有或可预见的法令障碍、确保竞争秩序以及建立可遵循与可预测的法律规范,使当局推动电子商务的各项措施都能符合依法行政的基本原则,同时兼顾网络使用者利益的保障,达到蓬勃电子商务的目的。

(4) 重视电子商务法律机制与产业自律的配合

电子商务法律机制应与产业自律规范相配合,在电子商务法律架构中,产业及其他公私团体应多方努力共同议定国际或本地区的行为规范、模范合同以及自律公约共同遵守,以维护公共利益及消费者权益。

(5) 适应网络特性加强知识产权的保护

为适应网络特性,必须尽快制定合理的知识产权法律,塑造一个有利于网络信息服务应用的环境。

(6) 支持全球性的网域名称系统

网域名称(domain name)对于电子商务的发展具有很重大的意义,所以必须建立一个全球性的网域名称的注册、分配与管理系统。②

(7) 打击网络犯罪维护电子商务交易秩序

网络犯罪会严重影响与打击企业及消费者使用电子商务的信心。为避免窃盗、诈欺、洗钱等经济犯罪在网络上进行,应针对刑法等相关法令的修正,成立计算机犯罪防治中心专门负责,同时积极参与国际组织,结合国际力量,共同打击网络犯罪。③

2. 在市场秩序方面

台湾地区主张网际网络为一自由开放市场,对于电子商务市场秩序,应由民间企业主导,让各种电子商务的创新应用能在自由经济体制下逐步落实。如果当局必须介入管理,则应秉持中立的原则,维持市场信息的透明化。

---

① 例如:美国《统一商务法典》(Uniform Commercial Code; U.C.C.) Article2B 修正草案、澳洲政府所公布《电子商务法律纲要》(Electronic Commerce: Building The Legal Framework)等;同时重视与国际组织法规的一致性,尤其是联合国所公布的《联合国国际贸易法律委员会电子商务模范法》(UNCITRAL Model Law on Electronic Commerce)等。

② 它必须充分反映网际网络的地域特色与多重功能的特质,而且必须为国际共同承认;此外,应具备未来可转换的弹性,并能为世界各经济体提供平等的待遇。

③ 台湾地区"经济部"商业司编:《1999 中华台北电子商务年鉴》,台北:"经济部"2000 年版,第 18 页。

3. 在技术标准方面

制定技术标准,应采科技中立的立场,技术标准应通过自由市场决定。①

4. 在金融财税方面

(1) 电子商务的租税议题

由于网际网络缺乏清楚的国界与边境,所以其交易程序的快速与交易匿名性等现象,使得依据实体商品与地理区域为设计基础的现行课税法律架构,在适用上更显得格格不入,从而有特别就电子商务设计并维持明确、一致、中立、无歧视性租税制度的必要。此外赞成当货物利用电子方式订购而以实体货物运送时,不应因其利用电子商务形式而被征收额外的进口税捐;但原有进口税捐的免税措施则继续予以维持。②

(2) 制订能弹性适应市场需求的电子付款政策

当局应避免采用僵化与强制性的管理政策,而应提供适当的培育环境促进电子付款系统的发展日益成熟。③

5. 在隐私保护方面

发展电子商务的关键之一就是促使上网者个人及交易资料的隐私获得充分保障;当局在网络隐私权保障政策推动上,将采取积极措施并推动产业界采行保护隐私权的自律规范,鼓励产业界开发科技装置,并采取安全措施来保护使用者的隐私。④

6. 在网络安全方面

台湾地区支持1997年经济合作发展组织的加密政策指导原则,并积极推动制订电子认证机制、信息安全管理及稽核制度,并订定信息安全共通规范,以及建立公开金钥认证体系。

---

① 例如台湾地区支持透过 ISO、IEC、ITU、W3C 等相关国际组织,倡导由产业主导制订标准,并防止各经济体界定标准或非关税障碍,造成自由贸易障碍。同时,为便利电信和信息科技的流通,更积极协助企业加入制订标准的国际组织,并参与国际间相关认证协议的协商,以进一步简化国际间认证处理的程序。

② 适应网络交易的特质,在制订电子商务租税制度时,避免采用会扭曲或阻碍电子商务的发展的租税制度,或产生歧视特定形态的交易效果。在执行层面,应考量稽征方式简单说明了且能有效收取税收,并以技术上易于执行、低稽征成本为原则。并注意避免电子商务的租税与台湾地区税管辖权产生冲突及双重课税。

③ 观察智慧卡、电子钱等新兴付款方式,鼓励开发更新颖的电子付款技术,并结合现行金融体系发展出可信赖的、安全的、高效率的电子付款系统。长期政策将与产业密切合作,配合国际组织的政策与趋势,发展出能弹性适应市场需求的电子付款政策。详参台湾地区"经济部"商业司编:《1999 中华台北电子商务年鉴》,台北:"经济部"2000 年版,第 19 页。

④ 为配合国际组织与各先进国家对隐私权的保护政策与法令,应提出适合电子商务的隐私保护政策。

7. 在电信建设方面

电信建设以提供市场所需要的网络频宽与服务为原则,提供高品质的网络通讯服务,同时逐步开放电信服务事业,促进电信市场自由化。并遵守世界贸易组织基础通信协议、信息技术协议(ITA)及双边协议,排除非关税障碍。

8. 在内容管理方面

网络上内容管理应遵循保障人民言论自由的原则,尊重市场机制运作,维持当局的低度管理。同时当局应推动网络内容业者制订自律规范,就网络内容进行明确分级标示,赋予使用者信息自主选择权,并利用如过滤软件等科技装置来解决儿童保护等相关课题。

9. 在教育推广方面

为适应电子商务发展的人力资源需求,应规划建立长期的人才培育计划、终身学习体系及短、中期现有在职人才的电子商务知识培育课程。①

10. 在中小企业方面

电子商务应努力提供中小企业提升国际竞争力的良机,应积极辅导及协助中小企业发展电子商务应用,迈向国际市场;并重视中小企业参与电子商务的权益,积极确保其公平参与的环境。②

二、政府的相关调整措施

有鉴于全世界的电子商业交易市场随着网际网络的发展而急速成长,各国家、地区政府对网际网络、电子商务或电子化企业等议题都投入了很多精力,可见各国家、地区对数字经济发展的重视,也可看出各国、各地区希望在 21 世纪持续提升经济优势的企图。而台湾地区政府机关、研究机构与产业界也对此提出阶段性调整方案,在此试简析如下:

(一)"行政院"产业自动化及电子化推动方案

从 1980 年起,台湾地区就陆续推动"产业自动化服务十年计划"和"产业自动化十年计划",全面辅导制造业、商业、农业、营建业进行生产合理化、标准化、计算机辅助工程设计制造及整厂整线自动化,以带动产业

---

① 在推广方面,初期以普及网络人口为基础,快速推动全民上网;日后则针对不同产业的上中下游供应链,推展深入的应用。

② 有关中华台北电子商务政策纲领,详见 http://wwwdoc.trade.gov.tw/BOFT/web/report_detail.jsp?data_base_id=DB008&category_id=CAT367&report_id=469(visited 2004/7/30)。

设备全面更新、提升生产效率、降低生产成本、稳定产品品质,促进产业升级。①

在面对电子商务带来的产业革命潮流时,为掌握国际市场的先机,台湾地区"行政院"鉴于推动 B to B 的电子商务发展对提升产业竞争力的重要性,积极推动"'国家'信息通信基本建设推动方案"(NII)②以建构网络建设、教育及法制等方面的优良环境;另一方面将进行的"产业自动化计划"扩大为"产业自动化及电子化推动方案",还继续推动生产、仓储、运送及营销四方面的自动化工作外③,并选择重要行业积极推动供应链及需求链的电子商务。④ 其相关措施主要的有⑤:

1. 产业推动电子化有关研究发展的投资准予抵减奖励⑥,厂商执行本方案投资自动化及电子化的设备,准予适用购置自动化设备优惠贷款及中小企业的相关优惠贷款的政策。

2. 由"行政院""国家"信息通信基本建设项目推动小组,推动网际网络基础建设及网际网络商务相关法规。

3. 由"财政部"在金融交易、税捐稽征及通关作业方面加以配合。

4. 由"交通部"推动邮政、电信及运输业的相关配合事宜。

5. 由"经济部"技术处协助财团法人机构,实现产业自动化及电子化相关的技术能力。⑦

6. 运用研究机构、大专院校及产业公会的资源,辅导厂商进行自动化,并选择特定行业推动电子化及建立相关标准。

7. 由"经济部"协助成立产业电子化运筹管理学会,带动学术界及各

---

① 近年来台湾地区每年的自动化设备投资均超过新台币 2500 亿元,自动化设备普及率与自制比率达 65.5% 及 47% ,台湾地区产业自动化及企业计算机化已提升至相当水准。详参"产业电子化白皮书", http://www.find.org.tw/0105/download/ebook.pdf (visited 2004/7/30)。

② 根据资策会统计,截至 2003 年为止,台湾地区上网人口约有 648 万人,但除了少数信息业者已配合跨国性公司深入应用企业对企业(B to B)电子商务外,其余产业还没有积极进行。

③ 台湾地区"经济部"商业司编:《1999 中华台北电子商务年鉴》,台北:"经济部"2000 年版,第 54 页。

④ 该方案拟订于 5 年 6 个月内推广 5 万家企业、200 个体系以上,深入应用企业间电子商务(business-to-business electronic commerce;B2B EC),其中至少 80% 为中小企业,并优先完成信息业 B2B 电子商务示范体系。另针对目标产业,积极发展生产、仓储、运送和营销模块以及其整合技术,建立示范点 40 处;并于 5 年内自制造业、商业、金融证券业、农业及营建业等产业,辅导 2000 家厂商建立整体自动化的能力。

⑤ 《产业自动化推动方案》,http://proj. moeaidb. gov. tw/iaeb/htm/02-plan/project. htm#01 (visited 2004/07/30)。

⑥ 就产业推动电子化所生的费用,准予适用《促进产业升级条例》第 6 条中有关研究发展的投资抵减奖励;自动化设备的投资准予适用有关自动化的投资抵减奖励。

⑦ 并运用业界科专计划,优先支持国际性公司及台湾地区企业建立示范体系。

界人才,投入电子商务相关管理及策略的研究。

8. 利用信息月、产业自动化及电子化相关活动,扩大宣传产业自动化及电子化。

9. 通过科技人才培训及运用方案、加强信息软件人才培训方案等专业人才培训计划,培训推动各产业计划所需要的人才。

(二) 经济部商业电子化方案

随着网际网络的发展,电子商务虽然日趋兴盛,但网络交易上仍有许多商业问题存在①,为了整合业者,促进电子商业发展,台湾地区"经济部"于1998年推动"网际网络商业应用4年计划",以营造良好的电子商业环境,提供消费者或企业更快速、经济且安全可靠的支付方式,将商业交易带向新的领域等为首要目标②,并于1999年推动"电子商业国际化推动三年计划",结合商业团体及网际网络信息服务厂商的力量,提供产业上、中、下游企业进行作业与信息流程的整合,加速电子商务的发展,以期达成以网际网络技术为基础,整合商业应用技术,建立网际网络商业环境。③

(三) "国家"信息通信的基本建设(NII)

1. "国家"信息通信基本建设(NII)推动小组的组成

"行政院"于1994年8月成立"国家"信息通信基本建设项目(NII)推动小组,由部、会、署及省、市副首长组成,并聘请三十位业界领袖与学者专家组成民间咨询委员会,由当局结合民间的力量共同推动台湾地区NII建设。④

2. "国家"信息通信基本建设(NII)的分工

NII推动小组下设七个组,包括:资源规划组、网络建设组、应用技术及推广组、人才培育及基础应用组、行政及便民服务自动化组、国际合作

---

① 例如缺乏安全的支付机制、软硬件设备与信息技术不一致、交易量少、欠缺完整有效的推广运作机制、小型企业进入的障碍仍高,等问题存在。
② 其目标为整合相关计划的成果,以网际网络技术为基础,整合商业应用技术,建立网际网络商业环境,使之具备观念、技术、法规、规范、秩序以及可以衡量环境发展的指针。并分年度逐步推动,4年共40个行业、50000家以上的上、中、下游企业导入应用网际网络,以扩大上、中、下游信息整合,使产业运作得有如一家大公司。详见《网际网络商业应用四年目标》,http://www.ec.org.tw/organize/organize_main.asp(visited 2004/3/15)。
③ 台湾地区"经济部"商业司编:《1999中华台北电子商务年鉴》,台北:"经济部"2000年版,第55页。
④ 主要参与NII推动工作的政府单位为:"经济部"、"教育部"、"内政部"、"财政部"、"交通部"、"法务部"、"经建会"、"国科会"、"法规会"、"研考会"、"新闻局"、"主计处"、"卫生署"等。1997年12月"行政院"院会通过"'国家'信息通信基本建设推动方案",1998年依此方案拟定"NII中程推动工作计划",全面展开台湾地区NII建设工作。

组和综合业务组。①

此外,1997年间,NII推动小组更进一步成立"法规推动工作小组"推动法规研修工作,企图健全NII建设的法规环境。其中针对知识产权、网络商务应用、大众传播媒体、个人资料隐私权、电信通讯与媒体整合问题、网络计算机犯罪、政府资料公开等问题,研析修法及立法的相关事宜。

三、相关组织运作的情形

审视目前台湾地区民间推动电子商务多为自发性的组织或是寻求商机的策略联盟,部分当局所支持或筹设的协会则以承接当局项目,规划一系列有关于电子商务相关训练课程或是研讨会,以达到教育大众并推广电子商务的目的。以下仅就相关组织作简要介绍如下②:

(一)台湾地区电子商业联盟

该联盟③成立主要目的为整合全台湾地区电子商务厂商资源与技术,为扩大企业用户提供多元化的电子商务导入方案。该联盟特别强调能提供多元化的电子商务解决方案。而这些方案横跨了物流业、配销业、零售业、旅游业、制造业、保险业、信息业、饭店业、娱乐业、金融业等,能提供 all in one 的 total solution(全方位服务)及教育训练于全台湾地区中小企业用户使用。主要活动则为通过每月的定期活动,提供给其客服团成员有关电子商务全方位的技术与教育训练。④ 并于1997年7月依据"经济部"商业司因特网商业应用四年计划成立网络商业运用资源中心,其主要目的在于辅助"经济部"商业司电子化相关计划之推动与执行,为"经济部"商业司提供企业电子化服务的平台。其主要有四项服务功能:1.项目计划;

---

① 资源规划组由"经建会"召集,其主要任务为拟订网络及通讯产业发展策略;网络建设组由"交通部"召集,其主要任务为:加速网络建设并加强网络的维护;应用技术及推广组由"经济部"召集,其主要任务为:推广各行各业网络科技的应用;人才培育及基础应用组由"教育部"召集,其主要任务为:加强人才培训与教材引进;行政暨便民服务自动化组由"研考会"召集,其主要任务为:研拟政府行政管理及便民服务自动化的整体架构及推动策略;国际合作组由"经济部"召集,其主要任务为:规划台湾地区在网络及电子商业等议题的立场;协调整合跨组,其业务负责各项会议的协调、记录、报告等工作以及各种行政措施等。

② 台湾地区"经济部"商业司编:《1999 中华台北电子商务年鉴》,台北:"经济部"2000年版,第374页。

③ 成员目前除了包括 IBM、CISCO 等全球知名大厂外,还包括岛内的入口网站——蕃薯藤。另外还有一些本土的系统整合业者及信息服务商像是泛伦、高格等。而联盟的总执行单位是启台信息;协办单位为零壹科技,则负责提供联盟的通路行销与技术教育训练。

④ 台湾地区"经济部"商业司编:《1999 中华台北电子商务年鉴》,台北:"经济部"2000年版,第374页。http://www.moea.gov.tw(visited 2004/7/30)。

2. 企业 e 化知识库；3. 网络应用情报网；4. 服务专区。①

（二）台北市消费者电子商务协会

台北市消费者电子商务协会是以非营利为目的，依法设立之社会团体，以推广电子商务之应用、建立自律有序、公平效率、明确安全的电子商务环境、协助消费者和会员间纷争的协调与解决为宗旨。其任务如：1. 协会政策之拟定；2. 会员之认证与监督；3. 核发电子商务各消费者保护之相关认证标章；4. 订定会员管理办法；5. 办理各项电子商务相关之研讨及展示活动；6. 提供消费者申诉管道，协调会员解决。②

四、电子商务业者自律公约草案的提出

为落实前述台湾地区提出的"中华台北电子商务政策纲领"中所揭示重视电子商务法律机制与产业自律的配合原则，并推动消费者保护方案的重要措施，台湾地区"资策会"科法中心并特别制订《电子商务业者自律公约》③，在此试简介如下：

（一）电子商务业者自律公约的目的

提供企业经营电子商务指导原则，架构活络有序的电子商业环境。④

（二）电子商务业者应遵循宣示

凡签署此自律公约的电子商务业者，都宣示自发性遵循自律公约所揭示各项消费者保护政策与电子商务经营原则；并愿意持续相互砥砺督促，共同提供消费者更完善电子交易环境。

（三）电子商务业者应提供身份资料

电子商务业者应于网站诚实提供本身各项身份与营业资料，以利消费者辨认其真实身份，进而建立交易安全信心。⑤

---

① http://www.ec.org.tw/ (visited 2004/7/30)。

② http://www.sosa.org.tw/index.asp (visited 2004/7/30)。此外，尚有台中市消费者电子商务协会与高雄市消费者电子商务协会。

③ 期望经由电子商务法律机制与产业自律规范相配合。在电子商务法律架构内，透过电子商务业者及其他公私团体的努力；议定国际或岛内的行为规范，并经由自律公约的提出，与业界自发性遵守与自我约束，共同达成维护公共利益及消费者权益的愿景。

④ 藉由电子商务业者(以下简称电子商务业者)的自律建立消费者保护规范原则，确立消费者的信心，消除其对电子交易方式的不信任，更能积极性为业者开创商机，建立消费者与业者双赢的局面。虽目前(2004)台北市消费者电子商务协会计划推动《滥发商业电子讯息(垃圾邮件及简讯管理)法》，企图以法架构加以管制电子商务，惟其精神仍以业者自律为其前提。

⑤ 电子商务业者提供的身份资料至少应包括下列项目：1. 电子商务业者名称(公司登记名称及登记字号，商业登记名称及登记字号)、经营业务种类、负责人姓名；2. 营利事业登记证及登记字号、电子商家主营业所地址、通讯联络方式(至少应包括：电话号码、传真号码、E-mail 地址)；3. 其他适应行业特性依法应向消费者揭露事项。

（四）电子商务业者应完整提供交易条件信息

电子商务业者应于网页诚实并完整的提供消费者交易条件相关信息，其揭示应以明显且消费者易于取得的方式作出。[①]

（五）电子商务业者的责任

电子商务业者经营电子商务，应确实对消费者提供下列服务或履行下列义务：

1. 合同成立后，对消费者发送确认合同成立的通知。
2. 提供符合合同内容要求的品质、数量、样式的商品或服务。
3. 妥适运送货物的要求。[②]
4. 合理退货、换货机制的建立。[③]
5. 电子商务业者应确实履行保证售后服务的内容。
6. 电子商务业者应于合理期限内保存交易资料。
7. 对消费者合理要求应迅速给予响应。

（六）网络广告与宣传的原则与规范

自律公约要求网络业者应履行下列义务：

1. 电子商务业者应确保其广告内容的真实性，而且对消费者所负的责任不得低于广告的内容。
2. 电子商务业者承诺不刊登色情、暴力或违法的广告。
3. 广告内容应具体、明确、禁止夸大或过于抽象。
4. 同业广告的创意应予以尊重，并承诺不侵害知识产权，同时杜绝抄袭行为。
5. 电子商务业者承诺拒绝以不实的攻击做为广告内容，同时不利用广告进行不公平竞争。

---

① 电子商务业者提供的交易条件信息至少应涵盖下列范围：1. 所提供商品或服务的价格、种类、性质、数量及样式；2. 消费者应支出费用总额与内容，例如：运费、手续费、税款；3. 要约与承诺的传送方式、生效时间、要约有效期间、合同成立时点；4. 付款时间及方式；5. 货物寄送与服务提供的方式与时间；6. 保证与售后服务内容；7. 消费者得退货、换货或终止合同的时间、方式与限制，及双方的权利义务；8. 网络上的目录提供或线上服务如需付费，需明白向消费者揭示；9. 若该笔交易价格或其他交易条件设有期限、数量等限制条件，应于交易之初即明白向消费者揭示；10. 消费者抱怨及申诉管道，例如：电子邮件、传真、电话；11. 其他依法应揭露的事项。

② 其要求：1. 电子商务业者对消费者所订购的商品应按其性质、交易习惯为必要的包装，并选择安全、适当及迅速的运送方式；2. 运送商品如有迟延时，应依有效通知方式立即通知消费者。

③ 其要求：1. 电子商务业者承诺提供消费者法定期限或更长期限的无条件退、换货；2. 商品若未具备合同所约定的内容、品质、条件，或因运送过程中所致的污损、毁坏，消费者得不负担任何费用要求退换；3. 电子商务业者提供的商品若属线上传递的数字化商品，应明白载明所采行的销售原则与相关的退货、换货条件。

6. 在寄送电子广告邮件时,应尊重消费者的自主选择权。①

(七)消费者个人资料及隐私权的保护

电子商务业者对消费者个人资料与隐私权的保护及尊重,应成为企业内部一致遵循的原则。②

(八)安全的付款机制

电子商务业者应提供消费者至少一种在当前科技下,安全而可信赖的合法付款方式。

(九)安全的交易环境

电子商务业者应致力在技术与管理层面,确保其交易环境及信息系统的安全性。

(十)客户申诉与抱怨处理

电子商务业者应设置专人处理消费者申诉与抱怨,而且对消费者的申诉与抱怨应积极进行处理,并在适当时日内迅速给予消费者妥适回复。

(十一)标识

电子商务业者应在网页上揭示标识,载明本商店宣示遵守电子商务业者自律公约;并提供本公约网页连结,方便消费者查阅公约内容。

(十二)法律遵循与规范

本公约所规范的交易行为应遵循台湾地区所制订的相关法规及国际规范的规定;且承诺提供消费者不低于法律规范标准的保护。

电子商务业者应在网页明白揭示,因消费纠纷产生诉讼的第一审管辖法院。

(十三)其他事项

为适应网络的发展与进步,应定期审视公约内容进行调整修正;签署的电子商务业者应配合公约修正予以更新,以维护消费者信心的确立与健全电子商务发展。

---

① 一旦消费者要求停止寄送时,即应立即中止电子广告邮件的寄发,且应明白向消费者揭示中止方式。

② 电子商务业者搜集及运用消费者的个人资料时,应注意遵循下列原则:1. 电子商务业者应于网页明确向消费者揭示关于消费者个人资料的搜集方式,例如:客户资料窗体,与搜集个人资料的使用目的;且承诺只在揭示的使用目的下使用消费者个人资料;2. 电子商务业者就因交易所获悉的消费者信息应严格保密,且在未经消费者同意前,不得将其提供给第三人;3. 电子商务业者对于消费者针对商家所搜集个人资料为下列要求时,在反映直接成本的原则下,电子商务业者应给予妥适的响应:(1)查询及请求阅览;(2)请求补充或更正;(3)请求停止计算机处理及利用,或请求删除;4. 其他依法保护消费者个人隐私应遵循的事项。

五、电子商务法制环境建构

除了前述的相关发展外,台湾地区还配合网络发展的需求积极地在建构所需的法律环境,主要有:

(一) 相关法规措施的规划

随着网络与电子商务的发展,各种法律问题逐渐发生,为了解决因网际网络的特性所生的各种现行法未规范的法律问题,提高行政效率,台湾地区"'国家'信息通信基本建设(NII)推动小组"于1997年4月23日指示由"经建会"召集相关部会组成"NII法制推动工作小组"①,协调NII发展的相关法规的研修②,以下仅就相关法规简析如下:

1. 有关知识产权相关法规部分

(1) 著作权法部分

相较于传统的纸张、书本等有形媒介,在网络上传送的数字化信息具有容易大量重制,且重制多次品质不变的特色,再加上它可以快速交换讯息的性质,对重制、公开发表、合理使用等传统著作权观念产生相当大的冲击。③ 至于现有著作权法制的公开播送权、公开上映权、公开演出权等,其在现有法律上的意义是否足以用来涵盖并规范网际网络上的传输行为,也还有疑义,从而也导致现有著作权法的难以有效调整。换而言之,如何平衡网络的传输特性与著作权人的权益保护,已成为网际网络所带来的新兴课题。

举例而言,为因应暂时性重制之争议,台湾地区《著作权法》于2003年7月9日修正,该法第3条规定所谓的重制是指:"以印刷、复印、录音、录像、摄影、笔录或其他方法直接、间接、永久或暂时之重复制作。于剧

---

① 其主要秉持以下原则:1. 法制建立的主要目标在于加速网际网络的建设,以促进网际网络普及应用与信息流通;2. 应优先让市场机制与技术本身解决相关问题,而视政府的介入与相关法令的调整为最后手段;3. 法规的调整以解决现有或可预见的将来法令明显的障碍、活络网络应用、确保竞争秩序、建立可遵循与可预测的法律环境、保障网络的使用者个人资料与隐私为主要范畴,并使行政机关得依法行政又得保障使用者权益。

② 自成立时至2000年3月"NII法制推动工作小组"共完成22种法案、11种行政命令的检讨其中包括刑法、信息公开法、数字签章法、电信法、有线电视广播法、商标法、著作权法、仲裁法、计算机处理个人数据保护法、公平交易法、消费者保护法、银行法、公司法、所得税法、税捐稽征法、营业税法关税法、贸易法、证券交易相关规定、网域名称(domain name)登记规范等,检讨结果现阶段台湾地区必须制订电子签章法与信息公开法共2项新增法律,修订11项法律,并调整7项行政命令。

③ 例如,网络信息的流通,会对于著作造成不可避免、暂时性的重制(例如过程中所经过服务器的重制,个人计算机中暂存内存的重制),或是个人利用上的重制,如均必须获得授权,将使网络资源共享的本质无法实现。但若未善加规范,将使网络上著作的保护落空。

本、音乐著作或其他类似著作演出或播送时予以录音或录像;或依建筑设计图或建筑模型建造建筑物者,亦属之。"依此规定,可知台湾地区著作权法明白揭示暂时性重制仍属重制,唯著作权法虽然保护著作人的权益,也同时兼顾社会公共利益,故仍订立了许多合理使用的规定,来限制著作人的权利,让一般利用人在合理的范围内,取得利用著作的权限。使用计算机和激光视盘机造成的暂时性重制状况,当然也适用合理使用的规范。是以,台湾地区《著作权法》第22条规定:"著作人除本法另有规定外,专有重制其著作之权利。表演人专有以录音、录像或摄影重制其表演之权利。前两项规定,于专为网络中继性传输,或使用合法著作属技术操作过程中必要之过渡性、附带性而不具独立经济意义之暂时性重制,不适用之。但计算机程序不在此限。前项网络中继性传输之暂时性重制情形,包括网络浏览、快速存取或其他为达成传输功能之计算机或机械本身技术上所不可避免之现象。"简而言之,于网络传输过程中,或者合法使用著作时,所生操作上必然产生的过渡性质或附带性质的暂时性重制情形,不属于重制权的范围。也就是说,在这种情况下产生的暂时性重制,不会发生违反著作权法侵害重制权的问题。①

整体而言,目前台湾地区著作权法的基本方向,主要着重在默示授权同意或扩张合理使用范围的安排,使网络上个人使用或机器自动的重制不致违法;此外,并配合世界知识产权组织(WIPO)著作权条约的调整方向,增列著作权人公开传播权的规范;参考世界知识产权组织著作权条约,增列著作权辅助侵害规定,禁止制造、贩售破解他人著作权保护的装置;以及仿效国际规范,对于非故意的网络服务业者,限制其责任范围。②

(2) 网域名称(Domain Name)部分

除著作权部分外,网域名称的保护问题,则是另一个随着网际网络的快速成长与日益商业化而发展的问题,基本上网域名称或大陆所称的域名是被用以辨识网站的名称,就像一般好听易记的电话号码一样,也成为工商业争逐的目标,因此,网域名称的争议亦相当的多。目前就网域名称所遇到的问题③,台湾地区现参考美国NSI的网域名称争议处理政策修正

---

① "台湾地区暂时性重制规定之相关说明",请参照台湾地区"经济部"智慧财产权局,http://www.tipo.gov.tw (visited 2004/7/30)。

② NII 相关法规, http://stlc.iii.org.tw/stlc_c.htm (visited 2004/7/30)。

③ 如利用他人公司或产品名称登记为网域名称(Domain Name)法的争议,或网域名称(Domain Name)申请程序过于简单,有网络纠纷发生时,不易追查当事人,造成网络犯罪侦查的困难应予强化等。

现有规定[1],并在 TWNIC 接受网域名称登记时将对申请人身份确实查核,以利于网络犯罪侦查,并拟定相关公约以解决现有的问题。[2]

就涉及商标部分,其基本方向为认定网域名称在符合商标认定的标准前提下亦具有商标的性质。所以,使用相同或近似他人注册商标名称作为网域名称,并在网站促销与该他人同一或类似商品,均可能构成商标侵害[3];然而虽以相同或近似他人注册商标名称为网域名称,并在网站促销,但商品与该他人商标所指定商品非属于同一或类似者,则不构成商标侵害。

2. 有关消费者保护相关法规部分

仅次于前述知识产权部分的,则为消费者保护的课题,谨略述其主要发展如下:

(1) 电子商务消费者保护纲领

为确保交易公平,保障消费者权益,建立消费者对电子商务之信心,促进电子商务健全发展,并提供各目的事业主管机关研拟电子商务中消费者保护措施之准则,台湾地区于 2001 年 12 月公布《电子商务消费者保护纲领》,提出十项指导方针:1. 透明及有效之保护;2. 公平之商业、广告及行销活动;3. 在线信息揭露机制;4. 电子商务合同之提供与保护;5. 隐私权保护;6. 交易安全之保障;7. 安全付款机制;8. 消费争议处理:消费者应能取得公平、有效、及时、经济且易于取得之公平、有效、及时、经济之机制;9. 教育、宣导与自觉;10. 加强国际合作。[4]

(2) 消费者保护法

为促进电子商务的发展,维护合法业者的权益,建立消费者交易的信

---

[1] 网域名称委员会于第 11 次会议(2001.01.30)通过财团法人台湾地区网络信息中心网域名称争议处理办法及财团法人台湾地区网络信息中心网域名称争议处理办法实施要点,以处理注册人于财团法人台湾地区网络信息中心及受理注册机构注册的网域名称与第三人所生的争议,http://www.twnic.net.tw/(visited 2004/7/30)。

[2] 有《台湾地区网际网络使用公约》、《ISP 与用户共享规约》、《不受欢迎邮件处理公约》等,详参 NII 相关法规,http://stlc.iii.org.tw/stlc_c.htm(visited 2004/7/30)。

[3] 故以相同或近似他人网站名称作为商标注册,就网站名称的独创性、知名度、商品的关联程度等事项斟酌,商标注册有致公众误信之虞者,网站所有人得申请评定商标注册无效。

[4] 台湾地区"行政院"台 90 闻字第 063444 号函核定,请参台湾地区"行政院"消费者保护委员会,http://www.cpc.gov.tw/(visited 2004/7/30)。

心,就消费者保护的相关问题①,应建立一套健全的体制来面对它,因此台湾地区就这个问题,鉴于现有消费者保护法应仅能提供最低程度的规范,为平衡保障消费者及企业经营者的权益,将另定特别法来解决。②

(3) 隐私权的保护部分

随着计算机科技进步、通讯技术革新发展,网络信息化社会已日渐形成,人们越来越依赖科技所发明的工具,以进行人跟人间的沟通,因此,个人私领域部分已逐渐暴露于公众当中,隐私被窥探可能性随之大增,在面对个人资料遭受侵害威胁之下,"信息隐私权"③(Information Privacy)的概念即产生。面对如何确保个人的隐私与资料的安全,并避免因计算机网络发达与电子商业的盛行损及个人资料的保护,台湾地区拟扩大《计算机处理个人数据保护法》保护范围,并对于搜集与利用的条件规范明确化④,以解决隐私权保护的问题。

《计算机处理个人数据保护法》自1995年8月11日制定公布全文45条后,修正条文仍然没有通过立法的程序。⑤

3. 网络金流法制规划

电子商务既然叫商务,则最后付款的选择方案也自然重要,谨略述台湾地区近来这方面的法制发展情形如下:

(1) 付款工具部分

由于电子商务能否蓬勃发展取决于是否能提供方便、快速、安全的电

---

① 例如,网络购物是否属于邮购买卖,适用邮购买卖相关规定保障消费者权益、ISP 是否应为其线路上传输的广告负媒体经营者的连带责任、数字化商品的提供者应否负无过失责任、线上递送的数字化商品的消费者在收到数字产品后是否仍可以不具理由在 7 日犹豫期间内退货等相关消费者保护的疑义,就此疑义台湾地区方向为:网络购物应可以归类于消保法邮购买卖的规定中,不应排除 7 日犹豫期间的适用,消保法应以保护消费者权益为主旨,不适宜作负面表列;数字化商品属于《消费者保护法》第 7 条规定的商品,提供者应负无过失责任;ISP 应为其线路上传输的广告负媒体经营者的连带责任,但以明知或可得而知为要件(中 86 年 5 月 29 日台 86 消保法字第 00648 号函),详参台湾地区"经济部"商业司编:《1999 中华台北电子商务年鉴》,台北:"经济部"2000 年版,第 40 页。

② NII 相关法规,http://stlc.iii.org.tw/stlc_c.htm(visited 2004/7/30)。

③ 即没有通知当事人并获得其"同意"之前,资料持有者不可以将当事人为某特定目的所提供的资料用在另一个目的上。廖纬民:《论信息时代的隐私权保障——以信息隐私权为中心》,载《信息法务透析》1996 年第 11 期,第 22 页。

④ 台湾地区"经济部"商业司编:《1999 中华台北电子商务年鉴》,台北:"经济部"2000 年版,第 43 页。

⑤ 修正条文中增列未经当事人的书面同意,不得转让或贩售个人资料,以防止消费者权益受损,及公务机关应妥善维护国人个人资料,不得牟利的规定。详参"立法院"议案关系文书,院总第 1570 号,委员提案第 3095 号,http://npl.ly.gov.tw/index.jsp(visited 2004/7/30)。

子付款方式作为网络交易的支付工具,因此付款安全机制当属一重要问题。①

以信用卡为网络购物的支付工具来说②,台湾地区已有制定"个人计算机银行业务及网络银行业务服务合同模板"③,以业者自律的方式提高交易安全的保障。而就电子钱包的法律问题,因涉及金融监理,台湾地区已在《银行法》中增列第 42 条之一④,除就现金储值卡加以定义外,同时在考虑货币信用管理下,只有银行才可以在取得"中央"主管机关许可下,发行现金储值卡,并且需依"中央"银行的规定提列准备金。同时授权"中央"主管机关洽商"中央"银行订定相关管理办法。

(2)网络银行部分

近年来,因网际网络的快速发展、银行申办全面性电子化银行业务的强烈需求、同时考虑交易安全及消费者权益的保障,台湾地区"财政部"于 1998 年责成银行公会进行"金融机构办理电子银行业务安全控管作业基准"⑤及"个人计算机银行业务及网络银行业务服务合同模板"⑥的研拟工作,作为开放银行办理电子银行业务标准的配套措施,其作业范围包括个人计算机银行(PC Banking,意指客户通过专属网络及加值网络与银行联机)及网络银行(Network Banking,指客户通过网际网络与银行联机)等电子化银行业务。⑦

在前述的安控基准及合同模板陆续公布后,至 2000 年,台湾地区的

---

① 关于安全保密方面,国际实务上约有 SSL(Secure Socket Layer)与 SET(Secure Electronic Transactions)2 种安全机制,但台湾地区目前的发展还不普遍。
② 虽然在主管机关已经公布的《信用卡定型化合同》第 9 条的规定中,要求持卡人想通过网际网络直接进行信用卡电子交易服务时,必须事先与发卡银行签订相关合同。然而该定型化合同中并没有针对信用卡电子交易服务做进一步规范,而且主管机关也没有针对信用卡电子交易服务再行公布模范合同条款供业者在缔约时遵循,所以仍然有相当多的问题存在。
③ NII 相关法规,http://stlc.iii.org.tw/stlc_c.htm(visited 2004/7/30)。
④ 《银行法》第 42 条之一规定(现金储值卡的许可及管理):"银行发行现金储值卡应经主管机关许可,并依'中央'银行的规定提列准备金;其许可及管理办法,由主管机关洽商'中央'银行定之。"前项所称现金储值卡,是发卡人以电子、磁力或光学形式储存金钱价值,持卡人得以所储存金钱价值的全部或一部交换货物或劳务,并得作为多用途的支付使用者。
⑤ 参见台湾地区"财政部"台财融第 87721016 号函,复于 2000 年 8 月 14 日修正。
⑥ 参见台湾地区"财政部"台财融第 88725263 号函。
⑦ 其涵盖的内容,在交易安全方面:"金融机构办理电子银行业务安控基准"主要是分电子转账交易指示类及非电子转账交易指示类两种交易,就其交易面及管理面的安全需求及安全设计订定电子银行的基本标准,规范范围涵盖讯息隐秘性、完整性、来源辨识、不可重复、不可否认等安全要求以及管理面的安全防护措施与系统安全标准等作业管理规范。另外,在银行及客户间权利义务关系上,则透过合同模板提供消费者基本保障。该合同模板主要在规范银行与客户间相关之权利义务关系,包括一般性共通约定、电子讯息传输的相关事项、危险责任的分配、损害赔偿责任的限制,及透过合同条款赋予电子讯息等同于书面文件的效力。

银行已经可以依据"财政部"所颁布的合同模板以及电子银行安控基准所示办理业务的最低要求标准,申请开办网络银行相关业务。①

(3) 贸易法部分

网络的发展是属跨国界的交易形态,而依据贸易法的规定,经营数字商品的国际贸易是否需向国贸局办理进出口登记,以及对于通过网络传输侵害知识产权的商品国际贸易局有无管理依据,都属于相关的课题。就这一部分而言,在解释上由于在台湾地区的贸易法中,其所规范的对象应为有形货品,并不包括数字商品,所以解释上网络上数字商品的进出口应不在贸易法规范之列。②

另外就关税部分来说,在美国所提出的"全球电子商务纲要"中是主张数字商品免课征关税,台湾地区就这部分也认为,对于数字商品课予关税在实务的执行上有其困难性,所以对于美国所主张数字商品免征关税的部分原则上予以支持。

4. 电子商务市场与租税优惠部分

(1) 租税优惠措施部分

为鼓励电子商务的发展,以租税政策的优惠方式是为有效的政策工具,台湾地区于是依据《促进产业升级条例》第 8 条第 3 项规定:"新兴重要策略性产业的适用范围、核定机关、申请期限、申请程序及其他相关事项,由'行政院'召集相关产业界、政府机关、学术界及研究机构代表定之,并每 2 年检讨 1 次,做必要调整及修正。"于 2001 年 2 月制订并于同年 12 月修改《新兴重要策略性产业属于制造业及技术服务业部分奖励办法》,藉以并建立电子商务产业良好投资环境,以全面提高台湾地区产业国际竞争力。

(2) 上市上柜的法规部分

为了鼓励优秀的网络公司发展,并且保证有充裕资金投入网络事业,台湾地区已经研拟完成"柜台买卖第二类股票",这些都是以网络业者为适用对象量身定做的配套法规,以放宽旧有公司设立年限、缩小公司最低资本规模额度、取消公司营利能力限制及简化审查程序,使网络业者得以通过上市上柜规定,以利公开资金之募集。

---

① 台湾地区"经济部"商业司编:《1999 中华台北电子商务年鉴》,台北:"经济部"2000 年版,第 49 页。

② NII 相关法规,http://stlc.iii.org.tw/stlc_c.htm(visited 2004/7/30)。

5. 网络基础建设与安全机制及信息流通

(1) 电信法

为了实现电子商务蓬勃发展的目标,电信基础建设的完备就处于相当重要的地位,积极推动电信自由化便成为发展目标之一。放宽外国人投资第一类电信事业限制的规定、电信保密器仅以厂商为管理对象、授权主管机关订定相关技术规范等,这些都是台湾地区在电信法上发展的方向。此外,台湾地区开放电信业自由化的脚步,更是在加速进行中。①

(2) 刑法部分

网际网络盛行之后,相关的网络犯罪也随之兴起。针对网络犯罪的部分,现行法规已修正将电磁记录视为文书(《刑法》第220条)并增列相关之处罚规定。此外,于2003年6月25日,更增定第36章为《妨碍计算机使用罪》专章。

(3) 行政信息公开法

随着社会的快速变迁及政府职能的扩充,人民无论是参与公共建设、监督政府施政作为,还是纯做市场消费,都需要大量正确的信息,而当局正是最大信息拥有者,此外,网络中文内容确实有不足,如作为信息主要来源之一的行政信息,欠缺公开的机制,人民取得内容将非常不易,所以为了中文信息的流通,使身为重要资料来源的当局得以提供相关信息资料,及促进信息公开化、透明化,使信息合理利用,特于2001年订定《行政信息公开法》以建立行政信息公开之法制基础,其第5条更明订行政信息以公开为原则,不公开为例外,以促进人民权益之保障。②

---

① 参台湾地区"电信总局""电信自由化专区",http://www.dgt.gov.tw/chinese/Review/review.shtml (visited 2004/7/30)。

② 《行政信息公开法》第5条:"行政信息,除依前条第一项规定应主动公开者外,属于下列各款情形之一者,应限制公开或提供:一、公开或提供有危害'国家'安全、整体经济利益或其他重大利益者。二、公开或提供有碍犯罪之侦查、追诉、执行或足以妨害刑事被告受公正之裁判或有危害他人生命、身体、自由、财产者。三、行政机关作成意思决定前,内部单位之拟稿或准备作业或与其他机关间之意见交换。但关于意思决定作成之基础事实,不在此限。四、行政机关为实施监督、管理、检(调)查、取缔等业务,而取得或制作监督、管理、检(调)查、取缔对象之相关数据,其公开或提供将对实施目的造成困难或妨害者。五、公开或提供有侵犯营业或职业上秘密、个人隐私或著作人之公开发表权者。但法令另有规定、对公益有必要或经当事人同意者,不在此限。六、经依法核定为机密或其他法令规定应秘密事项或限制、禁止公开者。行政信息含有前项各款限制公开或提供之事项者,应仅就其他部分公开或提供之。"

3 以电子数据交换法制为基础的电子贸易

3.1 无纸化交易环境的形成

随着数字化环境的发展,网际网络的日益发达,使用者可通过网络即时交换讯息并进行交易,这一科技的迅速发展,在相当程度上削弱了地理界限的意义,也使整个世界相对变小而无国界。

科技的进步对现代商业所可能产生的影响,已远超过我们所能想像。在中世纪,传统的有纸贸易(paper-based transactions)取代以物易物的互易贸易,这一项革命性的突破,使贸易结构也随之经历了相当大的变化。如今,网际网络所引发的突破将更加剧烈,长久以来广为接受的有纸化贸易,正在被与之相对应的电子化贸易所替代,而向无纸化社会发展,在数字交易环境中,所有的商业活动也将在虚拟市场(virtual marketplace)中进行。

在此数字交易环境中,交易的当事人间不用纸与笔,便可以完成其交易,传统的书面(writing)形式和签章,都将被通过计算机网络中所传输的数字讯息所取代,这一变化所隐含的法律意义在于:书面形式与签章的概念需要重新加以界定。事实上,如果任何交易或合同,其书面形式与签字的纸式原件(original paper copies)能逐渐被电话之类的事物所取代[①],那么它们当然可以被数字信息和电子加密形式所取代,而通过计算机网络

[①] Hamley v. Whipple, 48 N.H. 487, 488 (1869),在该案中,the New Hampshire's highest court 裁决:以电报进行的要约和承诺符合"诈欺法"(Statute of Frauds),而且行为人在书写要约和承诺时,是用带有一个普通笔杆的一公尺长的金属笔,还是用一条1000公尺长的金属线所形成的"笔",二者之间并无区别;在另一个案中,此一思考模式亦被适用在用于用手指握笔的方式书写过的"纸"上,用普通的红墨水书写与用一种更微妙的液体,所谓的电流书写,应该是没有差别的,然而 the New Hampshire's highest court 依然受到"纸"此一传统概念的限制,其认为书写必须是在有形物体下加以进行的。但在 Pike Indus., Inc. V. Middlebury Assocs 一案中,法院裁决:以电报方式所作的签章不能被认为构成"诈欺法"(Statute of Frauds)所指的签章。换而言之,即使电报可能被视为符合该法要求的有效书写形式,但透过电报所作的签章仍然不能构成有效签章。该案所揭示的旨趣在于:当相应的法律规范缺乏确定性时,电子交易仍存在着潜在的危险与无序。

迅速传播。

然而,当国际贸易合同的缔结,是通过以电子、光学或类似的方式来生成、储存或传递商业贸易信息来进行时,电子数据交换(Electronic Data Interchange,简称 EDI)[①]、电子邮件(E-mail)等数据信息,就已经取代了曾经是贸易信息的主要媒介——纸张,而提供了更快捷、更经济,甚至于可以更安全的交易方式,其中 EDI 更被认为是国际贸易发展过程中的一个重要里程碑,因其能有效地促进商业的交易流程,简化交易当事人的关系并降低交易成本。

基本上,EDI 本身的执行过程是一种商业上的改造过程(re-engineering),让使用 EDI 的人运用新的科技来改变其交易方式;然而此交易方式却也产生了许多新生法律问题,如其如何传送当事人间的意思表示?而这一传送的意思表示的法律效力如何?是否可以满足书面形式及签章的要求?再者,如果交易间的各当事人就此通过网际网络完成的交易发生争议时,各当事人对其主张能提供什么证据?都值得我们加以研究。所以,若能以日益发展成熟的 EDI 经验为师[②],肯定会有助我们具体掌握、使用电子数据讯息的国际贸易合同,因进入"无纸化"环境所涉法律问题,进而对于整体贸易电子化相关的发展,有更清楚的了解与适应。

3.2 电子数据交换的产生背景及发展

一、电子数据交换的产生背景

电子数据交换的历史可追溯到20世纪60年代末,欧洲和美国几乎同时提出电子数据交换的概念,早于1968年,美国运输业的许多公司便联合成立了一个运输数据协调委员会 TDCC(Transportation Data Coordinating Committee),着手研究开发电子通讯标准的可行性,他们的方案形成了电子数据交换的基础。70年代以后,由于全球危机的发生,西方工业国

[①] 由于 EDI 的发展与实施的方法各有不同,对其并无统一的定义,有说 EDI 是贸易伙伴计算机系统间,以最少人力介入方式交换标准化格式的资料(联合国 EDIFACT 准则);企业经由计算机网络联机,以标准化格式传送交易信息,如订单、汇票、清单或其他纪录。Smedinghoff, Thomas J F\Et Al, Eds. *Online Law: the SPA'S Legal Guide to Doing Business on the Internet*. 3rd ed. Boston: Addsion Wesley Developers Press, 1997, pp.108—110.

[②] EDI 是1种透过计算机,在当事人之间传送标准化商业文件的电子手段,由于使用 EDI 可以减少甚至消除贸易过程中的纸面单证,因此,它又被俗称无纸贸易,见单文华:《电子贸易的法律问题》,载《民商法论丛》1998年第10卷,第2页。

家结束了使用廉价石油发展工业的时代,转向以电子与计算机技术为核心的信息工业时代。①

所谓电子数据交换,于传统意义下是指直接与特定企业联机(例如集团企业内或相关公司间)或通过 VAN(Value Added Network;加值网络)联机,构成某种计算机网络,而在该网络中交换产品下单、接单的电子数据交换。具体而言,就是通过规格化的计算机间交换日常交易信息。就EDI 方式的企业间,相较于人工操作而言,能较迅速、确实且容易地完成产品下单、承诺等商业交易行为。例如,产品买卖过程中的下单、接单、存货的确认及送货日期的排定、产品交付、价金请求、营业额的计算等事务,都可交由电子数据来处理,因无书面之累,可在瞬间确实地进行。

传统的 EDI②,原来是以封闭性电子数据的交换为前提,一般是由大企业架构自己的计算机网络,再要求原来交易对象采用同一计算机系统,对新交易对象则多以采用相同系统计算机为交易条件,美国称这种状况为轮轴与轮辐(Hub and Spoke)。然而因为各集团间的计算机网络规格不同,所以无法与集团企业外的不特定企业交流,因此产生诸多不便。近来,为克服这一缺点,有所谓的开放性电子数据交换,是利用网际网络等开放式网络(如 Web 或 E-mail),而可能与集团企业以外的不特定企业交换电子数据,而此时,随各类加值网络系统的诞生,以及宽频网络(Broad Band Network)的逐渐建制完成,EDI 的概念已逐渐融入电子商务的概念中。③

二、电子数据交换的国际组织规范发展

第二次世界大战后,贸易的极速扩展,使贸易的相关文件种类总数增

---

① 汪涛主编:《EDI:国际贸易新手段》,中国经济出版社 1997 年版,第 6—7 页。
② EDI 的使用甚早,只不过在早期未纳入 Internet 的架构前,因成本高又不便利,使用者甚少。在过去 40 年,使用者为超过 10 万人;参见王全德:"Internet 电子商务发展现况",http://www.psd.iii.org.tw/inews/focus/ec_trend/main.htm(visited in 1999/05/25)。
③ 由于 EDI 已由封闭式逐步走向开放式,因此极易与电子商务产生混淆,然而所谓电子商务(E-Commerce)是使用整合后的科技来简化交易外部的流程以促进贸易,而 EDI 正是被运用来达成 EC 的目的的工具之一,基本上,EC 正在朝向更广泛的科技利用发展,其中包括了 INTERNET 在内,而这些的科技与 EDI 相同的都是被用来企图促进资料收集储存的努力以及用以创造一个快速而更具有生产力的工作环境。参见 Nahid Jilovec, *The A To Z of EDI and Its Role in E-Commerce*, 2nd edition, LLoveland:29th Street Press, 1998, p.25。

加,而且文件不同也妨碍交易履行的顺利和迅速进行,导致输出成本增加。① 因为为了货物的输出入,输出业者或输入业者在必要的情况下,须向输出入管理提出输出入申请书,取得输出入许可证。② 根据美国贸易程序简易化委员会于 70 年代所进行的调查,做成及处理一件贸易交易所需文件的时间,输出时为 37 小时,输入时为 28 小时,而一组文件的做成费用,输出为 375 美金,输入为 325 美元。输出入交易大多为相同的交易对象,重复同样的交易,而且货物的交付,价金的支付等合同履行的顺序,多依照交易习惯来进行。③ 而每次交易都如前述般须做成多数的文件,将来贸易交易的件数及金额大量增加后,为了贸易程序的合理化,认为需要引进计算机代替文书。

然而早期的 EDI 虽然在特定企业与特定企业间或业者间,通过引进网上的闭锁型 EDI,试图加以解决此问题,但因仍需配合交易对方所使用的 EDI 标准作安排,因此当面临同时多位不同的交易对象时,就面临了须使用不同终端机来从事 EDI 讯息收发信作业的窘境,结果,以 EDI 收受的信息约有 75% 需要再输入,并且在这类信息通信过程中,约有 5% 的错误率需要再输入,因此进一步开发不同企业间能开放使用的国内标准,并能满足全球化贸易营运需求的国际标准十分必要。

承前所述,随着国际贸易上愈来愈多的 EDI 使用④,使得建立这种交易行为的国际法律架构变得需要。相对的,国际组织像是国际商会(International Chamber of Commerce;简称 ICC)、欧洲联盟执行委员会(The Commission of the European Communities)及联合国(The United Nations)等,也

---

① 因此联合国欧洲经济委员会在 1960 年设置贸易手续简易化作业部会,讨论贸易制度的简易化及贸易相关文件的标准化问题。认为现行贸易交易中主要文件文件应予 EDI 化的必要性,其主要文件有:
1. 买卖当事人间的订货单、买卖承诺单、发货单、装运通知书。
2. 送货人及运送人间的货柜预约书、码头收据、载船证件、保证书等。
3. 货主、被保险人及保险人间的保险申请书、保险证明、保险费请求书等。

② 输出入程序约 40 种文件,港口的载船程序约 80 种文件,卸货需 30 种文件。以上程序均需各种文件,有部分文件有法律或规则等,详尽的规定及样式,记载项目的署名或记名验件,通常诸如此类的文件须记载买卖当事人的企业名称、住所、商品种类、数目、价格、交付场所、日期、船名、号码、价金支付条件等 4、50 项内容,并由负责人签名盖章。

③ 朝冈良平、伊东健治、鹿岛诚之助/菅又久直:《图解よくわかる EDI》,东京:日刊工业新闻社 1998 年版,第 128—129 页。

④ 这部分可参考,Ritter, Jeffrey B., "Current Issues in Electronic Data Interchange: Defining International Electronic Commerce", *J. INTL. L. BUS.* 1992, (13): 3.

持续展开了对于 EDI 相关法律问题的探讨并谋求解决之道①,在此试简述如下:

(一) 国际商会

在 1987 年,国际商会(International Chamber of Commerce；ICC)采取了所谓的 UNCID 规范。虽然其原本是要来创造 1 个模范合同,但后来却发展成了一套规范合同问题的统一基础行为规范。UNICD 规范特别提供了一标准方法来处理,诸如:确立当事人间的注意义务、在传送中当事人身份的认定、传送的认知、内容的确认、交换资料的保护及记录的创造及维持等问题；至于像是风险分担、损害赔偿及争端解决等部分,则仍留待未来的决定。基本上,UNCID 规范是第一个,并且是唯一被国际社会所广为接受的 EDI 规范,而且该等规范也被明示或默示地包含在大部分的基础合同中。例如,UNCID 规范便对于发展中的英国 EDI 协会基础合约有十分显著的影响,这可以证诸于这些规范已被纳入了合约用户的使用手册中。②

此外,值得注意的是,为因应近年来电子商务的快速发展,国际商会于 2001 年 11 月 27 日公布更新第二版《数位保障的国际商务共通使用方法》(General Usage in International Digitally Ensured Commerce, GUIDEC v. II)准则③,强调辨识与验证当事人身份与交易本身的信赖架构,且提出信息系统安全的相关原则,如:公钥加密技术及其他如生物辨识等新技术等。④

(二) 欧洲联盟执行委员会

早在 1987 年 10 月 5 日,当时的欧洲议会(the Council of Europe)便已建立了 1 套"交易电子数据交换系统"(Trade Electronic Data Interchange Systems; TEDIS)程序,用以规范数据处理系统间(计算机)的商业或行政格式的传送。该程序调和了商业资料的电子传送与用户间的隔阂,并提

---

① 国际贸易委员会(International Chamber of Commerce)是唯一一个对该问题的研究,已建立 1 个有用并受国际所接受的结果的组织。即其建立了 Uniform Rules of Conduct for Interchange of Trade Data by Teletransmission (UNCID),该法规已成为其他国际组织、国家或私人团体为发展更详尽 EDI 合同的模板,这部分可参考 Pisciotta, Aileen A. & Barker, James H., "Current Issues in Electronic Data Interchange: Telecommunications Regulatory Implications for International EDI Transactions", J. INTL. L. BUS. 1992, (13): 71。

② Boss, Amelia H., "The International Commercial Use of Electronic Data Interchange and Electronic Communications Technologies", BUS. LAW. 1991, (48): 1792。

③ ICC 于 1997 年前曾公布第一版的 GUIDEC,主要探讨如何建立在交易信息传递中当事人的信心,即信息的完整性、可用性与秘密性等议题。

④ http://www.iccwbo.org/home/guidec/guidec_two/foreword.asp (visited 2004/7/23)。

高了计算机软件及硬件制造商对 EDI 标准的需求。①

后来在 1989 年 4 月 5 日,该议会同意让"欧洲自由贸易协会"(European Free Trade Association, EFTA)的会员参与 TEDIS 的计划及授权欧洲联盟执行委员会去协商与这些国家间的协议。在 1989 年,TEDIS 计划提出了一份报告,其中详细分析了从事 EDI 交易所生的法律问题②,该报告建议:应统一各国分歧的法律来克服这些困难及其他的障碍,以利在欧洲建立统一的 EDI 贸易制度。主要的有:报告建议委员会应对于合同形成、网络使用者的责任及可信赖的第三人及类似的服务表示意见;在合同形成方面,应注重合同形成的时间及地点、中间媒介、一般条款及要约的撤回;在网络使用者的责任部分,主要是关于风险分担的处理;而在可信赖第三人问题上,则应特别考量可信任的 EDI 记录的保存责任问题。③

1998 年,欧盟首次提出了《关于电子商务的欧洲建议》,此后又于 1998 年发表《欧盟电子签名法律框架指南》和《欧盟隐私保护指令》。1999 年 12 月 7 日,欧盟通过《统一数字签名规则》,明确规定了在某一成员国签订的电子商务合同,其效力在其他任何 1 个成员国都应被承认等重要问题。2000 年 6 月 8 日,欧盟更采取电子商务指令(Directive 2000/31/EC),藉以厘清关于电子商务之部分法律概念及建构于国际市场原则下,促使信息社会服务利益之协调机制,唯针对电子商务所涉之管辖权问题争议,则未予规定。④

(三) 联合国国际贸易法律委员会(United Nations Commission on International Trade Law, UNCITRAL)⑤

早在 1991 年,UNCITRAL 在对总秘书处(Secretary-General)所提报告

---

① Kotch, Kevin J., "Addressing the Legal Problems of International Electronic Data Interchange: The Use of Computer Records as Evidence in Different Legal Systems", *Temp. Int'l & Comp. L. J.* 1993, (6): 454.

② 这份报告除了讨论 12 个会员国间的国际法问题外,更提出了 3 项妨碍 TEDIS 计划的障碍:(1) 利用已签署纸张文件的义务;(2) 为证据目的而回避 EDI 的传送;(3) 决定正确 EDI 传送的时间及地点的问题。在 TEDIS 计划开始之初(1988—1989),6 项工业承诺统一 EDI 的协调工作。而 TEDIS 的第 2 阶段计划在 1991 年生效。其目标是确保 EDI 系统可顺利地在欧洲社会建立并使必要达成该目标的资源可以流通。在第 2 阶段,TEDIS 计划将结合主要工业项目及所有 EDI 程序的制定方法。一些法律目标及准则提供了评估这些成就的方法。

③ "Electronic Data Interchange: Report of the Secretary General, U. N. Commission on International Trade Law", 24th Sess., p. 6, U. N. Doc. A/CN.9/350 (1991).

④ 相关数据请参,由欧盟信息社会总署(DG)所设置之信息社会网站; http://europa.eu.int/information_society/topics/ework/index_en.htm (visited 2004/7/23)。

⑤ 这部分请详见: Uzelac, Alan, "Comparative Theme: UNCITRAL Notes on Organizing Arbitral Proceedings: A Regional View", *Croat. Arbit. Yearb.* 1997, (4): 135.

的响应中,便已决定将电子数据交换的法律问题,列为优先的项目。因为在当时,UNCITRAL已检视了很多关于电子数据交换的法律问题及国际组织努力发现解决这些问题的报告。

例如在1985年的第18次会议委员会议中,UNCITRAL通过联合国秘书长所提的报告中,已发现使用计算机资料做为证据的障碍比预期中来得要少,但相对的对于签名及纸张的需求,却仍为一个严重的阻碍。因此,UNCITRAL于当时便已建议各国政府应设法排除这些障碍,并呼吁国际组织要更新法律条文,将电子资料交换列入考虑,以便在国际贸易下尽可能广泛地使用自动化数据处理之情形下,确保法律安全。

其后,在接下来的二次会议中,UNCITRAL斟酌了由其他国际组织所准备的EDI报告,进而在1988年第21次会议中尝试将国际电子合同予以合法地定型化。1990年,第23次会议中,UNCITRAL在检视了以EDI所涉主要法律问题为主题,针对欧洲及美国的发展所作成的综合研究报告后,正式要求其秘书长,进一步就如何调和不同基础的交换合同提出报告,并斟酌发展统一国际交换合约的可行性。[①] 1996年,UNCITRAL第29次会议通过《电子商务模范法》,藉以协助各国利用电子商务或便利其利用;此外,为使电子环境下履行签字功能基本原则基础得以扩充,并期使电子签章具有功能等同之情况下,促进依赖这种电子签章发生法律效力,于2001年制订《电子签章模范法》及《贸易法律委员会电子签章模范法颁布指南》,以扩充《电子商务模范法》之适用。[②] 为促进电子商务之发展,更计划于2004年10月11日至22日间,由第四工作小组,在维也纳召开第44次会议,研究《国际合同中使用电子公约通信草案(draft convention on the use of electronic communications in international contracts)》,藉以消除电子通信使用中之障碍,并加强国际合同的法律确定性及商业上的可预见性。[③]

(四)联合国促进数据交换贸易工作小组(United Nations Working Party on the Facilitation of Interchange Trade)

除前述UNCITRAL外,联合国促进数据交换贸易工作小组是在联合

---

① "Report of the United Nations Commission on International Trade Law, U. N. Commission on International Trade Law", 23th Sess., U. N. Doc. A/CN.9/333 (1990).

② 贸易法律委员会电子签章模范法及其颁布指南(2001),请参 http://www.uncitral.org/en-index.htm. (visited 2004/7/24)

③ A/CN.9/WG.IV/WP.110—Legal aspects of Electronic Commerce,请参照, http://daccess-ods.un.org/TMP/9955063.html (visited 2004/7/24)。

国欧洲经济委员会下运作成立。① 首先,在 1990 年 3 月间,该工作团体组成了一个特别法律顾问团,就 EDI 问题提出了具体的行动计划;其中工作小组的努力方向区分成五个领域:基础交换合约(interchange agreement)、票券(negotiable document)、国际法律障碍(national legal barriers)、电子认证(electronic authentication)及为贸易数据交换而发展的用户名录(developing a user directory for trade data interchange)。② 这些工作均成功的引导 EDI 的交易环境趋向于成熟。

三、电子数据交换于国际贸易上的应用

由于 EDI 是建立在完善计算机处理与先进通讯网路基础上的作业方式,是集合计算机技术与科学处理于一体的新贸易方式③,更是能满足广阔国际贸易市场需求的模式。基本上,就 EDI 在国际贸易上的最大效益而言,应在于节省国际贸易交易过成中大量使用文书资料的成本,因为国际交易除了海外的交易对象外,还涉及许多与交易相关的当事人,在各种不同文件中,填写相同事项,都是 EDI 可发挥其长处的条件,不仅在交易成本的降低④,也可使进出口货物较快速的移转并改善顾客服务。根据联合国贸易调查委员会(UNCTAD)的调查,大量的文书工作,复杂的格式以及相关的迟延与错误的成本,大约占最终货品价值的 10%。1 宗典型的国际贸易交易可能涉及 30 个不同单位,60 份原始文件以及 360 份文件印本,这些文件都必须被检查、传送、重新输入到不同的信息系统处理及归档,联合国贸易调查委员会认为交易成本,将可因流程的合理化及无纸贸

---

① 从 1970 年代中期起,该工作团体已准备、收受及检视关于 EDI 法律问题的报告。虽然,该工作团体主要的功能是发展 EDI 的国际标准,但其了解,在国内及国际障碍除去前,其无法有效实现国际电子交易。该工作团体在私人团体间所参与制定制式 EDI 合约对 UNCID 条文的发展是非常重要的;"Legal Problems and ADP Systems in International Trade", U. N. Doc. TD/WP. 4/GE. 2/R. 123 (1978)。

② Boss, Amelia H., "The International Commercial Use of Electronic Data Interchange and Electronic Communications Technologies", *BUS. LAW* 1991, (48): 1787。

③ 汪涛主编:《EDI:国际贸易新手段》,中国经济出版社 1997 年版,第 10 页。

④ 早期,关于处理这些因不同交易机制共同化所生交易成本之支出问题,每年所花费的成本,粗估约在 1400 亿美元左右,请参 Kevin J Kotch, "Addressing The Legal Problems Of International Electronic Data Interchange: The Use Of Computer Records As Evidence In Different Legal Systems", *Temp. Int'l & Comp. LJ* 1992, (6): 451。此外,以台湾地区为例,透过环节贸易无纸化,将有效提升台湾地区之运筹效率,使得贸易文件占整体贸易成本比例由 7% 降为 5%,每年约可节省 57 亿新台币。请参照,"台湾地区 2008 发展重点计划", http://hirecruit. nat. gov. tw/twinfo/2008_plan_08c. asp (visited 2004/7/24)。

易的推广而节省 25% 的成本。[①] 然而,通过 EDI 不仅可以在贸易伙伴间传送商业讯息,更可以不需人工的参与而自动的完成商业交易过程,其不仅是简单的进行讯息资料交换,对讯息传递过程所引发的订货、安排生产、运输、保险、结汇、报关等贸易过程,都可以通过电子化的手段来完成。在此试就其交易流程简析如下(详下图):

(一)交易前资料的交换

企业间在建立交易关系之前,必须先经过一段相互试探与了解的过程,我们将这一过程中交换的企业与产品资料称为主资料(Master Data)。如下图所示,买家与供货商之间,首先交换各自的企业信息以相互了解;其后买家探询产品资料;供货商则提供产品信息。

这整个过程中交换的讯息有四个分别简介如下:

讯息名称	使用说明	内容概述
交易当事人资料 Party Information	● 二交易伙伴之间在建立交易关系之初交换的讯息,其目的在促进相互之间的了解 ● 资料有所改变,应再交换一次交由对方更新用 ● 交易伙伴之间也可共同更新一集中数据库而为共同利益者所共享	地址、联络窗口、相关作业管理、商业、财物等等
产品资料查询 Product Inquiry	● 依买主需求针对一特定商品或一组特定商品发出 ● 此一信息的回复可以是产品报价型录 Price/Sales Catalogue;也可以是产品资料 Product Data	其商品需求在讯息中由买家规定,供货商即可针对买家指定商品报价

---

① 到 20 世纪末将可达到每年 4000 亿美元,见 Kalakota & Whinston 著:《电子商务概论(Frontiers of Electronic Commerce)》,查修杰、连丽真、陈雪美译,跨世纪电子商务出版社 1999 年版,第 239—240 页。

（续表）

讯息名称	使用说明	内容概述
产品报价型录 Price/Sales Catalogue	• 供货商发出给客户 • 供货商针对所有商品报价，也可是特定商品的事前变价警示 • 此一讯息也可由买家发给供货商以指定如标签包装等特殊要求 • 若产品资料有所改变、删除，应再交换一次以为对方更新之用 • 交易伙伴之间也可共同更新一集中数据库，而为共同利益者所共享	• 产品信息、物流、财务信息
产品资料 Product Data	• 交易伙伴之间交换产品相关资料 • 本信息不常交换	• 本信息最大不同在于其提供技术及功能说明 • 且不含任何商业约定和条件

在正式交易前，或交易伙伴关系建立之前，交易伙伴间相互间参考资料或产品资料的交换有其必要性，以上四个交易前交换的讯息，可以是交换信息，也可以汇集于一集中管理的数据库，供使用者集中查阅，视使用者需求与多寡而定。①

（二）电子数据交换的交易模式（Transactions）

企业间在建立交易关系之后，就开始来往交易。一般的交易行为不外乎买与卖，从采购商品到结账付款完成一个交易流程，交易模式共包含五个流程：订单采购、货物处理、运输控制、收货验收、请款对账。本文首先介绍订单采购流程。

1. 订单采购流程

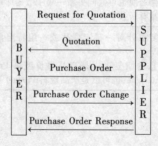

如上图所示，订单采购流程，始于询价单，终于订单确认。初次交易者可从头走一遍各信息交换的流程，经常性交易伙伴可以常态性从每日

---

① 资料来源：财团法人信息工业策进会系统工程处，《电子商务导航精华》，第11篇，参见http://www.ec.org.tw/net/ecpilot/pilot_main.asp 2002/4/2。

的订单交换做起。如果是长期大宗采购,也可以空白订单(Blank Order)模式作业。

讯息名称	使用说明	内容概述
询价单 Request for Quotation	• 询价单的使用是客户向供货商要求商品或服务报价时发出	• 此一信息的使用可参考产品资料或产品报价型录中的产品规格与编号 • 一潜在客户可要求供货商提供单一或多项商品或服务的报价 • 其中包含商品或服务之配送时程及取消条款 • 若为国际贸易使用则可要求提供通关相关信息及统计资料
报价单 Quotation	• 供货商回传给客户认为对产品或服务询价单的响应报价单应 • 报价单应响应客户先前在询价单中要求的特定信息 • 紧跟报价单之后可能即是客户的订单	• 响应询价要求的报价配送时程及条款外讯息 • 也可含测试资料如材积或数据测试方法等方法等 • 品质信息可系至每一单项产品或服务
订单 Purchase Order	• 订单由买家发给供货商指定购买产品与服务 • 订单可参考先前供货商传递的产品与服务报价单 • 此一信息设计,虽为每天每一配送地点单一订单息 • 但也可用于不同日不同地点的配送	• 订单指明产品与服务相关的量,及配送时间地点 • 订单内容也可参考产品报价型录中的产地与编号可参考产品报价型录中之产地与编号
订单修改要求 Purchase Order Change Request	• 订单修改要求由买家发给供货商指定购买产品与服务的细项修改或取消 • 订单修改要求的信息使用时机各不相同,应由交易双方约定,(例如有些业者未收到订单修改信息,即不必发出订单确认信息) • 订单修改要求不可更动订单号码、买卖双方的身份、产品品项编号 • 如果分行细项资料有修改,则全部分行细项资料应重传以避免错误	• 订单修改要求为对其产品、服务要求配送的修改或取消信息求为对其产品、服务要求配送之修改或取消资讯 • 若为国际贸易使用则可要求提供关税相关信息及统计资料易使用则可要求提供关税相关信息及统计资料

订单确认
Purchase Order Response
	• 订单确认由供货商发给客户以:
	  1. 收到订单或订单修改要求
	  2. 供货商接受订单或订单修改要求客户做某些修正,或告知部分或全部订单内容不能接受
	• 此一信息也可使用于回复订单修改要求订单修改要求
	• 买家发出的订单可由一订单确认信息回复也可由多个订单确认信息回复,视业态不同由业者自订一订单确认信息回复
		• 订单确认应含产品、服务配送时程信息品、服务配送时程信息
		• 若为国际贸易使用则可要求提供关税相关信息及统计资料易使用则可要求提供关税相关信息及统计资料
		• 应含运输、目的地细节及交货模式目的地细节及交货模式

这五个交易交换信息,也可以汇集于一集中管理的数据库,供交易双方集中查阅,视使用者需求与多寡而定。①

2. 货物处理流程②

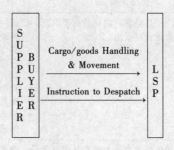

如图所示,本组货物处理流程信息是买方或卖方发送给物流业者(LSP, Logistics Service Provider,代客处理货物的物流中心、仓储业者)处理货物及配送、出货的指示,通常二讯息会相互配合。

3. 货物运输处理流程③

本组信息是买方或卖方发送给运输业者要求运输服务、发出运输指示及取得运送状况的信息组。

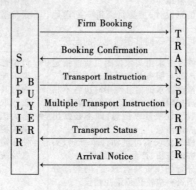

---

① 资料来源:财团法人信息工业策进会系统工程处,《电子商务导航精华》第12篇,参 http://www.ec.org.tw/net/ecpilot/pilot_main.asp 2002/4/2。
② 资料来源:财团法人信息工业策进会系统工程处,《电子商务导航精华》第13篇,参 http://www.ec.org.tw/net/ecpilot/pilot_main.asp 2002/4/2。
③ 资料来源:财团法人信息工业策进会系统工程处,《电子商务导航精华》第14篇,参 http://www.ec.org.tw/net/ecpilot/pilot_main.asp 2002/4/2。

讯息名称	使用说明	内容概述
托运预约 Firm Booking	• 企业或组织(买主、卖家)向运输或运输代理服务业者提供服务的要求 • 托运预约对运输或运输代理服务的要求 • 运输或船舶代理服务者根据此信息作业或拟订计划 • 运输或船舶代理服务者以托运预约确认(Booking Confirmation)回复此一信息 • 托运预约已可用以取消或取代前此发出的信息 • 由运送指示(Transport Instruction)作委托合同定案 • 这一委托可含数种货品 • 受托物可以是货柜也可不是 • 受托物装于单一货柜也可于多货柜;多货柜可装单一货物也可装多种货物 • 单一货物可与一项或多项海关代码有关 • 单项海关代码货物可装于单一货柜也可于多货柜	• 要求服务者所定的运送条件、原则 • 使用的交通工具、装载容器…… • 每批货的数量、材积 • 货物处理方式(食物、零下X度) • 运送地、对象
托运预约确认 Booking Confirmation	• 运输或运输代理服务业者发出此讯息用以确认托运预约 • 这一信息可表示接受、暂缓、有条件接受或拒绝	• 装载、卸货地点 • 装载、卸货时间 • 拒绝接受预约原因(例如无法处理放射物品)
运输指示 Transport Instruction	• 客户发送给运输业者发出此讯息用以指示将一批货物送往特定地点 • 该指示可涵盖单种货物也可为多种货物也可为特定的包装 • 这一指示可含数种货品 • 受托物可以是货柜也可不是 • 受托物装于单一货柜也可于多货柜;多货柜可装单一货物也可装多种货物 • 单一货物可与一项或多项海关代码有关 • 单项海关代码货物可装于单一货柜也可于多货柜 • 该货物的包装得借助物流条形码(SSCC) • 同一指示只能由唯一委托者发出,但却可有数个不同到货地点	• 装载、卸货地点 • 装载、卸货时用的交通工具、装载容器…… • 每批货的数量、材积 • 货物处理方式(食物、零下X度) • 运送地、对象
预约托运指示汇总 Multiple Transport Instruction	• 这一信息由货主提出,在先前已达成的交易条件下,预约或指示运输或货运代理业者提供服务的摘要汇总 • 这一信息收到托运交付合约即成立,通常是用于管理营运的便利	• 运输代号 • 运送日期 • 托运者 • 托运货物明细 • 运输业者
运送状况报告 Transportation Status	• 在货物运送的过程中,特定的时间点或地点,依先约定,由运输业者或代理业者发出给委托者 • 这个讯息,可以是: 1. 委托者要求 2. 依先前约定的时程 3. 状况 4. 意外状况	• 运输代号 • 运送日期 • 收货者 • 货物处理状况(遗失、损坏、拒收) • 运输业者

(续表)

讯息名称	使用说明	内容概述
到货通知 Arrival Notice	• 运输或运输代理服务业者发出此讯息用以告知委托者到货详细资料 • 这个讯息也可用以提供配送信息的证明 • 一到货通知对应一笔委托	• 运费(币别) • 预计到货时间 • 运送内容、批次、包装、材积、栈板(是否回收) • 运送起讫点 • 运送工具、环境(真空、温度……)

本组信息在国际性企业管理或国际贸易上十分有用,在幅员辽阔的大陆或国家(欧洲、美国、中国大陆)也能发挥一定的功效。尤其近年来在供应链管理运用上,如在途商品管理或物料管理(Material In Transit,MIT)方面都见其重要性。

4. 出货、验收处理流程①

本组信息旨在供买、卖双方于出货作业时互相通知,先是请对方准备收货;收货通知:请对方验收状况,俾便为请款对账的基础。

讯息名称	使用说明	内容概述
出货通知 Dispatch Advice	• 出货前明确说明在双方交易条件下出货或准备的明细状况 • 此一信息让买家知道出货内容、时间,使其有时间准备收货,并可与订单作交互检查 • 此一信息与买卖双方及代理人相关 • 此一信息发出后,在货到时可与物流资料(品项、数量、包装)交互勾稽 • 此一信息可为出货者发出,也可为退货者发出 • 国际贸易上是结账的第一步 • 信息中,每一包装单位(栈板、纸箱)都应明确指明,俾便货到时能与实际货物交互勾稽,不同之处立刻查出	• 出货地点、时间 • 一或多个到货地点 • 涵盖多少品项、订单,及其包装(栈板、纸箱……)、编码(栈板、纸箱、产品序号)

---

① 资料来源:财团法人信息工业策进会系统工程处,《电子商务导航精华》第15篇,参 http://www.ec.org.tw/net/ecpilot/pilot_main.asp 2002/4/2。

（续表）

讯息名称	使用说明	内容概述
验收通知 Receipt Advice	• 此一信息应为在收到实体货物后,买家向供货商或代理商发出 • 验收通知前明确说明在双方交易条件下验收货物内容,其目的: 　1. 确认收货 　2. 与出货通知对应,确认其验收内容是否与出货单一致,或是通知出货单内的控件是否被接受(运货单已签核) 　3. 通知收货内容与订单或计划内容不符 • 买家对内容不符或不接受的货品,向卖家所做的建议行动 • 买家根据出货单的错误所做的发票或贷方票据,内容不符或不接受的货品,向卖家所做的建议行动 • 收货者也可用以校正内部发票,用以转向最终的客户 • 此一信息的发出应在协议时间内,如收货后24小时 • 供货商可依此一信息资料,检视出货资料,调整发票、贷方票据、作内部控制、库存检验……	• 收货日期 • 收到货物之初货单号、日期 • 订单号码、日期 • 出货单数量、收获数量、不足原因(如损坏)、处理方式(如赔偿)

5. 对账、请款处理流程①

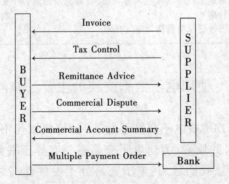

本组讯息旨在供买、卖双方于验收动作完成后的账款处理流程,除买卖双方外还包括付款银行及收款银行。

---

① 资料来源:财团法人信息工业策进会系统工程处,《电子商务导航精华》第16篇,参 http://www.ec.org.tw/net/ecpilot/pilot_main.asp 2002/4/2。

讯息名称	使用说明	内容概述
发票 Invoice	• 发票讯息由卖方传送给客户,声请在先前约定的条件下,支付货物、或劳务的费用 • 本信息在资料适切状况下也可当作 Proforma Invoice 或借、贷票据 • 方开出发票可以是一或多笔费用,相对应于一或多笔订单、出货指示…… • 在跨国交易时,信息内容可包含付款条件、运输细节及报关、统计所需资料	• 付款方式(如银行转账) • 订单号码、发货单号 • 买主代码 • 付款币别、加值税 • 付款条件(如发票收到后2个月内) • 付款明细项
税款控制 Tax Control	• 此一信息由供货商发给客户,说明税款的支付情形,可是一笔发票也可是一批发票 • 常与一张发票或一批发票一起传送 • 此信息也可是交易双方发给第三者、税务稽核,告知税款支付状况	• 供货商、买主统一编号 • 与之交互参照的发票资讯、税率、金额
汇款通知 Remittance Advice	• 在特定日期,提供付款的会计相关资料,及结账的会计资料,内容含支付款项的商品或劳务细节 • 此一信息双方可互发 • 汇款通知是通知对方,将付款项的细节,国内或国际交易都可用,其内容可涵盖一笔或多笔交易 • 每笔汇款通知只用一种货币,只有一个结算日期 • 可含订单资料认为交互参考	• 付款日期 • 收款银行、账号 • 收、付双方编号(统一编号、Location Code) • 付款币别、汇率 • 冲抵发票日期、金额、号码 • 支付、调整(如短交货扣款)明细

3.3 使用电子数据交换的主要法律问题

有论者认为,EDI 或电子交易不过是"计算机取代书面交易或利用电话、传真的交易",并质疑,为何电子交易需要有异于书面交易的合同、法律制度?就这一点,我们认为,电子交易处于发展建构之中,仍然存有许多盲点,而且电子交易是以包含硬件、软件的计算机技术、通讯技术为基础,但该技术容有限制,所以对于利用网络而言,当有异于传统的书面交易。所以,在讨论企业间电子交易合同时,应特别针对电子交易的特性[①]加以掌握。实际上,有关电子交易在法律实务上最重要的事项,是如何确保合同及整体电子交易的可信赖性与安全性。[②] 从法律角度看来,针对个别具体交易电子化分析其疑点、风险,及确保经过合意的安全性、信赖性的技术手段应如何赋予其法律上的效果,当是我们首要的任务。

基此,本文首先拟针对使用 EDI 所涉及的法律问题,举主要的说明如下:

一、书面形式的问题

书面形式的要求,乃现行国际贸易相关各国之国内立法及国际公约与国际惯例中最常见到的一项合同要求[③],而 EDI 的最大特点,便是以虚拟的电子化环境条件来取代原有交易系统之书面纸张文件,实现所谓之"无纸交易";然而,此与传统的书面合同之主要差异,为表现形式不同、存储介质不同与可信度不同[④],而如何使传统立法之文书形式要求与 EDI 交易中无纸之特性兼容,是吾等首应解决之法律问题。此外,就较为成熟的

[①] 其主要具有以下 2 大特性:(1) 第 1 特性为与公司内部内外系统网络化的特性。在对于与公司内系统的联机,已具有未来网络化的独立系统处理交易信息的交换。多与补充发单系统等存货管理系统或会计系统互动,与后述自动处理的特性相辅相成,负责经营、营业效率化的机能;在对于与公司外系统的联机,现有实施与价金支付连系的银行的利用、与运输公司、仓库公司等物流系统的联机。尤其在实现金融 EDI 时,可预测未付金管理的处理,将与诸金融体系相连系而运作。(2) 第 2 特性乃信息自动处理特性。亦即多数情况下,接单信息交换时,收到下单者的下单信息,可不假人手地将其换为接单信息、出货指示信息或更转换为未付信息作业,作为会计上利用。而信息自动处理有时伴随着商品、交易对象的数字化处理,而今亦被利用为交易信息的自动发信处理。见室町正实:"EDI 契约の実务上の留意点(上)",《EDI(电子のデータ交换)と法》,1996(NBL584):43—44。

[②] 例如,下接单信息交换系统发生障碍,致价金支付迟延或价金支付金额发生错误的情形下,此时买卖价金支付的法律纷争,也就是价金支付金额不足时,有债务不履行的损害赔偿请求权发生,过多时有返还请求权发生;价金支付不足时,可能对对方资金支付产生影响,使对方遭到银行交易停止处分等不利益。接单信息处理上有错误时,该错误的影响并不仅对于接个人,对于流通业者也产生影响。商品信息的错误,可能造成对方缺货,制造停止,甚至发生人、物的损害。所以,交易保全的相关事项,可以说是是电子交易中法律检讨上最重要课题。

[③] 使用 EDI 所涉之首要问题,在于传统之文件非仅具传送记载信息之功能而已,其常有表彰财产性价值的私权之功能,需透过该文书使该权利发生移转行使之流通证券。为了落实其交易的安全及确实,各国皆制定法律以为规制。将传统书面形式的文件体系转换为利用 EDI 技术体系方法有(A)实质性方式及(B)机能性方式。前者于不修正相关法律规则的情况下,尽量以电子方式模仿现行法下文书具有的部分机能;后者为了促进 EDI 技术的引进及普及,制定必要的法律完全以电子文书代替传统文书。

[④] 高云:《电子合同中电子邮件应用的法律问题研究》,载《电子知识产权》2002 年第 3 期,第 43 页。

海运电子提单①的发展而言,除 UCNITRAL 模范法外②,国际上还有一些为实现电子提单的努力正在进行中,主要的有:

(一) CMI 规则(The CMI Rules)

在 1990 年,国际海事委员会(The Committee Maritime International,CMI)就电子提单的适用采用了一套提单规则(CMI rules of bills of lading,1990)。③ 在 CMI 规则下,当事人间之合意为规则适用之大前提④,其后在电子提单之运用上,运送人于签发电子提单时,会连同一组私人密码(Private Code)或所谓的私钥交付予货主,此密码的持有可用以表彰持有人对货物的占有,而此种占有权并将在占有权人(货主)通知运送人取消原有钥匙,并依货主的指示另行签发一组新钥匙后,得以移转予其他利害关系人。为了能顺利达到前述的目的,CMI 规则同时要求所有当事人必须认同电子讯息具有与传统书面及签名相当的法律效力。然而即使使 CMI 规则已经尽可能的周密,在实际的执行面上,仍然无法完全处理所有的问题。例如,在何种情况下构成要约与承诺并没能加以涵盖,此外该规则也没有就系统故障时的责任归属问题,有任何的规定。⑤ 此外,国际商会于 1993 年所修订的《跟单信用证统一惯例》(ICC Uniform Customs and Practice for Documentary Credits,简称 UCP500),其第 20 条第 B 项也确认了 EDI 的效力。⑥

(二) 欧洲提单计划(BOLERO PROJECT)

1995 年 6 月,在香港、荷兰、瑞典、英国及美国的参与下,欧洲开始进行所谓的欧洲提单计划(Project Bolero, Bills of Lading for Europe)。通过运送公司、银行及电讯公司所组成的联盟的运作,该计划尝试解决将票券转换成电子形式时可能发生的法律问题。Bolero 系通过使用者及一集中

---

① 是指透过电子传送有关海上货物运送合同的数据,Livermore, John & Euarjai, Krailerk, "Electronic Bills Of Lading: A Progress Report", *J. MAR. L. & COM.* 1997, (28):55。

② 详请参阅 UN DOC. A/CN.9/426 (1996)。

③ CMI rules of bills of lading,请参 http://www.comitemaritime.org/cmidocs/rulesebla.html (visited 2004/7/24)。

④ CMI rules of bills of lading, Article 1: "These Rules shall apply whenever the parties so agree."

⑤ Dube, Jocelyn, "Second Place Canadian Perspectives on the Impact of the CMI Rules for Electronic Bills of Lading on the Liability of the Carrier Towards the Endorsee", *TRANSP. L. J.* 1998, (26):107; Kelly, Richard Brett, "The Cmi Charts A Course on the Sea Of Electronic Data Interchange: Rules for Electronic Bills Of Lading", *MAR. LAW. J.* 1992, (16):349。

⑥ 关于电子提单与电子数据之比较,请参 Zekos, Georgios I., "The Contractual Role of Documents Issued under the Cmi Draft Instrument on Transport Law 2001", *Mar. L. & Com.* 2004, (35):99。

线上登录中心(Centralized Online Registry)间 EDI 讯息的转换来运作。这其中,使用人(运送人)、货主、承揽人及银行间的收发讯息,都是以计算机工作站的方式从登录中心发出,但关系人彼此间也可直接交换信息。依据其设计,登录中心会在"交货记录内"项下载有详细的运送文件,任何经合法授权者均可进入系统查看这些详细资料。至于登录中心,则负责确认及鉴定这些信息并汇整信息。Bolero 计划中包含了高度安全控管的设计,用以保护信息的真实性。其中所采用的方式之一就是使用数据签章,这种签章方式不仅可用以辨识发信人的身份,并可预防信息在传递过程中被篡改。① 而为因应数字时代的到来,Bolero. net 于 1999 年亦公布了 Bolero 系统下的数字签章指南,其中即认为法律行为如有使用书面之必要者,如其电子签章经 Bolero 认证,则可符合书面及签名之需求。②

(三) 美国 1992 年海上货物运送法案(The Carriage of Goods by Sea Act 1992)

美国通过本法案的修正,来调整 1885 年海运提单法(The Bills of Lading Act)的规定;虽然主要在规范当事人有权起诉与否的问题,但也特别允许该法案条文可以适用于 EDI 交易。③

(四) 澳洲海运文件法案 1996(The Australian Sea-Carriage Documents Bill 1996)

本法案是最近一个接受电子提单的法案。其立法依据主要是援用 UNCITRAL 模范法有关"电子及计算机海运文件"的规定。法案中还明白表示,除以传统书面表彰的海运文件外,也同样适用于以数据讯息形式呈现的海运文件。④

这样看来,以 EDI 的观点分析书面的要件,若采用机能性方式来分析书面的机能,可认其有下述之目的:1. 使所有人能理解其信息;2. 留下易保存的永久性交易记录;3. 以复制方式使各当事人保有相同信息;4. 留下署名作成当事人最终意思的记录;5. 以有形的方式简易的保存信息;6. 对具有法律拘束力的意思留下有形的证据;7. 使当事人认识合同的效果;

---

① Nelson, "Bolero-An Innovative Legal Concept", Computers & L. 1995, (6): 17.
② http://www.bolero.net/decision/legal/(visited 2004/7/26).
③ Sturley, Michael F., "Proposed Amendments to the Carriage of Goods by Sea Act", HOUS. J. INT' L Lp. 1996, (18): 609.
④ Livermore, John & Euarjai, Krailerk, "Electronic Bills Of Lading: A Progress Report", J. MAR. L. & COM. 1997, (28): 59.

8. 易于会计课税的控制及监察。①

在传统的交易过程中之所以会要求签署合同或留下书面之文书,其主要之目的有二:其一,以书面作为合同成立生效要件;其二,以之作为证明合同存在及证明其内容之证据。基本上,欠缺有效性的合同,将不足以作为任何请求权基础之依据,而文书证据正是在传统交易中最容易为法院所接受之证据形式,而今,在电子交易的环境中,电子信息是否可以等同于传统之文书,具有同等的法律效力,这正是我们必须加以思考的法律难题。

基本上,针对书面性之解决,在 1991 年的联合国 EDI 小组便曾提出了两种解决之道:一种是透过扩大法律对"书面"一词所下之定义,以便把电子交易纪录纳入书面之范畴,来满足传统交易过程中所要求之书面性;另一种方法系透过当事人间之协议,将电子信息视同书面。② 因以协议方式来解决书面形式法律问题,仅限于国家的法律允许当事人对书面形式要求作出自由处分时方为有效,且仅能约束签订该合同或协议各方当事人,但不能有效地制约第三方的权利和义务。③ 故在 1996 年 6 月,联合国国际贸易法律委员会(UNCITRAL)在处理有关 EDI 及相关通讯方法之法律问题时,便采用《联合国国际贸易法律委员会电子商务模范法》(UNCITRAL Model Law on Electronic Commerce)之规定,藉由使用"功能等同(functional-equivalent)之方法"试图消除至今电子信息无法与纸张讯息有相同法律地位之障碍④,并于模范法第 6 条规定:"若法律要求数据必须为书面或以书面提出,以数据信息所为之数据,视为符合法律之规定"。⑤ 此系以书面形式的基本功能为标准,一旦电子形式具备了传统书面形式的基本功能,本着对同一功能的法律制度同等对待的法律原则,法律就确认

---

① 朝冈良平、伊东健治、鹿岛诚之助、菅又久直:《图解よくわかるEDI》,东京:日刊工业新闻社 1998 年版,第 130—131 页。

② "United Nations Commission on International Trade Law Working Group on Electronic Commerce", A/CN. 9/WG. IV/WP. 53 (1991).

③ 刘颖、骆文怡、伍艳:《论电子合同中的书面形式问题及其解决》,载《经济师》2003 年第 2 期,第 49 页。

④ EDI 的信息讯息与传统的书面纸张文件差距很大,联合国国际贸易法律委员会电子商务模范法采用"功能等同之方法",系分析法律对传统的纸张文件要求之目的与功能,只要 EDI 的信息讯息符合该要求,则赋予与书面文件等同之法律效力;"United Nations Commission on International Trade Law Working Group on Electronic Commerce", A/CN. 9/WG. IV/WP. 94 (2002)。

⑤ 该条之基本精神是避免 EDI 在法律适用上受到歧视,不得因 EDI 之形式而否认其法律效力。

电子形式的效力并给予书面形式同等的保护。① 不可讳言者,数据电文与纸面文件在物理性质上有所不同,二者无法相互完全替代,法律承认数据电文具有书面文件的效力,只是一种等价功能意义上的承认。② 法律上的规定并不能使一个不具备书面功能的形式变成"书面形式",只有某种形式具备了书面的功能,法律方能赋予其在"书面形式"上之效力;而行为形式的"功能"状况取决于物质条件,即技术水平的发展,因此,法律上意思表示的形式(包括合同的形式),实际上系由商业活动所追求的高效与安全的目标、当时的技术发展水平与立法者对该形式所具备功能的认识,故法律与技术的结合已不再仅限于知识产权的保护,而且已经扩展到交易方式的领域。③

以大陆之法规范而言,虽于《民法通则》中并未对合同形式作限制性之规定,然早期于《经济合同法》第 3 条中规定,"经济合同,除即时结清者外,应当采用书面形式";故最高人民法院在《关于适用涉外合同法若干问题的解答》中,明确表示订立合同未用书面形式的涉外经济合同无效。是以,如何确定合同的有效性问题,当显得相当重要。故此大陆乃于新修之合同法中,将数据电文(包括电报、电传、传真、电子数据交换)等可以有形地表现所载内容之形式者,均认为属书面形式,此系以条文之形式重新定义书面形式,扩大解释书面形式之载体,即不再局限于传统之唯一载体"纸"上,而是扩大到有形的、可读的、并可在一定时期内储存特定信息的载体上。另,于 2001 年《最高人民法院关于民事诉讼证据的若干规定》的第 22 条中,"调查人员调查搜集计算机数据或者录音、录像等视听资料应当要求被调查人提供有关资料的原始载体。"将其归为视听资料。唯大陆于 2004 年 8 月通过之《电子签名法》第 4 条却将数据电文视为符合法律、法规要求的书面形式,准此,似将数据电文认为非书面而仅透过视为书面之方式赋予其法律效果,以此观之,似与新修合同法之精神不一。④

以台湾地区之民法规定言,并未对书面加以定义,考其立法原意显系指纸本文书而言,虽于新修正之《刑法》第 220 条规定中,将足以表示其用

---

① 齐爱民:《电子合同典型法律规则研究》,载《武汉大学学报(社会科学版)》2002 年第 2 期,第 159 页。
② 刘颖、骆文怡、伍艳:〈论电子合同中的书面形式问题及其解决〉,载《经济师》2003 年第 2 期,第 49 页。
③ 卓小苏:《电子合同形式论》,载《法商研究——中南财经政法大学学报(法学版)》2002 年第 2 期,第 102 页。
④ 由法效果之观点而言,适用与视为应无不同,然于构成要件之基本认定上,则以本质不同为其前提。

意证明之电磁记录以文书论,但能否扩张解释民法现行"书面"及于电子文件,则不无疑问;虽亦有论者以为,或可参考其他法规之用语,直接认可电子文件之文书性,并援用诸如《会计法》第40条第2项之规定:"会计数据采用机器处理者,其机器贮存体中之纪录,视为会计簿籍。"《公司法》第169条第2项规定:"(股东名簿)采计算机作业或机器处理者,前项数据得以附表补充之。"及《公文程序条例》第2条第2项:"前项各款的公文,必要时得以电报、电报交换、电传文件、传真或其他电子文件行之。"然此种说法,仍令人存疑。盖这些技术性文件的属性毕竟不同于规范整体合同关系之合同文件。

这些问题在面临新科技时更为明显。试问电子交易是否构成一个"书面"合同?一个传真何以得被视为"已签章"?这些问题都无法从条文的规定中得到清楚的答案,但是却可能使得原本合法的合同变得无效或无法执行。这些因为欠缺清楚的规范所产生的诸如电子交易是否构成合同的疑点,以及电子合同是否可依 U.C.C. 2-201 来加以执行的问题,都会影响电子交易的发展,也可能使有诈欺意图的一方当事人可以任意地违约,再以"诈欺条款"作为挡箭牌来逃避责任。[①]

就当前国际发展趋势,台湾地区于《电子签章法》第4条中[②],也采用类似的立法。[③] 认为书面文件可以以电子文件取代[④],然而必须要满足四项条件:(1) 是电子文件能够完整呈现书面文件的内容及供人为或机器验证电子文件真伪;(2) 是法律另有规定不适用者;(3) 是经各目的事业主管机关公告不适用者;(4) 是当事人另有约定不适用者。而电子文件虽然可以取代书面文件作为通信及交易的媒介,但并非所有以电子方法

---

① 面对此科技变迁所引发的问题,使我们不得不对诈欺条款作一番省思,这个条文被认为是对抗诈欺的合理且有效的武器,预防不实的主张被执行并保护个人对抗不存在的口头合同,而达到这个目的的方法,在过去是通过可以实质纪录双方合同形成的证据来加以完成。因为最初诈欺条款的目的是要鼓励在合同成立时使用"书面",而该书面可在日后做为证据证明双方的目的及意图,此外,还可以阻止基于证据所称的口头合同而为的不实主张。

② 台湾地区于《电子签章法》第4条规定:"经相对人同意者,得以电子文件为表示方法。依法令规定应以书面为之者,如其内容可完整呈现,并可于日后取出供查验者,经相对人同意,得以电子文件为之。前两项规定得依法令或行政机关的公告,排除其适用或就其应用技术与程序另为规定。"

③ 参考《联合国 UNCITRAL 电子签章基本规则草案》、《伊利诺州安全电子商务法》section 5—125、《新加坡电子交易法》clause 4。

④ 传统赖以作为通信及交易行为基础的书面文件,其功能皆可利用现代信息及通信以电子方式制作、呈现、保存及传送,为使电子文件能广为各行各业应用,减少书面与电子作业并行的不便,以充分发挥数字化及网络化作业的效益,所以规定依法律规定书面文件制作者,可以以电子文件作出。

制作的电子文件,都可防止被篡改及伪造,必须以主管机关认可或约定的安全技术、程序及方法所制作的电子文件并且可供验证真伪的,才能推定为真正,才赋予与书面文件同等的效果。

就此,吾人以为若从语源学上对书面一词加以分析,可以看出其限定性含义是如何形成的,起初"write"是指用尖锐物刻标记[1],然而随科技之发展,于当事人以电报、电传及传真等透过电子媒介传送交易信息,只需于交易过程中产生一份文书,作为最终传递之结果,便可成为交易所能接受的手段。同样地,透过电子媒介传送之 EDI 或 E-mail,于当事人认为有必要时,同样可透过计算机打印出书面单据或将之储存于磁盘或其他载体,而这些纪录其上之讯息,应可视为"超文本"之形式。[2] 对此新兴科技所生之法律议题,于台湾地区《电子签章法》第 4 条中[3],亦认书面文件得以电子文件代之。唯电子文件虽可取代书面文件作为通信及交易的媒介,但并非所有以电子方法制作的电子文件,皆可防止被篡改及伪造,必须以主管机关认可或约定之安全技术、程序及方法所制作之电子文件且可供验证真伪者,始赋予与书面同等之法律效力。

二、签章之问题

当交易进入无纸化时,对当事人最重要的问题,系解决书面和签章问题,而此二问题间有密切关系,立法例中往往会要求当事人于文件作成书面后,另须亲自签章,以为该文件成立生效要件之一;而要求当事人签章之目的,在于(1) 确定当事人身份;及(2) 基于其签章,把有关书面文件或信息载明的权利义务归属于该特定当事人。[4] 是以,传统上只有手写签章[5]被认为符合法律之要求,因签章之目的在确认该文件,以证明当事人

---

[1] 《韦氏国际英语新词典》(第 3 版),将"write"界定为用笔或类似工具书写的文字或印刷物。该定义仍限于用笔或类似工具形成的标记或符号。

[2] 所谓超文本依《英汉双解网络词典》的注解,是一种向用户展示信息的方法,用超文本方式信息可以由用户安排以非顺序方式访问,而不需要考虑原来的组织方式。超文本是要使计算机能够适应人类非线性思维方式——人类思维和使用信息的方式是联想、关联,而不是像电影、书籍和演讲那样的线性组合;齐爱民:"电子合同典型法律规则研究",载《武汉大学学报(社会科学版)》,2002 年第 2 期,第 159 页。

[3] 台湾地区于《电子签章法》第 4 条之规定:"经相对人同意者,得以电子文件为表示方法。依法令规定应以书面为之者,如其内容可完整呈现,并可于日后取出供查验者,经相对人同意,得以电子文件为之。……"

[4] Lewis, Mark, "E-Commerce: Digital Signatures: Meeting the Traditional Requirements Electronically: A Canadian Perspective", *Asper Rev. Int'l Bus. & Trade L.*, 2002 (2): 63.

[5] 冯大同:《国际贸易中应用电子数据交换所遇到的法律问题》,载《中国法学》1993 年第 5 期,第 102 页。

愿在合同约定的条件下进行交易。①

在传统法制中,双方的签章为一般国内及国际认同的认证方式,签章的作用,主要在确定合同当事人的身份及确保其欲受法律拘束力的意思表示。然而,签章并非认证的唯一手段,如各国普遍存在的公证制度便是另一种常见的认证方式②,此外,也有用手印代替亲笔签名。其实,任何的认证手段都不是完美无缺的,而在多数国家,"签章"被法院局限于双方的签字,亲笔签字虽具有独特性,但也并非无被模仿伪造的可能,盖章更是任何一个执有印章的人都可以做到的,遇有争议时,这种认证方法的真伪,也有待于法院或仲裁机构依法鉴定。可见,使用 EDI 等现代科技手段进行认证,与签字等传统方式相比较,未必有更多的不可靠性。事实上,传统上签字要求关键在于它所用的符号是否为当事人基于认证该书面文件的明确目的而签署或采用的,而不在于是否为当事人手写的完整签名。简而言之,签字不一定要由签署者亲笔白纸黑字地写上,而是可以使用某种同样具有独特性的符号来代替。

早期,《联合国国际贸易法律委员会系将电子商务模范法》(UNCITRAL MODEL LAW on Electronic Commerce)第 7 条③扩大其含意,从而包含电子签章在内,其规定:"若依法律有使用签章的必要者,如以电子讯息为之,需具备如下要件:(1) 方式之使用足以辨识当事人及指出该数据电文之内容;(2) 且根据所有情事(包括所有相关的协议)该方法被用于上述目的是适宜的、可信赖的。"④然而,为使电子环境下履行签字功能基本原则基础得以扩充,明确以功能等同之基础,评价电子签章促进依赖这种电子签章发生法律效力,遂于 2001 年制订《电子签章模范法》及《贸易法律委员会电子签章模范法颁布指南》,以扩充《电子商务模范法》之适用。关于电子签章之意义,《电子签章模范法》第 2 条更进一步规定:所谓的电子签章系指在数据电文中,以电子形式所含、所附或在逻辑上与数据电文有关系的数据,它可以用于鉴别与数据电文相关的签字人和表明签字人

---

① 于静:"电子合同若干法律问题初探",载《政法论坛》,1997 年第 6 期,第 71 页。
② 例如外贸公司对外合同实践中,普遍使用合同专用章,虽不能代替签字却能起一定的认证作用。
③ 见 http://www.un.or.at/uncitral/texts/electom/english/m1-ec.htm,(visited 2001/8/15)。
④ Article 7.: "(1) Where the law requires a signature of a person, that requirement is met in relation to a data message if: (a) a method is used to identify that person and to indicate that person's approval of the information contained in the data message; and (b) that method is as reliable as was appropriate for the purpose for which the data message was generated or communicated, in the light of all the circumstances, including any relevant agreement."

认可数据电文所含信息。该法第6条第1项也规定：凡法律规定要求有一人签字时，如果根据各种情况，包括任何有关协议，使用电子签章既适合生成或传送数据电文所要达的目的，而且也同样可靠，即满足了该项签字要求。准此，原则上电子签章模范法仍承袭电子商务模范法之精神，且更进一步定义出电子签章之意义与内涵，值得肯定。

由上述的规定可知，既然相关当事人能依一种可信赖的方法正确地予以确定，那么与之相关的权利义务，也应自动地归属于当事人。

承上所述，早期，联合国国际贸易法律委员会虽有订立《电子商务模范法》，然而该法并没有触及数字签章是什么；嗣后虽于2001年制订《电子签章模范法》，该法架构下，亦仅于第3条规定："电子签章法之规定，除第五条之规定外，概不排除、限制或剥夺可生成满足第六条第一款所述要求或符合适用法律要求的电子签章的任何方法或法律效力。"然就具体而言，电子签章究竟具有如何的效力，仍值研究。就此我们可参考美国犹他州数字签章的立法规定（The Utah Digital Signature Act）。[①]

该法首先定义数字签章，所谓"数字签章"（digital signature）是指一种数字次序。行为人意图在特定讯息中通过单向功能运作讯息的方式签名，而将该讯息锁码。相较于联合国电子签章模范法之规定，犹他州之立法较强调锁码之功能，而联合国之规范则着重于当事人的可辨识性与传送讯息之确认性，以此观之，联合国之规范考量似较周全。唯就真实发生之效力而言，犹他州之法律仍不失为一值得参考的依据所在，兹就数字签章的效力[②]，略述如下：

（一）推定的法律效力

数字签章在下列情形下被推定是真实的：(a) 公开密钥[③]证书是由特许认证机构依照该法相应的规定签发的；(b) 该证书已经犹他州商务部备案；(c) 在进行数字签章时，该证书仍然有效。所以，如果一项数字签章符合上述三点时，该数字签章即被视为是真实的，因此而发生特定的法

---

① Biddle, C. Bradford, "Misplaced Priorities: The Utah Digital Signature Act and Liability Allocation in a Public Key Infrastructure", *San Diego L. Rev.* 1996, (33): 1143.

② 依 The Utah Digital Signature Act 46-3-401（一）、（二）款的规定。

③ 在非对称密码体制之下，有一对密切联系的密钥，一个是公开密钥（public key），该密钥为公众知晓以以认证数字签章的真实性；一个是私密密钥（private key），其与公开密钥不同，私密密钥仅为当事人或已经获得其授权进行数字签章的代理人知晓。

律效力。①

（二）可推翻的推定（Rebutable Presumption）

由于数字签章只是被推定为真实，它当然可以被相反的证据推翻，所以在下列四种情形下②，数字签章真实性的推定将被阻却：（a）有证据表明，由特许认证机构签发的证书中登记的公开密钥不能够证明处于争议中的数字签章的真实性；（b）有证据表明，基于违反本法任何规定之外的原因，公开密钥的真正签名人已经丧失该公开密钥的控制；（c）有证据表明，争议中的数字签章将因为不符合普通法（Common Law），而被视为不存在；（d）对争议中的数字签章的信赖将构成对一般商业惯例的违反。

此外，为避免由于数字签章法律效力的不确定性所引起的争议和分歧，该法还规定，任何以数字签章签署的电子文书与手写签章的有形文书，具有同样的法律效力③，以消除大众的疑虑并满足法院适用现行法律解释数字签章的法律效力的需求。就此而言，与联合国《电子签章模范法》第 3 条之原意，大致相同。

就台湾地区现行法而言，对签名或盖章并未作定义，但因台湾地区民法第 3 条系将签名、盖章与其他符号并列，故学者一般认为签名仍需有姓、名、别号、商号、堂名等文字，单纯的符号应不构成签名。故在使用电报或传真时，因其仍在原稿上使用具传统意义之签章，较无争议；然在无纸化交易环境下，无法透过电子媒介亲笔签字时，究竟何种方式之签章可满足无纸交易之需求，并能得到法律上之承认。

大陆方面的规范架构上，虽于合同法之修正建议草案中，有学者提出将签字定义为"当事人及其授权代表的亲笔签名，或者在运用计算机等机器的情况下，能被识别信息传递的合理方法"④，然于新修合同法中并未将此采为具体条文规范。⑤ 后于地方性之规范，却有较前瞻性之规定，以上海市及广东省为例，上海市方面，如 1999 年公布之《国际经贸电子数据交

---

① 依 The Utah Digital Signature Act 46-3-401（四）款的规定，任何数据签章均须附有时间戳记，除非由数码讯息另行指定，时间戳记所显示的日期和时间，将被视为该数字签章形成时间的初步证据，并因此发生，相应的法律效力。但是，由于时间戳记仅被视为初步证据，所以它可以被透过其他方法所获得的证据推翻。

② 依 The Utah Digital Signature Act 46-3-401（五）款的规定。

③ 依 The Utah Digital Signature Act 46-3-402 的规定。

④ 此显然采用了扩大解释的法律途径，参见该建议草案第 28 条第（2）款。载于梁慧星主编：《民商法论丛》1996 年第 4 卷，第 447 页。

⑤ 据大陆国家信息化办公室有关负责人透露，中国电子商务发展框架即将出台，将包括立法的总则、数字化信息的法律地位和网络合同的法律效力以及网络服务提供者的责任四方面；郑成思、薛虹：《台湾地区电子商务立法的核心问题》，载《互联网世界》2000 年第 10 期，第 10 页。

换管理规定》;至于广东省方面,早于 1996 年广东省即公布《对外贸易实施电子数据交换(EDI)暂行规定》,唯已于 2002 年失效;其后更于 2003 年 2 月 1 日实施电子交易条例。① 至 2004 年 8 月通过《电子签名法》后,该法第 14 条规定:"可靠的电子签名与手写签名或者盖章具有同等的法律效力"准此,以大陆法规范之架构而言,其签名并不因无纸化交易而受影响。

目前台湾地区系透过所谓电子签章的立法期能解决这方面的问题②,盖传统的签章其作为意思行使及查验文书真伪之功能③,应可透过电子签章达成,而为使电子签章能配合电子文件广为各行各业应用,减少书面与电子作业并行之不便,充分发挥数字化及网络化之效益,认其与传统之签章生同等之效力;然并非所有以电子方法制作的电子签章皆有相同的安全性,须依主管机关认可或依约定之安全技术、方法及程序所制作之电子签章,并满足独特性、辨识力、可靠性及验证电子文件内容正确性等四项条件时,始生等同之法律效力。然则,私法自治之空间与合同自由之精神,仍应尊重,故此并不排除交易当事人间之协议④,而得以合同条文约定。

三、证据法上之问题

在传统的交易过程中之所以签署合同或留下书面之文书,主要系在于满足发生争议时之证据要求。基本上,欠缺一个有效的合同将不足以证明任何请求权基础之存在,而书面证据正是在传统交易中最容易为法

---

① 关于美国法的介绍,可参 Epstein, Julian, "Cleaning Up a Mess on the Web: a Comparison of Federal and State Digital Signature Laws", *N. Y. U. J. Legis. & Pub. Pol'y* 2001/2002, (5): 491.

② 《电子签章法》第 9 条:"依法令规定应签名或盖章者,得经当事人约定以电子签章代之。但法律明定或经政府机关公告不适用者,不在此限。前项电子签章以当事人依约定之安全技术、程序及方法制作可资验证电子文件真伪者为限。"然而,另一个值得研究的问题在于,当契约当事人未依循电子签章法时,其所为之电子交易效力为何? Huey, Nathan A., "Do E-Sign and UETA Really Matter?", *Iowa L. Rev.*, 2003, (88): 681.

③ 传统签名或盖章的意义及功能如下:1. 证据:当签署者在文件上签章后,将留下可供鉴别签署者身份的证据,以明责任归属。2. 同意:在现有法律及习惯下,签署者对某文件签章,表示其同意文件的内容。3. 仪式:经由签章的行为,促使签署者审慎思考签署后必须承担的法律责任,以防止思虑不周的合同行为。

④ 联合国国际商务使用 EDI 模范合同,系联合国欧洲经济理事会(United Nations Economic for Europe)第 4 工作小组,于 1995 年 3 月于第 41 会期通过,公布供全球 EDI 使用者作为签订网络服务合同之参考,以规范在适用 EDIFACT 标准所设定之规格化电子数据交易行为,其主要内容包括:1. 讯息交换与传输标准;2. 安全控管程序与服务;3. 意思表示之生效;4. 使用 EDI 之有效性;5. 证据;6. 损害赔偿责任;7. 利用第三人提供服务之责任;详见洪淑芬:《联合国国际商务使用 EDI 模范合同简析》,参 http://stlc.iii.org.tw/publish/infolaw/8411/841126.htm (visited 2004/8/1)。

院所接受之证据形式,而今,在电子交易的环境中,由于书面合同并非必要,故法院在执行法律时便必须考虑到其他证据和其他可接受之替代证据。而当 EDI 被广泛应用于国际贸易实务上时,传统国际贸易上之合同、载货证券、保险单、发票等书面文件,都被储存在计算机中相对应的数据资料所替代,而这些电子数据是否具有证据能力?其是否具有证据价值?是值得吾等加以深思的证据法问题,也是国际贸易中推广 EDI 之重要障碍。这些电子数据与传统交易文书相较,其主要之差异在于:传统的交易文书为有形的书面,可长久保存,且其若被变更,亦很容易留下痕迹;而电子数据并非有形物,其系储存在计算机中,透过计算机输入指令时,很容易被更动而不易察觉。[①] 是以,这种无纸电子文件,其安全性与真实性受到相当之质疑,故其在诉讼上能否被采为证据,便成为一法律上之难题。

综观各国对证据法则之规定,主要之立法方式有三[②]:

(1)允许自由提出所有有关之证据[③],如德国、奥地利、日本等国之立法。在此立法下,电子数据证据原则上是可以被采纳为诉讼上之证据,唯法院仍有权衡量其具有之证据价值及可信度如何。

(2)限制于一定种类之证据,始具证据力,如智利、卢森堡等国之立法。在此立法下,电子数据证据目前都未被列入可接受为证据之清单中,尚无法被采纳为诉讼上之证据。

(3)主要是指英美法系国家的证据法。在这些国家的证据法中,由于有完整的证据接受法则,而其中传闻证据法则(Hearsay Rule)[④]排除所谓传闻之可接受性,以及最佳证据法则(The Best Evidence Rule)[⑤]对于所

[①] 薛德明:《国际贸易中 EDI 的若干法律问题探讨》,载《法律科学》1994 年第 3 期,第 72 页。

[②] 参见刘毓骅:《国际贸易中 EDI 应用的举证、签字和书面要求》,载《国际贸易》1994 年第 9 期,第 58 页。

[③] 冯大同:《国际货物买卖法》,北京大学出版社 1995 年版,第 295 页;单文华:《电子贸易的法律问题》,载《民商法论丛》1998 年第 10 卷,第 40 页。

[④] 所谓传闻证据法则,即为排除传闻证据之法则,依此规则只有原证人亲自之见闻所为之证言,才可作为证据。依该规则,对原证人以外的人明示或默示的事实主张以及在无证人作证之情形下,向法院提出之事实主张,不能被采纳为证明其所主张事实为真实的证据,见薛德明:《国际贸易中 EDI 的若干法律问题探讨》,载《法律科学》1994 年第 3 期,第 73 页;换言之,只有亲自见闻的原证人之证言,才能被接纳,因为只有对原证人始可进行反对询问。由于电子数据都是透过计算机自动处理并加以储存,不可能进行反对询问,因此经计算机打印出之数据均属传闻证据,而不予采纳。

[⑤] 此所谓最佳证据为原始证据,只有文件的原本才能作为书证为法院所采纳,对电子证据来说,只有所储存的磁盘或电子形式的数据才是原本,经计算机打印出之数据并非原本,所以不能采为证据。

谓原件(originals)之要求,往往构成 EDI 应用在证据法上之重大障碍。

在《联合国国际贸易法律委员会电子商务模范法(UNCITRAL Model Law on Electronic Commerce)》中,则藉由使用"功能等同之方法"之用语,试图消除至今电子讯息无法与书面纸张享有相同法律地位之障碍。另就有关证据效力方面之课题言,在数据讯息中产生二项最具争议之问题,即他们是否为"文书"(documents)? 可否被法院采为"证据"(evidence)? 联合国模范法第 5 条为解此问题,特别规定:"一数据不得仅因其为数据资料而否认其法律效力。"同样地,在《模范法》第 9 条中亦认为,应禁止使用"最佳证据法则"及"传闻法则"来改变该数据之法律认定及证据价值。值得注意者,大陆于 2004 年 8 月通过之《电子签名法》,亦与《联合国模范法》第 5 条同其规范意旨而于该法第 7 条规定:"数据电文不得仅因为其是以电子、光学、磁或者类似手段生成、发送、接收或者储存的而被拒绝作为证据使用。"

至于证据种类之问题,大陆地区虽有论者认为,电子证据应当归入书证一类。因为《合同法》等法律已经对书面作出了更宽泛的解释,使之涵盖数据电文。将电子证据作为书证不但全面体现了网络的特点和技术性,而且也由于电子证据作为书证具有更强的证明效力有利于确保电子商务的健康快速发展。① 吾人以为,可将视听资料作为间接证据,盖依《民事诉讼法》第 63 条之规定,视听资料是法定七种证据之一②;另依第 69 条之规定,人民法院对视听数据,应辨明真伪,并结合本案的其他证据,审查确定能否作为认定事实的根据。依此规定,一视听资料要成为能证明案件事实的证据,除应当由法院审查核实以外还必须有其他证据③或另外的视听数据相互印证,亦即视听数据不能单独、直接地证明待证事实。④ 申言之,审查判断电子证据的真实可靠性和如何与其他证据结合起来认定案件事实是最主要的工作;其为主要包括以下几点:(1) 审查电子证据的来源;(2) 审查电子证据的收集是否合法;(3) 审查电子证据与事实的联系;(4) 审查电子证据的内容是否真实等;如与其他证据相一致,共同指

---

① 李祖全:《电子合同的证据法学之思考》,载《常德师范学院学报(社会科学版)》2003 年第 3 期,第 52 页。
② 所谓"视听数据",是指利用录音录像磁带反映出的形象以及计算机储存的数据来证明案件事实的证据。
③ 此之"其他证据",应系指《民事诉讼法》第 63 条规定的书证、物证、证人证言、当事人陈述、鉴定结论、勘验笔录等证据。
④ 赵骏:《商业 EDI 活动的法律调整》,载《政治与法律》1998 年第 1 期,第 48 页。

向同一事实,就可以认定其效力,作为定案根据,反之则不能。①此为介于大陆法系与英美法系之间的做法。由于尚未有要求网络服务商对传输的电子文件储存纪录或转存之制度,部分地方法规已有相应之规定,以广东省为例,早期,广东省《对外贸易实施电子数据交换暂行规定》第13条规定即要求电子数据服务中心应有收到报文和被提取报文的响应与记录,唯该暂行规定已于2002年失效。其后,广东省于2003年复行实施《电子交易条例》,该《条例》第18条第1款第4项规定,认证机构应建立认证系统的备份机制和应急事件处理程序,藉以确保在人为破坏或者发生自然灾害时认证系统和数字证书使用的安全。

至于台湾地区在民事诉讼法中,并未对得为证据的范围作严格限制②,故电子文件不论储存于科技设备(例如计算机硬盘、磁盘或光盘)、计算机印出(print-out)文书,甚或尚在"暂时存取记忆体"(Random Access Momory;RAM)而得于计算机屏幕上阅读状态,若得举证,均应认其具有证据能力。③ 是以,电子文书于台湾地区民事诉讼程序举证时,大多系径以打印于纸本之文书向法院提出声明书证,若尚未打印书证而仅储存于磁盘等设备者,则因与文书有相同效用而为《民事诉讼法》第363条第1项之"准文书",亦可准用声明书证方式于诉讼中提出。④

于兹较为棘手者在于如何提出电子文书之原本?及如何证明其为真正?虽台湾地区于《民事诉讼法》第363条第2项规定:"文书或前项对象,须以科技设备始能呈现其内容或提出原件有事实上之困难者,得仅提出呈现其内容之书面并证明其内容与原件相符。"然就计算机运作流程举例言之,某甲于其计算机缮打订购单,缮打完成时,将之存盘于A磁盘中,再以E-mail方式将该文件传送予某乙;数小时后,某乙开启计算机并于电

---

① 陶岚、王芳:《试论电子合同的法律效力》,载《南昌高专学报》2003年第3期,第10页。
② 除《刑事诉讼法》第156条、第159条与第160条就被告自由、证人审判外陈述、证人个人意见或推测之词设有证据能力之规定外,民事诉讼法则未有明文。
③ "司法院"第九期司法业务研讨会结论及"司法院"第一厅研究意见均认为"计算机数据经由机器之处理录印,显现之文字或符号如能表示一定之意思,为一般人所得知,则可作为文书之一种,可采为书证之一",引自杨佳政:《电子交易中数字签章与电子文件之法律效力浅析》,载《信息法务透析》1998年第2期,第19页。是以,依台湾地区实务之见解,可供证据之用的文书,仅需其能表达当事人之意思或思想,不问其为中文或其他符号,均得谓为文书;至于其构成之物质为何?其作成之方法为笔书、印刷、木刻,均在所不同。见"司法院":《民事法律专题研究(四)》,"司法院"司法业务研究会第五期及第九期研究专题,台北:司法周刊杂志社印行1987年版,第520—522页。
④ 杨佳政:《电子交易中数字签章与电子文件之法律效力浅析》,载《信息法务透析》1998年第2期,第19页。

子邮件信箱中点取甲传送之文件阅览后存盘,并另存于 B 磁盘片中,嗣后某甲对于以 E-mail 向某乙购物径予否认。就本例言,若法院令某乙提出"原本"时,则某乙应如何举证?虽《民事诉讼法》第 363 条第 2 项规定,某乙于诉讼中声明书证时,得仅提出呈现其内容之书面并证明其内容与"原件"相符,然某乙究应证明与何处之原件相符?就电子文书制作与传输的顺序言,可能为:(1) 甲计算机中之暂时存取记忆体(RAM);(2) 甲计算机中之存盘之硬盘(hard disk);(3) 甲另存盘之 A 磁盘;(4) 电子邮件传输过程中经过的网络服务器(Internet server);(5) 乙计算机中之暂时存取记忆体(RAM);(6) 乙计算机中之存盘之硬盘(hard disk);(7) 乙另存盘之 B 磁盘。此时,究应以何为原件?以发文方之电子文件之储存载体?抑或首次传输至收受方之储存载体?容生疑义,为避免法院于适用时之困扰,此应透过立法明定为宜。[①]

于探讨证据法则问题时,应对于文书证据重新观察;书证据之使用乃至成为具绝对优势地位之因,系源自于人类对于文字阅读及理解能力的提高,从而让交易当事人对以文书为基础建构出来的交易环境产生信任,让立法者开始要求合同应以书面为之或司法之证据法则中强调文书之重要性的规定。然而电子文书之使用应不是单纯的选择问题,而系基于交易环境需求,在过去近百年的发展中,我们虽看到科技的变迁,但仍发现对于文书使用的坚持,此点不论在电话、电报、电传甚至到早期之计算机使用均然;直到网际网络的诞生,信息科技带入了网络即时互动的环境,当事人信任电子交易带来的速度、确定与安全性,甚至对电子数据之信任胜过对文书之依赖。再者,法律对于原件之要求,因电子文书是以数字形式,记忆在计算机中,不可能像传统的书面合同那样直接出示,唯现代的电子技术若能使电子文书具备原件之功能,如保持原样、不被篡改、电子签名等;从逻辑上来说,符合原件功能之电子文书,应按原件对待。[②] 准此,合同法或证据法应本诸尊重当事人真意之原则,来看待电子数据在证明合同关系存在之价值,而联合国对于 EDI 统合立法之努力,以及当前欧美国家在规范电子签章及电子记录效力上的立法趋势,亦显示合同关

[①] 至于乙若提不出原件,便只有让法院依其自由心证断定其所提出书面之证据力,但纵使乙可以证明与原件相符,亦仅系解决原件提出之问题,法院仍应综合判断该文书之形式与实质的证据力。详见杨佳政:《电子交易中数字签章与电子文件之法律效力浅析》,载《信息法务透析》1998 年第 2 期,第 20—21 页;《最高法院》22 年上字第 2536 号、41 年台上字第 791 号判例。

[②] 马琳:《略论电子合同形式的合法性》,载《中国工商管理研究》2003 年第 11 期,第 59 页。

系之建立,可透过数字环境来进行,不须依赖传统文书以为证据之方向。①

再者,面对我们应思考数字化交易中,究竟何种电子纪录(electronic record)或电子签章可以被接受,且具有证据力之判断上?基本上,过去对于文书的要求多侧重于真伪的认定,而在电子代理(electronic agent)介入后,人的因素只停留在传输设备之选择,个别交易(缔约)行为本身已脱离了当事人之意思,对合同关系存否之争执,将不能单纯的探讨当事人行为之有无,而应及于整个交易环境建构过程之理解;换言之,举证之重点已不是有无签章或文书而已,而应及于传输设备由哪一级指定,传输内容如何安排,以及实际传输过程如何的整体判断,此时面对科技中立与纪录之不可否认性,我们要思考的证据因素应已扩及于交易的过程,而非原本的要约或承诺行为如何而已。综上,面对电子交易的证据问题,或可透过公证机关藉由网络技术措施,建立网络服务器系统,充当"电子公证人",以降低风险;唯"电子公证人"至少需要采用下列三种信息技术:(1)身份鉴别软件;(2)完整性鉴别手段;(3)不可否认性鉴别手段。②

3.4 通过电子数据交换缔结合同所生的主要问题

一、使用电子数据交换当事人间的交易类型与合同关系

(一) 使用电子数据交换当事人间的交易类型

各种类型交易所牵涉的问题,将是我们探讨相关法制发展时所应先行了解的课题。基本上,这些贸易或交易之所以会面临诸多的问题,都是出自于无纸化交易环境的发展与影响,也是必须自国际贸易法制的角度给予全面性的思考。③ 在这个基础上,本节首先拟针对使用 EDI 的 3 大形态,加以说明如下:

1. "相对当事人间合同前置型":在这种类型中,特定二当事人间例如:超级市场及进货业者间交易;加工制造商及原料进货业者的交易等,继续交易关系的特定二当事人间的交易,属于所谓封闭性 EDI 交易。这种类型由当事人斟酌交易内容、EDI 化具体风险后,具体地规定各种技术事项或必要的保全等。然而在这种类型中要约当事人究竟是否是信息上

---

① 其实就合同效力的角度来看,电子合同与数字签章两者之间的关系至为密切,详见 Jonathan Rosenoer, *CyberLaw The Law of The Internet*, New York: Springer Verlag, 1996, pp.237—238.
② 陶岚、王芳:《试论电子合同的法律效力》,载《南昌高专学报》2003 年第 3 期,第 11 页。
③ 另,内贵田:《契约法の现代化》,1996(NBL584):4—16。

表示的要约人,只得由住所、姓名等个人识别信息中加以确认,这也有争议。

2. "会员规约制"电子交易类型:例如特定企业或团体于网络上设定电子市场,对电子市场会员提供商品、劳务信息、进行电子交易的类型。这种类型中,在网络上开设电子市场的企业或团体,多采用"会员规约"形式,规定有关传达情报的诸事项或交易条件,承认该会员规约者即得成为会员利用该电子市场。在这种类型中虽然多约定,如电子数据交换的合同何时成立,数据有障碍时、系统有故障等种种障碍发生时的处理方法,或有关的损害赔偿规定,然而在有约定不清楚时,应如何解决,值得加以探讨。

3. "合同非前置型"电子交易形态。例如将有关自己的商品或服务的信息于网际网络上的 Home Page,对于阅览该 Home Page 的不特定用者发出的商品买受要约信息作承诺信息答复的电子交易。这种类型随着网际网络的普及,可预见以消费者交易为对象将日益增加,所以需就消费者保护观点多加关注。①

(二) 使用电子数据交换当事人间的合同关系

要探讨通过 EDI 缔结合同所生的主要问题,在此首先应弄清楚的在于 EDI 当事人间的合同关系。我们认为,EDI 当事人间应存有原因合同(underlying trade agreement)与 EDI 交换协议(EDI Trading Partner Agreement)②:就前者而言,是指存在于当事人间有关货物、服务等长期反复性供给需求的合意;而后者,则是基于原因合同关系的合意,以 EDI 信息集结买卖合同、运送合同时,彼此通过 EDI 交换协议书,约定相关的事宜。③另外,因交易当事人常通过网络完成信息的交换,所以 EDI 交易当事人或利用人常与加值网络(Value Added Network;简称 VAN)业者间,缔结使用

---

① 见室町正实:《EDI 契约の实务上の留意点(上)》,《EDI(电子的データ交换)と法》,1996(NBL584):41—42。

② 基于 EDI 协议书,交换电子信息的当事人间有继续供给货物或服务的原因有存在与不存在的情形。前者在原因合同的有效期间终了时,EDI 协议亦终了。同一当事人间缔结新原因合同,基于该合同交换电子讯息时,须缔结新的 EDI 协议,因此不管原因合同是否存在,都必须作成可继续使用的 EDI 协议书。原因合同存在时,EDI 协议书最好规定 EDI 协议、原因合同与应交换电子数据的成立合同间相互关系、合同内容解释上发生争议时的优先顺位等。详见朝冈良平、伊东健治、鹿岛诚之助、菅又久直:《图解よくわかる EDI》,东京:日刊工业新闻社 1998 年版,第 134—135 页。

③ 例如,所谓 EDI 是不同组织间利用通讯网络,应用计算机交换商业信息的架构之定义。为了以 EDI 交换信息,当事人间须使用经合意的 EDI 架构而尽量服从广泛合意的标准。合意书为 EDI 交换协议书,通常包括:交换协议书的基本规定、EDI 体系的业务运作等条项及有关 EDI 讯息的当事人间法律问题等条项。而技术附属书规定情报信息的协议及信息传达的协议。

网络服务的加值网络使用合同。

原则上,EDI 的交易仍免不了必须按照传统合同法的构成要件来检视其合同的成立与生效,换而言之,我们仍然可以按照要约,承诺以及对价关系来检视 EDI 交易的流程。① 所以,法院在处理 EDI 的效力问题时,便必须斟酌这些预先架构的交易流程与内容,并将它纳入作为相关证据来用。然而,回到我们前文所提到的基础性考虑,对于一些较为谨慎的商人来说,使用传统性质的协议以作为 EDI 交易进行的基础,会是避免纠纷的最佳安排。

以美国的发展为例,在统一商法典(U.C.C.)有关买卖的规定被调整之前,由于 E-mail 或 EDI 的文件能否被法院接受作为合同成立或生效的证据,仍处于未定状态。所以,交易的伙伴间通常会预先签署书面的协议书(即前文所称的交换协议(interchange agreement)),以建立其彼此间所谓的 EDI 法律关系;此时,该交易伙伴间的协议或合同,就是着眼于建立电子交易关系的原则性合同或主合同(A General Contract),而在此原则性协议的基础上,各方再来进行其个别的交易。

就这种协议的主要内容来看,大约可区分为以下 3 阶段性安排:即①交易基础的合同:规定实体合同内容的合同(合意)。例如买卖、承揽等交易中,规定有关价金的事项、验货的事项、担保责任等的事项,此合意是传统的交易合同。② 数据交换协议:这是根据后述技术手册,运用手册规定的技术性合意交换有关交易的种种信息时,其法律效果、合意、信息(有时该当于意思表示)的传达、有关交易保全的事项、系统产生障碍时处理方式等事项。③ 技术手册:为了进行电子交易中的信息交换,需规定有关处理收受信息的事项、系统操作时间的规定、操作时间外收受信息的处理方法等,与营业额计算时期或未付金额的买卖价金支付的问题。②

二、通过电子数据交换缔结合同所生的主要问题

(一) 合同成立与生效的问题

就合同成立或生效与否的争议角度来说,我们可以发现,过去单纯着眼在判断文书资料的存否及其内容真否的争议,然而随电子交易过程的

---

① 通常在 EDI 的交易过程中,我们可以发现,其有关交易套件(Transaction Set)的传送是一种要约,而收受该套件则是一种承诺。至于汇兑的讯息与电子资金移转以作为支付的过程,则表彰对价关系。

② 详见室町正实:《EDI 契约の实务上の留意点(上)》,《EDI(电子的データ交换)と法》,1996(NBL584):43。

介入,这个问题逐渐发展为是否有传输或收受的事实的判断,也就是说已为电子资料真正与否的问题所取代;基本上,在判断的过程中,传统的合同问题是取决于执法者的举证分配与心证,如今执法者如果不能了解科技并藉助科技的发展,针对诸如加值网络业者或网际网络服务提供者课以证据法上的义务与地位,将难以顺利处理相关的问题,而这也是 EDI 交易未来对于相关法制会影响的部分。

整体来说,如果回到电子合同当前的立法发展,以美国 U.C.C. 所建构的相关法规来看,EDI 所涉及的交易合同成立与生效问题,实际上在判断过程中,必须纳入所谓的电子代理(electronic agent)所扮演角色的考虑。换而言之,依传统民事合同探求当事人的真意为原则的运作基础,来考虑 EDI 相关的合同问题并不恰当,相对的,以探求原有交易架构的安排是由谁所取舍,以及电子代理本身所传输内容的真正程度如何为着眼点,才较为恰当。

此外,时间的问题也很重要,例如,即使是对于一个按照双方的约定,已经确认收受的订单,双方仍可约定,若收受订单者未在一定时间内为明确的表示或作出特定的行为,下订单者仍可保留其撤回权。换而言之,就传统民法角度来讲,若双方并没有预先作原则性的约定,一方寄送要约于他方,而他方收受要约后,没有在合理的期限内为承诺,则要约的递送者可视同无承诺,然而在 EDI 电子交易的架构下,由于双方通常会事先针对要约的寄送与收受方式加以约定,所以当要约送达原收受者所指定的认证设施时,除非双方另就一定期间为约定,否则这种到达即已让要约生效,因此,为避免纠纷的发生,双方往往必须另行约定,说明是否该要约在一定期间内未获得积极的承诺或意思表示为妥。①

至于,对于使用 EDI 所产生合同成立或生效与否的证据问题而言,如何处理收受的确认,与如何处理所收受的内容真正应是二个须同时重视的问题。② 就网际网络服务提供的角色而言,由于还不能对加值网络业者提供足够的监控工具,所以,能否作为公正的第三者仍具有相当的问题;以台湾地区目前的网络交易环境来说,财金信息公司(原金资中心)及关贸网络,都属于可以扮演公正第三者的角色者,然而将来诸如 HINET 或 SEEDNET 是否也会随 EDI 的扩张使用,可能逐渐扮演类似的角色则与美

---

① 依台湾地区民法第 158 条的规定,要约定有承诺期限者,非于期限内为承诺,失其拘束力。另,内贵田:《契约法の现代化》,1996(NBL584):4—16。针对此部分亦有深入之探讨。

② 野村丰弘:《受癸注のEDI化の法的诸题の概要》,载《法とコンピュータ》,1995(13):42—43。

国所面临的问题相同,仍有待进一步的规划。

(二) 就合同内容争议的问题

至于就交易当事人之间有关合同内容的争议部分来说,在过去,因为交易双方各自备有自制的交易条件内容,所以当双方将各自主张的合同条件与内容彼此寄送给相对人时,就产生了所谓的格式之争(the battle of forms)①,面临这类问题时,往往法院必须出面来解释,究竟哪一种条件与内容是有效的;如今在 EDI 的环境当中,这种不协调的现象,则可以通过交易双方在建构 EDI 关系之初的协商与交易协议的安排来解决。换而言之,各方当事人都可以将其商业上的需求纳入书面当中,而此种方式将可以让交易的双方更加了解彼此,也更能避免误会及纠纷的发生。②

所以,在未来 EDI 的交易环境中,我们将可以预期,过去国际贸易纠纷所谓的格式之争(battle of form)将会逐渐减少甚至逐渐消失,而这也是 EDI 的发展将有助于未来贸易发展的基础。基本上这些容易引发争议的交易内容与条件,主要包括折扣问题、付款条件和退货条件。目前,通过 EDI 事先的协议及协议的签署,通常可以避免,或至少降低这类的争议,因为在 EDI 的协议架构下,通常会按照现有的交易关系纳入一些除外的情形藉以规范彼此的需要。

综上可知,目前 EDI 的发展,有助于降低纠纷的发生,但是另一方面随着新的立法出现,交易当事人也容易陷入错误的期待,而误认既有的交易经验全盘为新的法律制度所接受,所以配合整体 NII 的发展,交易的当事人仍应了解在电子交易的环境中,仍应由私法或私人知识的力量来主导,再辅以法律的机制,是较为适当的。③

(三) 真确性的问题

基本上,总结美国过去的经验,这方面所涉问题主要有二大部分:一是交易内容的真确性问题。二是传输过程及内容的真确性问题。而这些

---

① 格式之争,是指在贸易中双方通过交换彼此的标准格式文本进行交易,并且都坚持最后的合同是在自己的格式文本的基础上达成,从而引起的关于合同是否成立及如何确立合同条款的争议。详见王江雨:《买卖合同成立的一般规则与国际贸易中的格式之战》,载《民商法论丛》1997 年第 8 卷,第 573—574 页;另外,请参见 Kent D. Stuckey, Internet and Online Law §1.02[4][a](1998)。

② 另可参阅,早川武夫:《电子取引と书式の斗い(1)(英文契约解释とドラフティソグ 74)》,载《国际商事法务》,1996.12, 24 (12):1318—1319。

③ 例如,交易的当事人可以进一步的针对交易进行过程当中最重要事项加以约定;究竟要如何才能够认定一个订单业已寄送,又如何确认是否订单业已变更,这些都涉及电子讯息的传输过程;每一个电子代理所扮演的地位的认定与判断,EDI 的当事人最好事先加以约定。

真确性的存在必须取决于传输软件内容的规划,以及 EDI 认证功能的安排。① 就内容的真确性来说,首先,必须要证明其使用 EDI 文件的内容是完整而未经变更的;其次,传输或收受文书者,都应经过合法的授权来从事 EDI 的交易;就针对传输的真确性部分来说,必须证明这些数字文书的产生及传输,确实是从原始的起始点到达收受者的计算机,这点主要必须证明,是真传输网络的传输,确实未显现出 EDI 数据有经过变动的现象。在处理这类纠纷时,通常提供传输功能的加值网络及网际网络服务提供者扮演非常重要的角色。

目前,由于加值网络业者已可以有效提供解决上述二项真确性问题所需要的证据,更可以提供 EDI 使用者许多能掌控整个交易过程的详细报告,所以,法院通常可以传唤加值网络业者,以公正第三者的身份来证明 EDI 的文件是否业已送出并到达。至于,EDI 架构下所具有的功能性认证安排,则通常被用作数字文书已经收受的证据。但我们必须了解,该计算机上的认证安排,只能被用来证明确有文书收受的事实,而不能证明其电子文件内容的收受。换而言之,若因变更或计算机传输过程的瑕疵导致该文件内容有缺漏时,上述的收受认证功能并不足以确认其内容的真正。②

(四) 损害赔偿的问题

至于 EDI 交易中所涉及的损害赔偿问题,其中最值得关切的应该是涉及加值服务与网际网络服务提供者以及电话提供者之间接责任问题,基本上,目前的实务上并不认为这些加值服务和网际网络服务提供者当然的必须为这些损害负责,各当事人的责任范围可以以下图说明:

---

① 例如,有关于 EDI 文件传输者,即网际网络服务提供者(Information Service Provider;简称 ISP),目前台湾地区规定所有的网际网络服务提供者都是属于第二类电信事业,受电信法的规范,但是网际网络服务提供者会因其客户的违法行为,而受到牵连,因此,网际网络服务提供者的责任为何,有待厘清,目前美国以立法排除网际网络服务提供者的责任,见冯震宇:《电子商务法律问题何其多》,载《能力杂志》1998 年第 11 期,第 62 页。

② 这里所说的功能性认证与核发数字签章的认证有所不同者:前者是公证人证明有文书存在的事实,但不保证其内容真正,而后者则有户政机关核发印鉴,认证包括了签章本身的真正。

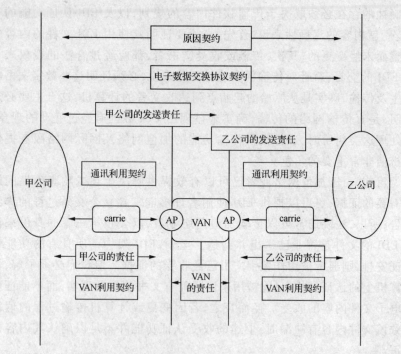

此外,加值服务和网际网络服务提供者往往也在其服务合同中,将自己这方面的责任排除;电话提供业者也有同样的情形。基本上,这是因为要求传输业者负责,往往会导致加值服务和网际网络服务提供者或电话传输业者服务成本的提高,从而对 EDI 交易产生妨害,进而迫使这些 EDI 的交易伙伴必须考虑采用其他的讯息传输方式,而通常这些替代方案都不能有效地取代目前已经存在的数字化交易环境。

3.5 应用电子数据交换的解决方案

综上所述,在对有关 EDI 相关问题进行探讨后,我们认为,发展至今,EDI 的日渐普及代表了国际贸易合同电子化的日益成熟,而 EDI 的推动,主要是以民间力量为主,通过合同协议来解决主要问题,进而促使国际性规范的调整或诞生,而各国再进一步通过国内法的调整,来处理不能由合同协议解决的相关问题。所以,对上述的系统提供者与系统使用者之间最好通过一个妥善的网络服务合同①,来规范彼此间的权利义务关系,并就若干争议事先约定,以杜纠纷。至于交易当事人之间,或可参考联合国国际商务使用 EDI 模范合同②,签订一交易主体合同,以弄清当事人之间的法律关系,这种方法在实务上运用了多年,应该是目前较为可行的;再者,还可通过国内法的调整,作为当事人间的具体规范依据,这种法律对策虽然具体明确,然而一国的国内法调整,还难以适应国际贸易当事人间跨国的属性,无法完全解决这个国际性的议题。这样看来,或可通过国际贸易电子商务平台的提出,通过网际网络的科技,调整个别企业、国家与区域间不同格式,开发一个企业对企业(Business to Business)的交易平台,将国际航运与金融交易相关的贸易文书电子化,取代以往实务上国际函电照会查询及书证往返的方式,如果可行的话,当是未来最好的法律对策,在此试就这三个方案,说明如下:

一、传统前置电子数据交换合同模式:协议书的签订

承前所述,电子数据交换协议书的签订,应该是可以解决 EDI 当事人间纠纷的有效机制。从目前美国的实务经验来说,下列的事项应是最值得在建构 EDI 交易关系时,特别加以协商的:第一,是有关交易当事人间具特殊要求事项的性质与范围;第二,有关如何克服法律不完整之处以及促进 EDI 交易的可执行程度;第三,针对传输过程所发生的疏漏或因为加值网络(VAN)或网际网络服务提供者的介入所引发问题的风险加以分配;第四,配合其他重要交易的内容与条件,在协议中强调 EDI 实施的方式与格式在法律上的重要性;第五,澄清交易协议将用以涵盖电子信息交换的整个过程;第六,澄清与 EDI 无关的交易部分,仍需通过其他合同来加以处理;最后,应在协议中尽可能的减少对于交易内容与条件的混淆或错误的解释。③

---

① 关于网络服务合同,基本上应包括下列内容:1. 网络服务业者的主给付义务及从给付义务;2. 使用者的主给付义务及从给付义务;3. 债务不履行的情事及责任事由。

② 联合国国际商务使用 EDI 模范合同,是联合国欧洲经理事会(United Nations Economic for Europe)第 4 工作小组,于 1995 年 3 月第 41 次会期通过,公布供全球 EDI 使用者作为签订网络服务合同的参考,以规范在适用 EDIFACT 标准所设定的规格化电子资料交易行为,其主要内容包括:1. 讯息交换与传输标准;2. 安全控管程序与服务;3. 意思表示的生效;4. 使用 EDI 的有效性;5. 证据;6. 损害赔偿责任;7. 利用第三人提供服务的责任。详见洪淑芬:《联合国国际商务使用 EDI 模范合同简析》, http://stlc.iii.org.tw/publish/infolaw/8411/841126.htm (visited 2004/8/1)。

③ Street, F. Lawrence, *Law of The Internet*, §1—4(b) (1998).

目前已有各方面提出的标准 EDI 交易模板,可供各方参考。例如,美国律师公会(American Bar Association)便有针对此方面所作的努力,在美国律师公会所规划的架构下,各方将签署原则性的交易协议,此外,再针对不同的交易个案签署所谓的附件协议,以避免重复原有的交易内容。对于中小企业来说,往往无法承担缔结原则性交易协议的成本,此时,美国律师公会建议他们可以签署所谓的电子资料暨电子信函(Electronic Data And Electronic Letter)。① 基本上,这是一种简略式的交易协议,通常只强调交易的内容和条件,而不去触及其他诸如通讯传输过程中的责任及有关文件所涉及的特殊争议问题,换而言之,只着眼于较关键的 EDI 合同问题。

综合上述,在此介绍一份电子数据交换协议书②,作为参考:

○○(以下称甲)及××(以下称乙)中,甲为下单者,乙为接单者,基于甲乙间另外记载的有关商品的继续交易(以下称"基础交易关系")的个别合同,以交换电子信息方式使其成立时,缔结以下协议。

第一条 数据交换的实施

甲与乙合意以数据交换方式,成立关于本件交易的个别合同。

第二条 操作手册

1. 实施信息交易的必要系统、送信程序、信息架构、传达信息的种类、系统激活时间及其他细节,由甲乙间另外制订的信息交换操作手册(以下称"操作手册"规定)。

2. 甲及乙相互确认操作手册及本协议相符,与此协议具相同效力。

3. 因变更系统或其他事由需变更操作手册时,甲乙间应事前进行协议以合意变更的费用负担问题。

第三条 确保信息交换的安全及信赖的程序

甲及乙,为了确保信息交换的安全,将照以下各点的全部或部分的顺序履行,并合意由操作手册规定履行顺序的内容。

---

① Ibid. 至于早期使用 Edi Agreement 所涉问题,请参 Boss, Amelia H. , "Current Issues In Electronic Data Interchange: Electronic Data Interchange Agreements: Private Contracting Toward A Global Environment", *J. INTL. L. BUS.* 1992, (13): 31。此外,针对电子合同缔结之复杂性,ABA 亦于 2002 年制订缔结电子合同指导原则,参 ABA http://w3.abanet.org/home.cfm(visited 2004/7/25)。

② 参考,室町正实:《EDI 契约の实务上の留意点(上)》,《EDI(电子的データ交换)と法》,1996(NBL584):39—40。

1. 发信人同一性的确认顺序
2. 发信人制作权限的确认顺序
3. 传送途中信息变质的确认顺序
4. 有无信息内容错误的确认顺序
5. 其他甲及乙合意的事项

第四条　信息的传达

信息的传达，依操作手册规定的方法，寄至对方的信箱中。

第五条　无法阅读的信息的处理

1. 传达的信息无法读取或读取技术上有错误时，收信人得知后，应以××方式，立即通知对方。
2. 有前项通知时，视发信人撤回该信息。

第六条　收信确认

1. 甲或乙可要求对方经传达的下单信息或接单信息作收信确认，其确认方法没有特别约定时，以××方式作出。
2. 收到前项收信确认时，视该下单信息或接单信息传达完成，没有收到确认时，视为没有传达。

第七条　信息的确定

甲与乙合意传达的信息依第三条各款规定的确保安全的顺序制作、传达时，对各经确认的事项确定收信信息内容。

第八条　个别合同的成立

有关本件交易的个别合同，于接单信息传达时成立。但乙要求甲方作第六条的收信确认时，个别合同于受领收信确认时成立，且甲乙间有另外规定时，依其规定。

第九条　信息的保存及交付

1. 甲与乙应保存有关发信及收信的资料，在对方请求时，应交付予对方。但印制、复制或其他费用产生时，该费用由请求者负担。
2. 保存及交付细节由操作手册规定。

第十条　费用负担

本合同规定操作信息交换的费用负担另外规定。

第十一条　系统管理

1. 甲及乙为了顺畅、安全地交换信息，应各自管理系统。
2. 系统异常、故障发生时的措施，由操作手册另订。

第十二条　与基本合同的关系

甲乙间缔结有关本件交易的×年×月×日的基本合同中，规定事项与本协议规定事项相异时,本协议的规定具有优先效力。

第十三条　有效期间

本合同有效期间由×年×月×日至×年×月×日,期间满×个月前无由甲或乙向对方以书面拒绝更新或变更内容时,以同一条件续约×年,以后相同。

二、单一国家或地区立法模式:国内法规的调整

早期,大陆地区广东省人民政府为加强对外贸易中实施电子数据交换(EDI)的管理,以简化程序、降低成本、增加企业竞争力,根据有关法律、法规及国际惯例,于第八届107次常务会议通过《广东省对外贸易实施电子数据交换(EDI)暂行规定》[1],以规范使用EDI所涉的相关问题,唯此暂行规定已于2002年4月4日失效。其后,广东省第9届人民代表大会常务委员会第38次会议于2002年12月6日通过电子交易条例,于2003年2月1日起施行,藉以为规范电子交易活动,维护电子交易正常秩序,保证电子交易的安全、可靠,保障电子交易各方的合法权益,促进电子商务的发展,当是最为具体明确的方案,在此试举其重要规范,说明如下:

(一)定义说明电子商务、电子网络、电子交易、电子记录、电子签名、公钥、私钥、数字签名、数字证书、电子合同、电子商务认证机构、电子交易服务提供商等。[2]

(二)有关书面性问题的规范:以安全的电子签名方式签署的电子记录为安全的电子记录。安全的电子记录是真实、完整、未被修改的电子记录,与书面记录具有同等效力。[3]

(三)对签章问题的规范:在电子交易过程中,安全的电子签名与书面签名具有同等效力。[4]

(四)电子交易基本原则之宣示:电子交易活动应当遵守公平交易、平等自愿、诚实信用的原则。藉以鼓励在电子交易活动中使用安全的电子签名签订电子合同。[5]

---

[1]　汪涛主编:《EDI:国际贸易新手段》,中国经济出版社1997年版,第117页。
[2]　《广东省电子交易条例》第33条。
[3]　《广东省电子交易条例》第9条。
[4]　《广东省电子交易条例》第8条。
[5]　《广东省电子交易条例》第3条。

三、多边单一规范或会员模式：国际贸易电子商务平台及集中交易机制的建构①

承前所述，如果能建立一套企业对企业（Business to Business）的电子商务平台，通过网际网络的科技以开放的模式，整合个别企业、国家与区域间不同格式的交易平台，而把国际航运与金融交易相关的贸易文书电子化②，取代以往实务上国际函电照会查询及书证往返的方式通过电子信息交换网络（EDI Network），将国际贸易手续建构在网际网络上进行，应是解决 EDI 交易当事人的一根本性的方案。在此试介绍这项由欧洲耗时五年开发成功的电子贸易商务平台 Bolero.net 如下，认为参考③：

（一）Bolero.net 的特色

Bolero.net 主要有以下特色：

1. 其提供一个以网络为基础、无纸的商务模式，设计成为国际标准的一个国际贸易实务作业平台。

2. 以网际网络为基础，支持国际贸易上所有当事人之间企业对企业（B-to-B）电子商务上的资料交换，将与贸易有关的文书证件，如 L/C、B/L、保单及商业发票等改以电子化方式处理。

3. 其发展出具高度可靠性与安全性的"核心传讯平台（Core Messaging Platform, CMP）"以解决传统上对于通过网络传递讯息时安全性的质疑。

4. 提出"Bolero 规则全书（Bolero Rule Book）"，使电子资料交换具有法律效果上的确定性。

5. 利用所有权档案室（Title Registry）系统，允许并监控货品的所有权

---

① 本书此部分的论述是引自市研处陈在方所撰稿的《国际贸易电子商务平台》一文。
② 根据世界贸易组织（WTO）与联合国的联合研究显示，国际贸易界耗费在书面交换程序上的成本，每年高达 4200 亿美元。而改善贸易程序除了系统间兼容性以及时效性的问题外，安全性也是极为重要的课题。依照国际海事组织（International Maritime Bureau）的估计，约有 20% 的载运货物的文件是记载有误的，这就造成了海关程序上可观的迟延。登记错误的文件造成了货品卡在海关，流动资本停滞。若能以电子文件的方式传递此种文件，并以电子格式的方式控制其品质，则能节省可观的成本。准此，如何建立一个网路交易之公平法律机制，即为企业对企业於网路交易之重心所在，Ponte, Lucille M., "Boosting Consumer Confidence in E-business: Recommendations for Establishing Fair and Effective Dispute Resolution Programs for B2C Online Transactions", *Alb. L. J. Sci. & Tech.* 2002, (12): 441。
③ 据 The Tower Group 的报告显示，Bolero.net 在所有正在发展中而与国际贸易相关的电子商务平台中，将是最有可能被广泛接受的。从 Bolero.net 的背景、条件以及发展方向上来看，的确如此。国际贸易的程序一直在变革，而网络时代来临后更将会加速步调。从事国际贸易的厂商应密切注意数字化时代的发展，以为适应。

以电子文件交换的方式迅速而安全的转移至全球各处的当事人。

综上,其提供了开放、中立而跨产业的商务模式、独特的法律架构以及完整的安全性,由可信赖的中立者执行其服务,企图解决无纸化交易导致的问题应运而生的方案。

(二) Bolero.net 的内涵与特性

1. 背景

其原本隶属于联合国欧洲委员会的筹办计划①,是一个中立的组织,不受特定企业、市场及国家的利益干扰。② 目的是建立一个安全、有保障的电子贸易文件交换的服务,主事者还希望 Bolero.net 能成为国际贸易交易的标准,并把文件交换服务的使用者与提供加值服务的合作伙伴组织成为一个电子贸易社群(the electronic trade community),并架构出一个全新的市场。

2. 商务模式

其具有跨平台的特性③,目前提供"核心传讯平台(CMP)"与"所有权档案室(title registry)"两种服务;贸易体系中的所有成员间,都可以通过该系统,以电子传送的方式交换包括物权证书(document of title)在内的所有的文件以及资料。

3. 法律架构

国际贸易以电子商务方式进行最大的问题之一,就是其法律上的不确定性。尤其是跨国交易所涉及的货款支付以及物权移转的问题非常复杂。其以适用于全球十八个主要的司法领域为目的,研拟出"Bolero 规则全集(the Bolero Rule Book)"。这是一个多边合同(multiparty contract),用以规范电子贸易文件交换的法律效力与纠纷的解决方式,所有参与使用者都必须同意接受该规则的拘束。让从事电子交易的当事人能够预期,

---

① 1994 年在环球银行财务通讯协会"S.W.I.F.T."(Society for Worldwide Interbank Financial Telecommunication)和海运业者的再保团体联合运送俱乐部"TT Club"(Through Transport Club)各出资一半的条件下承接,并从 1999 年 9 月 27 日开始正式营运。SWIFT 代表国际银行界,TT Club 代表海运、港口、后勤相关业者,共有约 1 万 2500 名会员,服务的对象包括绝大部分参与国际贸易的成员,因此他们的合作相当具有代表性,正适合发展全球通用的电子交易平台。

② 过去 2 年来全球有 500 余家不同产业的公司及公会团体配合服务实验,并于 1999 年由 120 家国际企业,包括 15 家全球前百大企业进行最终测试,共同从功能及法律层面提供服务,进行评估改良。

③ 这是它优于企业间自订电子文件交换系统之处。以往的自订模式需要个别企业间的双边 EDI 协议,必须架构昂贵的软硬件,以互相传递安全保密的电子讯息。而其提供一个开放的模式,所有使用的企业间,都可经由任何私人网络通讯协议(IP)系统或网际网络与核心传讯平台(CMP)连结。此因 Bolero.net 的通讯协议是以现存的网际网络标准为基础所架构的。

在 Bolero.net 上所传递的电子讯息的法律效果与争端解决能与传统的文书方式相当,以解决电子商务的法律效果不明确的问题。

4. 安全性的问题

其对首次申请加入的企业,都进行严格的征信查核[①],该系统提供组织间传递电子讯息所需要的认证、加密与资料整合服务且对于其提供的服务负法律上的责任与义务,负责赔偿厂商在传递信息时,由于该系统因违反安全保证所造成的损失。[②]

5. 运作方式与提供的服务

由 SWIFT 管理系统的骨干"核心传讯平台(CMP)",让使用者能通过网际网络来交换电子信息及贸易文件,并操作"所有权档案室(title registry)"以监控物权提单的交换转让作业,并保证该系统的安全性,以法律架构作为支撑,由可信赖的第三者来维持其运作。[③]

(三) 具体应用个案

Bolero.net 在 1999 年,有 120 家国际性大公司参与试用,例如,由 Cargill 公司利用该系统将咖啡豆由巴西运往美国;三井将 Subaru 车辆由日本运至比利时;Otto Versand 将香港时装运至汉堡等。台湾地区的长荣海运公司(Evergreen Marine Corporation)也已宣布成为 Bolero.net 的使用者。此外,2003 年 10 月,日本 UFJ 银行与韩国 KEB 银行,亦签署并宣布将透过 Bolero 系统以强化日韩之间的网络交易。[④]

---

① 使用者于传递信息时,使用一种电子签章锁以作为认证,传递中亦加密(encrypting)以防信息外泄及被删改。每一项网络服务与邮件信箱都需要电子锁才能使用。每一个讯息都需经由数字签章,使收信人确知发信人的身份。

② 其讯息传送与安全保证由 SWIFT 负责执行,保证经由其交换的贸易文件的安全性。SWIFT 本身的主要业务原本就是传送各参加国间非公开与专有的国际金融业务通讯,该组织目前服务全球 6500 个金融组织与 189 个国家。该系统于 1999 年共传送超过 10 亿项讯息,平均每日处理全球超过 5 兆美元的金融支付指示,由该组织负责 Bolero.net 的讯息传送将稳定使用者的信心。

③ 所有使用者间的讯息交换及其效力都必须经由核心传讯平台(CMP),所有的讯息在核心传讯平台(CMP)上获得承认,并依照使用者的要求发出通知。其所提供最主要的服务是透过核心传讯平台(CMP)提供完整的服务,其第一个加值服务为所有权档案室(title registry),该系统首创提供传送电子提单(bill of lading)的能力。

④ http://www.bolero.net/news/pressrel/ufjkeb.php3 (visited 2004/7/25)。

4 电子合同的成立与生效

4.1 电子化交易环境的形成

自网际网络(internet)在近年被普遍地使用以来,各国无不对之投以相当的关注,因为伴随着整个社会环境的信息化,数字化环境的发展已全面冲击到世界上的每一个角落,这种冲击甚至被誉为自工业革命以来之另一次工业革命。

目前,电子商务的发展主要对国际贸易的发展带来了许多重大的影响,而为了适应这些影响,国际贸易实务上首先发展出了电子数据交换(Electronic Data Interchange)制度,这个制度在私法自治的领域内,通过标准合同的制定与授权机制的建立,以及通过数字化贸易文书之使用:包括电子订单、电子发票、电子信用证、电子汇票等,将贸易的流程导引进入了电子化的程序;而此时,诸多法律问题也应运而生。就其影响层面,我们可以将问题归纳如下:

一、无纸化(Non-Paper)的交易环境

例如书面形式、电子签章、证据法[①]、合同的成立生效与履行、管辖[②]、危险分担与网络关税[③]等。

二、新形态的支付工具(instrument)与媒介(mechanism)

例如电子票券与电子提单的出现,使计算机从仅仅是一种登记有纸

[①] 有关电子文书的内容真正与否、如何证明证明之、电子 data 其是否具有证据能力、其与传闻证据法则间的关联性如何等相关问题,应如何解决实在值得研究。

[②] 由于网际网络空间性的全球性使司法管辖区域界限变得模糊,网络空间的不确定性亦让传统司法管辖权的基础产生动摇,所以应探寻新的管辖模式,当是一重要的课题,见王德全:《试论 Internet 案件的司法管辖》,载《中外法学》1998 年第 2 期,第 30 页。

[③] 虽美国于 1997 年提出的电子商务政策纲领中表示,透过网络递送的数据化商品免税;然此涉及各国主权行使的争议问题,各国的态度不一,且应如何适应,实应研拟相关政策。

化财产权利凭证的工具,逐步演变成一种财产所有权存在形式的客体。

三、无国界的即时(Real Time)互动(Interactive Movements)

跨国界交易、虚拟主体与机构、计算机自动筛选与人工智能的媒介、交易不可否认性等问题。

四、纠纷处理的模式调整

传统国际贸易的管辖多是通过缔约当事人间的约定来确定,但因为电子贸易的无纸化特性,有时因为当事人在缔约时意思不明、或因举证不易、或因不公平条款而使得当事人无法依照约定确定管辖时,即是利用网际网络所进行的电子交易应如何定其管辖的问题。

基本上,我们可以说,国际贸易电子化的现象,已经全面影响到原有法制结构的有效性。当国际交易合同的缔结是通过网际网络来进行时,也将新生许多法律问题,如何传送其间的意思表示?而这一传送的意思表示的法律效力如何?再就国际贸易的交易内容而言,原本 GATT 下的发展是着眼于商品(goods)的交易,而后及于服务(services),如今随软件与信息(information)本身的交易发展成为跨国交易的重要内容,所谓线上(on-line)信息授权(licenses of information)交易,带入了所谓第三类型的交易标的(subject matter),也改变了传统买卖合同对缔约行为、缔约过程、履约方式、损害赔偿、纠纷处理等法律规范的要求。[①] 为此,《美国统一商法典(Uniform Commercial Code;简称 U.C.C.)》首先经过修正提出了 2B 条(Article 2B),试行对于电子代理、自动化计算机系统的成立方式,以及牵涉到电子签章的运用部分,加以涵盖。这一条并在经过各方热烈的讨论后,被进一步调整成为完整的统一计算机信息交易法(Uniform Computer Information Transaction Act),该法案并于 2000 年正式完成定稿,开放给各州采用。

数字化的科技带来了新的工业革命,也对国际贸易合同原有的信任

---

① 在该条于 1998 年 4 月份提出的草案中,各方提出的意见,几乎将前揭提及的交易环境数字化所衍生相关法律问题都予以涵盖,虽然在美国法律的实务上,U.U.C. 并非规范国际贸易的依据,然而其发展正引领着全球走向贸易合同法制的创新领域。因为 U.U.C. 属各州自行引用,透过其州内立法来规范非州际贸易或非国际贸易的交易者,然而 U.U.C. 的相关规定,仍可经由联邦法院的援用,在所谓联邦习惯法(Federal Common Law)的领域中,发展出其地位。由于 U.U.C. 已然成为美国当前处理交易事项最重要的法源,因此,这次的增订,配合其他诸如 Article 2、Article 4、……的修正,已经为美国新的国内国际贸易法制奠基,更会随美国在 WTO 积极推动的电子商务交易架构而扩散。

基础、法律的基本原则与交易惯例产生根本性的冲击。在传统的国际贸易合同法制结构中,国际公约、国际惯例与国内法律分别提供了规范国际贸易合同的法源基础。如今,国际惯例或法规在此方面都已经有了长足的发展①;举例而言,数据讯息最受争议者在于其是否为"文件"(documents),可否为法院采为证据,在《电子商务模范法》(UNCITRAL Model Law on Electronic Commerce)第5条即规定:"一资料不得仅因其为数据资料即否认其法律效力。"另外在第9条还禁止使用最佳证据法则(The Best Evidence Rule)及传闻法则(Heresay Rule)。②

反观在国内法的发展部分世界各国呈现程度不一的状况;目前,美国与欧洲具有领先地位③,而日本、澳洲、加拿大等则正在迎头赶上;至于在亚洲,新加坡可能是最积极的④,它企图成为"网络贸易国际中心"(an international center for trade over the internet)⑤,并具体就区域性交易闸门(gateway)地位加以规划。

就两岸当前的发展而言,法制相关建设部分与上述国家相比,还有些许落差,所以将来整个国际贸易环境电子化后,将立即面临与外国或国际法律衔接或配合的问题。以合同的书面性为例,大陆虽然已关注到数字

---

① 例如,联合国国际贸易法律委员会(THE UNITED NATIONS COMMISSION ON INTERNATIONAL TRADE LAW;UNCITRAL)于1996年6月提出了《电子商务模范法》(UNCITRAL Model Law on Electronic Commerce),在这个模范法试图消除至今电子讯息无法与纸张讯息具同等法律效力的障碍,所以对电子合同、电子文件的效力、书面性签名及仲裁等问题,提出规范标准以供各国参考。此外,联合国国际贸易法律委员会亦于2001年制订《电子签章模范法》及《贸易法律委员会电子签章模范法颁布指南》,以扩充电子商务模范法之适用。

② 依大陆民事诉讼法相关规定来看,视听资料虽可作为证据,却不可单独、直接地证明待证事实,只能作为间接证据。

③ 对电子商务的规范美国倾向采放任制,而欧洲采严格控制。

④ 新加坡于1998年6月29日通过电子交易法(Electronic Transactions Bill 1998),使其成为继德国、马来西亚、意大利等国之后,另一以整体立法规范电子交易的国家,冀望透过该法能为新加坡创造安全可信赖的电子商务环境,并清楚界定交易当事人间的权利义务关系,其主要参考法源为美国伊利诺州的电子交易法草案、美国统一商法典(Uniform Commercial Code)、联合国国际贸易法律委员会电子商务模范法(UNCITRAL Model Law on Electronic Commerce)、德国多元媒体法、美国犹他州与马来西亚的数字签章法等;广泛包含各项争议的集中立法方式,故本法案可谓是集目前世界先进电子商务与数字签章立法的大成。

⑤ 为建立有利于电子商务发展的法律与政策环境,新加坡于1997年1月成立电子商务政策委员会(EC Policy Committee),该委员会辖下的"法规与执行研究组"(the Legal, Regulatory and Enforcement Study Group),于1998年4月间即提出电子交易法草案,而国会仅用2个多月的时间即完成电子交易法的立法程序,可见新加坡的企图心。见杨佳政:《新加坡通过电子交易法》,参见 http://stlc.iii.org.tw/publish/infolaw/8708/870801.htm (visited 2004/8/1)。

化环境对合同的影响，所以在 1999 年合同法修正时，即反映于部分条文①；然而以电子提单的使用为例，如果海商法仍坚持提单为缴回证券，那如何满足电子数据交换架构下使用电子提单的要求？② 如果再不积极研拟并调整现有国际贸易合同相关法制，则挡不住的实务发展将引发诸多新类型的法律问题，甚至促使国内厂商必须迁往他国以满足其依法作业的需求。

再者，由于国际贸易通过电子数据交换的发展所采用的诸多无纸文书，都是通过合同的安排，来串起合同当事人间在数字化交易环境下的法律关系，这种借重私法自治功能来建构数字化交易关系所显示出的自律机制，也正是当前电子商务环境下所追求的基本精神。然而要注意的是，如何确保这种自律机制的良性运行，又如何提供参与者发生纠纷时顺利解决纠纷的机制，以利交易环境的发展，却是当前重要的课题。尤其在跨国即时交易的背景下，各国对于上述数字化国际贸易环境所需要的法律基础，还没有统一的建制步调，如何让业者能无虑地采用这种交易机制，实在是一个迫切的课题。③

综上，电子交易合同关系的成立，随电子数据交换的发展，因扩大了国际贸易的内涵而进入电子交易的纪元，电子交易合同法制也随交易环境的数字化而有所调整，这种动力源于自律的要求，并透过私法自治的功能来加以运作，然而如前所述，诸多问题仍有待法律制度的配合。所以，要想解决电子交易合同可能因电子化而涉及的问题，应以传统的国际贸易合同的国际性规范与国际贸易惯例为基础，再参酌国际间配合合同电子化的发展所作的努力，期通过国际合作建构出一致性的规范，为电子合同法制的发展奠基，更为电子商务合同树立良好的法律适应经验。

4.2 传统国际贸易合同的法源

基于电子交易法制是具有全球性意义的法律，在进一步探讨电子交

---

① 如《合同法》第 11 条："书面形式是指合同书、信件和数据电文（包括电报、电传、传真、电子数据交换和电子邮件）等可以有形地表现所载内容的形式。"第 16 条、第 26 条、第 33 条、第 34 条，也是相关的规定。

② 详参郭瑜：《国际货物买卖法》，人民法院出版社 1999 年版，第 160—167 页。

③ 目前，国际间已有数项重要的发展值得加以关注；例如希望于 2005 年达成 APEC 地区贸易无纸化为目标，将在商品贸易上，将要求国内海关的通关过程无纸化及各国间海关资料交换的无纸化以台湾地区目前在货物通关过程自动化方面，已取得相当大的进展，通过关贸网络（Trade-Van）的联结，不论在收单、分估、验货、征税、放行等步骤都广泛使用计算机传输取代各式书面文件。

易法制如何配合调整之前,自然需要对传统的国际贸易相关法制先有所掌握;基本上,传统国际贸易法的渊源主要有两个:即国际立法与国际交易惯例。前者是指各国共同制定的规范性规则,其内容是通过国际公约或模范法的形式来具体呈现①;而后者则是当前由各国及其业者所普遍采用的各种习惯性做法。至于国际交易合同法制,则是以此为基础慢慢建构出来的交易法制。在此谨以国际贸易合同为课题,针对主要的国际性规范与贸易惯例,举主要的说明如下:

一、相关的主要国际性规范

长久以来,人们一直在期盼统一国际贸易有关之法律,特别是统一作为交易基础的合同规范,以排除往来间之法律障碍。是以,国际组织先后展开了统一运动,在经过 20 几年的努力,并于其中尝试提出多项国际规范后,联合国于 1980 年提出了《国际货物买卖公约》(United Nations Convention on Contracts for the International Sale of Goods;CISG)②,此乃国际贸易法统一化运动的重大成果。此公约对统一不同社会制度、不同法系及不同国家在货物买卖领域的法律原则,有重大之建树,然其管辖的范围仅限于国际货物买卖领域,未能真正满足统一合同规范之需求。从而,国际统一私法协会乃进一步于 1994 年 5 月通过了第一版之《国际商务合同通则》(Principles of International Commercial Contracts;UNIDROIT),并于其中确立了国际商事合同领域内的各项法律原则,此可谓为国际合同法统一化过程中之另一重大成就。③ 其后,于第一版之国际商务合同通则实行 10 年后,国际统一私法协会于 2004 年 4 月 19 日至 4 月 21 日之年度会议上,由管理会(Governing Council of UNIDROIT)采行国际商务合同通则之最终标准,通过第二版之国际商务合同通则。相较于 1994 年之国际商务合同通则,2004 年之国际商务合同通则新增五个章节,分别为:代理人权限(Authority of Agents);第三人权利(Third Party Rights);抵消(Set-off);权利移转(Assignment of Rights),义务承担与合同承担(Transfer of Obligations and Assignment of Contracts);消灭时效(Limitation Periods)。此外,条

---

① 国际公约是各缔约国之间达成的国际多边协议,各缔约国承担将其纳入各本国的义务;模范法也是国际间的协商,但它由各国单方接受为本国法。
② 又名 1980 年维也纳公约,其制定可溯及 1930 年,目前已是近 50 个国家之内国法,其能为不同社会、法律及经济制度的国家所接受,证明其相当成功。
③ 吴兴光:《国际商法》,中山大学出版社 1997 年版,第 35—36 页。

文数亦由 120 条增为 185 条。①

唯随网际网络时代的来临,信息经济、数字经济与电子商务经济的理论正逐渐将传统的交易环境推向全球化、科技化与多元个性化的方向,这对于用来规范并促进变迁中交易行为之法律而言,是一大挑战,而如何配合全球化的法制发展趋势,以利新世纪交易之进行,已成为法律研究之重要课题。基此,联合国国际贸易法律委员会(United Nations Commission on International Trade Law; UNCITRAL)乃于 2001 年起着手研议《藉数据电文缔结或证明之(国际)合同公约草案初稿》(Preliminary Draft Convention on [International] Contracts Concluded or Evidenced by Data Messages)②以为因应;是以,吾人拟自既有国际贸易规范出发并就此新发展趋势加以评价之。

(一) 联合国国际货物买卖公约之相关规定

《联合国国际货物买卖公约》③之制定可溯及 1930 年代的国际贸易统一运动,其中虽有 1964 年《国际货物买卖统一法公约》与《国际货物买卖合同成立统一法公约》之提出,然参加此两公约之国家为数不多,因此在地区与内容上有局限与不足,尚难谓其为世界性之公约。是以,在 1966 年第 21 届联合国大会上,联合国国际贸易法律委员会正式成立,担负起制定国际货物买卖关系之工作,并于 1974 年通过了《国际货物买卖时效期限公约》(Convention on the Limitation Period in the International Sale of Goods),1977 年完成了国际货物买卖公约草案,并决定将此两公约合并,定名为《联合国国际货物买卖公约》。④ 然于草拟 CISG 之过程中,所面临之最重大立法技术问题系来自于大陆法系(Civic Law)与英美法系(Common Law)的冲突,其后透过折衷方式,建构出一套独立的国际贸易法律体系;然而,尽管 CISG 系透过整合两大法系法律原则之方式来建构相关规范,然此不意味着 CISG 是由不同条款所拼凑成者。基本上,CISG 系本诸促进国际商业交易之目的,配合当时之交易惯例加以折衷,并本诸一致性、国际性与诚信等原则,以追求 CISG 之永久适用,故其虽非各法律争点

---

① http://www.unidroit.org/english/home.htm#(visited 2004/7/31).

② 本草案系根据联合国国际贸易法律委员会电子商务工作小组第 38 届会议决议而来,嗣于 2002 年 3 月 11 日至 25 日,假纽约举行的第 39 届会议中提出公约草案初稿,"United Nations Commission on International Trade Law Working Group on Electronic Commerce", Thirty-ninth session, A/CN.9/WG.IV/WP.95.(2002).

③ 详参"United Nations Convention on Contracts for the International Sale of Goods", http://www.uncitral.org (visited 2004/8/1).

④ 赵威:《国际商事合同法理论与实务》,中国政法大学出版社 1995 年版,第 45—46 页。

最适当之解决方式,但其所创造者却是能为大陆法系与英美法系所共同适用之一般原则。①

《联合国国际货物买卖公约》不仅反映出国际法统一运动的发展趋势,更是规范国际货物买卖行为最权威的国际公约;该公约于1980年3月通过,并于1988年1月1日正式生效。② 综言之,其宗旨系以建立新的国际经济秩序为目标,在平等互利的基础上发展国际交易,促进各国间友好关系。该公约共分为四大部分③,全文101条;按其规定,公约适用于下列之货物买卖:

1. 缔约国中营业地分处不同国家之当事人间;
2. 由国际私法选法之结果导致适用某一缔约国之法律者。

而所谓货物买卖,各国法律虽有不同规定,唯公约则倾向仅限于有形动产及尚待生产与制造之货物,始有其适用。④

就买卖合同而言,公约仅适用于合同的缔结与买卖双方的权利、义务而不涉及合同之效力、合同对所有权之影响与货物对人身造成伤害之产品责任等问题。至于公约所未涵盖之问题,则仍可依照双方业已同意的惯例或合同适用之本国法。⑤

(二) 国际商务合同通则之相关规定

另一个值得重视的国际发展,系国际统一私法协会于1980年代起所投注之努力。盖在多数国家的经济朝向全球化发展之同时,商业交易急遽的增加,也导致国际社会欲建立符合跨国商业交易之法律环境,藉以规范商业交易之需求剧增。是以,在历经14年努力后,国际统一私法协会⑥

---

① UNIDROIT, "Principles of International Commercial Contracts (1994) with comments", http://www.unidroit.org/english/principles/contracts/main.htm (visited 2004/8/1).

② 大陆亦为该公约之缔约国,唯作了二项保留:即1. 针对采用书面形式之保留:公约对于国际货物买卖合同之形式,原则上并未加以限制,无论当事人以书面或口头缔结合同,均属有效成立,就此大陆坚持国际货物买卖合同,必须采用书面形式,该公约对大陆不适用。2. 关于公约适用范围之保留:就公约第1(1)b款之扩大适用范围规定,对大陆无效。详见董新民:《国际商务法律》,中国审计出版社1996年版,第74页;张勇:《国际货物买卖法》,南开大学出版社1997年版,第47页。

③ 公约包括四大部分,即适用范围、合同之成立、货物买卖与最后条款。

④ 公约以排除法列举了不适用公约之货物买卖类型:(1) 股票、债券、票据、货币及其他投资证券交易;(2) 船舶、飞机及气垫船之买卖;(3) 电力之买卖;以及(4) 卖方之主要义务在于提供劳务或其他服务之买卖。

⑤ 王传丽:《国际贸易法——国际货物贸易法》,中国政法大学出版社1999年版,第36—37页;郭瑜:《国际货物买卖法》,人民法院出版社1999年版,第64—68页。

⑥ 国际统一私法协会,系根据1926年通过的多边条约设立,现有包括所有西欧国家、美国、加拿大,以及一些社会主义国家和亚非一些国家之成员国,该会起草了许多公约与模范法。见施米托夫:《国际贸易法文选》,中国大百科全书出版社1993年版,第253页。

于1994年提出第一版之《国际商务合同通则》[①],该通则系由前言及七大章节所组成,包括:"通则"、"形成"、"效力"、"解释"、"内容"、"履行"、"不履行"七大部分。[②] 实行十年后,国际统一私法协会复于2004年4月修正第一版之国际商务合同通则而通过第二版之《国际商务合同通则》并新增五个章节,如:第三人权利、抵消、权利移转等,总条文数也增加65条条文。该通则兼容了不同法律体系的通用法律原则,同时吸收了国际商事活动普遍适用的惯例与最新立法成果,以下谨就其内容,试举其要者说明如下:

1. 适用范围

本《通则》适用于所有国际商务合同,不仅包括提供商品、服务的一般国际贸易,还可包括其他类型之经济交易。[③] 固然《国际商务合同通则》未经国家之立法授权,则不具法律拘束力,但其至少可提供下列之功能:(1)可为内国或国际立法者立法时之参考;(2)解释及补充国际规范;(3)提供当事人草拟合同之参考;(4)作为规范合同之原则;(5)作为内国法之代替。[④]

2. 基本原则

《国际商务合同通则》之总则部分共12个条文,除有基本定义之规定外[⑤],更进一步概括地确立基本原则等重要事项,揭示了国际贸易领域中的三大基本原则:

(1)缔约自由原则:当事人有权自由缔结合同并有权自由决定该合同之内容。[⑥]

(2)信守合同原则:除由规则明订或经当事人之同意变更或终止合同,双方当事人应受有效缔结之合同之拘束。[⑦]

---

① 详参"UNIDROIT Principles of International Commercial Contracts", http://www.unidroit.org/english/principles/contracts/main.htm (visited 2004/8/1)。

② Cheng, Chia-jui, *Basic Documents on International Trade Law*, Boston: Hingham, 1986, pp. 211—235.

③ 吴兴光:《国际商法》,中山大学出版社1997年版,第36页。

④ Bonell, Michael Joachim, "The UNIDROIT Principles of International Commercial Contracts: Why? What? How?", *Tul. L. Rev.* 1995 (69): 1121;刘晓红亦表示通则可以拟补国际条约之不足、可用来解释或补充现有之法律档,亦可由当事人选择作为合同准据法或由诉讼和仲裁机构用以解释合同准据法,详参刘晓红:《论合同之债法律冲突解决方法及最新发展——兼论〈国际商事合同通则〉的效力与适用》,载《国际法学》2000年第1期,第37—38页。

⑤ 详参"UNIDROIT Principles of International Commercial Contracts", Article 1.12。

⑥ 详参"UNIDROIT Principles of International Commercial Contracts", Article 1.1。

⑦ 详参"UNIDROIT Principles of International Commercial Contracts", Article 1.3。

(3) 诚信与公平交易原则:国际贸易交易中,须遵守诚信与公平交易之原则,且此为强制性规定,当事人不得排除或限制之。①

3. 有关合同成立之相关规定

(1) 有关意思表示成立之方式,除对要约为承诺之方式外,若有充分显示双方当事人合意之行为时,亦可认为合同业已成立。②

(2) 有关要约之生效:就对话之要约,采了解主义;而非对话之要约,则采到达主义。③

(3) 有关要约之效力:于要约经撤回或拒绝时,要约人所为之要约失其效力。④

(4) 有关要约之拒绝:要约经相对人拒绝后,失其效力。⑤

(5) 有关承诺之时间:口头要约需立时承诺;反之,需于要约人所定之时间内为之,如无约定时间,则需以合理之时间内为之。⑥

(6) 有关承诺之迟到:关于要约之迟到,除要约人适当地通知承诺人该迟到事由,该迟到之承诺不因之而失效。⑦

(三)《藉数据电文缔结或证明之(国际)合同公约草案初稿》之相关规定

伴随着对电子商务发展的动力,国际贸易领域亦在联合国之主导下,展开了新的规划,相关研究指出了未来交易电子化发展的最大障碍将在于跨国法制之调和问题⑧,而此正具体显示出当前相关法制所呈现出来的紊乱现象。是以,联合国国际贸易法律委员会第四工作小组(电子商务),继起草了《电子商务模范法》(UNCITRAL Model Law on Electronic Commerce)、《电子签章模范法》(UNCITRAL Model Law on Electronic Signatures)后,为避免各国立法歧异造成交易障碍,进而提出《藉数据电文缔结

---

① 详参"UNIDROIT Principles of International Commercial Contracts", Article 1.7。
② 详参"UNIDROIT Principles of International Commercial Contracts", Article 2.1.1;此规定与 CISG 相较,不限于要约与承诺为意思表示合致之唯一方式。
③ 详参"UNIDROIT Principles of International Commercial Contracts", Article 2.1.7;此规定与 CISG 相似,详参"United Nations Convention on Contracts for the International Sale of Goods", Article 15。
④ 详参"UNIDROIT Principles of International Commercial Contracts", Article 2.1.3 & Article 2.1.4;此规定与 CISG 相似,详参"United Nations Convention on Contracts for the International Sale of Goods", Article 16—18。
⑤ "UNIDROIT Principles of International Commercial Contracts", Article 2.1.5。
⑥ "UNIDROIT Principles of International Commercial Contracts", Article 2.1.7。
⑦ 详参"UNIDROIT Principles of International Commercial Contracts", Article 2.1.9.(2)。
⑧ 参见 Amelia H. Rose, "Electronic Commerce and The Symbolic Relationship between International and Domestic Law Reform", *Tul L. Rev.* 1998,(72):1931。

或证明之(国际)合同公约草案初稿》(以下简称《公约草案初稿》)①,就其功能言,应可视为《联合国国际货物销售公约》在电子交易环境下的补充版本,于兹试举其要者说明如下:

1. 适用范围

就《公约草案初稿》第 1 条之规定言,提出之初本有两方案以供选择: A 案不论当事人之国籍与合同之性质,凡以数据电文②为方法所缔结或证明之民商事合同,均有本公约之适用;至于 B 案,以合同缔结时,当事人之营业地不在同一国家,而以数据电文为方法所缔结或证明之国际合同,始有本公约之适用。③ 就其适用之地理范围而言,若采 A 案,则所有以数据电文所缔结或证明之任何合同均涵括在内,而不论当事人之营业地是否在不同国家;若采 B 案,则限于当事人之营业地不在同一国家之国际性合同,始有其适用。④ 而于最新之版本,则限于特定情况下适用于营业地位于不同国家的当事人之间对现行或计划中合同使用数据电文始有适用。⑤

而对本《公约》之实质性适用范围而言,首应加以厘清者在于"电子缔

---

① 早于 2000 年国际贸易委员会第 33 届会议上,就电子商务领域未来工作即有共识认为应将重点放在下列 3 个议题上:(1) 以"联合国国际货物销售合同公约"角度考虑的电子缔约问题。(2) 网络争议解决之议题。(3) 所有权凭证尤其是运输业的所有权凭证的非物质化。由于公约最易达到电子贸易所需要的法律确定性与可预见性,故将公约之拟定列为首要议题,"United Nations Commission on International Trade Law Working Group on Electronic Commerce", Thirty-ninth session, A/CN. 9/WG. IV/WP. 95. (2002).

② 所谓"数据电文",系指经由电子、光学或类似方法生成、储存或传递的数据,这些方式手段包括但不限于电子数据交换、电子邮件、电报、电传或传真;详参 Preliminary draft convention on [international] contracts concluded or evidenced by data messages Article 5(a). United Nations Commission on International Trade Law Working Group on Electronic Commerce, Forty-third session, A/CN. 9/WG. IV/WP. 108 (2004).

③ 详参 Preliminary draft convention on [international] contracts concluded or evidenced by data messages Article 1; United Nations Commission on International Trade Law Working Group on Electronic Commerce, Thirty-ninth session, A/CN. 9/WG. IV/WP. 95. (2002).

④ 合同之国际性可从各种角度界定,国内与国际立法采用了各种界定方法,从以不同国家的当事人的营业地或惯居地为准(如联合国国际货物买卖公约),到采用较为一般之标准,如于合同具有"与一个以上国家的重要关联"或"涉及国际商务"等(如联合国国际贸易法律委员会电子商务模范法)。

⑤ 备选案文 A:(a) 有关国家为缔约国;(b) 国际私法规则导致适用某一缔约国的法律;或(c) 当事人约定适用本公约。备选案文 B:有关国家是本公约缔约国,而且对根据这些缔约国的法律适用下列国际条约之一的现行或计划中的合同使用数据电文:(1)《国际销售货物时效期限公约》(1974 年 6 月 14 日,纽约)及其议定书(1980 年 4 月 11 日,维也纳);(2)《联合国国际货物销售合同公约》(1980 年 4 月 11 日,维也纳);(3)《联合国国际贸易运输港站经营人赔偿责任公约》(1991 年 4 月 17 日,维也纳);(4)《联合国独立担保和备用信用证公约》(1995 年 12 月 11 日,纽约);(5)《联合国国际贸易应收款转让公约》(2001 年 12 月 12 日,纽约)。"United Nations Commission on International Trade Law Working Group on Electronic Commerce", Forty-third session, A/CN. 9/WG. IV/W p. 108 (2004).

约"之概念,其不应被认为与传统之书面合同有着根本性差异[1],而应认其为经由电子、光学或类似方法所缔结之合同,为一种新的缔约方式,并非以任何特定主题为基础之分类方式。[2] 是以,《公约草案初稿》主要目的在试图解决涉及使用数据电文所产生的合同缔结问题,而不涉及要约与承诺等行为之实质要件探讨;亦即,任何特定电子合同所产生的实质性问题,仍将继续沿用传统的法律作为管辖之依据。至于在公约所辖合同之类型,公约草案初稿并不局限于国际货物买卖合同,而扩及于任何以电子方式缔结或加以证明之合同。[3]

2. 与合同缔结相关之问题

在电子合同中,与缔结有关者除合同缔结之一般性问题外,应特别针对因使用电子数据方法缔约所衍生之特殊问题加以研究;前者主要系在探讨要约与承诺、发出与收受等传统行为观念,如何因应交易环境之电子化;至于后者,虽不是全新的问题,但因其已超过原《联合国国际贸易法律委员会电子商务模范法》所倡议之"功能等同"观念所能解决者,例如法律应如何评价自动化计算机系统(automated computer systems)?电子代理(electronic agents)应用于电子合同之情形下,当事人之权义关系应如何处理?均属之;于兹试分述如下。

(1) 数据电文在合同缔结中之使用

《公约草案初稿》第 8 条与《联合国国际贸易法律委员会电子商务模范法》第 11 条均规定,除当事人另有约定者外,要约与承诺双方当事人均可透过电子通信或其他类型的数据电文来表示同意。[4]

---

[1] Pompian, Shawn, "Is the statute of Frauds Ready for Electronic Contracting?", *Va. L. Rev.* 1999, (85): 1497.

[2] Kidd, Donnie L. & Daughtrey William H., Jr., "Adapting Contract Law to Accommodate Electronic Contracts", *Rutgers Computer & Tech. L. J.* 2000, (26): 269.

[3] 唯有 2 个例外,分别是(a) 为个人、家人或家庭目的而缔结之消费者合同(b) 授予有限使用知识产权之权利相关的合同。前者,工作小组虽然注意到将某些消费者交易与商业交易加以区分的实际困难性,但仍认为,公约应不及于此;至于后者之限制标准,非以贸易货品之性质(无论是有形货物或虚拟货物)为区别,而以当事人所缔结之合同性质与意图为准,仅于买受人得不受限制地自由使用该产品时,始有此公约之适用。详参 Preliminary draft convention on [international] contracts concluded or evidenced by data messages Article 2; Preliminary draft convention on [international] contracts concluded or evidenced by data messages Article 9; United Nations Commission on International Trade Law Working Group on Electronic Commerce, Forty-third session, A/CN. 9/WG. IV/WP. 108 (2004)。

[4] Preliminary draft convention on [international] contracts concluded or evidenced by data messages Article 8; United Nations Commission on International Trade Law Working Group on Electronic Commerce, Forty-third session, A/CN. 9/WG. IV/WP. 108 (2004).

(2) 要约之拘束力问题

为厘清要约之拘束力问题,《公约草案初稿》于第 11 条中特别针对"要约之诱引"加以辨明,并具体规定,若缔结合同之要约,非向一个或一个以上特定人提出,而仅系可供信息系统使用人查询之用者,除要约人同意受其拘束者外,应视为"要约之诱引",当事人不因要约而受其拘束。①

此外,随着科技之发展,自动化计算机系统(automated computer systems)与电子代理(electronic agents)应用于电子合同之情形,有日趋普遍之现象,就现有之国际规范而言,仅于《联合国贸易法律委员会电子商务模范法》针对信息之归属设有一般原则性之规定,此尚不足以解决自动化交易系统之法律定位;故公约草案初稿第 12 条,确认自动化系统之缔约效力,对透过自动信息系统与人之间的交互动作或者通过若干自动信息系统之间的交互动作订立的合同,不得仅仅因为无人复查这种系统进行的每一动作或者由此产生的约定而被否认有效性或可执行性。② 公约草案初稿并要求透过自动化计算机系统表示能够提供货品或服务之当事人,应向使用该系统之其他当事人提供适宜、有效且便于使用之技术方法,让这些当事人能于缔结合同前发现或纠正错误。③

(3) 发出与收受数据电文之时点认定

关于合同缔结过程中的收受与发出问题④,依《联合国国际货物买卖公约》第 24 条之规定,要约与承诺均以"到达"(reach)时,始生效力。⑤ 就传统通信之方式而言,不论以口头或书面,就其时点之认定,较无疑义;唯

---

① 在有纸化环境下,报纸、广播和电视中的广告、价目表之寄送,因其承诺约束之意图不明显,一般均被视为要约之诱引。相同地,当事人透过网络提供货物或服务,亦应视为要约之引诱,而不构成具拘束力的要约。Preliminary draft convention on [international] contracts concluded or evidenced by data messages Article 11;"United Nations Commission on International Trade Law Working Group on Electronic Commerce", Forty-third session, A/CN. 9/WG. IV/WP. 108 (2004).

② Preliminary draft convention on [international] contracts concluded or evidenced by data messages Article 12;"United Nations Commission on International Trade Law Working Group on Electronic Commerce", Forty-third session, A/CN. 9/WG. IV/WP. 108 (2004).

③ 此规定系参照欧盟 2000/31/EC 号指示第 11 条第 2 款之规定所订立,《加拿大统一电子商务法》(Uniform Electronic Commerce Act of Canada)第 22 节及《美国统一电子交易法》(United States Uniform Electronic Transactions Act)第 10 节,亦设有类似之规定;详参 Preliminary draft convention on [international] contracts concluded or evidenced by data messages Article 14;"United Nations Commission on International Trade Law Working Group on Electronic Commerce", Forty-third session, A/CN. 9/WG. IV/WP. 108 (2004)。

④ 在联合国国际货物买卖公约(CISG)与国际商务合同通则(UNIDROIT)之规定中,均以要约到达要约人时,发生效力。详参"United Nations Convention on Contracts for the International Sale of Goods", Article 15.;"Principles of International Commercial Contracts", Article 2.3。

⑤ 详参"United Nations Convention on Contracts for the International Sale of Goods", Article 24。

于电子通信方式中,如何确定"收到"(receive)数据电文,即生疑义。是以,联合国国际贸易法律委员会于电子商务模范法中,便针对发出与收受数据电文之时点,另设规定。① 此应足以涵盖瞬间即至的电子通信情况,故公约草案初稿基本上亦反映了此立法精神,即除当事人另有约定者外,数据电文的发出时间是数据电文,进入发端人或代表发端人发送数据电文的人控制范围之外的某一信息系统或离开发端人或代表发端人发送数据电文的人控制范围之内的信息系统时;至于收到之时点,除非考虑到具体情形和数据电文的内容,发端人选择发送数据电文的该特定信息系统是不合理者外,当数据电子进入收件人的信息系统时,即应推定收件人能够检索该数据电文;故数据电文的收到时间系以是数据电文能够为收件人或由收件人指定的任何其他人检索的时间。②

3. 形式之要求

有关电子合同之书面形式要求,《公约草案初稿》于第13条中规定,本公约任何规定均不要求合同须以书面缔结或以书面证明之;凡法律要求本公约所适用之合同应当采用书面形式者,只要系争数据电文所含信息可以接取(accessible)以备日后查用者,即能满足该项要求。③ 此规定乃参考《联合国国际货物买卖公约》而来,盖依该《公约》第11条之规定,有关国际货物买卖合同无需以书面缔结或证明之,故可经由口头、书面或其他方式来缔结④,《公约草案初稿》亦体现此形式自由之原则并将其适用范围扩大于一切合同。此外,《公约草案初稿》亦采用《联合国国际贸易法律委员会电子商务模范法》中功能等同之观念⑤,赋予数据电文具有等同于书面之效力。

此外,对电子合同之签字形式要求规定,凡法律要求合同或当事人被要求作出或选择作出的有关合同的其他任何通信、声明、要求、通知或请求应当签字的,或法律规定了没有签字的后果,对于该项数据电文而言,在下列情况下,即满足了该项要求:(a) 使用了一种方法来鉴别该人

---

① "UNCITRAL Model Law on Electronic Commerce", Article 15.
② Preliminary draft convention on [international] contracts concluded or evidenced by data messages Article 10; "United Nations Commission on International Trade Law Working Group on Electronic Commerce", Forty-third session, A/CN.9/WG.IV/WP.108 (2004).
③ Preliminary draft convention on [international] contracts concluded or evidenced by data messages Article 9; "United Nations Commission on International Trade Law Working Group on Electronic Commerce", Forty-third session, A/CN.9/WG.IV/WP.108 (2004).
④ "United Nations Convention on Contracts for the International Sale of Goods", Article 11.
⑤ "UNCITRAL Model Law on Electronic Commerce", Article 6.

的身份和表明该人认可了数据电文内所含的信息;而且(b)从所有各种情况来看,包括根据任何相关的约定,该方法对于生成或传递数据电文而要达到的目的而言,既是适当的,也是可靠的。①

二、国际贸易电子化相关的国际贸易惯例

所谓国际贸易惯例,是由各国商业惯例及由诸如国际商会、联合国欧洲经济委员会、国际法律协会及其他国际组织所制定的各种标准所组成。② 一般来说,国际贸易惯例的渊源主要有二:第一,是国际商会或国际法协会等民间国际组织所编纂有关国际贸易活动的统一规则和惯例;第二,是各种贸易协会和国际经济组织所制定具有权威性的某种行业、商品交易的标准合同格式或一般的交易条件。③ 其成立之始是由一国或多国单方设立的规则,而后该规则被其他国家以明示或默示的赞成或遵守而形成。④

基本上,传统国际贸易交易主要是通过私法自治(合同自由)与国际贸易惯例来运作;如《跟单信用证统一惯例》(Uniform Customs and Practice for Documentary Credits)等。所以,当数字化环境来临时,国际贸易惯例部分的配合调整自然也有必要,在尊重私法自治与合同自由的前提下,1993年国际商会⑤提出的《跟单信用证统一惯例》,便于新修正条文中正式纳入了电子数据资料与电子签章的有效性。⑥ 在通常使用的跟单信用证部分,原则上,除非当事人在信用证中另有约定,否则这些数据都具有等同原件或原签章的效力。⑦ 这样看来,新类型电子支付系统或工具的操作系统已经完备,而电子数据交换的快速发展也证明了对这方面调整的价值。

然而,单纯的私法自治并不足以解决所有国际贸易纠纷发生时所面

---

① Preliminary draft convention on [international] contracts concluded or evidenced by data messages Article 9; "United Nations Commission on International Trade Law Working Group on Electronic Commerce", Forty-third session, A/CN.9/WG.IV/WP.108 (2004).
② 张圣翠:《国际商法》,上海财经大学出版社 1997 年版,第 146 页。
③ 李双元:《国际经济贸易法律与实务新论》,湖南大学出版社 1996 年版,第 19 页。
④ 邓建华:《国际商法》,中国金融出版社 1995 年版,第 13 页。
⑤ 国际商会是在非政府间的制法机构中最为重要与成功的 1 个,成立于 1919 年,是商业组织与商人的 1 个联盟,它在许多个国家设有国家委员会或会员,它是 1 个名副其实的世界商业组织,是联合国经济及社会理事会的咨询机构。施米托夫:《国际贸易法文选》,中国大百科全书出版社 1993 年版,第 255 页。
⑥ 关于签章的定义、范围及作用:UCP 500 第 20 条中规定,任何单据都可以用手签章或传真签字、穿孔签字、印戳、用符号或使用任何其他机械或电子证实的方法签章。
⑦ UCP 500 第 20 条 b 款中规定,除非信用证中另有规定,单据正本是指任何经影印、自动或计算机系统处理的单据与复本。

临的问题,因为当事人间的同意并不代表在发生纠纷时司法或行政机关都应该配合,更不代表立法已经完备,因而就有前述《联合国电子商务模范法》(UNCITRAL Model Law on Electronic Commerce)[1]提出的举措。但是联合国电子商务模范法的提出,显然是着眼于当事人间所使用电子数据的法律效力,其中固然强化了解决当事人选择电子支付工具的法律效力,然而国际贸易付款过程本身的复杂性,以及多边当事人之间因此所涉及的其他法律关系,却往往不是单纯的探讨约定或合同的效力所能解决的。[2] 所以,面对电子商务的快速变迁且缺乏法规、规则及惯例,国际商会于 2000 年提出《国际商会电子贸易及清算统一规则暨指导》(ICC Uniform Rules and Guidelines for Electronic Trade and Settlement; URGETS)作为规范。在此就这两个规范,举主要内容介绍如下:

(一)《跟单信用证统一惯例》(Uniform Customs and Practice for Documentary Credits, 1993)

基本上,自 20 世纪 80 年代以来,《1980 国际贸易条规》(International Rules for the Interpretation of Trade Terms 1980,简称 INCOTERMS)与《1983 跟单信用证统一惯例》(Uniform Customs and Practice for Documentary Credits, 1983),即国际商会[3]第 400 号出版品(I.C.C. Publication No.400,简称 UCP400),就是对于国际贸易影响最大的两套国际贸易惯例,并已为世界各国及地区广泛的承认与采用。但是,因新的运输方式和运输工具出现与新的通讯技术的发展,使电子数据交换系统在货物买卖中得以广泛使用,在国际货物买卖领域中发生了"无纸革命",出现了电子载货证券及电子单据,使得以纸单证为代表的传统单证发生变化[4],国际商会在 1993 年 5 月正式颁行了《1993 年跟单信用证统一惯例》,即国际商会 500 号出版品(简称 UCP 500),其中除了对信用证本身及银行的责任与义务,有更

---

[1] 在这个模范法中主要针对电子合同、电子文件的效力、书面性签名及仲裁等问题,提出规范标准以供各国参考。
[2] 例如,新形态电子支付的本身所涉及的财金法律或规范问题,就不是自治或惯例所能解决者。
[3] 国际商会的主要职能有四个,即:在国际范围内代表商业界,特别是对联合国和政府专门机构充当商业发言人;促进建立在自由和公平竞争基础上的世界贸易和投资;协调统一贸易惯例,并为进出口制定贸易术语和各种指南;为商业提供实际服务。董炳和、李振瑞:《国际商务法律与惯例》,山东人民出版社 1996 年版,第 87 页。
[4] 董炳和、李振瑞:《国际商务法律与惯例》,山东人民出版社 1996 年版,第 88 页。

明确的规范外①,对于单据部分也作了广泛的修正,以弥补 UCP 400 的不足,其中还对数字化的电子文书②有所着墨,举其要者如下:

1. 关于单据正本的定义

UCP 500 第 20 条 b 款中规定,除非信用证中另有规定,单据正本是指任何经影印、自动或计算机系统处理的单据与复本。其是针对 UCP 400 规定过于笼统加以调整,并将计算机系统的单据文书也作为单据正本。

2. 关于签署的定义、范围及作用

UCP 500 第 20 条中规定,任何单据都可以用手签署或传真签字、穿孔签字、印戳、用符号或使用任何其他机械或电子证实的方法签署;其并进一步规定,上述的任何一种签署,都可以满足单据已被证实、确认的要求,从而使单据有效、合法。③

此外,国际商会在国际贸易条规部分也有显著的调整,基本上,国际贸易术语解释通则的制定目的,是在就国际贸易中经常使用的贸易术语解释,提供一套国际规则,以降低因不同国家对这类术语作不同解释所产生的不确定性。因为合同当事人不一定了解其贸易伙伴各自国家中的贸易惯例与法规,常因此而产生误解、争议、甚至诉讼,所以,国际商会便须通过出版此规则,提供国际贸易各方的参考,来达到减少因上述问题而生的纠纷。当各方长久以来以此作为交易的基础时,这些术语就发展成为所谓的国际贸易惯例。

如今,随着数字环境的来临,企业间使用电子数据交换系统,对原有贸易术语与其适应性的影响,也同样对国际贸易条规造成冲击,因此,国际商会同样通过出版 1990 年修订本④,试图达到符合电子数据交换电子贸易环境要求的目的。在 1990 的修订版本中,即针对卖方所须提供单据(例如商业发票、报关的单据、运输单据等),及交易期间,通过使用电子数

---

① 如对跟单信用证本身而言,取消使用以汇票开状申请人为付款人的汇票,并于欠缺明确表示时,信用证视为不可撤销;另针对银行的责任言,要求银行应依据国际标准银行实务以确实单据是否相符,而单据不符的单据,银行可联系开状申请人,以确定申请人是否对不服之点放弃抗辩权,至于非规定的单据银行并不负审单责任。

② 主要是将电子单据与纸单据同时并用,使电子单据在法律上与纸单据处于相同的地位,以解决国际贸易中由于电子数据交换系统的使用而产生的问题。董炳和、李振瑞:《国际商务法律与惯例》,山东人民出版社 1996 年版,第 88 页。

③ 详见 UCP400 与 UCP500 第 20 条规定的区别,林季红、李蓉:《信用状实务指南》,台北:世界文库 1997 年版,第 228 页。

④ 国际商会于 1936 年首次出版一组解释国际贸易术语的规则,其后又于 1953、1967、1976、1980 作了修改与增补,最近的一次修改为 1990 年 4 月国际商会的第五次修订,而同年 7 月 1 日生效。

据交换系统来传输讯息时,如何确认买卖双方的法律地位,都加以调整。这些做法对于国际贸易合同法制如何适应电子合同环境的发展,具有相当的意义。

以电子数据交换程序下处理的载货证券为例,传统上只有已装船的载货证券(on board bull of lading)才是卖方根据 CFR 及 CIF 等贸易条件来提示而可被接受的单据,而载货证券被认为有三个作用:(1)已在船上交付货物的证据;(2)运送合同的证明;(3)将书面单据转让给他方,即可转让在运输途中的货物物权的工具。[①] 其中针对载货证券的物权移转作用而言,由于传统国际贸易实务是要求受货人于目的地提取货物时,必须出示、缴回载货证券,从而使电子数据交换程序必须将载货证券电子化的安排,显得特别困难。

其次,运送单据不仅用来证明货物已交代运送人,还必须证明货物于交付时,是处于良好的状况,这就是所谓的清洁载货证券(clean bill of lading);相对的,若运送单据上有表明货物未处于良好状况的批注,就是不洁的载货证券,按照原有信用证统一惯例的规定,银行在押汇时,是不可以接受的。[②] 所以,国际商会就在 1990 年版的《国际贸易术语解释通则》中,将这一意料中的发展加以考虑,其中原则性的认为,如果买卖双方已经约定以电子媒介来进行交易或通讯,则交货单据、运送单据等文书,都可以通过约定由相当的电子数据交换系统的讯息来取代。

(二)《国际商会电子贸易及清算统一规则暨指导》(ICC Uniform Rules and Guidelines for Electronic Trade and Settlement; URGETS)[③]

鉴于电子商务的快速变迁且缺乏法规、规则及惯例,国际商会(ICC)会员认为,相对于以纸张为基础的交易,提供电子贸易及清算统一规则暨指导来规范电子商务应为一合宜的选择。但是,这个规则是国际商会为了提供一个架构来促进经由电子讯息交换的企业对企业交易的一致性而设,并不适用于个人为其私人、家庭或家属的目的所为的交易,将被使用

---

① 林季红、李蓉:《信用状实务指南》,台北:世界文库 1997 年版,第 108 页。
② 详见 UCP500 第 32 条的规定,林季红、李蓉:《信用状实务指南》,台北:世界文库 1997 年版,第 232 页。
③ 详见 ICC Uniform Rules and Guidelines for Electronic Trade and Settlement, URGETS (2000)。资料来源:亚洲贸易促进会驻巴黎办事处 2000 年 5 月 25 日法(89)经字第 533 号函。

于提供一般规则及最佳惯例,以促进从纸张交易到电子企业对企业的交易①,就其具体规定说明如下:

1. 电子贸易及清算统一规则暨指导的适用

(1) 其目的是想提供一个架构来促进经由电子讯息交换的企业对企业交易的一致性。②

(2) 在电子贸易及清算统一规则暨指导为电子合同的一部分时,除有反对的表示以外,对合同的所有当事人都有拘束力。③

2. 电子贸易及清算统一规则暨指导的解释

应将有关(1) 电子交易所含习惯、惯例及相关用语;(2) 为全世界电子交易系统的一致性、明确性及统一性的需求及技术等因素列入考虑。④

3. 电子贸易及清算统一规则暨指导中重要名词的定义

(1) "电子合同"(Electronic Agreement):是指当事人基于发生法律效力的意思,通过电子讯息的交换,将双方的权利及义务所合意的条款记录于该电子合同中,以形成一个或更多的电子交易。

(2) "电子贸易交易"(Electronic Trade Transaction):是指一交易是通过电子讯息交换所为的行为。

(3) "电子信息"(Electronic Message):是指资料电子转换的内容,不论其是通过开放或关闭的联网方式所使用。

(4) "认证信息"(Authenticated Message):是指一个在商业惯例中所普遍被认同的程序及方式所确认的电子信息。⑤

---

① 因为是仅对那些经由电子讯息所执行的交易及因此而生的行为提出观点,所以并没有要改变适用的法律,而且当事人采用电子贸易及清算统一规则暨指导,应就其适用的范围内,参考现有的本国法及国际条约,使企业以将电子贸易及清算统一规则暨指导纳入合约的方式赋予完全的法律效力,并且允许电子商务连系去适用电子贸易及清算统一规则暨指导到他们自己发展的商业惯例中。所以,所有使用者应了解电子贸易及清算统一规则暨指导的本质是机动的,而且未来将视实际需要做修订以支持电子交易的发展。

② 就所有的 ICC 商品,是采自愿性地采用电子贸易及清算统一规则暨指导,其必须受限于所适用法律的强制规定。

③ 而且在下列情形中,将适用:(1) 若没有特别规定电子贸易及清算统一规则暨指导的版本的,对含 URGET 的电子合同所适用的版本为该电子合同订立当时所生效的 URGET 版本;(2) 结合电子贸易及清算统一规则暨指导的电子合同当事人得以双方的合意,以明示特定条款的排除或在电子合同中订立相反于电子贸易及清算统一规则暨指导的条款的方式来修正或排除电子贸易及清算统一规则暨指导的任何条款的适用。

④ 其他对用语的解释,如:(1) 在单数内的文字包括复数且复数内的文字包含单数,但文内有相反的规定者,不在此限;(2) "包括"是指包含但不限于;(3) 中性用语包含任何性别的用语;(4) 承认不代表接受但仅是表示收到电子讯息而已。

⑤ 或是在电子讯息中藉由当事人所合意的程序或方法得以同时确认发件人的身份、来源及资料的真实性。

(5)"确认"(Acknowledgement):是指一种流程可以使收件人在收受一电子讯息时,检查造句及语意,并由该当事人发送一电子通知确认其收受。

(6)"交易日"(Business Day):在国际贸易,当事人应在其合同中定义其交易日。①

4. 电子贸易及清算统一规则暨指导中有关电子合同有效性规定

(1)电子要约及承诺的效力—电子要约或承诺于以可以被该系统操作的格式进入收件人的信息系统及以一被认证的格式收受时发生效力。

(2)电子合同是一有拘束力的行为,且当事人不得以其是以电子讯息的方式而生为由,反对通过电子讯息发生合同的效力。

(3)准据法的适用:若一方当事人知悉一电子合同或电子信息的内容或应用是违反准据法者,应通知他方当事人。

(4)若准据法要求书面或原件,则当事人应同意该电子信息已符合此要件,且不得否定其于法律程序或仲裁中的证据力。

(5)对电子信息的格式及认证(Form & Authentication of Electronic Messages)问题,加以规定。②

(6)对电子信息收件人的响应(Response to Receipt of Electronic Messages)问题,加以规定③。

(7)电子信息的保全(Security of Electronic Messages)问题:包括代理

---

① 然而在没有这种约定时,适用下列的规定:如果有记载履行地的,所谓交易日是指收受电子讯息的当事人指定地一日历天中 24 小时内相关行为一般被履行的时间;如果没有载明地点时,所谓的交易日是指收受电子讯息的当事人实际所在地 1 日历天中 24 小时内相关商业行为通常被履行的时间。

② 其规定:1. 电子讯息为一有拘束力的行为:当事人不得仅因其是经由特定的通讯方式成立的原因而行使任何违反电子讯息的权利;2. 当事人应同意可以接受的认证的方法以确保所有的电子讯息可以判认发件人、收件人及所有当事人间为认证而要求的其他信息;3. 当事人应同意电子讯息可被接受的格式以确保每一方当事人可以读取所有的电子讯息及检查任何关于传送、收受及真实性的资料。

③ 具体而言:1. 若需要承认电子讯息者,其须由收受方以一电子讯息,根据合约条款确认收受来加以完成;2. 电子合同的当事人同意利用一指定的人来收受电子讯息者,由该指定的人收受者视为已收受;3. 收受电子讯息后应有下列适当的行为:当事人收受电子讯息应操作任何此等讯息及采取任何必要的行为,或于不超过收受电子讯息日后的两个工作日内为相反的响应。若一方当事人怀疑一讯息有迟延或中断,其应通知他方当事人;4. 确认并非要件除非在电子讯息中或当事人间有特别的规(约)定;5. 当事人应就确认的形式及内容予以合意,而且如果缺乏这种合意时,确认应为一电子讯息,而该电子讯息应参考最初的电子讯息及收受讯息的日期及时间;6. 若需要做确认的,该确认应自收受电子讯息的当日或次一工作日前,于原始讯息收受地发出。

人的责任、保全与错误的问题。①

(8) 保密性及资料的保护(Confidentiality and Protection of Data)问题,加以规定。②

(9) 电子信息的记录及储存(Recording and Storage of Electronic Messages)问题,加以规定。③

(10) 电子信息的作业要求(Operational Requirements for Electronic Messages),设有规定。④

(11) 清算(Settlement)问题:电子合同的一方当事人同意利用电子交易清算者,则有义务使该清算生效。

(12) 其他(Miscellaneous)的约定:包括不可抗力、除外规定、变更与可分性的规定。⑤

(13) 准据法的规定:若没有准据法的约定,电子贸易及清算统一规

---

① 其规定:1. 就代理人的责任(Responsibility for Agents):每一方当事人应就其代理人的行为负责,包括保密条款及电子合同的他方当事人所信赖的认证服务等;2. 保全程序(Security Procedures):当事人应记明、实现及维护保全程序及方法以确保电子合同合理的保护,使其不让未经授权人进入、篡改、延迟、毁损或损失的风险来确保记录的真实性;3. 错误及拒绝(Errors & Rejections):若保全方法及其他程序的使用造成在电子讯息中的拒绝或发现错误者,收件人应不得超过收受该电子讯息后的次个工作日通知该讯息的发件人,但若另有相反的规定者,不在此限。被拒绝的电子讯息的收件人在收到发件人进一步指示前不得对讯息有所行为。如果一个先前遭拒或错误的电子讯息由发信人重送者,该重送应明白说明其为更正后的电子讯息。

② 主要的有:1. 保密性(Confidentiality):当事人应确保电子讯息所含的资料,经发件人载明需保密,或经双方当事人同意保持机密者应以机密的方式维护且不得揭露或传送予任何未被授权的人或供做非当事人意欲以外的目的使用。在授权下,进一步的传送此等机密资料应比照相同保密的程度。但若资料已是公开可得者,不在此限;2. 加密(Encryption):当事人应载明每种形态讯息可接受的保护等级;3. 个人资料(Personal Data):若电子讯息的传送或收受包含个人资料者,每一方当事人应知悉数据保护法或其个别国家自治团体所制定保护个人资料的标准。

③ 其规定:1. 讯息的保存(Retention of Messages):当事人在电子交易下所发出或收受的所有电子讯息的完整及依照年序的记录应由一方当事人安全地保存,此包括任何背书及任何依照国内法律或准据法所为的规定或时间限制内,在正常通讯、储存、及展示过程中所产生的变更;2. 保存的形态(Format for Retention):电子讯息储存的方式为:对发件人而言,应以允许该讯息可以传送格式的方式来储存,而对收件人而言,则应以收受的格式储存;3. 讯息的还原(Retrieval of Messages):当事人应确保电子讯息的记录可以人为能读取的格式还原;4. 讯息的真实性(Integrity of Messages):当事人应记明保证记录真实性的方法以确保该记录在传送及还原过程中未被篡改。

④ 1. 操作环境(Operational Environment):当事人应完成及维护一可以依照电子贸易及清算统一规则暨指导的规定操作的环境,其包括但不限于电子讯息的产生、传送、收受、读取、储存、还原、保全及认证等;2. 通讯的方式(Means of Communication):当事人应同意通讯的方式,包括通讯的标准及议定书。

⑤ 1. 不可抗力:电子合同的一方当事人对他方当事人因不可抗力的事由而无法履行合同时,不负赔偿责任;2. 除外规定(Exclusion of a Rule):除非电子合同中有相反的约定外,任何对本"电子贸易及清算统一规则暨指导"的除外规定,应仅构成对该情况的例外;3. 变更(Changes):任何电子合同的变更应以电子讯息的形式为之。如果以其他方式作出的,将产生把电子合同自这些电子贸易及清算统一规则暨指导的范围中移除的效力,但不影响基本合同。

则暨指导及电子合同应依商品或服务的出卖人其主要事务所在地的法律。

4.3 合同电子化的相关问题

一、概述

电子商务是商业的未来,当成千上万的网际网络使用者,通过网际网络来完成其交易时,合同也被搬上了网络;然而因为电子商务是通过网际网络来完成的,所以它不可能用传统的纸张方法来缔约,而一电子合同可以在几秒内穿越世界,但相同的纸式合同可能需数天或数星期。然而撇开速度及方便性不论,电子合同是否仍必须符合与传统合同相同的法律要件,便值得吾人加以探讨。① 是以,在此首将针对传统的国际贸易合同的意义、成立与生效要件,加以说明:

(一) 国际贸易合同的意义

在传统上,所谓国际贸易合同,是指国际商品买卖合同而言,意即当事人约定,一方自一国境内移转商品财产权于他方或其所指定的国境,而他方以约定方式交付价金的合同。② 分析其要点,我们可知:

1. 是当事人间的债权合同

合同是以当事人以发生私法上效果为目的所为的合意;其中以发生债的关系为目的,由两个以上相互对立的意思表示一致所为的合同,称为债权合同。所以,国际贸易合同,是以发生国际贸易债权债务关系为目的的合同,所以属于债权合同的一种。

2. 是以商品为买卖标的

国际贸易的对象,在传统上多以传统商品的买卖为标的,也多为有形的国际贸易,然而,随着知识产权商品的出现,国际贸易的标的并不限于传统商品。

3. 是以移转商品财产权于他方或其指定的国境为目的

按移转财产权与交付价金互为对价关系,在国际贸易所涉交易上,其对价关系是商品的财产权自一国境至另一国境,因而产生与国内交易合同不同的对价或移转与运送交付的方式。然而,在国际贸易中的知识产

---

① Lupton, W. Everett, "The Digital Signature: Your Identity by the Numbers", *Rich. J. L. & Tech.* 1999 (6): 10.

② 林诚二:《民法债编各论》,台北:瑞兴图书股份有限公司1994年版,第168—170页。

权商品的移转,仅需通过电子媒介的下载,即可达到交易的目的,未必会有有形商品移境的情形。

4. 是依约定方式支付价金

国际贸易合同因是在不同国境间进行交易,涉及不同国家货币汇兑及支付信用制度的问题,所以对价金支付的方式,常作特别约定。

5. 是法律行为的一种

法律行为是以意思表示为要素,而依意思表示的内容发生一定私法上效果的法律事实。所以,国际贸易合同是法律行为的一种。

(二) 国际贸易合同的成立与生效要件

1. 国际贸易合同的成立要件

(1) 一般成立要件

国际贸易合同为法律行为的一种,因而法律行为应具备的一般成立要件,如当事人、标的及意思表示,三者缺一,则法律行为不能成立。所以,国际贸易合同也需具备这些一般成立要件,才能成立。

(2) 特别成立要件

所谓特别成立要件,就是指各个法律行为特有的成立要件,国际贸易合同之所以有别于其他法律行为,在于国际贸易合同必须通过当事人就标的及价金相互同意而成立,所以,当事人间就标的及价金的意思表示一致,是国际贸易合同的特别成立要件。此外,如果当事人就一定方式的履行有特别的约定,例如书面的要式[①]或交付标的物时,则该合同除须具备上述的要件外,还需要履行一定的方式,才能成立。

2. 国际贸易合同的生效要件

(1) 一般生效要件

在理论上,国际贸易合同虽然因具备上述的要件而成立,但仍然需要具备一般生效要件,才可生效。也就是说,国际贸易合同仍须其当事人具有行为能力、标的适当(合法、确定、可能、妥当)及当事人的意思表示健全无瑕疵(无不一致或不自由的情形),才足以生效。[②]

[①] 在国际交易行为,其合同的成立,并不以有合同书为必要,通常以口头合同行之;但在正式订货场合,因数量大、金额多、交货期限长,而双方当事人又居于不同国境内,为避免日后产生疑义纠纷,一般非长期性采购,则以传真或正式面对面签订一基本约,再依此基本约进行个别合同。林诚二:《民法债编各论》,台北:瑞兴图书股份有限公司 1994 年版,第 171 页。

[②] 依大陆《民法通则》第 55 条的规定,任何法律行为皆须符合下列有效要件:(1) 行为人具有相应的行为能力;(2) 当事人的意思表示真实;(3) 不违反法律或社会公共利益。彭万林主编:《民法学》,中国政法大学出版社 1996 年版,第 100—102 页。国际贸易合同也是法律行为的一种,故也应符合此要件。

(2) 特别生效要件

所谓特别生效要件,是指法律就各个法律行为是否有效所作的特别规定。

二、合同电子化的相关问题

(一) 电子合同之法律概念

自因特网被普遍使用以来,数字化环境之冲击,已全面性地影响到原有法制结构。针对逐步成型之电子合同概念言,虽联合国贸易法律委员会早于 1996 年便曾于《联合国贸易法律委员会电子商务模范法》(United Nations Commission on International Trade Law)①中提出"功能等同"(functional-equivalent)之概念②,试图来解决传统民事法中所涉要约与承诺、发出与收受等传统行为概念,因应交易环境电子化之调整问题,但此概念之提出尚不足以解决因自动化计算机交易系统与电子代理普遍应用于电子合同中所新衍生之问题③,盖其已超过前述"功能等同"观念所能涵盖之范围。是以,联合国际贸易法律委员会第四工作小组(电子商务),为避免各国立法歧异造成交易之障碍,乃进一步提出《藉数据电文缔结或证明之(国际)合同公约草案初稿》(以下简称公约草案初稿)④,尝试解决此种新的缔约方式所新生之法律问题。

面对此国际发展趋势,如何藉由电子签章立法之初备,探究其与电子合同所赖民事法规间之调和关系,并就电子合同实务中可能面临之民事基础法律问题,参考国际社会之立法精神及实践经验,以为未来法制调适与因应之需,实有探讨之必要。基此,本节拟就当事人、标的与意思表示之问题,分述如后。

---

① "Report of the United Nations Commission on International Trade Law, U. N. Commission on International Trade Law", 29th Sess., U. N. Doc. A/51/17 (1996); Uzelac, Alan, "Comparative Theme: UNCITRAL Notes on Organizing Arbitral Proceedings: A Regional View", *Croat. Arbit. Year B.* 1997, (4): 135.

② http://www.uzp.gov.pl/zagranica/ONZ/UNCITRAL_english.html (visited 2004/8/1).

③ 如自动化计算机系统与电子代理之应用之问题等。Bellia Jr., Anthony J., "Contracting With Electronic Agents", *Emory L. J.* 2001, (50): 1047。

④ Preliminary draft convention on [international] contracts concluded or evidenced by data messages Article 1; Report of the Working Group on Electronic Commerce on the work of its forty-third session, A/CN.9/548 (2004).

(二) 电子合同之当事人问题

1. 关于当事人身份之确认问题

在传统合同之缔结过程中,合同之双方多透过人类五官为用,并按传统书面交易方式藉对照印鉴或署名,以确认当事人身份并将有关书面文件或讯息载明的权利义务归属于该特定当事人。① 唯于电子交易中,数字讯息上所显示出之发文者,与实际上制作并发出讯息者是否同一,并无法按传统方式来辨认,虽可依预先安排之密码,透过电子方式加以辨认。② 唯当事人间用以确认身份之电子签章其法律属性与法律效力为何? 即生疑义。

就台湾地区而言,传统书面合同关系中,多藉由对照签名或印章以辨认当事人之身份,故台湾地区民法第 3 条中规定,依法律规定有使用文字之必要者:(1) 应由本人亲自签名;(2) 并得以印章代其签名;(3) 如以指印、十字或其他符号代签名者,并需经两人签名为证,始与签名生同等之效力。③ 然而,若应用电子签章于依法律规定应签章之文书时,其本质上究系属"本人之亲自签名"、"印章"抑或为"以其他符号之代签名",即生疑义。虽台湾地区现行法并未就签章加以定义,但因民法第三条系将签名、盖章与其他符号并列,是有论者以为签名仍须有姓、名、别号、商号、堂名等文字,④故于解释上尚难认电子签章属"本人之亲自签名"或"盖章"。至于电子签章是否得认其属"以其他符号之代签名"? 吾人以为,此于实际应用上,易生困扰。当应用电子签章取代传统签章时,若依台湾地区民法第 3 条第 3 项之规定,则需经当事人以外之两人签名证明,始生与签名同等效力,并为法律行为生效之依据⑤;于电子交易合同中,该二人若复以电子签章为之者,则各再需经两人签名证明,此于实际应用上,实不可行。而为解决应用电子签章于依法律规定应签章文书时之难题,特于《电子签

---

① 林瑞珠:《当前贸易电子化所面临之法律新课题——以两岸法律因应为例》,载《万国法律》2002 年第 123 卷,第 25—36 页。
② 室町正实:《EDI 合同の实务上の留意点(中)》,载《EDI(电子的データ交换)と法》,1996,(NBL585):34—35。
③ 通说以为,台湾地区民法第 3 条固以规范法定要式行为为其目的;唯于当事人约定之法律行为,亦得类推适用之。参王泽鉴:《民法总则》,台北:三民书局 2001 年版,第 80—81 页。反对说,参郑玉波:《民法总则》,台北:三民书局 1998 年版,第 63 页。
④ 林诚二:《民法总则讲义》(上册),台北:瑞兴图书 1995 年版,第 106—107 页;另可参 71 年台上字第 4166 号判决。
⑤ 参民国 31 年上字第 3256 号判例:"不动产物权之移转或设定,应以书面为之,此项书面得不由本人自写,但必须亲自签名或盖章,其以指印、十字或其他符号代签名者,应经二人签名证明,否则法定方式有欠缺,依法不生效力。"

章法》第 9 条中规定,"依法律规定,应签名或盖章者,经相对人同意,得以电子签章为之。"此可认为系创设一种新的签章之方式。至于大陆方面,2004 年 8 月通过之《电子签名法》即对当事人身份确认有所规范,该法第 13 条第 1 款第 1 项认为可靠的电子签名应属于电子签名人专有;此外,由第 16 条及第 20 条之规定,当事人之电子签名如需认证,应提供真实、完整和准确的信息,并需对当事人之身份进行查验,准此,亦可间接推知当事人身份之确认。

基本上,电子交易合同中如何确认合同当事人身份,并确保传送讯息与收受讯息为真正,诚属不易①;在电子数据交换运用于电子交易架构时,为免除不必要之争议,当事人多透过合意之方式以签章密码等方式来辨认发文者并确认责任归属。② 而于实务运作经验上,有许多辨认之方法,其中较单纯者为密码之设定或采用电子邮件再确认方式,亦有以生理外貌辨识、指纹辨识、瞳孔虹膜辨识、声纹辨识、DNA 比对辨识等技术,作为辨认当事人身份之方式。③

至于认证之问题,在传统以书面为基础之合同关系中,常透过公证机构来确认当事人之身份,而于电子合同之缔结中,国际间之发展已普遍采取建立电子商务认证中心,建立起类似印鉴管理和登记制度担当起对电子文书的真实性证明和鉴定责任。④ 面对非技术因素,如主体欺诈风险、放弃风险、内容异议风险与举证所造成之风险;公证应是控制电子合同特殊风险的有效手段,除对接收、发送电文的行为进行现场公证外,建立"电子公证人"系统、"电子认证"系统,以作为电子证据取证手段。⑤ 对此,台湾地区与国际间之立法趋势相若,配合数字签章与认证科技之发展,以因应电子交易之匿名性所导致当事人身份辨认问题,在当事人同意或选择之基础上⑥,一方面透过数字签章作为辨认当事人身份之表征,他方面则透过凭证机构来对签

---

① Berman, Andrew B., "International Divergence: The 'Keys' to Signing on the Digital Line—The Cross-Border Recognition of Electronic Contracts and Digital Signatures", Syracuse J. Int'l L. & Com. 2001, (28): 125—128.
② 室町正实:《EDI 合同の实务上の留意点(中)》,载《EDI(电子的データ交换)と法》,1996(NBL585): 34—35。
③ 吴嘉生:《电子商务法导论》,台北:学林文化 2003 年版,第 365 页。
④ 章宏友:《关于电子合同若干问题的法律思考》,载《武汉冶金管理干部学院学报》2003 年第 1 期,第 71 页。
⑤ 郑远民、易志斌:《试论公证在电子合同中的应用价值》,载《北京理工大学学报(社会科学版)》2002 年第 2 期,第 93—95 页。
⑥ 例如,德国(1997 年)、马来西亚(1997 年)、意大利(1997 年)、新加坡(1998 年)、韩国(1998 年)及美国各州之立法。

章之真正性加以认证①,以达保护交易当事人之目的。②

2. 关于当事人行为能力之欠缺问题

在传统合同之一般生效要件中,通常会要求当事人应具有完全之行为能力③,大陆《合同法》第9条中亦规定:"当事人订立合同,应当具有相应的民事权利能力和民事行为能力。"而在电子合同中,理亦应要求当事人具完全行为能力,合同始生效力。唯如何得知悉他方是否具有完全行为能力? 在传统透过面对面(face to face)的交易模式中,当事人可以经由外貌、言语或行止等,来判断交易相对人是否为完全行为能力人;唯于电子交易中,就相对人行为能力有无之判断,则具事实上之困难,而如何在促进电子交易发展之前提下,兼顾无行为能力人与限制行为能力人交易上之保护,则值得吾等进一步探讨。

以台湾地区之现况而言,或可参考《邮政法》第12条或《电信法》第9条之规定,以为讨论的基础④,此二规定虽分别就无行为能力人或限制行为能力人所为之邮政事务与电信行为,设特别规定"视为"有行为能力人;唯在电子交易过程中或有利用电信之行为,但尚不能对"使用电信发生之其他行为",视为有行为能力人所为。⑤ 是以,就电子交易合同之缔结,于电子签章法或其他专法未设有特别规定之情形下,似不宜类推适用邮政法或电信法之规定,而应依民法中有关当事人行为能力之规定,以为效力认定之基础。换言之,应认为无行为能力人所为之意思表示无效;限制行为能力人未得法定代理人之允许,所订立之合同,须经法定代理人之承认,始生效力;此容或造成相对人之不利益,进而影响电子交易安全与信

---

① 设置认证中心的重要性在于由其扮演公证第三者角色,使数位签章的签署者难以否认其曾为的意思表示,并为其所发出的讯息负起应负的法律责任,如此电子交易安全方可获得保障,见洪淑芬:《数字签字——公开金钥认证机构介绍》,载《信息法务透析》1996年第11期,第15页。

② 周忠海等:《电子商务法新论》,台北:神州出版社2002年版,第50页。

③ 参施启扬:《民法总则》,台北:三民书局2000年版,第198—199页。另,《中华人民共和国合同法》更进一步将之明文化,参该法第9条规定:"当事人订立合同,应当具有相应的民事权利能力和民事行为能力。"

④ 《邮政法》第12条之规定:"无行为能力人或限制行为能力人,关于邮政事务对中华邮政公司所为之行为,视为有行为能力人之行为。"至于《电信法》第9条则规定:"无行为能力人或限制行为能力人使用电信之行为,对于电信事业,视为有行为能力人。但因使用电信发生之其他行为,不在此限。"

⑤ 对此有论者以为,限制行为能力人或无行为能力人通过网络订立的合同,对于相对人应视为有行为能力,因网络具开放性,相对人又须面对不特定多数人,加以交易不是面对面进行,因而相对人难以辨认对方之真伪;吴楠:《电子合同中若干法律问题探析及应用建议》,载《学术界》2003年第2期,第224页。

赖之保护,必要时可依台湾地区民法第83条之规定,认限制行为人用诈术使人信其为有行为能力人或已得法定代理人之允许时,应认其法律行为有效,藉以达到权衡限制行为人保护与电子交易安全维护之目的。

综上,对当事人行为能力欠缺之问题,如何在交易安全、信赖之维护与限制行为或无行为能力之保护间,加以权衡?吾人虽能于既有法规中找到一些探讨方向,然传统之书面合同法制系用以拘束当事人之行为,电子合同法制所强调者却倾向于规范当事人之缔约过程;是以,在处理电子合同成立与生效之问题时,不应过度强调科技本身所带来之变动,而应强调科技对人与人间在信息交流与交易关系之互动上所显示之价值,故较佳之处理方式仍应就电子合同环境所赖之私法体系,作一较全面的检讨。

3. 关于自动化计算机系统与电子代理之应用问题

传统合同的缔结是建立于双方当事"人"之意志上,但在电子合同中,此种观念将受到挑战,盖当吾等将自动化计算机系统(automated computer systems)与电子代理(electronic agents)①之制度应用于电子合同之缔结时,是否能缔结一个等同于传统民事法架构下之成立并生效之合同关系?便成为值得吾等加以探讨之课题。例如,某量贩店甲公司以自动化计算机系统管理库存商品,而甲公司销售之特定产品,系向乙公司购买,唯该特定产品之下单或接单则系透过EDI,交由各该公司之自动化计算机系统自动进行。此时,甲公司与乙公司间所缔结有关该产品之各别买卖合同中,并未另立书面文书,亦无人为之交涉或意思决定的介入,全系交由自动化计算机系统来进行交易,此正是典型的电子自动缔约行为;换言之,整个过程均系经由当事人或使用人设计、选择,或程序设计之计算机用以发出或响应相关电子讯息或工作,而不经人为之审视。② 以本例言,电子代理并不是具有法律人格的主体,而是一种能够执行人的意思的、智能化的交易工具。一般的应用工具,只是人体部分功能的复制或延伸,而"电子代理人"则不同,它是商事交易人的脑与手功能的结合与延伸。从构成

---

① 所谓电子代理,指一旦被一当事方所启动,便可在所编制的程序参数范围内开始运作、响应或与其他当事方或其他当事方的电子代理人进行相互联系。见"United Nations Commission on International Trade Law Working Group on Electronic Commerce", Thirty-ninth session, A/CN. 9/WG. IV/WP. 95. (2002)。

② 而此电子讯息相较于传统之代理人而言,容有相当之差异。首先,其签名不能以墨水或亲笔为之。第二,该讯息可能系由计算机之自动行为而非自然人所产生。例如,一个计算机库存管理系统,在没有人为介入下,在其资料呈现出低库存时,开立了一张EDI订单。同样地,一个计算机资金管理系统可能在特定银行之户头超过先前同意之门槛时,自动签发电子资金移转。第三,一电子讯息可能由本人而不是其代理人发出。

上看,它是具有自动化功能的软件、硬件,或其结合;从其商业用途看,它可用于搜索某一商品或服务的价格,完成在线买卖,或对交易发出授权。①

此时法律应如何来评价自动化计算机系统(automated computer systems)与电子代理(electronic agents)应用于电子合同之情形?目前,实务上多以当事人间之协议为基础,来解决自动化计算机系统与电子代理之定位问题;然若交易当事人未有合意时,则为立法者或法院所必须面对并加以解决之议题。此于美国学说之论述中或有主张同意理论(The Consent Theory)②、信赖理论(The Reliance Theory)③、侵权理论(The Tort Theory)④、市场信心理论(The Market-Confidence Theory)⑤、信任理论(The Trust Theory)⑥等,至于两岸究应如何建构足以衔接既有法规发展之制度,实有赖进一步从事比较法与法律继受之研究。

就现有之国际规范而言,仅以《联合国贸易法律委员会电子商务模范法》针对信息之归属设有一般原则性之规定,然吾等以为,此尚不足以解决自动化计算机系统与电子代理之法律定位;是以,公约草案初稿第12条乃规定,除当事人另有约定者外,即使未经自然人复查计算机系统运作之每一个动作或因此产生之约定,合同仍可透过自动化计算机系统与自然人间之交互运作,或透过若干自动化计算机系统间之交互运作来缔结。⑦ 由此规定观之⑧,计算机的自动化处理并不是没有体现当事人的真

---

① 李祖全:《电子合同的证据法学之思考》,载《常德师范学院学报(社会科学版)》2003年第3期,第53页。

② Lerouge, Jean-Francois, "The Use of Electronic Agents Questioned Under Contractual Law: Suggested Solutions on a European and American Level", *J. Marshall J. Computer & Info. L.* 1999, (18): 403.

③ Raz, Joseph, *The Morality of Freedom*, New York: Clarendon Press, 1986, 173—176.

④ Gilmore, Grant, *The Death of Contract*, Columbus: Ohio State University Press, 1995, 95—112.

⑤ Farber, Daniel A. & Matheson, John H., "Beyond Promissory Estoppel: Contract Law and the Invisible Handshake", *U. Chi. L. Rev.* 1985, (52): 903, 927.

⑥ Raz, Joseph, "Promises in Morality and Law", *Harv. L. Rev.* 1982, (95): 916.

⑦ Preliminary draft convention on [international] contracts concluded or evidenced by data messages Article 12.1.; "United Nations Commission on International Trade Law Working Group on Electronic Commerce", Forty-third session, A/CN.9/WG.IV/WP.108 (2004).

⑧ 《公约草案初稿》并要求透过自动化计算机系统表示能够提供货品或服务之当事人,应向使用该系统之其他当事人提供适宜、有效且便于使用之技术方法,让这些当事人能于缔结合同前发现或纠正错误,以达衡平之目的。此规定系参照欧盟2000/31/EC号指示第11条第2款之规定所订立,《加拿大统一电子商务法》(Uniform Electronic Commerce Act of Canada)第22节及《美国统一电子交易法》(United States Uniform Electronic Transactions Act)第10节,亦设有类似之规定;Preliminary draft convention on [international] contracts concluded or evidenced by data messages Article 12.2.; "United Nations Commission on International Trade Law Working Group on Electronic Commerce", Forty-third session, A/CN.9/WG.IV/WP.108 (2004).

实意思,而只不过是这种真实意思被格式化、电子化、自动化了而已,且所反映的是当事人订立合同时的真实意思[1];立法者同意电子合同系可透过自动化计算机系统来完成,并进一步认为经由计算机程序代为处理商务之人(不论自然人或法人),应就该自动化系统所生成之数据电文负终局责任。[2]

针对上述问题,两岸并未设有相关之规定,吾人以为其可能之解决方案,或可透过技术规划[3]、合同当事人之明示同意、代理制度与理论之探讨[4]、拟人(人格)化理论之建构[5]、工具说[6]、电子签章法之调整或电子交易之特别立法(如美国之 UCITA[7] 或 UETA[8]),加以解决。唯就台湾地区现有之法规范言,电子签章法中并未对此设有规定,而台湾地区民法第103条以下关于代理之规定,系以"人"为适用前提;故解释上应认为自动化计算机系统与电子代理虽得自行发出或收受意思表示,但其并无独立之意思,且其所为之发出或响应动作,若均系基于当事人或使用人所设计、控制的,在某种程度上,似可认为系人的意志之延伸,而得将之视为"工具";基此,将透过自动化计算机系统与电子代理所为之行为,仅是当事人思维和行为的一种延伸,行为的后果也理应由人承担[9],与该当事人所为者具同等法律效力。具体而言,人类与计算机分工,计算机作为人类意思之延伸,计算机之表示行为,乃系基于人类本身之意思或间接地以人

---

[1] 吕国民:《电子合同订立的若干问题探析》,载《财经问题研究》2002年第5期,第79—80页。

[2] "United Nations Commission on International Trade Law", Thirty-fourth session, A/CN. 9/484 (2001)。

[3] Hermans, Bjorn, "Intelligent Software Agents on the Internet: An Inventory of Currently Offered Functionality in the Information Society and a Prediction of (Near) Future Developments", http://www.firstmonday.dk/issues/issue2_3/ch_67/(visited 2004/8/01)。

[4] Kerr, Ian R., "Spirits in the Material World: Intelligent Agents as Intermediaries in Electronic Commerce", *Dalhousie L. J.* 1999, (22): 190, 239—247.

[5] Solum, Lawrence B., "Legal Personhood for Artificial Intelligences", *N. C. L. REV.* 1992, (70): 1231, 1238—1240.

[6] Preliminary draft convention on [international] contracts concluded or evidenced by data messages Article 12.1. "United Nations Commission on International Trade Law Working Group on Electronic Commerce", Forty-third session, A/CN. 9/WG. IV/WP. 108 (2004).

[7] UNIF. Computer Info. Transactions Act 107.

[8] Uniform Electronic Transactions Act 2(6)中,对电子代理之定义"单独使用计算机程序、电子方式或其他方法,以发动一行为或是响应、执行电子记录,而其全部或一部并无人类对其再为检查或再为其他行为"。

[9] 于海防、韩冰:《电子合同订立过程中的若干问题研究》,载《烟台大学学报(哲学社会科学版)》2002年第2期,第158页。

类之意思为根据①,故得将其视为工具。

综上,关于自动化计算机系统与电子代理之问题,本书所强调者在合同当事人与参与者间互动关系之重新界定,而非本诸于传统"代理人"之法则,强调其个别行为在商品或劳务交易过程中之法律属性与定义而已。尤其,随着科技之进步,此自动化计算机系统与电子代理在可预见的未来将具"自主行为"的能力,而不仅拥有"自动行为"之能力;即透过 AI 人工智能之发展,其可能吸取经验,改变自己程序中的指令,甚至设计新的指令,此应如何评价? 也许在不久的将来,生化机器人(cyborg)②亦不再只是电影中之虚拟人物或是科技的想像时,此时 cyborg 是不是"人"? 而我们又应如何因应? 对此,吾人以为法律所应侧重者乃代理之功能,而唯一真正重要的人,则系指导"电子代理"行事之本人,此方不致发生无法解决之哲理困扰,故针对此新兴之法律问题,实应进一步调适相关民事法规以为规范。

(三) 电子合同之标的问题

相对于传统合同多以传统之最终商品买卖为交易之标的,电子合同常以知识产权商品为交易标的,故如前述所谓第三类交易标的在电子合同中,即扮演着相当重要之角色。一般人对智慧财产商品之了解,往往将之解释为一种无形资产(Intangible Assets)。而当前大多数国家之做法,系在法律上将无形资产界定为两个主要类别;一类是工业财产,另一类为属于人文艺术创作之著作。③ 对于传统以实体物为合同标的之法律环境而言,民事法之规定有其依附之物理实体及人类感官辨识能力之逻辑,唯今因面对标的之抽象化属性,原有法律规范是否仍足以延续其规范逻辑,殊值得吾人加以重视。④

就现行法律规范观之,合同之标的必须可能、确定、适法与妥当。此

---

① 依德国民法有关意思表示之解释,一般系采所谓基于意思表示受领人客观理解之层面或观点为标准,因此在设置者利用计算机及程序使一项意思表示进入法律交易中之情形,即使设置者对于此一意思表示之内容及其相对人为何人,均毫无所悉,此项利用计算机程序及所为之意思表示,亦得归属于设置者本身而成为意思表示。亦即,数据处理系统之设置者,使相对人足以正当信赖其数据处理系统所完成并传达之意思表示具有拘束力下,即得将之归属于设置者而作为其意思表示。详参杨芳贤:《电子商务契约及其付款之问题》,载《中原财经法学》2000 年第 5 期,第 297—298 页。

② 此名词系由 Manfred Clynes 与 Nathan Kline 于 1960 年所提出,为 cybernetic organism 的缩写,指的是利用辅助器械,来增强人类克服环境的能力。苏健华:《科技未来与人类社会——从 cyborg 概念出发》,嘉义市:南华大学社会学研究所 2003 年版,第 62 页。

③ 工业财产(Industrial Properties)又称产业财产权,通常在欧美系指专利、商标、工业设计(industrial design)等。与智慧财产相关之艺术创作主要包括文学、音乐、摄影、电影、绘画、珠宝、唱片、录音带、多媒体传播等。通常这些智慧财产系透过著作权法(Copyright Law)来加以保护。

④ 周忠海等:《电子商务法新论》,台北:神州出版社 2002 年版,第 54 页。

在以传统最终商品为交易标的,固无问题;然就以传统商品、劳务以外之智慧财产商品为标的之电子合同是否可为相同之解释?则不无疑义。吾人以为,传统民法系以"物"为权利之客体,至于所谓之"物",应系指人身以外,凡人力所能支配并可独立满足人类社会需要之有体物或无体物均属之[①],故在解释上自不以有体物为限,从而以无体物为交易标的之合同,其成立生效似可无异于一般之有体物交易。[②] 然无可讳言者,现行法律规范之执行,均本诸对有体物交易内容之理解所为之规范[③],故适用上难以期待执法者对无体物交易给予特别之考量;如网络上的计算机软件下载合同,究属网络授权合同抑或买卖合同?对当事人之影响甚巨,盖若为买卖合同,则将涉及所有权之移转,而软件授权合同则仅生使用权之授予而已[④];对此,虽有论者以为,无论在传统套装计算机软件或在线商业软件交易中,如消费者所欲交换之经济利益,为无限期、继续使用软件之权利,该软件是否受著作权之保护、是否为民法上之物、究竟系以附载媒体如磁盘片交付或以直接下载传输到消费者计算机方式代替交付,皆无关紧要,换言之,消费者所强调者,乃在于经济利益之获致,并以"合同主要目的"为判断依据,认为此一合同非属授权合同,而应适用、类推适用买卖之规定。[⑤] 唯吾人以为,一般软件交易形式上虽以套装方式交易,然仅生授权之效果而与买卖关系中所生移转财产权之"完全交付"显系有别,而美国之所以会特别针对计算机信息商品之交易研拟专法,正是基于对于此类数字商品之特殊性所给予之必要考量。

早于1988年美国司法界就已发现到这个问题[⑥],以 Micro Data Base Systems, Inc. v. Dharma Systems, Inc. 案为例言[⑦],此涉及一个四方计算机软件合同之债务不履行事件。在系争合同中,MDBS 除同意支付 Dharma12 万 5000 美元的授权费用(License Fee)以取得使用 Dharma 既有软件之授权外,其另行支付同样金额给 Dharma 要求其调整该软件以符合 MD-

---

① 林诚二:《民法总则讲义》(上册),台北:瑞兴图书 1995 年版,第 242—250 页。
② 周忠海等:《电子商务法新论》,台北:神州出版社 2002 年版,第 54—55 页。
③ 陈汝吟:《论因特网上电子契约之法规范暨消费者保护》,台北大学法律学研究所硕士论文,1998,第 85 页。
④ 杨桢:《论电子商务与英美契约法》,《东吴法律学报》,2003, 15 (1):65—66。
⑤ 吴瑾瑜:《网络中无体商品之民法相关问题——以在线递送付费商业计算机软件为例》,载《政大法学评论》,2003 (74):61—107。
⑥ 周忠海等:《电子商务法新论》,台北:神州出版社 2002 年版,第 55—57 页。
⑦ Micro Data Base Systems, Inc. v. Dharma Systems, Inc., Nos.97—2989, 97—3138, 1998 U.S. App. LEXIS 10725, (7th Cir. 1988)。

BS 的需求。① 基本上,这是很典型的计算机软件交易合同,然若细查所谓顾客受领软件之交付应于何阶段完成验收②,即可了解此合同之法律属性。第七巡回上诉法院就本案提出其观点,认为在合同关系中,当买受人受领软件时,若未能告知出卖人其受领之商品有瑕疵,并表达拒绝受领之意思者,将构成受领给付,虽本案之标的为信息软件调整合同,仍有统一商法典(Uniform Commercial Code)中买卖合同之适用。③ 以本案而言,合同之标的会因劳务内容究为原始软件之开发抑或系针对原有软件之调整而有差异,若为"原始软件之开发",我们通常会视为承揽合同,需待工作物之交付,承揽人之义务始完成;然若以"原有软件的调整"为劳务供给之内容,法院认其属性仍应倾向于买卖,故于商品有瑕疵时,买受人便应在受领时即时检验,或于合理之期间内为必要之检查并就瑕疵为主张,否则即构成受领。

基此,即便同样是软件劳务供给合同,法院会因给付义务之差异而将其归类为承揽或买卖等不同属性之法律关系?这种法律属性上之差异,亦生不同的法律评价;而这是当时美国各界关切《统一商法典》增修第 2B 条(Article 2B),及日后不得不单独针对信息软件交易发展出独立之《统一计算机信息交易法》(UCITA)与《统一电子交易法》(UETA)的重要立法背景。④ 事实上,美国针对电子合同中因交易标的之改变所作之调整,应可作为未来在实务上及立法修正上之重要参考。

(四)电子合同之意思表示问题

承前所述,电子合同与传统合同在缔结合同之方式容有不同,在传统合同中,其缔结通常基于当事人之意思,透过口头或书面方式为之,然于电子合同中,并未如传统之缔约方式般有口头交谈或书面签署之过程,是

---

① 授权费用系立刻付款,而服务费用(Professional Services)则系约定三次分期付款。依约定第一期的 5 万元在计划开始时支付,第二期则在修改后的软件送交 MDBS 及 Unisys 工作初步测试(Beta Testing)时才支付。
② 在履约的过程当中,MDBS 先付了第一期款,而且 Dharma 也将 Beta Version 送交 MDBS,让 MDBS 转交 Unisys 以利测试。Unisys 并未向 MDBS 或者 Dharma 表达任何瑕疵之意思。
③ 此与 MDBS 从 Dharma 处购买汽车而支付 2 万元买汽车本身,1000 元给 Dharma 来调整该车以符合 MDBS 之特殊需求应无不同。
④ U.C.I.T.A. 系模仿统一商法典,而实际上一开始即是 U.C.C. 一条新的条文,但起草人了解信息产品之特性不能符合第二章条所规定货品买卖法律规定。故起草人重新命名该法为 U.C.I.T.A. 来表示该法案之范围仅着重在计算机信息取代原先其被称做 2B 之提案,参考 Miller, Fred H. & Ring, Carlyle C., "Article 2B's New Uniform: A Free-Standing Computer Information Transactions Act", http://www.2bguide.com/docs/nuaa.html (visited 2004/8/2);有关其发展见 http://www.ucitaonline.com (visited 2003/05/28);关于 UCITA 的优缺点,可参 Yacobozzi, Ruth J., "Integrating Computer Information Transactions into Commercial Law in a Global Economy: Why UCITA is a Good Approach, but Ultimately Inadequate, and the Treaty Solution", *Syracuse L. & Tech. J.* 2003, (2003):4.

以,当事人间之意思表示于何时成立生效？当事人发出之意思表示,是否有撤回之可能？当事人之意思表示有瑕疵时,应如何处理？均值得吾等加以探讨,以下拟先就电子合同与传统合同之缔约流程异同以图表略示如下,并说明之：

传统合同缔结流程

A. 当事人对话方式

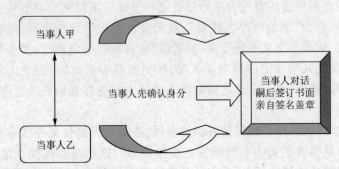

B. 当事人非对话方式

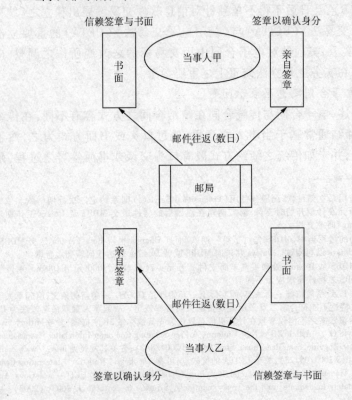

电子合同缔结流程

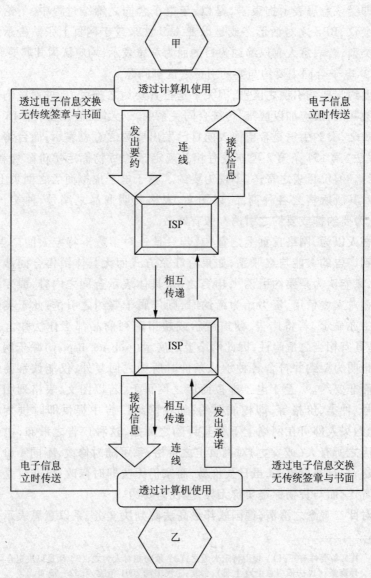

1. 电子合同中之意思表示成立与生效问题
（1）电子合同中之要约意思表示
① 电子合同中要约之意义
在传统合同之缔结中,所谓"要约",系指希望与他人订立合同之意思

表示,为以缔结合同为目的,而唤起相对人承诺之意思表示。① 要约之成立必须具备下列要件:(1) 内容具体确定;(2) 表明经受要约人承诺,要约人即受该意思表示拘束。② 是以,于电子合同之缔结过程中,不论系以视讯会议、BBS之对话形态或是以E-mail往来或于网页上张贴告示之非对话类型,若表意人有以缔约为目的而为意思表示,均应认为其属要约。

② 电子合同中要约与要约引诱之区别问题

要约与要约引诱之区别,因关乎是否具要约之拘束力,进而影响当事人权益甚巨,故应加以区辨;传统合同关系中,于大陆《合同法》第15条中规定观之,要约引诱是希望他人向自己发出要约之意思表示;而台湾地区于《民法》第154条第2项亦设有相关规定,认"货物标定卖价陈列者,视为要约。但价目表之寄送,不视为要约。"然于电子虚拟商店之网页上,若商家对其所贩售之各种商品,以图文、表格列明商品之编号、种类、价格等,究为要约抑或要约之引诱?殊有疑义。

吾人以为,网络首页上之宣传,若只是针对多数不特定人的广告,希望看到广告的人能与之联系,如果有联系方式而无具体销售合同涉及的内容,只能认为是要约引诱③;申言之,未具体表示合同之内容,或表意人注重相对人之信用、资力始为缔约时,则仅属于要约之引诱;此于英美判例法中亦显示,若将广告、橱窗展示或超市陈列商品都当作法律上之要约,是具有相当之危险性,因此网络上之展示(website display)除于网络上特别指明为要约并符合各种承认条件时所为之回复外,仅能认系要约之诱引而非要约。④ 至于电子虚拟商店之网页上,若以图文、表格列明商品之编号、种类、价格等,即构成要约;如在网络广告中提供即时供货的服务,让购买人即可在网络上下载其订购之商品,这种广告之散布,电子虚拟商店之所有人(或卖主)对网页上之价格,系可随时修改,不同于价目表之寄送,一旦寄发出去,虽日久价易,商家仍无法即时修改;已非仅是价目表之寄送,而与货物标定卖价无异,应视为要约。⑤

对此二观念之澄清,德国联邦最高法院判决实务,系以意思表示受领

---

① 其具备要件有三:(1) 须由特定人为之;(2) 须向相对人为之;(3) 须足以决定合同之必要之点。孙森焱:《民法债编总论》(上册),台北:三民书局2001年版,第52—53页。
② 大陆《合同法》第14条之规定,亦同其要旨。
③ 朱宁先、朱成化、朱顺先:《电子商务的电子合同及其法律思考》,载《管理科学》2003年第5期,第94页。
④ 详参杨桢:"论电子商务与英美契约法",《东吴法律学报》,2003,15(1):50—51。参阅孙森焱:《民法债编总论》(上册),台北:三民书局2001年版,第50—52页。
⑤ 详参黄茂荣:《电子商务契约的一些法律问题》,载《植根杂志》,2000,16(6):17。

人,本诚信原则,并参酌交易惯例,可得理解之客观意义为准①;台湾地区未于《电子签章法》中设有相关之规定,吾等或可参考公约草案初稿第 11 条之规定②,对经由数据电文传送缔约之提议,若非向一个或一个以上之特定人提出,而仅系供信息系统使用人查询之用者,除当事人表示愿受该意思表示拘束者外,视为要约之引诱,当事人间不生要约之拘束力。此规定与两岸民法之概念相类似,唯更能描述出电子合同之特性,应可供台湾地区未来立法之参考。

③ 电子合同中要约之生效时点

于传统合同缔结时,关于要约之方法,台湾地区民法并未设有特别规定,一般仅将其区分为对话与非对话之要约,而在其生效时点上设有不同之规定。准此,在电子合同之缔结过程中,只需该电子讯息在客观上为具有法效意思之表示意思、表示行为,且为本人所发出者,则应认其属要约之一种。就此,大陆《合同法》有相关之规定值得重视,其虽未特别针对要约之方式加以明定,然依该法第 10 条规定,当事人订立合同,有书面形式、口头形式和其他形式以观③,合同之形式包括"电子数据交换与电子邮件",是以,当讯息系经由自动化计算机系统或电子代理人所发送时,法律虽未明文规定其法律效果,然在解释上,当该程序系由其所有人或使用人所设计或控制时,则仍可认为该行为人或使用人有使其发出具法效意思之表示行为的意图或真意;准此,该自动发送之要约应与其所有人或使用人自己之行为无异,从而应认具有法律上之效力。台湾地区《电子签章法》中并未就此设有相关规定,究应如何厘清当事人间因使用电子交易系统行为所生之权利义务关系,以确立责任与风险分配,实有赖进一步立法。

④ 电子合同中要约之生效时点

在传统合同之缔结过程中,行为时间的认定相当重要,常被用来作为法律责任归属的基准④;于电子合同中,要约生效与否应如何认定?遇有纠纷时,应如何确认该电子讯息出处之归属?实值得加以探讨。

---

① 详参杨芳贤:《电子商务契约及其付款之问题》,载《中原财经法学》2000 年第 5 期,第 316 页。

② 详参 Preliminary draft convention on [international] contracts concluded or evidenced by data messages Article 11; "United Nations Commission on International Trade Law Working Group on Electronic Commerce", Forty-third session, A/CN.9/WG.IV/WP.108 (2004).

③ 唯有论者以为其他形式是公证、鉴证、批准、登记等形式;江平:《中华人民共和国合同法精解》,中国政法大学出版社 1999 年版,第 11 页。

④ 见"行政院"研考会研拟:《电子签章法草案总说明》,1999 年 12 月 23 日"行政院"第 2061 次院会审议通过。

在传统合同中,就意思表示之生效时点,依台湾地区民法之规定于对话之意思表示,其生效时点应于相对人客观上可得了解之时[1];至于非对话之意思表示[2],本法采用受信主义,以其通知达到相对人时发生效力。另依通说及判例之见解[3],此所谓之"到达",应系指意思表示到达相对人之支配范围内,相对人随时可得了解其内容之状态而言。

准此,于缔结电子合同时,若系透过视讯会议或 BBS 等网际网络之对话方式来缔约时,因其仍具有传统面对面或声音传递之特色,在解释上应采了解主义,于相对人了解时发生效力,此于认定上较无问题;至于,以 E-mail 往来或于网页上张贴告示之非对话类型,应如何解释要约生效之时点,则容生疑义。就电子文件之发出时点言,大陆《合同法》第 16 条第 2 款中规定,"采用数据电文形式订立合同,收件人指明特定系统接收数据电文的,该数据电文进入该特定系统的时间,视为到达时间;未指明特定系统的,该数据电文进入收件人的任何系统的首次时间,视为到达时间。"台湾地区则参考《联合国电子商务模范法》[4],于《电子签章法》第 7 条中规定,"除当事人另有约定或行政机关另有公告者外,电子文件以其'进入'发文者无法控制信息系统之时间为发文时间",此具体针对电子文件之发文时点设有规定,应认为系针对电子交易所设之特别规定。[5] 至于大陆于 2004 年 8 月通过的《电子签名法》第 11 条,亦采相同之立法模式;此外,该法第 10 条亦规定,如当事人约定数据电文需经确认收讫者,其收受时间之确认,则以发件人收到收件人的收讫确认时,视为已经收到。

至于涉及纠纷时,应如何去判断电子讯息的出处或归属?对此,《联合国电子商务模范法》中设有明确之规范[6];此外,新加坡电子交易法主要

---

[1] 参台湾地区民法第 94 条之立法理由:"谨按向对话人之意思表示,应取了解主义,自相对人了解其意思表示时,即生效力是属当然之事。唯对话不以见面为必要,如电话等虽非见面,亦不碍其为对话。"

[2] 参台湾地区民法第 95 条之立法理由:"谨按非对话人之意思表示,即向不直接通知之相对人为意思表示是也。此种表示,应于何时发生效力,立法例有表意主义、发信主义、受信主义(到达主义)、了解主义四种。本法采用受信主义,以其通知达到相对人时发生效力。"

[3] 参 54 年台上字第 952 号判例:"所谓达到,系仅使相对人已居于可了解之地位为已足,亦不问相对人之阅读与否,该通知即可发生为意思表示之效力。"58 年台上字第 715 号判例:"所谓达到,系指意思表示达到相对人之支配范围,置于相对人随时可了解其内容之客观之状态而言。"

[4] UNCITRAL Model Law on Electronic Commerce Article 15, Time and place of dispatch and receipt of data messages.

[5] 对此规定容或解释为特别规定优先于民法之适用,抑或解释为对民法规定之补充,以说明"到达"之认定基准。

[6] UNCITRAL Model Law on Electronic Commerce Article 13, Attribution of data messages.

系依循下列原则处理①:(1)当发文者确有寄送电子纪录时,则应认定该纪录为发文者所有;(2)虽该纪录不是直接由其寄发时,于特殊情形下该讯息仍将被视同(deemed)为发文者所寄发②;(3)当这些纪录被视同为发文人所寄送时,则收文者可以认为该纪录系发文者故意寄送;唯该收文者明知或可得而知其传输有错误发生时,则无此规定之适用。对此,两岸均未立法未加以规范,然证诸前述新加坡立法,显见攸关当事人权益,值得两岸未来立法之参考,以避免当事人间之纠纷。

(2) 电子合同中之承诺意思表示

① 电子合同中承诺之意义

在传统合同之缔结中,所谓"承诺"系指受要约人同意要约的意思表示,以与要约人订立合同为目的,所为之意思表示。唯承诺尚需具备下列之要件,始成立生效:(1)承诺需由受领要约人为之;(2)承诺需向要约人为之;(3)承诺之内容需与要约之内容一致;(4)承诺需于承诺期限内为之。是以,于电子合同之缔结中,不论系以视讯会议、BBS之对话形态或是以 E-mail 往来或于网页上张贴告示之非对话类型,若受要约人有以同意要约为目的而为意思表示,均应认为其属承诺。

此外,于传统合同之缔结方式中,尚有所谓"意思实现"之情形,系指依习惯或事件之性质承诺无须通知者,此时,只要有可认为承诺之事实时,合同即可成立。③ 此与大陆《合同法》第 26 条规定,"承诺不需通知的,根据交易习惯或者要约的要求作出承诺时生效。"相若;实际上承认,承诺可以通过表示以外的方式,如实际行为作出的可能性。④ 至于意思实现中之"有可认为承诺之事实",是否须以行为人主观上有承诺之认识为必要?学说上容有争议,有论者以为,不以行为人主观上有承诺之认识为必要,只要依"有可认为承诺之事实"推断出有此效果意思即可⑤;亦有论者以

---

① 本份法案可参阅 http://agcvldb4.agc.gov.sg(visited 2004/8/02)。
② (1) 如果是透过发文者所授权之人或其设计的信息系统所寄发,或该信息系统自动(operate automatically)寄发时,(2) 若收文者系依原有双方决定采用之程序来确认是否该纪录为发文者所寄发时,或者(3) 收文者之所以能收受数据讯息,系透过发文者特别安排之第三者,而该第三者得以透过发文者所采之方法来发现该电子纪录是否为其所有时。唯在(2)和(3)之情形下,如收文者明知或可得而知(knows or ought to have known)该纪录并非发文者所寄发,或者该收文者业已收受通知,表示若其将该电子纪录视同为发文者所寄送系错误时,(2)和(3)之规定并不适用。
③ 详请参台湾地区民法第 169 条。
④ 杜颖:《电子合同的效力问题探析》,载《黑龙江省政法管理干部学院学报》2002 年第 3 期,第 28 页。
⑤ 孙森焱:《民法债编总论》(上册),台北:三民书局 2001 年版,第 27—29 页。

为,仍应以行为人主观上有承诺之认识为必要,仅无须相对人为受领之意思表示而已。① 基此,在电子交易合同中,若有某甲利用电子邮件寄送一套电子书予乙,乙在开启信箱阅览后,知悉为某甲之商品并开启所附之电子书档案,同时将其下载并储存至他处作为使用之准备②;此时,乙下载该电子书并储存至他处之事实,应可认为系有"可认为承诺之事实",合同基意思实现而成立。若系利用在线订位系统订购火车票、电影票等,当该机构为订票人预留票券时,则其已为履行合同之准备行为,亦属意思实现,合同应可成立。

② 电子合同中承诺之方法

在传统合同之缔结中,承诺既系以订立合同为目的所为之意思表示,故应以意思表示为之,至于其方法以明示或默示为之者均无不可。③ 唯在电子交易合同中,双方当事人可能会有因传输错误或要约人无法确知相对人是否已为承诺之困扰,故有立法者认为应以"明示同意"为妥;④ 然就台湾地区现行法中并未设有类似之规定,吾人以为,除要约人有特别约定者外,不论以明示或默示方法为之,原则上皆属有效;唯尚需具承诺之主观意思,至于承诺意思之有无,则应依客观事实认定之。至于应以何种方式为之,除要约人有特别约定者外,应无限制,故当要约系以电子讯息为之时,承诺人并不一定要以电子讯息方式为之。

---

① 王泽鉴:《基本理论——债之发生》,台北:三民书局2001年版,第146—147页。

② 有时候为了确定使用者的真正意思,或为了让使用者陈述一些事实数据,以便于决定是或不是、或如何采取下一个步骤,网站会使用点选式的点选按钮或窗体,如果使用者依照网站上的指示,依照自己的意思点选某一个特定按钮或选项,网站就认为使用者已经同意选项所代表的约定或使用者已经作了窗体上所记载之陈述,见钟明通:《网际网络法律入门》,台北:月旦出版社1999年版,第148页。

③ 凡是以语言、文字或当事人了解的符号或其他表示方法,直接表示意思者皆为明示的意思表示。若以各种方法间接表示意思者,为默示意思表示,然此与单纯沉默不同,盖前者为一种积极的行为,只是经由表示其他意思的方式,或以事实行为表示某种特定的效果意思,如在饮食店中取食菜肴食用;而后者仅系单纯的不作为,并非间接的意思表示,是以原则上不生法律效果,唯依当事人约定或在习惯上有时亦将沉默视为或解释为"意思表示",如当事人约定对于要约不于一定期间内拒绝者,视为同意(承诺)。施启扬:《民法总则》,台北:三民书局2000年版,第235—236页。

④ 故于美国《统一商法典》第2B条草案,以"明示同意"(Manifesting Assent)作为计算机信息合同成立之有效要件,所谓明示同意,需要可观要件判断,在欠缺无法得知相对人承诺下,则需符合下列条件:(1)可鉴证过去有表示显然同意的记录;(2)对授权合同同意的一方,曾参与确定表示同意的行为;(3)上述表彰显然同意的记录,已经显然提供或表现被授权人已经承诺;(4)授权人仅是保留该信息、记录,虽未反对,尚难谓为显然同意。杜维武:《美国关于信息授权与管辖权相关问题(上)》,载《法令月刊》,1999,50(3):19。

③ 电子合同中迟到之承诺

在传统合同之缔结中,依台湾地区《民法》第159条之规定,承诺之通知,按其传达方法,依通常情形在相当时间内可达到而迟到者,要约人应向相对人即发迟到之通知;要约人怠于为此通知者,则其承诺视为未迟到。此规定于电子合同中亦然,如因网络服务业者之主机故障、邮件服务器故障、计算机当机或遭病毒侵入皆可能造成承诺之迟到,此时要约人应向相对人即发迟到之通知,若怠于为之者视为未迟到。

④ 电子合同中承诺之生效

关于承诺生效之时点,就理论上约有以下四种理论:(1)宣告理论(declaration theory):据此理论,当相对人书写其承诺时,承诺即生效力;(2)发信主义(dispatch theory):即为信箱原则(mailbox rule),承诺于相对人将其承诺传送于要约人时,发生效力①;(3)到达主义(receipt theory):即为受信主义,需要约人收到承诺时,承诺始生效力;(4)了解主义(information theory):于要约人了解承诺存在时,承诺始生效力。②

在传统合同中,就意思表示之生效时点,依台湾地区民法之规定于对话之意思表示,其生效时点应于相对人客观上可得了解之时;至于非对话之意思表示,本法采用受信主义,以其通知达到相对人时发生效力;而大陆《合同法》第26条之规定,亦以到达要约人时,发生效力。基此,在电子合同之缔结中,若以视讯会议、BBS之对话形态以相对人客观上可得了解之时,在认定上较无问题;然若以E-mail往来或于网页上张贴告示之非对话类型时,应如何解释承诺生效之时点,即生疑义。大陆《合同法》除于第26条中规定,采用数据电文形式,缔结合同时,承诺到达之时点依第16条第2款之规定,应满足下列要件:(1)承诺的意思表示已进入要约人的支配范围;(2)承诺的意思表示已脱离承诺人的支配范围;(3)承诺的意思表示处于可期待要约人能了解的状态;故在电子合同的情况,承诺生效的

---

① 例如,在美国传统以书面交换为前提之统一商法典(U.C.C.)规范中,原则上系以承诺之发送时点为准,亦即采"发信主义";此际,一如以邮寄方式发出承诺,以投入邮筒之时点为承诺发生效力之时点,且认为意思表示已于此时合致而成立合同,此乃所谓之"信箱法则"(Mailbox Rule)。在邮件信箱规则下,相互合意的成立时期,原则上即为承诺之发信时点。例如,以邮件发出承诺之情形,于投至邮筒时,该承诺即发生效力。另可参吴嘉士:《电子商务法导论》,台北:学林文化2003年版,第453—456页。关于信箱原则之理论基础介绍,可参Watnick, Valerie, "The Electronic Formation of Contracts and the Common Law Mailbox Rule", *Baylor L. Rev.* 2004, (56): 175。

② Viscasillas, del Pilar Perales, "Recent Development Relation to CISG: Contract Conclusion under CISG", *J. L. & Com.* 1997, (16): 315.

时间应指承诺到达要约人在虚拟空间的支配范围,如电子信箱、计算机系统等;①另,依《合同法》第 33 条之规定:"当事人采用信件、数据电文等形式订立合同的,可以在合同成立之前要求签订确认书。"而以签订确认书时,合同成立。在实践中,电子合同订立过程中要约、承诺以及确认书签订生效日期采取的安全措施是数字时间戳,这是一个经加密后形成的凭证文档,以该机构收到文件的时间为依据,电子合同成立的时间以承诺到达生效或签订确认书的数字时间戳为准。②

　　此于台湾地区《电子签章法》制定时,参酌《联合国电子商务模范法》之规定③,于第 7 条中明文,除当事人另有约定或行政机关另有公告者外,电子文件以下列时间为其收文时间。(1) 如收文者已指定收受电子文件之信息系统者,以电子文件"进入"该信息系统之时间为收文时间;电子文件如送至非收文者指定之信息系统者,以收文者"取出"电子文件之时间为收文时间。(2) 收文者未指定收受电子文件之信息系统者,以电子文件"进入"收文者信息系统之时间为收文时间。④ 此规定以收文者是否已指定收受电子文件之信息系统为区别标准,具体针对电子文件之收文时点设有规定,应认为系电子交易之特别规定。至于大陆之《电子签名法》,则以该法第 10 条及第 11 条为其规范依据。

　　至于电子合同之缔约过程中,因与传统交易之方式有异,在交易技术之发展,常设有"再确认"之机制,其法律属性及法律效果为何? 亦生争议。对此,台湾地区并未于电子签章法中加以规定,是否得援引民事法之相关规定? 若是,应如何认解释? 于兹略以图示并说明如下:

---

① 如果对"到达"做如此解释,则不论是对纸面合同,还是对电子合同,不论在现实空间,还是在虚拟空间,到达主义能够最恰当地在要约人与承诺人间分配风险。在纸面合同的情况,承诺生效的时间应指承诺到达要约人在现实空间的支配范围,如信箱、收发室、办公室、亲属等。刘颖:《论电子合同成立的时间与地点》,载《武汉大学学报(社会科学版)》2002 年第 6 期,第 655 页。

② 孙在友、苏哲:《论电子合同的法律效力》,载《天津工业大学学报》2002 年第 6 期,第 49 页。

③ UNCITRAL Model Law on Electronic Commerce Article 15, Time and place of dispatch and receipt of data messages.

④ 有论者以为此种立法方式似乎兼采英美法之发信主义与台湾地区法之到达主义,反而对相对人不公,见冯震宇、黄珍盈、张南熏:《从美国电子交易法制论台湾地区电子签章法之立法》,载《政大法学评论》,2002 (71):232。

企业经营者先为要约

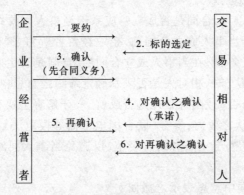

企业经营者先为要约之引诱

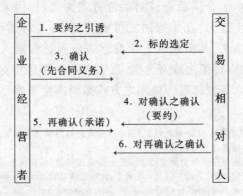

于兹试就当事人间之交易流程,分析如下:(1)若企业经营者先为"要约"消费者对交易标的为选定行为后,企业经营者往往会透过确认机制发出"确认",由消费者对该确认为"承诺",基要约承诺意思表示合致,而成立合同关系;此时企业经营者将复行"再确认",消费者对此可能之表示有二:(A)若消费者欲缔约并确认该交易,则合同生效;(B)若消费者因不欲缔约而不确认该交易,则合同关系不生效力。(2)若企业经营者仅为"要约之引诱",于消费者为"标的选定"行为后,企业经营者往往会"确认"消费者是否欲缔约,若消费者欲缔结合同则可对企业经营者发出"要约"①,企业经营者将可透过"再确认"机制并为"承诺",使合同关系基意思表示合致而成立;对此,消费者可能之表示有二:(A)若消费者欲缔

---

① 此时,若消费者表示不欲缔约,因自始无要约之存在,并不生要约拘束力亦不成立合同。

约并确认该交易,则合同生效;(B)若消费者因不欲缔约而不确认该交易,则合同关系不生效力。

基此,吾人以为,合同是否成立?应系于当事人间要约承诺意思表示之合致与否。于当事人成立合同前,企业经营者所为之"确认"①,解释上得认系先合同义务。② 在当事人成立合同后,合同是否生效?则系于企业经营者为"再确认"时,相对人是否表示确定缔约之意思;唯此究系为确认解除权之行使与否③或随意条件是否成就?④ 于解释上实有疑义。故吾人以为,实应对确认之效力,参考《联合国电子商务模范法》⑤或新加坡之电子交易法之规定⑥,于立法时纳入规范,以避免当事人间对合同生效力认定上之争议。

2. 电子合同中意思表示之撤回

承前所述,在传统合同中,若依台湾地区《民法》对意思表示生效时点之认定标准,当电子合同系透过对话之方式为之时,因采了解主义,于相对人了解时,即生效力,几无撤回之可能。至于,非对话意思表示之效力发生,因采受信主义,从而表意人于意思表示到达相对人之前,均得撤回其意思表示。盖以传统之邮寄为例,意思表示于到达相对人之前,原得以电话、电报或传真等较邮寄为快速之方式撤回该意思表示。⑦ 若依此解释

---

① 依《德国民法典》第312e条之规定,企业经营者负有提供交易相对人于发出订单前辨认和修改合同内容输入错误之技术措施。

② 企业经营者是否应提供消费者预防或更正错误之机会,虽台湾地区并未就此设有规定,于解释上或可回归诚信原则"先合同义务"之概念;此亦证诸联合国 Preliminary draft convention on [international] contracts concluded or evidenced by data messages Article 14 (16); "United Nations Commission on International Trade Law Working Group on Electronic Commerce", Forty-third session, A/CN.9/WG.IV/WP.108 (2004)。

③ 关于企业经营者再确认之机制,或可评价为确认是否行使解除权,惟其究为法定或意定解除权之行使,则生疑义;(1)如认属法定解除权之行使,虽得以《消费者保护法》第19条为据,然该法仅适用B2C之消费关系中,若非B2C之消费关系时,尚难谓其有该规定之适用;(2)如为意定解除权,于B2C之消费关系中此意定解除权与法定解除权生竞合关系,若消费者确认缔约时,是否属意定解除权之抛弃,对法定解除权之影响又为何?则生疑义。

④ 关于企业经营者之再确认机制,解释上或可评价为对合同附一随意条件之附款;所谓"随意条件",系指依当事人一方的意思决定其成就与否的条件。参施启扬:《民法总则》,台北:三民书局2000年版,第268页。

⑤ UNCITRAL Model Law on Electronic Commerce Article 14, Acknowledgement of receipt.

⑥ 即(1)当双方未就确认之型式(form)加以约定时,则收文者任何行为通知方式(communication)均能满足其要求;(2)当电子纪录必须取决于该确认之收受时(conditional upon receipt of the acknowledge),则除非已收受该确认,否则应视同尚未寄送;(3)当合同未有上述条件(condition)且在预定的期间内也未收受任何确认时,或者未在合理期间内收受前述之确认时,则发文者可以要求相对人在合理期间内配合,且要求若未在收到通知后配合办理,则发文者得视同该电子纪录从未寄送。本份法案可参阅 http://agcvldb4.agc.gov.sg (visited 2004/08/02)。

⑦ 此于大陆《合同法》第17条与27条之规定亦然。

于电子合同中,发文与收文者双方之讯息,若瞬间即至对方当事人处,在解释上几无撤回之可能。①

唯有学理认为,于不甚侵害合同当事人间衡平之情形下,意思表示之撤回、变更仍得被承认②,例如,当事人间特别约定,要约得于相对人为承诺前撤回或变更之;再者,电子技术与软件系统是由人设计并实现的,在软件设计方面,应参照传统交易方式,依据合同法从实际出发,相应修改设计软件,使参与人有由于失误而可以反悔的机制,以保护双方当事人合法的权益。③ 再就意思表示之发出与收受时点认定上,依台湾地区《电子签章法》第7条第1项之规定,除当事人另有约定或行政机关另有公告者外,电子文件以其进入发文者无法控制信息系统之时间为发文时间;参酌该条第2项之规定,当电子文件进入发文者无法控制信息系统后,发文者于下述情形下,仍有可能撤回其意思表示:(1) 如收文者已指定收受电子文件之信息系统者,以电子文件"尚未进入"该信息系统前;电子文件如送至非收文者指定之信息系统者,以收文者"尚未取出"电子文件前。(2) 如收文者未指定收受电子文件之信息系统者,以电子文件"尚未进入"收文者信息系统前,发文者仍可撤回其意思表示。

故此,本书以为,在不妨碍当前传统合同理论之适用前提下,参酌前述学说之精神,先本诸合同自由之原则来解释,而于当事人未特别约定时才回归信息科技本身之即时性的考虑,似乎是较佳选择。④ 而台湾地区《电子签章法》第7条之规定,亦与此精神契合;这种规范架构正系本诸合同自由来因应科技变迁的做法,准此,不论事先当事人之意思,或是当事人对于信息系统之选择,都已成为建构规范的主要依据。

3. 电子合同中意思表示之瑕疵

在传统合同之缔结中,若当事人有错误、被诈欺与胁迫之情事时,当事人得撤销其意思表示?在电子合同之缔结过程中,若有类此之情事时,其法律效果为何?当系另一值得探讨之问题。所谓"错误",乃表意人为

---

① 周忠海等:《电子商务法新论》,台北:神州出版社2002年版,第66页。
② 从电子讯息交换旨在迅速处理交易事务之目的观之,允许撤回、变更之期间,应依其内容等等而做更严格之限制;见野村丰弘:《受奖注的EDI化的法的诸题的概要》,载《法とコンピュータ》,1995 (13): 38—39。
③ 朱宁先、朱成化、朱顺先:《电子商务的电子合同及其法律思考》,载《管理科学》2003年第5期,第94—95页。
④ 实务上,有以合同限制之。如个人计算机银行业务服务合同范本第6条中即规定:"电子讯息系由计算机自动处理,客户发出电子讯息传送至银行后,即不得撤回、撤销或修改。"详黄茂荣:《电子商务契约的一些法律问题》,载《植根杂志》,2000, 16 (6): 13。

意思表示时，因认识不正确或欠缺认识，以致内心的效果与外部之表示行为不一致之情形；依德国学说究其原因，可分为输入有误、使用有误之数据、系统或程序错误及传送错误①；原则上，以台湾地区法律为例，基于错误而为电子讯息之发文者，应可依台湾地区《民法》第 88 条有关错误之规定来主张撤销；唯基于交易安全之考量，于意思表示之内容有错误或若表意人知其情事即不为该意思表示者，若表意人欲将其意思表示撤销时，须以其错误或不知其情事，非由表意人自己之过失者为限，始得为之；至于，因传达人或传达机关传达不实者，亦得适用台湾地区《民法》第 89 条之规定，撤销之。②

在实务运作经验上，为避免发生此问题，科技界乃试图建构较不易发生错误之系统。例如，透过对话方盒要求再确认之机制，或由收受电子信息者发送确认信息之电子邮件予发文人，作为电子讯息内容之最终确认方式，以解决当事人间之争议。唯此种安排对于未来法律之影响如何？则值得进一步观察，以欧洲联盟有关电子商务之指令为例，便已注意到此问题，并特别规定，当事业经营者系透过网页从事交易时，若该网页之使用者只能依机械式行为选择同意与否，而不能享有其他选择，则合同将因① 使用者对事业经营者发出同意，② 事业经营者针对此同意以电子方式发出确认信息，③ 使用者收受该确认信息，④ 以其后使用者受领确认信息经再度确认，始成立。③ 准此，欧盟明确表示，当事业经营者已尽其努力避免错误时，若使用者仍因本身之疏失而陷于错误，则基于衡平之理念，实不应由业者承担风险。④ 基本上，这种规范架构系在权衡科技发展及交易安全后所做出的交易风险重行分配，其对电子交易之经营者课以确认当事人真意的较积极义务⑤，此更于《公约草案初稿》第 14 条中更进一步规定，若未提供预防或更正之机会，则该合同关系尚不成立生效；然此意味着得恣意任由使用者本身之轻忽，导致交易因错误之主张，而陷于不确

---

① 杨芳贤：《电子商务契约及其付款之问题》，载《中原财经法学》2000 年第 5 期，第 306 页。
② 参阅台湾地区民法第 88 条与第 89 条之立法理由；详黄茂荣：《电子商务契约的一些法律问题》，载《植根杂志》，2000，16（6）：10。
③ 电子商取引の法整備をめざすEU 指令案の公表，1999（NBL 659）：5。
④ Baistrocchi, Pablo Asbo, "Liability of Intermediary Service Providers in the EU Directive on Electronic Commerce", *Santa Clara Computer & High Tech. L. J.* 2002, (19)：111.
⑤ Preliminary draft convention on [international] contracts concluded or evidenced by data messages Article 14.；"United Nations Commission on International Trade Law Working Group on Electronic Commerce", Forty-third session, A/CN. 9/WG. IV/WP. 108 (2004)。

定。至于当电子合同之缔结系导因于被诈欺或胁迫时,其问题之本质与传统依文书或口头为意思表示之情形相同,吾人以为,亦应认其得依台湾地区《民法》第92条之规定为撤销。

综上,关于意思表示之瑕疵,得否撤销之问题,由于台湾地区《电子签章法》中并未设有特别之规定,是否可以直接适用民法之相关规定?实有赖进一步之说明或立法,以厘清当事人间之权利义务关系并确立责任与风险分配。

(五)结语

电子化交易之发展,对于传统合同法制之影响已然具体浮现,而有待吾等进一步的去调整相关法制以为因应。整体言之,电子合同法制显然正朝向"促进具社会容许性之行为"(the promotion of socially acceptable behavior)的方向发展[1],这种发展特色所呈现出者,将是人类互信与多元价值的尊重,系基道德规范所呈现出之共识,应系过去法律发展鲜少经历者。[2] 就电子合同所涉问题而言,本文以当事人、标的及意思表示为主轴的探讨,试图显现出电子化环境所带来的影响。

先就当事人部分言,远距的互动首先挑战了人类传统彼此辨识对方的经验,动摇了传统法制所建构出的交易当事人互信基础,从而也带动了电子签章法制的诞生,一方面透过数字签章作为辨认当事人身份之表征,他方面则透过凭证机构来对签章之真正性加以认证,以达保护交易当事人之目的。此外,如何在交易安全之维护与限制行为人或无行为能力人之保护间权衡的问题,吾等虽能在民法之相关规定中找到一些探讨方向,然较完善之处理方式仍应进一步调适相关民事法规,以为规范。至于,自动化计算机系统与电子代理之应用,乃电子合同之缔结过程中使用计算机软硬件之必然结果,而如何跳脱出传统以"人"为基础的代理概念,发展出以预先设计之"自动"系统或具人工智能之"自主"系统为内容,并以之为界定当事人间之权义及责任归属之依据,正是近来国际间法制之重要发展,而值得吾人加以借镜并立法因应者。

至于交易标的所涉问题部分,因智慧财产商品异于传统商品及服务之本质,促使传统贸易的外围法制均呈现涵括不足之现象,这其中又以如何满足确认交易标的及当事人间之权益关系界定问题为最;对此,美国司

---

[1] 见 Denning, Dorothy E & Lin, Herbert S eds., *Rights and Responsibilities of Participants in Networked Communities*, Washington: National Academy Press, 1994, pp.25—30。

[2] D. Casey, Jeff Magenau, "A Hybrid Model of Self-Regulation and Governmental Regulation of Electronic Commerce Timothy", *Santa Clara Computer & High Tech. L. J.* 2002, (19): 1.

法实务以类同于买卖合同关系来处理计算机软件研发之做法,以及新修《统一计算机信息交易法》(UCITA)与《统一电子交易法》(UETA)之提出①,除印证了国际社会对如何规范信息交易标的之不确定性外,更提供我们值得借镜之法制调整经验。

最后,以意思表示为核心之探讨,所衍生之要约与要约引诱之区别、非对话意思表示之生效时点认定与意思表示合致过程中之撤回与撤销等问题,乃前揭本文所涵括之重点。原则上,本书以为,欲完善之电子合同法制,就重要的基础性问题应透过立法加以规范,除对要约与承诺之成立生效时点之认定外,如何去判断电子信息的出处或归属?如何评价"再确认"之机制?均有待法律给予更明确的规范。台湾地区《电子签章法》中虽有相关之规定,然容有不足,从而较佳之处理方式仍应就电子合同环境所赖之私法体系,作一较全面的检讨与补充为是。

综上,以国际间的发展趋势而言,虽有论者以为,电子合同所涉之法律问题,并非电子环境所特有的,而系传统合同关系中都会遭遇的问题;是以,应否针对电子合同提出新公约,容有质疑。② 但从科技的发展与实际交易经验中,我们发现"功能等同"之概念,实不足以涵括所有新兴之法律问题,是以,联合国国际贸易法律委员会提出新公约草案,试图解决此种新的缔约方式所新生之法律问题。而此国际之发展趋势正逐步影响各国之立法态度,我们亦可从美国 UCC2B、UCITA、UETA 与 E-SIGN 之立法过程中③,加以验证。相对于此,台湾地区之因应则嫌不足,除于《电子签章法》设有部分规定外,另于消费者保护法中将因特网之交易纳入访问买卖之类型中,以保障消费者之权益④;然就本节所提出之问题,虽或可类推适用民法相关之规定,实难获得周延的解决。⑤ 吾人以为,面对此一新兴科技法律争议,立法者与执法者虽不宜采取冒进的激进行为,或可利用"停看听(wait and see)"的策略,只要不是太大的社会伤害,何妨停一下、

---

① 台湾地区学者关于 UCITA 及 UETA 之介绍,可参吴嘉生:《电子商务法导论》,台北:学林文化 2003 年版,第 466—469 页。

② "United Nations Commission on International Trade Law Working Group on Electronic Commerce", Thirty-ninth session, A/CN.9/WG.IV/WP.96. (2002).

③ 杨桢:《论电子商务与英美契约法》,载《东吴法律学报》,2003,15(1):41—72;冯震宇、黄珍盈、张南熏:"从美国电子交易法制论我国电子签章法之立法",载《政大法学评论》,2002(71):185—236。

④ 详参《消费者保护法》第 2 条第 1 项第 10 款之规定。

⑤ 如自动化计算机系统与电子代理之应用问题、以计算机软件为电子契约交易标的之问题、非对话意思表示之生效时点认定等。

看一下、给其他的解决方案有解决的机会,让新的科技法制有反应新文化、新价值观的机会①;同时,藉由停看听,促使国际之规范内国化,藉以达到建构完善法律制度之基础。

---

① 范建得:《新工业革命时代的科技法制》,收录于《知识经济与法制改造研讨会专辑》,台北:元照出版社2002年版,第50—52页。

5 论电子交易的管辖

前 言

信息时代的来临,开拓了人类活动的视野,也开展了人际关系的新境界,而于人类穿越时空限制,在虚拟空间(virtual space)彼此攀谈、互动甚至交易之际,传统世界的人性与争议,亦随之而生。正如同在工业革命发生后,我们看到了法律如何自生活过程的价值冲突中发展成形,乃至制度化;也看到了贸易打开国际族群交流之门后,国际性法制的发展;方今,信息科技带来了跨国与社会虚拟化冲击,将会是另一次革命性的挑战,盖此除延续自国家地域管辖争议之挑战外,各国法制因应尚未确定及族群价值观的差异,均加深了管辖冲突的必然性。

以电子合同之民事管辖课题言,于传统电子数据交换交易中,当事人间往往透过前置协议来决定双方之通讯设备与网域或网址名称,从而形成以协议来取得管辖基础,此虽较无争议,唯自律安排应否加以承认,则成问题。此外,随网络交易机制之发展逐渐取代人工操作及信息商品发展到成为电子交易之标的时,合同当事人之认定与合同成立生效时点之确定,往往也成为影响管辖决定因素之重要课题。目前,台湾地区虽已开始就这类问题有所着墨,但如何自既有相关理论出发,掌握信息社会之特殊性,进而提出可能解决方向的全面性思考,似乎仍有其努力之空间,故吾人拟针对涉外电子合同之民事管辖课题之缘起及其可能之解决方案为一探讨。

5.1 概说传统管辖权

一、管辖权的意义与类型

所谓管辖权,应具有两个层次的意义,其一为国际私法上的管辖权,即按照国际私法的原则决定该事件应由何国家具有管辖权,这种管辖权就是"国际管辖权"(international jurisdiction)①,这应属于国际私法的问题;另一方面,则是在该案件决定由何国法院管辖后,该案件应由哪一个法院管辖的问题,这种管辖权就好似"国内管辖权"(local jurisdiction)②,这应属国内民事诉讼法的问题。

基此,就管辖的类型言,可大概分为国际管辖权与国内管辖权两大范畴,而就前者言,其类型可区分为:(1)领域管辖(属地管辖)、国籍管辖(属人管辖)、保护性原则管辖与普遍原则管辖;(2)直接管辖与间接管辖。而后者则可区别为:(1)民事管辖与刑事管辖;(2)法定管辖、合意管辖、应诉管辖与指定管辖;(3)土地管辖、职务管辖与事务管辖;(4)专属管辖与任意管辖。③

通常各国对其国内管辖的实行多设有规定,却少有对于国际管辖权加以规定者,而国际间也还没有超国家的国际私法或国际管辖权的超国家规定,从而在面临国际管辖问题时,往往必须由每一国家按照自己认为合目的或适当的规定,来决定自己国家的法院是否拥有国际管辖权。④ 以传统对合同相关事项的管辖为例,大多便是通过当事人间的约定来决定,然而于国际民事管辖权未有明文的前提下,该合意是否应被承认、是否涉及剥夺国家的审判权均已成为问题,也挑战着传统的管辖原则。

二、传统确立国际管辖权的基本原则

基本上,各国决定国际民事管辖权的传统原则如下:

(一) 属人管辖原则(The Principle of Personal Jurisdiction)

此原则是以当事人的国籍作为法院行使管辖权的主要按照依据。因为国籍是个人基于忠顺关系而隶属于某国家的地位,个人因与一国家连结而具备国民资格⑤,一国法院根据当事人的国内国籍以确定管辖权,应有其正当性。

(二) 属地管辖原则(The Principle of Territorial Jurisdiction)

属地管辖,也叫地域管辖或领土管辖,是指在涉外民、商事案件中,如当事人、诉讼标的物,或者该法律关系、法律事实发生在该国,除享有司法

---

① 苏远成:《国际私法》,台北:五南出版社1990年版,第124页。
② 刘铁铮、陈荣传:《国际私法论》,台北:三民书局1998年版,第688页。
③ 蔡馥如:《网络管辖之研究》,台北大学法律研究所硕士论文,1999,第17—21页。
④ 陈启垂:《民事诉讼之国际管辖权》,载《法学丛刊》,1997(166):75。
⑤ 郭豫珍:《涉外民事之国际管辖权的确定》,台北:政治大学法律研究所硕士论文,1994,第155—166页。

豁免者外,该国法院对其有管辖权。至于确定属地管辖的因素,主要可分为三类:(1) 当事人的住所、居所或临时所在地;(2) 诉讼标的物所在地或被告财产所在地;(3) 行为地,如于合同关系的法律适用中的债务履行地。

(三) 合意管辖原则(Agreed Jurisdiction)

此原则主要是在民、商事领域,尤其是在国际贸易关系中常被援用的原则,合同当事人可以按照意思自主的原则来选择管辖法院,此即为合意或意定管辖之谓;但本原则的适用应仅限于非专属管辖的事件,并且只有在法律允许当事人以合意选择法院时,当事人才适用。

(四) 专属管辖(Exclusive Jurisdiction)

基本上,专属管辖是前三个原则的例外,凡属于专属管辖的事项,将排除前三个原则的适用。一般而言,专属管辖的事项多涉及一国的利益或公共秩序;适用专属管辖的事项至少包括:不动产诉讼、知识产权诉讼、婚姻家庭和继承诉讼等。

5.2 电子交易中管辖权问题的缘起与冲击

传统所谓民事管辖权,应具有两个层次的意义,其一为国际私法上之管辖权,即依国际私法之原则决定该事件应由何国加以管辖,此等管辖权为"国际管辖权"(international jurisdiction)[1],应属国际私法之问题;另一方面,则是于该案件决定由何国法院管辖后,该案件应由哪一个法院管辖之问题,此等管辖权即为"国内管辖权"(local jurisdiction)[2],此应属内国民事诉讼法之问题。

通常各国对其内国管辖多设有规定,却鲜少有对于国际管辖权加以规定,从而在面临国际民事管辖问题时,往往须由每一国家依自己认为合目的或适当之规定,来决定自己国家之法院是否拥有国际管辖权。[3] 以涉外民事合同相关事项之管辖为例,大多透过当事人间的约定来决定,然而于国际民事管辖权未有明文之前提下,该合意是否应被承认?其是否涉及剥夺国家之审判权?均已成为问题,也挑战着传统之管辖原则。

面对信息时代之来临,我们发现网际网络最独特之地方,应在其跨越

---

[1] 苏远成:《国际私法》,台北:五南出版社1990年版,第124页。
[2] 刘铁铮、陈荣传:《国际私法论》,台北:三民书局1998年版,第688页。
[3] 陈启垂:《民事诉讼之国际管辖权》,载《法学丛刊》,1997 (166): 75。

国界之国际属性,然而究竟网络上的虚拟空间是否仍能按国家主权之概念来建构其管辖原则？容有争议。吾人以为,网络空间的全球性使司法管辖区域的界限变得模糊,要在一种性质完全不同之空间中去划定地域疆界,将会是传统管辖理论所面临的第一个难题。盖在一般真实世界的立法都具有地域性(territoriality),而这个地域也就是立法国主权效力所及的领域①,它的管辖区域是明确而有具体物理空间之地理边界；然而网络是一种虚拟的空间,本身并无边界可言,它是一种全球性的系统,无法划分为不同之区域,而即便加以划分亦毫无意义,因其为虚拟无形且无法存有实际的对应关系,我们所能看见的只是一些有形的计算机终端机及连结之线路。是以,真实世界的国家主权概念,是否能及于虚拟世界,不无疑义。再者,网络空间的不确定性,使传统的管辖基础理论产生动摇,在传统管辖理论中,当事人之住所、国籍、财产、行为等之所以能成为取得管辖之基础,系因其与某管辖区域存有物理空间上之联系,如行为之发生地、国籍之归属地、当事人之意思等；然而,一旦将这些因素应用到网络空间,它们与管辖区域所存有物理空间之关联性顿时丧失,我们无法在网络中找到实体住所或有形财产。

面对此冲击,究应如何加以解决？有学者主张网络空间的"非中心性倾向"②和"新主权理论"③,试图从根本上否定国家司法主权,甚至认为虚拟世界具独立之主权概念,此说主要在强调网络空间的新颖性与独特性,对现实的国家权力则持怀疑之态度,并担心国家权力介入会妨碍网络的自由发展,试图以网络自律管理来取代传统的法院管辖。相对于此,亦有学者主张国家主权应可及于虚拟世界,并认为网际网络仅为一种媒介,其运用不影响国家主权行使之依据,反而有利于真实世界中既有价值之实现。④ 本书以为,新原则之确立固为未来努力的目标,而如何就现有之体

---

① 陈荣传：《虚拟世界的真实主权》,载《月旦法学杂志》, 2001 (77): 154。
② 所谓"非中心的倾向",系因网际网络上每一台计算机都可以作为其他计算机之服务器,故在此空间中没有中心没有集权,所有计算机都是平等的。是以,每个网络使用者只须服从它的 ISP,而 ISP 之间则透过协议的方式,以协调统一各自的规则,至于其间发生的冲突便交由 ISP 以仲裁者的身份解决之。王德全：《试论 Internet 案件的司法管辖权》,载《中外法学》1998 年第 2 期,第 28 页。
③ 而"新主权理论"则认为,网络空间中正在形成一个新的全球性市民社会 (Global Civic Society),这个社会有自己的组织形态、价值标准与规范,完全脱离政府而拥有自治的权力。Frederich, Howard H., "Computer Networks and the Emergence of Global Civic Society: The Case of the Association for Progressive Communication", http://www.eff.org/Activism/global_civil_soc_networks.paper (visited 2004/8/06).
④ 详参陈荣传：《虚拟世界的真实主权》,载《月旦法学杂志》, 2001 (77): 155—158。

制及国际间的发展,去探求解决之道,更是当务之急。准此,就涉外电子合同之民事管辖而言,当前国际贸易合同领域中为解决电子数据交换所生管辖问题,而发展出的贸易惯例或自治协议,诚有其价值。① 其次,国际间相关理论之发展也同样能提供给我们参考之空间;例如,美国法律学会(American Law Institute)就全面性电子商务发展需求,及配合信息商品买卖所尝试新修之美国统一计算机信息交易法(Uniform Computer Information Transactions Act;U.C.I.T.A.),便就管辖之处理,提出一些极具参考价值的规定。以下谨就国际间之相关立法与理论之发展略述如次。

5.3 国际立法与美国实务的发展

一、国际立法的状况

就国际立法之现况言,国际上关于国际民事纠纷管辖权分配,常以多边或双边条约、协议规范之。② 是以,在国际交易进入电子化后,接续着传统透过多边与双边条约、协议,来解决国际管辖权纷争之倾向,目前已有相关的国际条约或双边条约、协议正持续发展中,而这其中又以海牙国际私法会议之态度(The Hague Conference on Private International Law)最为积极。③

该会议先于1999年10月提出了《民商事管辖权及外国判决之承认与执行公约草案初稿》(Preliminary Draft Convention on Jurisdiction and Foreign Judgments in Civil and Commercial Matters;以下简称为《海牙公约草案》)④,嗣于2001年6月加以修正。⑤ 此《草案》仍系遵循1968年《布鲁

---

① 日本即采此态度,即在涉及合同之场合先遵循当事人约定,见道恒内正人:《サイバースペースと国际私法——准据法及び国际裁判管辖问题》(特集コンピュータ ネットワークと法)ジュリスト,1997(1117):63。

② 例如1940年3月19日之《蒙特维地亚国际民法公约》,其第56条第1项规定:"对人之请求权,应向构成诉讼标的法律行为之准据法国的法官,提起之。"1962年海牙之《荷兰与德意志联邦共和国关于相互承认与执行民商事司法判决及其他执行之条约》等,均对管辖权之归属加以规定。

③ 其早于1971年即曾制定一项关于承认与执行外国民事与商事判决公约,惟其并未对管辖权作出直接的规定,且该公约仅三个国家参与尚不具普遍性。

④ Preliminary Draft Convention on Jurisdiction and Foreign Judgments in Civil and Commercial Matters. Oct.30, 1999, http://www.hcch.net/e/conventions/draft36e.html (visited 2004/8/06).

⑤ Summary of the Outcome of the Discussion in Commission II of the First Part of the Diplomatic Conference, June 6—20, 2001, Jurisdiction and Foreign Judgments in Civil and Commercial Matters, 19th Session, http://www.hcch.net/e/workprog/jdgm.html (visited 2004/8/06).

塞尔公约》①(Brussels Convention)及 1988 年《卢加诺公约》②(Lugano Convention)中,关于管辖决定及外国判决之承认与执行等基本原则。目前,《公约草案》虽尚未定案,但已对于未来解决管辖之问题提供一良好之指引;细究之,其主要之目的在于解决管辖权归属及缔约国法院所为判决之承认及其执行力之问题。首先,对管辖权之归属,分就普通管辖及特别管辖设有规定;再者,对国际贸易合同所特别重视之合意管辖部分,依《公约草案》第 4 条之规定,原则上系允许缔约双方当事人得经由合意,就一定法律关系而生之争议,约定管辖之法院③;唯此合意管辖之约定,须以书面形式为之,或经由其他足以传递能供日后参考用信息之其他任何沟通媒介为之,或本诸系争当事人皆遵循之惯例,抑或本诸系争当事人应知或可得而知,且为系争特定贸易或商务领域中,同性质合同当事人皆遵循之惯例者,始生效力。④

至于,因合同关系所生之特别管辖部分⑤,依据《公约草案》之规定,会因系争事务为商品或劳务之供给而有别。原则上,在涉及商品供给时,以货物之全部或一部供给地之法院享有管辖权;在劳务之提供时,以其劳务之全部或一部提供地之法院享有管辖权;至于在商品与劳务混合供应时,则以其主义务(principal obligation)之全部或一部履行地之法院享有管辖权。唯对于企业与消费者间所签订之合同(B2C Contract)而生之管辖权

---

① Brussels Convention on Jurisdiction and Enforcement of Judgments in Civil and Commercial Matters, Sept. 27, 1968, 1990 O. J. (C 189) 2.

② Lugano Convention on Jurisdiction and Enforcement of Judgments in Civil and Commercial Matters, Sept. 16, 1988, 1988 O. J. (L 319)9,重印于 28 I. L. M. 620 (1989)。

③ 且此合意管辖,除当事人另有约定外,具有排他效力。Preliminary Draft Convention on Jurisdiction and Foreign Judgments in Civil and Commercial Matters Article 4.1.

④ Preliminary Draft Convention on Jurisdiction and Foreign Judgments in Civil and Commercial Matters Article 4 : "An agreement within the meaning of paragraph 1 shall be valid as to form, if it was entered into or confirmed—a) in writing; b) by any other means of communication which renders information accessible so as to be usable for subsequent reference; c) in accordance with a usage which is regularly observed by the parties; d) in accordance with a usage of which the parties were or ought to have been aware and which is regularly observed by parties to contracts of the same nature in the particular trade or commerce concerned."

⑤ Preliminary Draft Convention on Jurisdiction and Foreign Judgments in Civil and Commercial Matters Article 6. : "A plaintiff may bring an action in contract in the courts of a State in which—a) in matters relating to the supply of goods, the goods were supplied in whole or in part; b) in matters relating to the provision of services, the services were provided in whole or in part; c) in matters relating both to the supply of goods and the provision of services, performance of the principal obligation took place in whole or in part."

问题,应如何解决?则是当前《海牙公约草案》最具争议之问题。① 由于当初在制定《海牙公约》第 7 条时,并未将电子商务相关争议纳入考量,故该条是否得以适用到 B2C 之电子商务合同中? 于 2001 年 6 月之《公约草案》修订过程中,虽有部分与会代表团提出不同的替代提案,然因所持观点分歧②,导致公约难以定案。③ 在经过冗长的讨论仍不得结果之情况下,不得不决定先就商业交易中所涉《选择法庭协议公约(Convention on Choice of Court Agreements)》提出草案④,故于 2002 年 4 月 24 日之第 19 次大会(19th Session of the Conference)中决议成立非正式工作小组(Informal Working Group),针对此先提出草案,交 2003 年 4 月 1—3 日间召开之总务及政策特别委员会(The Special Commission of General Affairs and Policy)讨论;此《选择法庭协议公约草案》业经前述总务政策特别委员会于 2004 年 5 月间正式确认。⑤

在 2003 年 3 月非正式工作小组提出的《选择法庭协议公约草案》中,除延续着海牙公约草案重视当事人自主之精神外,更进一步透过列举无效之立法建议,来强化合意管辖之效力。⑥ 相对于原有之海牙公约草案,

---

① 就消费者间所签订之合同之管辖权规定略谓:原告得于其住所地所在国之法院提起诉讼,若(a) 原告起诉之请求所根据之合同系与被告在该国所进行之交易或专业活动有关或被告之行为或活动导向该国(direct to the State),特别是被告经由公开之方式招揽生意;及(b) 消费者采取了在该国订约所必要之步骤者。Preliminary Draft Convention on Jurisdiction and Foreign Judgments in Civil and Commercial Matters Article 7.

② Summary of the Outcome of the Discussion in Commission II of the First Part of the Diplomatic Conference, June 6—20, 2001, Jurisdiction and Foreign Judgments in Civil and Commercial Matters, 19th Session, http://www.hcch.net/e/workprog/jdgm.html (visited 2004/8/06).

③ 就此,若透过第 19 届大会前后之发展来观察,可知其结论认为应倾向扩大既有公约草案解释涵盖及于电子商务或网络所涉相关问题;http://www.hcch.net/e/workprog/jdgm.html (visited 2004/8/06).

④ 依据前述 2003 年 4 月间之总务及政策会议决议文显示,《法庭协议公约(Convention on Choice of Court Agreements)》除在适用范围上局限于商务事项外,更特别强调仅在处理选择法庭地之协议,不影响嗣后其他与管辖及外国判断之承认与执行相关事宜。http://www.hcch.net/e/workprog/jdgm.html (visited 2004/8/06).

⑤ 其详情参见, Preliminary Document No. 8 of March 23 (corrected) for the attention of Special Commission of April 2003 on General Affairs and Policy of the Conference; available at http://www.hcch.net/e/workprog/jdgm.html (visited 2004/8/06).

⑥ Working Group Draft Text On Choice of Court Agreements Article 5 Priority of the chosen court: "If the parties have entered into an exclusive choice of court agreement, a court in a Contracting State other than the State of the chosen court shall decline jurisdiction or suspend proceedings unless"— a) that court finds that the agreement is null and void, inoperative or incapable of being performed; b) the parties are habitually resident in that Contracting State and all other elements relevant to the dispute and the relationship of the parties, other than the choice of court agreement, are connected with that Contracting State; or c) the chosen court has declined jurisdiction. http://www.hcch.net/e/workprog/jdgm.html (visited 2004/8/06).

选择法庭协议公约草案于第四条中以成立要件之方式来叙述当事人合意之效力,认为交易当事人若存有关于专属管辖法院(exclusive choice of court)之选择时,原则上应赋予该法庭所属缔约国享有管辖权;此外,在解释当事人之合意是否为专属管辖法院之选择时,依《选择法庭协议公约草案》第2条第1项(b)款之规定,指定任何一缔约国之法院(courts in a Contracting State)或某特定管辖法院(a specific court)之安排,除有其他约定者外,均应被视为专属管辖之约定(shall be deemed to be exclusive unless the parties have provided otherwise);由此之规定,可见对当事人合同自主精神的重视与强调。至于在2004年5月完成的修正草案中,则将本条改列于第5条并删除第4项外,其内容大致相同。①

二、美国管辖权理论与司法实务的发展

在当前国际间的发展趋势中,除了前述配合国际贸易电子化发展之需求所做的国际性努力外,美国之经验应是最值得大家关注的发展。

(一) 美国确立管辖权的传统理论

司法管辖的有效行使,影响当事人的权益很显著,由于美国各法域规定不同,因此其司法管辖权基础,也可能不同;但其中民事事件主要可分为对人诉讼(jurisdiction in personal)②、对物诉讼(jurisdiction in rem)③与准对物诉讼(jurisdiction quasi in rem)。④ 在此试就其司法管辖基础的理论,略述如下:

1. 美国对人诉讼的司法管辖权基础

通常,美国法院在审理一个案件的实体部分前,须先对该案件取得管辖权。而所谓的"对人管辖权",是指一案件在法院审理前,法院所享有对于被告加以管辖的权利。而法院的管辖权有二:(1) 普通管辖权(general jurisdiction)与(2) 特别管辖权(specific jurisdiction)。前者,是基于其在法庭地的"出现"(presence)而取得;而所谓的"出现"则必须检视被告的行

---

① http://www.hcch.net/e/workprog/jdgm.html (visited 2004/8/06)。
② 所谓对人诉讼,是指法院有权决定当事人间权利义务,而且法院的决定仅在当事人之间发生效力;一般来说,法院是基于对当事人于法院内送达或其他宪法上所规定足够的接触,而主张有管辖权。陈隆修:《国际私法管辖权评述》,台北:五南出版社1986年版,第102页。
③ 所谓对物诉讼,是指当诉讼标的物位于法院管辖区域内时,法院可对该物主张对物诉讼的管辖权,而其效力及于全世界。陈隆修:《国际私法管辖权评述》,台北:五南出版社1986年版,第103页。
④ 所谓准对物诉讼,是指法院决定特定人对于法院管辖区域内特定物的权利。陈隆修:《国际私法管辖权评述》,台北:五南出版社1986年版,第106页。

为是否是"持续且有系统"在法庭地出现后加以决定。① 一旦法院对被告取得一般管辖权,则法院得就被告的任何诉讼主张管辖权。此外,即便被告并没有"出现"于法庭地,只要法院享有特别管辖权,该被告仍有接受该法庭地管辖的可能。至于在决定该特别管辖权是否存在时,法院仍须审视被告、法庭地及该诉讼行为间的关系。

(1) 传统"权力及到庭"的架构

简而言之,法院只能基于"权力及到庭"的基础对被告行使管辖权。因此,如果没有被告的到庭或被告的财产,法院无法对该被告行使管辖权。按照美国一般的管辖法则,法院对于居住于法庭地内的被告享有管辖权,这是在著名的 Pennoyer v. Neff② 中所确立的法则。

(2) 对人管辖权的发展

为满足美国《宪法》第 14 修正案中"正当程序条款"的要求,各州也分别制定了所谓的"长手臂法"(Long-Arm statutes),其中主要允许"地方法院对发生在当地的诉因(cause of action),而且该诉因足以影响当地原告的情况下,对被告可主张管辖权"。③ 这样,法院即使在被告没有出现于法庭地的情况下,只要依据对人管辖权,或者被告与法庭地间的接触符合该法的规定,该法庭地便可以对非住民的被告主张专属管辖权,而不致违宪。

在此之前,法院在对非住民的被告主张专属管辖之前,往往会要求被告"实体出现"(physical presence)在法庭地,然而当"实体出现"的要件难以满足社会变化应有的弹性时,将"对人管辖权"的分析扩张到包含"最低接触"在内的观念自然成为必要。以下则是美国法院就此方面所树立的一些较重要的原则:

① 最低接触原则(The Minimum Contact Test)

所谓"最低接触原则"是指"凡于该法院的管辖领域内,具有正当化的

---

① 见 International Shoe Co. v. State of Washington, 326 US 310 (1945)。

② Pennoyer v. Neff, 95 U.S. p.714 (1878)。该案中原告涉及了一件由加州的被告向其请求回复被告位于奥勒冈州的土地的诉讼。最高法院以奥勒冈法院欠缺对 Neff 的"对人管辖权"为由,予以确定。在该案中,Field 法官,制定了一项所谓"全或无"(all or nothing)之标准,也就是一州无疑地对其主权所及领域内的人民享有管辖权,而对于非其领域内人民则没有。因此,法院认为,系争当事人 Neff 既非奥勒冈州居民,又并非志愿在奥勒冈法院出庭,因此,奥勒冈法院对其并没有管辖权。虽然此原则看似简单,但实际上其管辖权最终的决定,仍须受宪法正当程序条款的限制。

③ Byasse, William S, "Jurisdiction of Cyberspace: Applying Real World Precedent To The Virtual Community", *Wake Forest L. Rev.* 1995, (30): pp.197,201。

相关活动,其受法律的保护及拘束,并且在符合正当法律程序①的要求时,应认为已具有最低接触的情况,从而认为法院对之具有属人管辖权。"这个原则在1945年的 International Shoe Co. v. Washington② 一案中确立,并作为美国管辖理论中的基本原则。至于应该如何适用与解释"最低接触原则",则产生出了所谓的二分原则:

通常管辖原则:以该非本州岛居民的行为是否"持续且有系统"为判断标准;如果该非本州岛住民的商业组织与本州岛法院管辖区域有"实质关连",不论其是否与本州岛管辖区域有接触,都可受本州岛法院的管辖。

特别管辖原则:决定行为是否与本州岛法院管辖区域有"接触"的要件包括:a. 先前双方的协商;b. 预期的未来结果;c. 合同的文字;d. 双方实际的交易过程。但同时也须考量该非本州岛住民可合理预见是否会受该州法院管辖。

② 公平与实质正义的原则

本原则应是肇始于 Milliken v. Meyer③ 一案,而在经过包括前述 International Shoes 在内案件的援用后,当法院采用最低接触原则时,公平原则已进一步发展成为对最低接触原则再予以补充修正的要件。④ 换而言之,被告的行为除了必须充足最低接触原则的要件外,法院还须考量传统上合理的诉讼送达与实质的正义原则。⑤ 这也是宪法所保障的正当法律程序所要求的。按照这个原则,判断非本州岛住民与本州岛法院管辖区域

---

① 所谓"正当法律程序条款"(due process),又称为"正当程序条款",为美国联邦宪法第5修正案第一款所阐明, the Due Process was declared to be a source of constitutional limits on adjudicative jurisdiction in a case invalidatimg a judgment both entered and collaterally attacked before the Fourteenth Amendment was ratified. See, e.g., Philip Kurland,另见, Pennoyer v. Neff, 95 U.S. p.714 (1877)。

② International Shoe Co. v. Washington, 326 U.S. 310 (1945)。该案判决理由中阐明,属人管辖权的有无,传统上是基于事实上的权限而定之,本案除了具备合理、公平的信赖及合乎实质正义的概念外,并符合正当法律程序的要求,在被告与法庭地间具有最低接触的情况下,法院判定对本案具有属人管辖权。见 Breen, Michele N., "Personal Jurisdiction And The Internet: 'Shoehorning' Cyberspace Into International Shoe", *Seton Hall Const. L. J.* 1998:(8):764—765。

③ Milliken v. Meyer, 311 U.S. pp.457,463 (1940)。

④ Meyer, Christopher W., "World Web Advertising: Personal Jurisdiction Around The Whole Wild World", *Wash & Lee L. Rev.* 1997, (54):1269。

⑤ 依据 Milliken 案法院的见解,所谓的实质正义(Substantial Justice)原则,意指"若正当程序原则所要求对人的判决,没有出现在法庭地领域内,但如果被告与本法庭地领域有特定的最低接触以维持本诉讼,就不会侵害公平与实质正义的传统要求。如果被告与本州法院管辖区域的接触目的不清楚,则须被告'能预见'其行为与本州法院管辖区域有关连,而被告的行为是有目的的指引(direct)其行为到本州法院管辖区域"时,本州法院仍可对的管辖。See World—Wild Volkswagen Corp. v. Woodson, 444 U.S. (1980)。

虽有"充分的接触"后,仍然需要按照下列因素作出衡平考量:(A)由被告举证,本州岛法院管辖是否公平?(B)本州岛法院管辖区域解决本案争端是否有利益?(C)原告可否因本州岛法院管辖获得便利性与有效性的利益?(D)跨州司法系统是否会因此获得最有效解决争端的利益?(E)在促进实质社会政策上可否分享本州岛法院管辖的利益?①

③ 商业流程理论(Stream of Commercial Theory)

"商业流程理论"通常被大量使用于商品责任诉讼的案例中,例如某产品在他州制造或销售,但导致本州岛人民损害的情形。但在 Asahi 这个重要案例中,②主审法官则认为"仅预见商业流程仍不足以主张本州岛法院管辖,被告须有其他行为可特别指引到本州岛法院管辖才行"。换而言之,本理论的适用仍然必须受制于最低接触原则。

④ 长臂管辖法

长手臂法(Long-Arm Statutes),又称为"单一法规管辖原则"(Single-Act Statutes)③,主要是指一个州得就属人管辖权通过立法让该州的法院取得对域外被告的属人管辖权。最早采用该原则并制订法律是1965年伊利诺州法律修正案第110节第17条第1项规定,该条文规定如下:"任何人,无论是否为该州公民,或有无住、居所于该州,只要本人或其他代理人有下列行为,并足以构成诉因者,该州法院对之即有管辖权:(A)于法院地内进行的任何商业活动;(B)于法院地内进行的任何侵权行为;(C)在法院地拥有、使用或占有任何不动产。"④

2. 美国对物及准对物诉讼的司法管辖基础

对物及准对物诉讼的司法管辖基础,是法院在对于法院管辖区域内的对象所有人欠缺对人诉讼的司法管辖权时,法院具有决定该物的归属

---

① 参阅杜维武:《美国关于信息授权与管辖权相关问题(下)》,载《法令月刊》,1999,50(4):30。整体而言之,美国法院管辖权有无之判断,仍系采事实导向而以个案认定之方法,期能求取公平正义之落实。Gray, Tricia Leigh, "Minimum Contacts in Cyberspace: The Classic Jurisdiction Analysis in a New Setting", *J. High Tech. L.* 2002, (1):85.

② Asahi Metal Industry, Co. v. Superior Court of California, 480 U.S. (1987). 唯亦有不同的判决见解,例如 Inset Systems, Inc. v. Instruciton Set, Inc. 一案,即认为通过网络及其免付费电话,会使该州住民看到,一旦将广告置于网络上,该广告即持续对任何网络使用者提供。因此应认为 ISP 是有目的将其经营业务的行为置于本州,所以应受其管辖。

③ CASENOTE: Bensusan Restaurant Corp. v. King: An Erroneous Application of Personal Jurisdiction Law to Internet-based Contacts (Using the Reasonableness Test to Ensure Fair Assertions of Personal Jurisdiction Based on Cyberspace Contacts), Pace L. Rev. 1998, (19):149.

④ 郭豫珍:《涉外民事之国际管辖权的确定》,政治大学法律研究所硕士论文,1994,第185页。

或其他法律关系的特定权力。传统上,对物诉讼与准对物诉讼的唯一管辖基础,是该物必须位于法院管辖区域内;换而言之,仅需该物置于法院管辖区域内,法院即有决定该物的归属或其他法律关系的权力,至于法院对非居民的当事人是否有对人诉讼的司法管辖权,则在所不问。①

(二) 美国网络管辖的司法实践

在美国法上,虽然有上述原则可供参考、灵活适用,但实际上仍然会遇到诸多困难,例如在适用前述最低接触原则时,网际网络上的商业活动便很难满足确定要约地、承诺地或其他商业活动地等"行为地"的要求。以下就目前已有的相关案例及理论见解加以评介:

在1996年以前,诉讼事件中的原告通常都会到被告所在地提起诉讼,但在网络普及后,被告则越来越需要至原告的法庭地应讯。通常法院就一个非住民被告的法庭地交易或许有蓄意损害原告的行为,都可以合法对被告行使对人管辖权。但当系争案件的事实不完全符合上述情形时,是否仍可对被告主张管辖权?容有疑义,以下试就相关网络案件评述如下:

1. 对人管辖的相关实务见解

基本上,美国相关实务见解认为,现代科技的进步使得人们可以延伸其交易的空间,因此,我们不能仅以被告未实际出现在法庭地而使其规避该法院的管辖。虽然地域的出现经常可以加强被告与该州的潜在关系并增大预见在该地被诉的合理性,但不可避免的,现今的情况已非昔比,愈来愈多的交易是通过电子通讯所完成,而进行交易时并不一定会出现在该州。②

美国实务见解还认为,在目前电子通讯时代,一州的域外管辖权系必要的,法院并持续将焦点放在被告与法庭地间的关联,是否符合公平正义的要求。对此,法院倾向于认为,只要被告的行为是有意的形成自己与法庭地间的关连,则不论其是利用何种媒介来从事这些行为,对人管辖权原则应可扩张适用在非住民的被告上。

另一个重要的问题是电子链接是否可以作为一州对于非住民被告行

---

① 蔡馥如:《网络管辖之研究》,台北大学法律研究所硕士论文,1999,第44页。
② Etienne-Cummings, Shamita, "CASENOTE: Vanishing Boundaries: Extending The Long-Arm Statute Into Cyberspace CompuServe Incorporated v. Patterson, 89 F. 3d 1257 (6th Cir. 1996)", *S. Ill. U. L. J.* 1997, (22): 217.

使对人管辖权的依据所在。在 CompuServe Inc. v. Patterson[①] 案中,第六巡回法院创下一个先例。在该案中,虽然被告与俄亥俄州间的接触几乎都只是通过电子通讯的传送来进行,法院仍然认为俄亥俄州南区地方法院得对非住民的被告主张对人管辖权。[②]

此判决确立了由下载人、销售合同、电子邮件、传统邮件及软件销售所组成的电子链接(electronic link)足以满足法院对不具住民身份的被告行使对人管辖权的基础,而不再坚持要求被告必须出现在法庭地。经过第六巡回法院这个判决,法院将能对在法庭地藉由网络获得经济利益的人行使对人管辖。换而言之,对人管辖权是可以扩张到那些藉由网络在法庭地进行交易的个人或企业。

近来,也有一些判决设法解决是否应将对人管辖权扩张适用到非住民的被告上的争点。由于这些被告实际上与法庭地相距很远,而且所有与法庭地的接触几乎是通过电子行为来完成;当实体出现之要件不再需要时,被告的意图,即其有目的地将其行为指向法庭地的住民时,就变得很重要。虽然,大多数法院要求被告与法庭地的接触须以网络以外的方式作出[③],但第六巡回法院则前瞻的将对人管辖权扩大到被告与法庭地间的电子接触。

后来在 Pres-Kap, Inc. v. System One, Direct Assess, Inc.[④] 与 Bensusan Restaurant Corporation v. King[⑤] 两个案件中,都与 CompuServe 之主张近似,都是强调被告透过网络行销、贩售商品或服务或其他计算机上线服务

[①] 1991 年,CompuServe 与 Patterson 透过"Shareware Registration Agreement"(SRA)签署一合约,在其网站上销售 Patterson 的网络浏览软件。双方间的生意关系从 1991 年维持到 1994 年。在 1993 年,CompuServe 也开始在其网站上广告及销售浏览软件。Patterson 控告 CompuServe 侵害其商标,因 CompuServe 的软件及名称与其近似。在 Patterson 的控告后,虽然 CompuServe 改变了其软件名称,Patterson 仍要求 CompuServe 负赔偿的责任。为了响应此诉讼,CompuServe 在俄州南区地区法院提起确认判决的诉讼,主张其并没有侵害 Patterson 的商标并且俄州法院对 Patterson 享有专属管辖权,因为本案的争端是起自 SRA,而 SRA 是受俄州法律管辖。然而 Patterson 则主张俄州无管辖权应驳回本案。

[②] 在本案的诉讼过程中,俄州南区地区法院接受了 Patterson 的主张,认为依 Patterson 与 CompuServe 的电子邮件来主张对人管辖权实太过薄弱。法院还采信了 Patterson 所提证物来证明其从未到访过俄州。在上诉时,第六巡回法院认为,Patterson 的接触及自俄州获得利益的事实,已使被告可合理预期其可能在俄州被诉。在这个先例下,第六巡回法院同意判决俄州南区地方法院应得对该与俄州的几乎全通过电子通讯接触的被告主张对人管辖权。

[③] CompuServe, 89 F. 3d p. 1268.

[④] Pres-Kap, Inc. v. System One, Direct Assess, Inc., 636 So. 2d pp. 1351—1353 (Fla. Dist. Ct. App. 1994).

[⑤] Bensusan Restaurant Corporation v. King, 937 F. Supp. pp. 295—300 (S. D. N. Y. 1996).

时,侵害原告商标的案例。其次,Panavision International v. Toppen[①]案,则是关于纽约居民向佛州公司租用计算机资料服务的争端,该案中,虽然所有的被告都使用网际网络或网际网络形态的计算机联机来从事日常的商业运作,但因每个被告与法院连结的方式不同,因此,每个法院对于最后是否要扩大对人管辖权的决定也有不同的看法。但判决结果则大多与前述 International Shoe 及其后的 CompuServe 所建立的对人管辖权准则相符合。[②] 在此试简要就这几个影响重大的案件分别评介如下:

(1) Pres-Kap, Inc. v. System One, Direct Assess, Inc.

在1994年,第三上诉法院在本案中,判决佛州法院对纽约州的被告(该被告是登录于一实体位在佛州迈阿密的计算机资料系统)主张对人管辖权是错误的判决。缘于1989年,原告 System One 与被告 Pres-Kap 签订了一个租赁合同,允许 Pres-Kap 的线上资料可以进入飞机、旅馆及汽车的预约,以收取月租费。System One 是纽约分公司,除了负责处理所有的后续系统问题外,还签署该合同。虽然,Pres-Kap 及被告的前身 Eastern Airlines 先前所存在的合同条款中载明佛州法院为合意管辖法院,而且该租用合同应适用佛州法律规定,但现存的合同对此并无任何约定。因此,当 Pres-Kap 以系统障碍为由,不再支付月租费时,System One 在佛州地方法院提起违约的诉讼。佛州法院认为租用合同及一些日常连线数据库的行为已符合了佛州法律所规定的"有目的获益及可预期性"及正当程序的要件。[③] 但上诉法院推翻了地方法院的见解。在应用正当程序的分析时,上诉法院发现 Pres-Kap 与佛州法院的接触仅为:(A) 邮寄所有上线费用至 System One 位于迈阿密的地址及(B) 提供上线的计算机资料系统架设在迈阿密。法院认为无论是单独或结合的接触,都不足以将此"以纽约州为主的交易转变成佛州的交易,而使被告在交易变质时,可以预期到其可能

[①] Panavision International v. Toppen, 938 F. Supp. p.616 (C. D. Cal. 1996).

[②] Resuscitation Technologies. , Inc. v. Continental Health Care Corp. , (U. S. Dist. 1997),也采用此见解。

在此案中,被告在印第安纳州并无财产或在之前曾从事任何的商业行为。所以在主张欠缺对人管辖权而该诉不成立的论证中,Continental 强调其与 RTI 是通过 RTI 存在的网站进行交易。地方法院认为,虽然 RTI 是经由网站开始与 Continental 接触,但此行为已经产生了预期的利益并完成了交易行为。经数月持续且频繁地发生电子接触,所以指出双方当事人是有意图在印第安纳州发生交易。因此,"毫无疑问地 Continental 已超过其家乡而在印第安纳州做生意",而使 Continental 在印第安纳州应讯是合理的。

[③] Pres-Kap, Inc. v. System One, Direct Assess, Inc. , 636 So. 2d p. 1353. (Fla. Dist. Ct. App. 1994)

在佛州被诉"。①

CompuServe 与 Pers-Kap 的不同在于 Patterson 不像 Pres-Kap,它是积极与法庭地接触。但可以肯定的是,Patterson 向 CompuServe 要求在其网站上行销其软件,并充分了解到 CompuServe 及提供其产品的计算机网络是架设在俄亥俄州。相反的,Pres-Kap 的争点是由租赁合同而生,而该合同是通过 System Ones 的纽约代表所签署。虽然二案中的被告都有从该案中的法庭地获得财务上利益的事实,但是,Pres-Kap 的商业交易行为是在其自己居住的州内。因此,Pres-Kap 一案并没有与 CompuServe 相冲突,应该认为该法院正确地限制了佛州法院的长手臂法的效力。

(2) Bensusan Restaurant Corporation v. King②

在 Pres-Kap 判决后两年,纽约州南区地方法院也因欠缺对人管辖权,而驳回了对密苏里州被告的诉讼(本案被告是使用网络被控商标侵权及不公平竞争)。这就是 Bensusan Restaurant Corporation v. King 案,本案法院在判决书中指出,单纯在网际网络上存在的网站,并不足以让法院据得对被告主张对人管辖权。③ 在该案中,被告像其他很多公司、大学及个人一样,架设了一个网站并允许任何可以发现该网站的人进入,它仅仅是通知那些愿意进入其网站的潜在客户及其商品,但被告并没有以电子方式传送其广告予任何人;所以,法院遵循最高法院在前述 Asahi Metal v. Indus. Co. v. Superior Court 的见解④,拒绝认定 King 是有意地使其自纽约州法庭地获益。法院指出:"架设一个网站,像是将商品推入市场潮流中般,可以是全国或全球的发行,但,若无更多的行为下,不能认定该行为是有目的的专注在某一州所在地的居民"。然而法院也指出,在欠缺被告确实向纽约州居民招揽生意的确实行为下,仅仅从其网站放置在网际网络上并让纽约州居民可以登录该网站的行为,并不能认定该行为是有意图地锁定特定州居民为对象。其次,被告的行为比较像是在商店橱窗张贴海报,允许任何经过的人可以看到它。任何进入该网际网络的人可以看一下被告的网站或电子海报,但被告自己本身则无法避免向任何特定地

---

① Pres-Kap, Inc. v. System One, Direct Assess, Inc., 636 So. 2d p. 1353.
② Bensusan Restaurant Corporation v. King, 937 F. Supp. pp. 295—300 (S. D. N. Y. 1996).
③ 本案的被告 King 是通过网络上的网站宣传其名为"The Blue Note"的俱乐部。原告 Bensusan,是一个纽约公司,拥有注册商标"The Blue Note"的权限,对其提起商标侵权及不公平竞争之诉。虽然,King 的网站在全球都可以登录,但地方法院认为 Bensusan 不能证实:(A) King 是特定向纽约州居民招揽生意;或(B) King 可以合理预期其应受纽约州法院管辖;CompuServe, 89 F. 3d p. 297。
④ Bensusan, 937 F. Supp p. 301 (S. D. N. Y. 1996).

区的人招揽生意。①

虽然法院在 Bensusan 的结论与 CompuServe 不同,但在 Bensusan 的理由并非与 CompuServe 相反。基本上,Bensusan 的事实与 CompuServe 不同,因在 CompuServe 案中的被告,其特别将俄亥俄州视为标的地,所以于俄州公司下载其服务及签订合约以在 CompuServe 的系统销售软件。② 而相反的,Bensusan 案的被告并没有以 Bensusan 为目标或特别向纽约州居民招揽生意而仅仅是单纯地通过下载一数据文件到位于密苏里的计算机服务器的方式,来刊登其广告,这时,对被告扩大主张对人管辖权,将会使公司因害怕其可能被每一州法院管辖,而阻碍公司在网际网络上刊登广告。而相对地,大众也会失去收到信息及从众多不同的商品及服务中选择益处。

(3) Panavision International v. Toppen③

但在 1996 年 9 月 16 日,加州中央地区法院却在 Panavision International v. Toppen 案中拒绝驳回一件欠缺管辖权之诉。该案牵涉到了一个非住民的被告,因使用网际网络而被控稀释商标、侵害联邦商标及不公平竞争的案件,而该案中的被告主张法院欠缺对人管辖权。

加州法院遵循了最高法院在 Calder v. Jones 案④中所建立的"结果分析"(effect test)说及第九巡回法院在 Ballard v. Savage 中⑤所建立的"莫非关系"(But For)说,来决定对人管辖权的范围。⑥ 虽然,加州法院并未判定 Toeppen 是经由网际网络在加州"做生意"(doing business),但法院确实清楚地建立了"Toeppen 行为的结果是其所计划的,且也对加州的公司

---

① Etienne-Cummings, Shamita, "CASENOTE: Vanishing Boundaries: Extending The Long-Arm Statute Into Cyberspace CompuServe Incorporated v. Patterson, 89 F. 3d 1257 (6th Cir. 1996)", S. Ill. U. L. J. 1997, (22): 226.

② CompuServe V. Patterson, 89 F.3d pp.1260—1261 (6th cir. 1996).

③ Panavision International v. Toppen, 938 F. Supp. p.616 (C. D. Cal. 1996). Panavision International,一个德拉瓦州合伙公司,主事务所设在洛杉矶,拥有"Panavision"及"Panaflex"等商标。在发现 Toeppen 注册了"panavision.com"后,Panavision 通知 Toeppen 其欲使用"panavision.com"为网址名称,而 Toeppen 则要求 $ 13000 元及注册其他 Panavision 的商标"Panaflex.com"做为其新的网址名称。Panavision 主张 Toeppen 注册 Panavision 的商标并不是要销售任何商品,而仅仅是想要在加州取得好处。

④ Calder v. Jones, 465 u. s. 783,787 (1984)。在 Calder 案中的被告都住在佛州,都受加州法院的管辖因其撰写及在全国性杂志发表所控的毁谤文章。

⑤ Ballard v. Savage, 65 F.3d pp.1495,1500 (9th cir.1995).

⑥ 在结果原则分析下,Toeppen 用来侵害 Panavision 商标的媒介变得与行使对人管辖权无关。甚者,加州法院基于 Toeppen 州外行为的目标及实际造成加州公司损害的事实来做分析,更发现如果没有 Toeppen 的与法庭地相关的行为,Panavision 所声称的损失则不会发生。

造成损害"。加州法院的判决与 Pres-Kap 及 Bensusan 二案的判决的不同,在于 Toeppen 案之所以会受对人管辖权的拘束,是因为被告的目的是企图侵害加州公司的权利,而不是因为被告使用网际网络。①

2. 对物管辖的相关见解

土地管辖为美国的管辖原则之一,而该原则于网络商业行为中应仍有所适用。因此,如果将网站架设于法院管辖区域内时,按照土地管辖的理论,法院应该可以主张对其有管辖权。② 但在有关案件牵涉到单纯的网络接触时,法院是否有管辖权时,法院的意见却有所分歧,所以学说及论理的方式重新探讨这些法院单独基于网站的存在而建立的管辖权案例是非常地重要。

(1) 与合同有关的网际网络接触

在多数案中,网际网络的接触都是与当事人间存在的合同相关,而这些合同可使法庭地的管辖变成适当。因此,大多数法院在这些案件中所持的见解都密切地反映出了传统对人管辖权制度,并且无过度扩张管辖权之虞。

在 Zippo Manufacturing Co. v. Zippo Dot Com, Inc③ 一案中,法院基于一些与法庭地公民间的合同及网际网络上的电子合同,确认了法院对于被告有对人管辖权。在针对特别管辖形态为分析时,法院订定了三个判断基准,以决定其得否对被告主张特别管辖权,即:(A) 是否与法庭地间存在有充分的"最低接触";(B) 而该接触是否与主张的请求有关;(C) 法院的管辖是否合理。④

---

① 其他要求 Panavision International 在伊利诺州法院起诉的决定都会对受损害的一方增加双重的负担。Panavision 的判决与第六巡回法院对 Patterson 主张对人管辖权的理论一致。两案中的 Toeppen 及 Patterson 都将其目标分别锁定在位于加州及俄州的原告,因此,在此二案中,扩大对人管辖权的主张是适当的。

② 例如,在 People V. Lipsitz, supreme court IA Part A (1997)案中,被告虽抗辩其没有在设立网页的地点进行商业行为,但法院认为基于土地管辖原则,法院仍取得管辖权。

③ Zippo Manufacturing Co. v. Zippo Dot Com, Inc, (952) F. Supp. 1119 (W. D. Pa. 1997);该案中原告, Zippo Manufacturing Co., 是一间宾州公司,而被告, Zippo Dot Com, Inc 是一间经营网站及提供新闻服务的加州公司。所有被告与宾州间的接触几乎都是在网络上发生。原告主张被告侵害其"Zippo"商标而对被告提起诉讼。

④ 本案的被告 King 是通过网络上的网站,宣传其名为"The Blue Note"的俱乐部。Bensusan,是一纽约公司,拥有注册商标"The Blue Note"的权限,所以对其提起商标侵权及不公平竞争之诉。虽然,King 的网站在全球都可以登录,但地方法院认为 Bensusan 不能证实:(A) King 是特定向纽约居民招揽生意;或(B) King 可以合理预期其应受纽约州法院管辖。

在 Digital Equipment Corp. v. AltaVista Technology, Inc.①一案中,合同的存在再度成为决定对人管辖权的因素。法院在实体审理前,先就管辖权问题做了说明。法院认为因双方当事人存有合同关系,而且诉讼的原因是直接基于该合同关系而生,因此,ATI 因可合理地预期到其可能在麻州应讯。而且法院在考虑 ATI 是与麻州公司从事商业行为及违反了与该公司的授权合同,故法院认为 ATI 是熟虑地与麻州居民作生意及有目的地想使其自己能占麻州管辖权的便宜。因此,法院判决 ATI 有听从麻州法院管辖的义务。虽然 ATI 所违反的合同已足够使法院基于"最低接触"判定有管辖权,但法院在本案中仍讨论到侵权行为也可作为允许法院享有管辖权的依据。换而言之,这些形式的不法行为及通讯,在造成伤害时,亦可形成另一种对人管辖权的基准。

(2) 网络的管辖权及广告

另一个足以影响合同管辖的判断者应是在商业行为领域中的广告行为。就此,已有部分包括巡回上诉法院的判决曾探讨及的且倾向认为:"若是单纯在网络或网站上的消极行为(passive activity),并不能使每一个网站所在地的法院主张对人管辖权"。以下仅分述其要者如下:

① 在纽约州或亚利桑那州法院认为无管辖权的案例

第九巡回法院在"Cybersell Inc. v. Cybersell Inc"案②中判定,亚利桑那州对佛罗里达州广告者的单纯透过网站与亚利桑那州的接触,并不能使其对该广告者有管辖权。在此判决下,法院运用了特别管辖权的三个检验基准,来决定对人管辖权是否适用于被告。

第九巡回法院提到的第一项特别管辖权的要求,为"被告与法庭地间是否有从事特定行为或交易,或有目的地从事一些可使自己从法庭地就

---

① Digital Equipment Corp. v. AltaVista Technology, Inc., 960 F. Suup. 456 (D. Mass. 1997);该案中 Digital Equipment Corp. (DEC)是麻州公司,经营网际网络的搜寻及服务,并拥有服务标章"AltaVista"。而 AltaVista Technology, Inc. (ATI)是加州公司,被授权使用"AltaVista"公司的部分名称及网址。本案是主张侵害商标及违反 ATI 及 DEC 间的合同。

② Cybersell Inc. v. Cybersell Inc, 130 F. 3d 414 (9th Cir.1997). 本案牵涉到两个名称皆为 Cybersell 的公司。原告,Cybersell AZ,是亚利桑那州公司,对佛罗里达州公司 Cybersell FL 提起侵害商标的诉讼。Cybersell AZ 成立于 1994 年 5 月并开始经营网络广告及市场服务。三个月后,其申请注册"Cybersell"为服务标章。而 Cybersell FL 在 1995 年夏天开始营业时,是一间提供其他希望在网络上刊登广告及行销的公司咨询的小公司。

在 Cybersell AZ 发现 Cybersell FL 的网页后,便通知 Cybersell FL "Cybersell"是一个经注册的商标,其不应使用。Cybersell FL 立即将其公司名称改为 WebHorizons,而其又变为 WebSolvers,但在其网页上仍声明"欢迎到 Cybersell"。这就是导致本案发生的原因。亚利桑那州地方法院同意 Cybersell 以欠缺管辖权的主张驳回本案,而 Cybersell AZ 提起上诉。

该行为获得利益的行为"。法院断定 Cybersell 并没有使自己有目的地自亚利桑那州法庭获取利益,因其行为与 Bensusan 案中的行为较为相似。

首先,法院断定 Cybersell 并没有在亚利桑那州从事任何商业行为。由于 Cybersell 的公告仅是消极行为,因此,法院认为该行为还不足以据之推断被告在法庭地有蓄意的行为。法院调查了事实后,还发现并没有亚利桑那州居民签署 Cybersell 所提供的服务,而且并没有任何合同、销售、电话、或收入从亚利桑那州所获得。此外,法院更进一步发现,并没有任何是真的网络通讯是自亚利桑那州收发。近来,法院更认为"单纯在网络上的广告行为,并不足以使广告者受到原告所在的法院管辖"。

② 在康乃迪克州法院认为有管辖权的案例

相对于 Cybersell 案,在下述两个判决中,则认为单纯在网际网络的接触,已足以满足"最低接触"要件,而可主张对人管辖权。在此试加以解析这些案件中的不同结果,以作为分析涉及网际网络接触相关的问题。

首先,康乃迪克地方法院在 Inset System, Inc. v. Instruction Set, Inc.[①]一案中的见解,可能是一扩张网际网络管辖的判决。因为在此案中[②],Instruction 的网站并没有进行任何其他行为,而且 Instruction 也没有在康州签订任何合同,也没有传送输入任何计算机档案或服务。基本上,Instruction 仅仅对那些想进入其网站的用户,单纯地以信息来维持其网站,换而言之,这种网络上的消极广告行为,实难遽认法院得因此对其享有特别管辖权。

在 Inset 案后,美国地方法院密苏里州东区分院,在 Maritz, Inc., v. Cybergold, Inc.[③]案中,在适用密州长手臂法规时,判定可以对被告主张对人管辖权。但在判断 Cybergold 的行为是否符合法规所规定的"交易行

---

① Inset System, Inc. v. Instruction Set, Inc., (937) F. Suup. 161 (D. Conn. 1996);本案中,原告 Inset 是一间康乃迪克州公司,对为麻州的被告 Instruction 提起商标侵权的诉讼。虽然 Inset 拥有联邦商标 INSET,但 Instruction 拥有 INSET 的网址及免付费电话的名称。

② 在本案中,法院判决因单纯地维持网站而进入一法庭地,可以认为依该法庭地长手臂法的规定,认满足管辖权的"最低连系"要件,可以对被告行使管辖权。

法院认为网站就像在报纸刊登广告,因此,本州法院根据长手臂法可对被告主张管辖权。其次,法院发现这种认定与 International Shoe 案中正当程序的限制相符。因为该广告是 Instruction 有目的使自己在康州境内享有做生意的特权。最后,法院决定其并非不合理地要求麻州的 Instruction 公司在康州防御诉讼。因为法院认为在二州的距离很近,而且本案的争点是有关康州的法律,因此,法院的结论为其主张管辖权并不会违反公平及实质的正义。

③ 被告是一间加州公司,设立一网站让用户可以将其姓名提供予被告,并收受被告提供网络服务讯息。因此法院判决认为虽然 Cybergold 与本州仅有透过网络的接触,但已使自己从密苏里州的对人管辖权中获益。Maritz, Inc., v. Cybergold, Inc., 947 F. Supp. 1328 (E. D. Mo. 1996)。

为"时,法院则采行了五个检测"最低接触"的基准:(1)与管辖区接触的性质;(2)接触的数量;(3)接触的原因;(4)州法院就此开庭对本州岛利益的帮助;(5)双方便利原则。

首先,法院特别强调网络接触特质的影响,其中法院注意到Cybergold利用其网站招揽用户,并有意持续地传送讯息给任何或所有的网际网络用户。因此,法院认定尽管Cybergold这种接触的性质是全新的,法院仍应得向其主张对人管辖权。其次,法院评估Cybergold接触的次数及判定其中311次由Cybergold传送出的广告讯息,是有意通过与密州贸易来谋求利益的行为。最后,法院在分析过这些接触与本案间的连系后发现Cybergold的"邀请"(invitation)确实与接触有关,法院指出:"通过计算机,企业可以同时和几个州交流,网络通讯不同于电话,就在于其传达的讯息可能被收讯人和其他一切想看到的人共享,所以当现代科技使全球交易更简单易行时,必须相对地扩张解释管辖权行使的范围"。

就本书的观点认为,Inset及Maritz二案似乎过度扩张了对人管辖权,从而恐有对现今快速发展的网络科技产生不良影响的可能。很显然的,该二案认为可以对于涉及单纯使用网络的所有用户的案件取得管辖的见解,已经忽视了美国最高法院在World Wide Volkswagen及Asahi案中所提到有关宪法的保障。[1] 所以,我们认为,法院较恰当的做法应是从最小连系原则中进一步分离出"公平(fairness)原则的要求",并按下列标准来衡量受理该等案件是否公平合理:1.被告所负的责任;2.受诉法院裁决争端的利益;3.原告基于善意的信赖;4.司法系统的利益;5.各州间扩展实质的社会政策所能分享的利益。[2] 但在Inset及Maritz案中,被告仅单纯地将其声明或广告放置在其网页[3],再者,法院既没有适当适用长手臂法的要件来判定其管辖权[4],又没有仔细检视该特定行为的诉因要件,便认为其有管辖权,似有欠妥适。是以,吾人以为若能参考O'Connor法官在Asahi案中,就特别管辖权与意图获益要件的分析,则可能使该二案中不利的结果及负面影响为之改善。

---

[1] 在World Wide Volkswagen及Asahi案中,法院都提到"必须被告能预见其行为及与法庭地间的关联,而使其可以合理预期可被法院管辖"。

[2] Christoper W. Meyer, "World Web Advertising: Personal Jurisdiction Around The Whole Wide World", *Washington and Lee Law Review*, p.1291(1997)。

[3] 虽然,二被告可能知道定位于任何管辖地的个人可以进入其网页,但被告并没有任何依Asahi案中所定的散布或其他与法庭间的其他接触行为。

[4] 但在Inset案中的长手臂法,是着重被告从法庭地招揽生意,而在Maritz中的长手臂法,是着重被告是否有在法庭地进行交易行为。

(3) 分析及可能的解决方法

在面临网际网络或通讯的问题时,我们可以发现,在对人管辖之问题上,法院透过限制或扩张各州的长手臂法以决定是否享有管辖权时,已经不是要求个人实际进入法庭地,但在有合同存在或发送毁谤的信息时,还是当被告的行为产生可预期其将享有在特定州的利益时,就应该认为有该诉讼行为的管辖权。所以,在每个案件中,很重要的是被告的某行为是否意图使其自己在法庭地内,就该行为获得利益,因而取得法律的利益及保护。然而,如何要求法院建构一公平的网际网络交易环境,似乎仍然值得我们努力。① 就此,应要求法庭地在诉因及州内接触行为间,有密切关系时始可主张管辖权,才不会有太多违反正当程序的疑虑了。

另外,一个特别管辖权的架构也需要法院进一步探讨被告的意图谋利及行使管辖权是否合理及公平。就此,我们或可参考O'Connor法官在Asahi案中的决定:首先,法官Bernnan的见解并不适当。因为根据其说法可能会使每个网站都受到每一州法院的管辖,因其可能仅仅单纯地将商品流通进入市场,便要受到该州管辖②,允许这样的结果将等于宣告全世界各地的任何法院,对全球性的网站经营者都可以对其主张对人管辖权。再就法官O'Connor的意见中,要求被告需有其他的接触行为使其有目的从法庭地中获益的要件而言,就网际网络的本质,把这一点纳入考量应是妥当的,因为的采用本要件将避免网站经营者就其单纯在网络的广告或刊行而受到所有法庭地的管辖。因此,一网站经营者若以某法庭地为目标,而通过特定行为与该法庭地接触或从该处获得经济利益时,就应有预期会在该法庭地进行诉讼。然而,除非其有做确定及有意的努力,并意图获益,否则网站经营者可以设立网站,而不必担心其会在一个任何或全部可以看到其网站的地方,都可能被主张对人管辖权。③ 最后,法官O'Connor的"商业流程"(stream of commerce)理论,包含了法院必须要探究合理性来决定管辖权是否合宜的精神。在这种理论下,法院应探讨网络通讯的本质,用以决定管辖权的主张是否合理。因此,除非网站是在全国性广

---

① 例如,要求"网络侵权行为人"在网际网络接触发生问题时,去防御他人所主张的不当广告、著作权侵权或毁谤时,似乎是公平的。但是,要求一个单纯的网站用户与其丈夫的几封电子邮件,而要求其就子女监护权的诉讼至该法庭地应讯,似乎是不公平的。

② 例如,将Bernnan法官的理论运用到网络交易时,只要网站的经营者知道其网页可能到被任何一州看到时,就会受到该法庭地的管辖。因此,几乎所有网站及电子通讯都可以创造管辖权,因其可同时地在无数个管辖地登录网络。

③ 这项要件也反映出International Shoe及其后认为"被告必须可以合理预期诉讼"的先例。

告,或其将注意力专注在某一法庭地,否则主张对人管辖权是不合理的。①

综合上述美国实务经验,我们不难发现在对物管辖问题上,所有法院的判决,都围绕着一个重要的课题,那就是网址能否成为定管辖的基础?其实,与当事人有关的因素要成为法院行使管辖权的基础,就法律标准而言,应具备下列两个要件:其一,是该因素自身有时间与空间上的相对稳定性(至少是可以确定的);其二,是该因素与管辖区域间存有一定的关联度。基此,要判断网址是否可以成为新的管辖基础,或许可以从这两个要件加以观察。

就第一个要件而言,有学者认为网址是具有相对稳定性,因为网址虽然存在于网络空间之中,然而其在网络空间中的位置是可以确定的,就Internet 本身来说,它是一个真实存在的物理结构②,应相当于居所在物理空间中的地位一样③;另一方面,由于网址是由 ISP 授予的,因此其与 ISP 所在的管辖区域的关联性是非常明确的,同时电子交易中的其他参与者所在其他管辖区域的关联性也是存在的。④ 其次,就网址与管辖区域间的关联度而言,其主要的途径有二:一是受制于 ISP 所在的管辖区域,这是网址存在的静态事实就能决定的关联,并且是充分的连系,正如同居所和居所地一样;再者是网址活动涉及到其他网络交易者时,与其相对人所在管辖区域的接触,是否使管辖该区域的法院获得管辖权,这便是上述案例所探讨的重点。

实际上,如果从接触程度来说,目前网站可分为六级⑤:第一级,是单纯广告型的网站,仅有简单的静态网页,作为广告而不从事商业交易;第二级,则是免费使用型的网站,该网站支持使用者的浏览器,可让使用者浏览其内容并免费选择下载的信息;第三级,则是互动性的网站,此网站会要求使用者提供基本资料或回答问题,并根据使用者的需求提供资料;第四级,则是付费使用型的网站,使用者必须付费后,才能使用该网站中的信息或服务;第五级,则是付费下载的网站,在付费后可以直接从网站上下载所购软件;第六级,则是线上交易型的网站,该网站可直接在线上

---

① 因为网站经营者对于登录其网站的人有极低的控制权,如果允许法院对经营者就其没有设计利用而造成的网站损害,主张对人管辖权是不公平及不合理的。
② 孙铁成:《计算机与法律》,法律出版社 1998 年版,第 249 页。
③ 王德全:《试论 Internet 案件的司法管辖权》,载《中外法学》1998 年第 2 期,第 30 页。
④ 刘满达:《网络商务案件管辖权的实证论析》,载《法学》2000 年第 2 期,第 39 页。
⑤ Eric Schneiderman & Ronald Kornreich, "Personal Jurisdiction and Internet Commerce", The New York Law Journal, 1997;转引自冯震宇:《网络法基本问题(一)》,台北:学林出版社 1999 年版,第 59 页。

进行电子商务交易,如网络下单或网络转账。原则上,若是属于较低层次的接触(如第一至第三级),因为多属静态型的活动,较少互动性,如 Ben-susan Restaurant Corporation v. King 案中,被告仅单纯为静态广告,所以法院认其无管辖权,至于较高程度的接触,如 Zippo Manufacturing Co. v. Zippo Dot Com, Inc 案中,因互动性高,又涉及线上交易,所以常为法院采为管辖的基础。

5.4 解决网络管辖权冲突问题的寻思

在传统国际贸易合同中管辖之决定,大多系由缔约当事人以合意约定管辖权之归属;此种约定管辖之模式,运用于电子化环境中固然可解决大部分关于管辖之纷争,然于国际民事管辖未明文规定之情况下,该合意是否应被承认?有无剥夺国家审判权之虞?此本有争议。再者,因贸易无纸化之特性,每有因当事人缔约时之意思不明或举证不易,致使当事人无法依约定以定其管辖权归属,此际是否得回归传统管辖决定之标准,或另寻其他依据,以决定之?均生疑义。于兹就传统管辖理论出发,试论及网际网络发展所生之冲击与因应之刍议如下:

一、传统国际贸易中的审判管辖理论的借鉴

(一)合意选择外国法院为管辖法院的情形

首先,基于当前两岸商务互动频繁,对于台湾地区而言,法律的研究应该同时将两地的发展加以涵盖,因此本节是特别将两岸当前的相关发展及民事诉讼法中的相关规定略述如后。

在大陆方面,针对合意选择外国法院的部分,在《中华人民共和国民事诉讼法》第244条中规定:"涉外合同或涉外财产权益纠纷的当事人,可以用书面协议选择与争议有实质关联的地点的法院管辖。选择中华人民共和国人民法院管辖的,不得违反本法关于级别管辖和专属管辖的规定。"因此可见,大陆的规定是允许涉外民事关系的当事人合意选择管辖法院的,但须受到两大限制:1. 不得违反民事诉讼法级别管辖和专属管辖的规定;2. 一些涉外民事纠纷由人民法院行使专属管辖权时,当事人不得

合意选择。①

具体而言,大陆地区的规定,具备下列条件的涉外协议管辖为有效:1. 涉外协议管辖的案件必须是涉外合同纠纷或涉外财产权益纠纷;2. 涉外协议管辖只限于第一审人民法院;3. 涉外协议管辖的协议必须以书面作出;4. 协议管辖法院须是与案件有关联的地点的法院,如涉外合同纠纷案件的关联地点为合同签订地、合同履行地、标的物所在地、原告住所地和被告住所地法院;5. 涉外协议管辖不得违反民事诉讼法关于级别管辖与专属管辖的规定。②

相对地,以台湾地区现行《民事诉讼法》第 1 条至第 31 条规定的管辖(如以原就被原则、主事务所、主营业所、各种特别审判籍等),是规定台湾地区第一审法院相互间的事务分配事项,其第 24 条的合意管辖,虽然也规定得合意定台湾地区第一审法院为管辖法院,然而考察其立法意旨最初无意将定外国法院为其管辖法院事项,并规定于上述条文之内。而当事人合意定外国法院为其诉讼事件管辖法院,实际上是合意将该诉讼事件归由外国法院审判,而不是仅仅合意改变台湾地区法院相互间的事务分配事项。这项合意,是否纯粹为上述法律所定合意管辖的适用范围?对此亦有疑义。因此,仅以《民事诉讼法》第 24 条规定,论断合意定外国法院为管辖法院的效力,容有疑义。③

就此,持"肯定说"者认为,当事人合意定外国法院为管辖法院时,法律既然未设有禁止规定,自无不可,但必须(1)该外国法律也承认当事人得以合意定管辖法院;(2)对于该外国法院的判决,国内法院也承认其效力;(3)且系争案件的属性非以专属管辖为限。④ 但亦有持"否定说"者认为,合意定外国法院为管辖法院,涉及法院的审判权事项,并不是仅仅为法院相互间的事务分配问题,也不是(台湾地区)《民事诉讼法》第 24 条原拟规范的事项,所以有认为法院管辖的规定,涉及国家的主权,合意定外国法院为管辖法院,等于限制国家法权的行使,应不承认其效力。⑤ 在台

---

① 如《中华人民共和国民事诉讼法》第 246 条中规定:"因在中华人民共和国履行中外合资经营企业合同、中外合作经营企业合同、中外合作探勘开发自然资源合同发生纠纷提起的诉讼,由中华人民共和国人民法院管辖。"
② 常怡主编:《民事诉讼法学》,中国政法大学出版社 1994 年版,第 451—452 页。
③ 参阅杨建华:《问题研析——民事诉讼法》(四),台北:作者 1995 年自版,第 13—14 页。
④ 石志泉:《民事诉讼法释义》,台北:三民书局 1987 年版,第 33—34 页;张学尧:《民事诉讼法论》,台北:三民书局 1970 年版,第 41 页;曹伟修:《民事诉讼法释论》,台北:曹游龙 1984 年版,第 100 页;姚瑞光:《民事诉讼法论》,台北:大中国 1991 年版,第 56 页。
⑤ 吴明轩:《民事诉讼法》,台北:作者 1981 年自版,第 85 页。

湾地区实务意见上,则有"最高法院"64 年(1975 年)台抗字第 96 号判决认为:"当事人……,按照法律其诉讼原应由台湾地区法院管辖,如以合意定外国法院为第一审管辖法院者,为保护当事人的利益,解释上始认以该外国的法律须承认当事人得以合意定管辖法院,且该外国法院的判决台湾地区也承认其效力为必要。"①按照这种实务上的见解,虽然与学者间的通说相同,但在当事人两者均为外国人者,则不加任何限制,直接承认其效力,这是因为两者都是外国人,合意不由台湾地区法院审判,与台湾地区的公私权益都没有影响。

也有学者认为:"民事诉讼所解决者,为私法上权利义务事项,私法上权利义务,当事人原则上得自由处分,是否行使其权利,应归诸权利人的自由意思,提起民事诉讼为行使权利的最后手段,权利本身既得不为行使或予以抛弃,则行使权利的手段,原则上自非不得由当事人自由选择。合意定外国法院管辖,虽非单纯定诉讼的管辖问题,而是排除受国内法院审判的权利,但衡诸处分权主义的原则,应无不许之理。且在判断私法上权利义务的争执,法律上承认仲裁制度,而仲裁制度即是按照当事人的合意,将私法上权利义务的争执,不归由法院审判,而由法院以外的人判断,仲裁制度既可承认,合意定外国法院管辖,自也可承认其效力。"②本书认为,这种见解似乎较为合理,并且合乎国际贸易的实际需求,可以说是较为允当的做法。

(二) 国际审判管辖权的理论的援用

除了前问以两岸为基础的探讨外,国际间相关理论的发展,同样是我们得以借鉴作为思考解决问题的基础。

1. 国际审判权的基本理论

关于如何定国际审判管辖的问题,传统的民事诉讼法学说是将其理解为有关国家主权之一作用,而属审判权(Gerichtsbarkeit)的对人的、对物的界限的问题,可由各国在行使其审判权的范围内,自行决定处理原则。

---

① 如当事人两者都是外国人,其诉讼原不应由台湾地区法院管辖(普通审判级不在台湾地区,也不专属台湾地区法院管辖),而又以合意定外国法院为管辖法院的,一经合意之后,就产生排斥得由台湾地区法院管辖的效力,至于该外国法院的法律是否承认当事人得以合意定管辖法院,以及该外国法院的判决台湾地区是否承认其效力,法院已没有考虑的必要,应听任该外国当事人的自由,而承认其合意管辖的效力。

② 但在专属管辖虽亦为法院相互间事务分配的问题,但其事涉公益,在台湾地区法院相互间还不承认他法院有管辖权,参考台湾地区《民事诉讼法》第 402 条第 1 款的宗旨,自不应承认合意定外国法院管辖的效力。参阅杨建华:《问题研析——民事诉讼法》(四),台北:作者 1995 年自版,第 15—16 页。

据此,向来采所谓逆推知说,认为可按照民事诉讼法有关土地管辖的规定为逆向推知。① 对此,晚近,国际私法上的学说则多认为:应基于追求达成裁判的妥适正确、迅速、经济及当事人间公平等诉讼制度理念,将国际审判管辖的问题本质,理解为属于由关联各国协力分担审判机能的问题,而循此为国际间的土地管辖的分配。但在分配之际,仍应综合审酌上揭诸理念而为具体的判定。基本上,涉外民事事件因牵涉诉讼程序的不同、准据法的差异、到庭的困难、移送制度的欠缺等因素,而与纯粹的国内民事事件有所不同,自应在参酌或类推民事诉讼法规定的同时,也并从国际协调的观点,按照实际需要的程度为适当的修正,而有不宜全面适用民诉法规定的情形。

2. 国际管辖权的基本理论

就国际管辖权的问题,学说上向来有"属地主义"与"普遍主义"的争执,属地主义是基于管辖权是主权表现的形式的观点;而普遍主义则基于国际社会互动且交流的需要来作考量,承认按照一般的法则来决定管辖权。

就普遍主义而言,本质与上述国际审判权所说的理论相似。现今学说上除上述的逆推知说外,还有所谓国际审判权协同分配说。在此叙述如下:

(1) 逆推知说

如前文所述,这种学说是按照民事诉讼法有关土地管辖的规定为"逆向推知",如果普通审判权或特别审判权在国内,则视为该国有国际审判管辖权。

(2) 国际审判权分配说②

所谓"国际审判权分配说",是以涉外民事事件牵涉诉讼程序的不同、准据法的差异、到庭的困难、移送制度的欠缺等,而与纯粹的国内民事事件有所不同,所以认应在参酌或类推适用民事诉讼法的同时,也从"国际协调"的观点,按照实际需要的程度作出适当的修正,而不宜全面去适用民事诉讼法的规定。

以此看来,下文所说的确定国际审判管辖权的标准,对于保障平等使用法院的机会,应该是必要并且有用的:

---

① 如果普通审判籍或特别审判籍在甲国内,则可据以推知甲国有国际审判管辖权;反之,如果普通审判籍或特别审判籍都不在甲国,则否定甲国的国际审判管辖权。
② 参阅丘联恭:《司法之现代化与程序法》,台北:三民书局1992年版,第98—102页。

① 个案利益衡量

定国际审判管辖权时,为保护弱者的权利,应就个案为利益衡量的考虑;例如,系争物之所在地、容易搜集证据之地或当事人据以生活或从事经济活动之地等都可为定国际审判管辖的标准。

② "以原就被原则"应予以缓和或排除

按照被告住所地原则,可成为定国际审判管辖的标准。因为这项标准能顾虑到原告通常已经做好了相当的准备而起诉及被告是处于可能因被诉而受突袭等现况,这种顾虑是符合当事人间的实质上公平及实现权利之方便。不过,在特殊情形,如果严格贯彻被告住所地原则,将导致实质上否定原告受救济机会的结果时,也应考虑原告所蒙受的不利益,另行探求被告住所地以外的定管辖标准。

③ 为提高涉外事件的审判的效率及迅速性,也应考量程序进行的难易及判决的实际效用(强制执行的可能性)

请求标的物的所在地、担保物的所在地,也可类推适用于国际审判管辖。

二、网际网络上审判管辖理论的适应

网际网络所造成的重要冲击之一,就是"距离之死"。我们可以想像一个蜘蛛网,信息的提供者位在网中央,信息则透过遍布的网络向世界延伸,透过网际网络,在蛛网中心的信息提供者,其商业活动可涵盖到世界各地,此交易形态,已跳脱出了以"空间"做为管辖基础的固有法律,而发生管辖权的适用问题。对此涉外电子合同之管辖问题,除修法以为因应外,当前比较实际的做法应是"类推适用现行民事诉讼法之相关规定"①,除藉由双方合意决定管辖法院外②,似亦可援引相关规定以决定其管辖法

---

① 请参阅,马汉宝:《国际私法总论》,台北:作者1997年自版,第180页;刘铁铮:《国际私法论丛》,台北:三民书局2000年版,第276页;林益山:《国际裁判管辖权冲突之研究》,载《中兴法学》,1993(36):7;林益山:《涉外网络契约管辖之探讨》,载《月旦法学杂志》,2001(77):23。

② 其实为解决网络管辖实际上的困难,网络上目前普遍采用的方式,便是以约定的方式决定其管辖权之归属,若双方未就管辖权有所规定,法院方适用传统的原则决定管辖权之归属,见冯震宇:《论网络商业化所面临的管辖问题(上)》,载《信息法务透析》,1997(9):31。

院[①],于兹试举例略述如下:

(一)以"被告之主营业所或主事务所所在地之法院"为管辖法院之可能性:当系争之被告国外厂商在国内设有主营业所或主事务所时,该主营业所或主事务所所在地之法院得否享有管辖权当成为问题;盖于网际网络之世界中,由于只需透过计算机即可遨游世界,企业经营者透过网站之架设,即可与世界各地的人为交易,无须实际至该地进行商业行为或设立事务所,故传统作为决定管辖基础之主事务所及主营业所等概念,似有视实际状况加以修正之必要。针对于此,大陆《电子签名法》第12条规定:"发件人的主营业地为数据电文的发送地点,收件人的主营业地为数据电文的接收地点。没有主营业地的,其经常居住地为发送或者接收地点。当事人对数据电文的发送地点、接收地点另有约定的,从其约定。"整体而言之,吾人以为,于决定网络交易中之管辖权决定时,所谓主事务所、主营业所,仍系指总揽事业事务之处所[②],唯应视实际状况而有所区别[③]:

1. 若被告于该地实际设有主营业所或主事务所,吾等认为该地法院享有管辖权,殆无疑义;至于网络上之网页,应被视为该公司之店面橱窗或能独立运作之分公司,则仍应就其实际之状况加以判断。

2. 若于未实际设有主营业所或主事务所者,且其事务之处理,皆系透过联机上网为之者,此时吾人究应以架设该网页之虚拟主机或实体主机所在地,为总揽事业之处所?或以实际运作该网站之企业经营者所在,为总揽事业之处所?或以网址之所在地,为总揽事业之处所?吾等以为,似应本诸既有管辖原则,辅以新的国际发展趋势及国际实务,依实际状况,就虚拟主机或实体主机所在地、企业经营者所在地或网址所在地等多方面与总揽事务相关之行为或处所等为多元之判断。

(二)以"被告可扣押之财产或请求标的所在地法院"为管辖法院之可能性:当被告有可供扣押之财产时,得否以该财产所在地法院为管辖法

---

① 关于网际网络上管辖权竞合或冲突之问题,法院于处理涉外之民事案件时,亦得依国际私法之原则处理,参阅冯震宇:《论网际网络与消费者保护问题(下)》,载《信息法务透析》,1998(7):34。另可参,Mann, Catherine L.,"symposium on intellectual property, digital technology & electronic commerce: the uniform computer information transactions act and electronic commerce: Balancing Issues and Overlapping Jurisdictions in the Global Electronic Marketplace: The Ucita Example",Wash. U. J. L. & Pol'y 2002, (8): 215。

② 杨建华等:《民事诉讼法新论》,台北:三民书局2000年版,第14页。

③ 相对于此,大陆民事诉讼法并无对主营业所或主事务所涉有设有法院得取得管辖权之规定,是以,如何于具体个案中,求取管辖之依据,恐仍须由私法自治取得一适当平衡之做法。另,或可透过类推适用《民事诉讼法》第22条之规定,解决法院取得管辖权之依据,唯仍须符合正当法律程序之要求。

院？亦容有疑义。盖所谓"可扣押之财产"于网络世界究系何指？在传统的实体世界里，"可扣押之财产"原系指被告所有之物或权利而言，而在面临强制执行时，则系指得为查封或拍卖之标的物而言①；基此，是否即可推定此些"可扣押之财产"也包括网页或网域名称？吾人以为，虽著名的网页与网域名称具有相当之经济价值，然而，其价值之判断基准不一，且其权利行使之范围，在法律上亦无法加以界定，况且于任一内国法院为执行时，于实务运作上恐有相当之困难，故尚难认当事人得对网页或网域名称为扣押。②

（三）以"债务履行地之法院"为管辖法院之可能性③：当合同当事人系因合同之履行而涉讼时，设若当事人间就债务之履行地有所约定，是否该债务履行地之法院，即享有管辖权。在过去，当交易之标的为实体商品时，不论买受人往取或出卖人赴交商品，均可透过合同以约定债务之履行地，此时债务之履行地应为实体世界中之某一地点，而容许当事人以该地之法院为管辖法院提起诉讼，此固无疑义。唯若以数字商品透过网际网络为交易时，鲜少系于实体地点为交付或往取以履行合同，常透过将信息或软件传输至指定之电子邮件信箱中，藉以遂行所谓之"债务履行"；此际，是否仍应援用前述实体世界中之原则以判断债务履行地？殊成问题。盖电子邮件地址所表彰者，仅系信息服务业者之邮件服务器所在位置，凡拥有该电子邮件地址之使用者名称与密码者，均得透过网络拨接，于任何地方来收发信箱中之电子邮件；故此，网络世界中所谓的"债务履行地"所对应者可能是现实世界中之任一地点。是以，较务实的做法似乎是以网络交易发生与履行所在之核心（媒介）设施所在地为其判断标准，亦即邮件（网络）服务器（mail server or web server）之所在地，或当事人透过设施实际收受该电子邮件等地点，来思考建立其管辖联结之可能，并依系争交易与核心设施间的实际关联性，来决定是否以设施或收受所在地法院为

---

① 姚瑞光：《民事诉讼法论》，台北：大中国出版社 1991 年版，第 28 页。

② 唯有以架设该网页之虚拟主机或实体主机之所在地，为网页之所在地，而得对具有价值之网页为扣押；亦得至网域名称权利取得地，对网域名称专用权为扣押。详见蔡馥如：《网络管辖之研究》，台北大学法律研究所硕士论文，1999，第 112—116 页。而就大陆之民事诉讼法而言，因法院管辖取得的依据，并无因可扣押之财产所在地为管辖取得之依据，从而，于此一案例之中，并无类推适用之可能；如于法理层次予以解释时，亦应兼顾正当法律程序之原则。当然，私法自治仍不失为一解决之道。

③ 参大陆《民事诉讼法》第 24 条。

管辖法院。① 此外,有论者以为,得以合同当事人订约时或履约时所委托的电子认证机构的主要营业地、以合同当事人履行给付以及接受给付时所委托的承担在线支付功能的网上金融机构的营业地、以合同当事人订约时或履约时所委托之网络服务提供者的主要营业地、以合同当事人履约时所使用的计算机信息系统中的网络服务器的所在地、以当事人履约时所使用的计算机终端设备所在地;此充分网络技术特点,或可于日后修改或补充合同法之参考。

承前论述,以两岸现有规范言,欲解决涉外电子合同管辖问题除得类推适用内国民事诉讼法之相关规定外,台湾地区《电子签章法》第8条中有关地点推定②之概念与《消费者保护法》中第47条以消费关系发生地之法院,均可作为决定管辖法院判断标准之参考。然而,在决定该法院是否有管辖权时,仍应就可能据以为管辖之基础参酌学理及国际间相关发展,视实际状况与关联性加以判断。准此,若于传统地域管辖理论下,似可认为当网址具备,该因素本身有时间与空间上的相对稳定性,且该因素与管辖区域应存有一定之关联性时,可以作为定管辖之基础,此亦有助于管辖问题之解决。再者,若能跳脱传统地域管辖之观念,将网络空间视为新管辖空间而存在时③,则吾等对网络空间内争端当事人之纠纷解决,则可透过网际网络的联系在相关法院出庭,亦可为解决管辖问题之机制(如美国密执安州,透过数字记录、视讯会议等高科技工具所设立之"网络法院"即为显例)。④ 此外,在美国目前有业者通过定型化合同的方式与客户就管辖法院与准据法等问题加以约定,于美国司法机关承认后,亦为美国计算

---

① 此外,有论者以为,得以合同当事人订约时或履约时所委托的电子认证机构的主要营业地、以合同当事人履行支付以及接受支付时所委托的承担在线支付功能的网上金融机构的营业地、以合同当事人订约时或履约时所委托之网络服务提供者的主要营业地、以合同当事人履约时所使用的计算机信息系统中的网络服务器的所在地、以当事人履约时所使用的计算机终端设备所在地;此充分网络技术特点,或可于日后修改或补充合同法之参考。王伟:"论在线履行数字电子合同的履行地确认机制",载《政法论丛》,2003(4):36。

② 《电子签章法》第8条:"……以与主要交易或通信行为最密切相关之业务地为发文地及收文地。主要交易或通信行为不明者,以执行业务之主要地……"

③ 有学者建议,应跳脱地域管辖的观念,而承认网络虚拟空间就是一个特殊地域,并承认在网络世界与现实世界存在有一个法律上十分重要的边界;若要进入网络的地域,必须透过网络或密码,一旦进入网络的虚拟世界中,则应适用网络世界的网络法,而不再适用现实世界的法律。如此一来,将可以不必就行为或交易发生地为何的问题,争论不休。Johnson, David R, & Post, David G, "Law and Borders—The Risk of Law in Cyberspace", *Stanford L. Rev.* 1996, (48): 1367.

④ 其实此类法院在美国并非先例,在美国北卡罗莱纳州早已设立了网络商务法院,该法院的高级法官可以通过电视会议技术对处于不同地点的原被告进行案件审理; http://www.cnc.ac.cn/news/news01/0201/news01_02011404.html (visited 2003/1/12)。

机信息交易法(U.C.I.T.A.)所接受①,此亦为一有效之解决方案。

5.5 结　语

　　涉外电子合同民事管辖理论仍在发展中,而待解决之问题亦然,一如其他发展中之网络法律课题,法规范之发展须依循逻辑推理来探求其与真实世界法规范之兼容性;而在立法努力跟上科技发展脚步的过程中,国际间的趋势、真实世界中的惯例,以及因应新兴科技所衍生的学理论述,都是吾等须小心以对者。以涉外民事管辖权争端解决方案言,如能透过国际合作签订"多边或双边条约"以决定管辖权之归属,当系最佳的解决之道,然国际间尚未有公约定案之提出,故现阶段尚无法透过此途径解决之;唯海牙《民商事管辖权及外国判决之承认与执行公约草案初稿》与《选择法庭协议公约草案》虽尚未定案,但其中已有共识之部分,仍值得吾等加以参考。再者,在决定该法院是否有管辖权时,吾等应就可能据以为管辖之基础参酌学理及国际间相关发展,视实际状况与关联性加以判断,以决定法院是否具备管辖之权限;是以,两岸对于涉外电子合同之民事管辖问题,除了修法因应外,当前比较实际的做法应是"类推适用现行民事诉讼法之相关规定"②,台湾地区或可参酌《电子签章法》第 8 条有关地点之推定,以决定法院是否享有管辖权;此外,或可参考美国实务之发展将"网址"作为定管辖基础,或承认"网络法院"之运作机制,均有助于管辖问题之解决。

　　最后,本诸自由市场经济原则,在法律变动过程中,尊重当事人的选择(autonomy)空间,则是另一个值得大家尊重的原则,其实这也本文在论及当前国际社会寻求解决电子合同涉外民事管辖问题过程中,所加以强调者。此可证诸于海牙公约草案与"Convention on Choice of Court Agreements"之规定,在尊重当事人合同自主之精神下,允许缔约当事人得经由合意定管辖法院,此与台湾地区民事诉讼法规定大致相符③,且于美国计

---

　　① 原则上,UCITA 亦承认当事人可以就准据法加以选择;详参冯震宇:《论电子商务之法律保护与因应策略》,载《月旦法学杂志》,2002(80):180—181。
　　② 请参阅,马汉宝:《国际私法总论》,台北:作者 1997 年自版,第 180 页;刘铁铮:《国际私法论丛》,台北:三民书局 2000 年版,第 276 页;林益山:《国际裁判管辖权冲突之研究》,载《中兴法学》,1993(36):7;林益山《涉外网络契约管辖之探讨》,载《月旦法学杂志》,2001(77):23。
　　③ 详见,冯震宇、陈家骏等:《电子交易法制相关议题之研究》,台北:经建会 2002 年版,第 190—191 页。

算机信息交易法(U.C.I.T.A.)亦承认当事人得以就管辖法院与准据法加以选择。① 是以,于当事人利用网络进行交易时,若得依民事诉讼法之规定,当事人得以合意定管辖法院②,此应可以解决大部分管辖法院决定之问题。

---

① 详参冯震宇:《论电子商务之法律保护与因应策略》,载《月旦法学杂志》,2002(80):180—181。
② 唯此合意管辖之行诸于书面并非为合意管辖之成立要件,通说以为此之书面仅为证明合意管辖之法定证据方式而已;详参骆永家:《民事诉讼法Ⅰ》,台北:三民书局1999年版,第25页;杨建华等:《民事诉讼法新论》,台北:三民书局2000年版,第32页。

6 电子合同之因应与建议

6.1 电子合同之法理新思维

网际网络的快速发展,为全球电子商务的成长注入了活力,更为传统国际贸易开创出一番新局。这其中,以俗称 B to B 的交易模式为核心的发展,在合同自由的基础上快速成长,并成为国际贸易电子化的主要动力。正如本书前文所说,国际上为迎接此电子交易时代的来临,已在以联合国为主的诸多国际组织架构下,制定出诸多的国际规范;相对地,传统国际贸易所赖的电子数据交换(Electronic Data Interchange)系统,也在国际商会等相关国际商业惯例拟定机构的研议下,迅速完成电子贸易所需的调整,并在过去数年间,引领全球贸易进入电子化的环境中。这种源起自国际间官方与非官方机构的统合努力,为具有全球化、无国界属性的电子交易奠定了良好基础,并成为电子商务主导国家,如美、欧、日等国家或地区调整其法制的重要依据。基本上,理想与技术水平俱高的国家,往往一方面主导了国际规范的形成,另一方面则迅速地调整其国内法制以与之衔接,进而将法制建构成另外一种竞争条件。例如美国于 1997 年提出于 WTO 的全球电子商务政策纲领,以及欧洲联盟建构的 Balero. net 电子贸易交易平台,都是这种企图的体现。此外,在与国际发展的接轨上,这些先进国家在国内法制的调整上更是不遗余力,以美国为例,其统一计算机信息交易法(U.C.I.T.A.)的提出,为其具全球主导地位的信息交易奠定了良好的基础。整体而言,本书认为,在掌握了电子合同法制的全球化发展趋势后,回到电子合同领导国家的比较法制研究,让我们更清楚地看到了这些高度工业国家如何透过国际法制建构过程的参与,以及国内法制的调整与衔接,落实了其追求电子交易竞争利益的政策目标。

但不可否认,技术、商业或政策面的思考都不能回避应面对的基础法学课题。换而言之,虽然我们看到了以电子贸易为核心所建构出以满足 EDI 需求为目标的诸多法制适应(如海运提单等),然而每个国家都不可避免地必须面对每宗交易最根本的合同法制调整问题,每一个电子交易环节虽然都涉及不同的交易关系与当事人,然而其权利义务关系的诠释,往往要回到一国自有的民商法体系来处理,因此,研究国际贸易合同各个环节所涉及的合同法基础问题,是研究电子贸易者不可回避的核心问题。近几年来全球电子商务的快速成长,已引导电子贸易进入多元少量的开放式交易环境,单纯的前置型协议或其他本着合同自由原则的安排,将难以解决牵涉日广的国际贸易法律问题。所以,在针对电子合同法制的问题作成研究后,作者却深刻感受到,在探讨电子合同法制问题时,除解决问题的技术导向外,更深层地跨学科思考,是很必要的。因为网络本身所带给社会的,绝非单纯的询答过程,而是一种源自科技变动,在人际关系多元而虚拟化的环境下,所呈现的复杂并创新的交易模式,如果我们仍然紧守着对于传统法律概念的坚持,以既有的知识来诠释 21 世纪应有的法律,我们将错失通过法律的积极价值引领社会进步的机会,甚至让自己成为电子交易发展过程中的绊脚石。总而言之,面临网络的时代,我们究竟要用怎样的态度来看待电子合同相关之法律问题,其实不是一件容易的事,有论者云就传统法制稍作调整即已足,或曰非积极调整法制不足以为功;本书则认为,应该从网络经济、信息经济或电子商务经济的角度来掌握电子贸易合同的发展及趋势,并充分掌握国内外的法律对应调整,进而具体分析相关问题的重心,认为深入进行体系分析或探讨的依据,应是基本的研究态度。

本书认为,先行了解并掌握网络规范的发展模式,应是未来各界研究电子合同法制问题的应有态度。而就网络规范的演进而言,其与社会规范息息相关并且相互影响,当然也会有所抵触。因此,我们或许可以从社会中群体的规范行为,推衍出网络规范的形成,大约可以分为五个阶段[①]:第一阶段,网络规范应仅仅是隶属于社会规范的一个子群体规范系统而已;然而当规模逐渐扩大,网络规范会从社会规范中筛选出适合于网络性质的部分,而偏离社会规范的核心,以形成其自我规范,这就进入第二阶段;至于第三阶段,是随着网际网络的发展与网络社群的成熟而出现,网

---

① 请参见 Major, April Mara, "Norm Origin and Development in Cyberspace: Models of Cybernorm Evolution", *Wash. U. L. Q.* 2000, (78): 59, 81—82.

际网络特殊属性①,将越来越明显,这时,既有的社会规范将无法全盘适用到网络世界,需要修正补充而发展出和既有本质不同的新规范;继而进入第四阶段,即网络规范渐脱离原有社会规范,形成半独立〈Quasi-Independent〉系统;最后,当网络规范规模持续扩张,除了继续受社会规范影响外,也会对社会规范发生影响,更随着网际网络和实体社会的结合,两个规范系统的依存关系会逐步密切合流。基本上,了解并重视网络规范和社会规范的依存关系,在未来网络世界的规制上有相当重要的地位。而本文于文末也拟以研究过程的所得,就此方面的观察,提出浅见,以供卓参。

以本文所侧重的电子合同问题而言,我们发现,整个法制调整的方向应是着眼于网上交易者的权利义务归属问题,而之所以要如此探讨,则又是起因于网络通讯结构本身所提供的虚拟机制;换而言之,是虚拟但具有人工智能的网络媒介②,导致我们必须重新思考网络上各方当事人的权责问题。因此,在思考电子合同法制以及合同当事人的权利义务关系时,我们基于前述本文论及的原则,应该跳脱出传统交易当事人的观念来看待问题,并应将网络上讯息传输者的角色与权责③一并予以考量,而这也正是前文联合国、ICC、美国 U.C.C. 及欧盟等相关法制在调整时所必须遵循的。

正如前文本书所说的,合同是一般人最熟悉的法律领域,它不但反映了现代企业界的共同价值观,更是符合一般人期待的互动方式,而这种互动方式往往表现在对于所谓明确的印刷(print)的信任上,至于所谓的印刷,则又往往是指所谓的定型化合同条款。基本上,这里所说的印刷应可以说是人类最早使用的原件,相对地,贸易中使用的定型化合同就可以被认为是一种为法律所认知的媒介方式,而这些使用或提供定型化合同的人,可以说是一种出版者,而出版者本身具有控制打印方式和设计合同的能力,从而这种合同常呈现出有利于出版者的现象。但前述的印刷对于

---

① 网际网络独特的属性如匿名(Anonymity)和信息流(Information Flow)。以匿名属性而言,网络使用者可以匿名的形式尽情发表想法,不像在实体社会中受到许多规范的限制,比在实体社会中享有更高度的自由。关于匿名的探讨,请参见 McAdams, Richard H., "The Origin, Development, and Regulation of Norms", *MICH. L. REV.* 1997, (96): 59, 97—102。

② 这一部分可由前文所论及的电子代理概念,加以观察。

③ 这方面包括五大方向:政策面、网络使用者的保护、传输机制提供者的权责、使用传输机制者的权责,以及联网后各方当事人的权责。这部分在美国国家研究委员会 1992 年即提出的研究报告中,即有很深的研究,参见 Denning Dorothy E & Lin Herbert S eds., *Rights and Responsibilities of Participants in Networked Communities*, Washington: National Research Council National Academy Press 1994, pp.25—30。

合同法本质所带来的冲击，绝非仅仅在于文义上的探讨，而是合同已随印刷的使用，发展成为一种使用信息去创造以及架构关系的一种媒介。这样看来，合同的价值最主要应在于它所创设的关系，而如果按照法社会学的观点来看，合同关系的发展应是伴随身份关系的演变而来，而在传统工业革命后发展出来的商品经济市场中，身份的价值似乎已经逐渐被稀释，这就是所谓"从身份到合同"之说；然而当社会迈入企业化的信息社会后，身份在信息化社会的交易中的地位，再次被凸显出来。因为在商品经济的交易环境中，交易当事人是通过合同来掌握与管理信息，进而从事经济价值或利益的交换；如今，在电子环境中，除每个人掌握信息的能力大为提高外，交易与互动的对象已经纳入了电子代理的功能与角色，从而，以认证功能为基础的交易架构，确认交易当事人在网络上的电子身份，将成为交易发生的前提条件。以 EDI 的使用为例，交易当事人通常必须先签署基础协议并纳入电子认证的安排，从而其后交易的发生均将通过身份认证的流程来进行，这时，与其说电子交易是在探讨个案物品或服务的提供问题，还不如说是在创设新的人际关系，好让交易能在这种关系上来进行。

综上，对于电子合同的探讨，应强调和同当事人与参与者间互动关系的重新界定，而不是其个别行为在商品或劳务交易过程中的法律属性的定义而已[1]；而这些考虑都已经呈现在美国调整电子合同相关法制的过程中。其实，随着工业革命进入以纸张为基础的交易环境以来，当事人已经习于通过合同书来规范其权利义务关系，然而此时他们处理合同关系的能力，却明显的受限于所获的信息；换而言之，在缔约过程中，各当事人选择或使用文字的方式，都会受限于其所获得信息间的互动，也就是说，每一个人是按照他和信息的互动后所获得的了解，来呈现出其打印于文书

---

[1] 这个部分主要牵涉到电子代理（electronic agent）的使用，以及科技本身所牵涉的即时互动与不可否认性问题。见 Raymond T. Nimmer, "The Uniform Commercial Code Proposed Article 2b Symposium: Article 2b: An Introduction", *J. Marshall J. Computer & Info. L.* 1997, (16): 211。再以安全性所涉电子资料的保护为例，所应强调的应不单纯限于特定使用者的权益，而是交易的效力与当事人之间的权利义务分配（attribution）问题。而欧洲在这方面所采的原则性保守态度，其争执重点主要在于是否欧洲联盟在 1998 年 10 月 25 日生效的全面性（comprehensive）隐私保护指令，The Directive on Data Protection 会影响美国与欧洲间信息交易的进行。参见 Cate, Fred H., "Data Protection Law And The European Union's Directive: The Challenge For The United States: The Eu Data Protection Directive, Information Privacy and the Public Interest", *Iowa L. Rev.* 1995, (80): 431。目前随美国商务部的提出"国际安全港隐私保护原则"（International Safe Harbor Privacy Principle），双方终于在 1999 年 7—8 月间初步达成共识。其内容请参见台湾地区"经济部"国际贸易局，"参与国际经贸事务项目小组电子商务工作分组"1999 年度第 2 次会议，会议资料。

上的内容。这时有些文字的使用或许已经有了一般的共识,然而许多具有法律意义的用字,如担保、给付不能、不可抗力等,却往往因当事人对相关信息的了解不同而有差异;此外,对于从事国际贸易的人而言,跨国交易的环境如果因为用语不一而被切割,则物流或金流的顺畅程度就都会严重受到影响。因此,国际间统一贸易合同用语及其意义的必要性就出现了;不论是通过官方性质的努力,如联合国国际货物买卖公约,或民间属性的整合,如国际商会的努力,发展至今,贸易合同的法制环境已经有其相当的确定性,而这些也是当前从事贸易的人员所了解,并藉以建构交易关系的基础;换而言之,贸易合同的签署本就不是单凭这几纸文书,而是在通过这个过程来交换彼此对于交易关系的期待,进而建构出稳定的关系。

因此,本书拟进一步指出,在面临国际贸易环境电子化的今天,对于数据电文是否可以取代文书的探讨,不应该拘泥于文书纸张(paper)与电子数据(electronic data)间的可替代性如何,更应在于需求产生的背景与当事人对于电子数据交换模式的期待。实际上,国际贸易环境的本身就属于极端强调惯例的地位者,换而言之,即使当前国际贸易法制架构下的国际性条约,如前述的借数据电文缔结或证明之(国际)合同公约草案初稿与选择法庭协议公约草案等,都在配合跨国交易的需求,借法制化过程求其一致与安定性。因此,不论纸张、电码或电波,还是当前的电子数据,贸易从业人员所关心的,在于如何与贸易相对人建立稳当的交易关系,而不是媒介本身的选择。基本上,只要他们能真正了解数据电文本身所代表的意义,并熟悉电子语言所表彰的内涵,他们就会接受以数据电文的形式来处理交易相关信息,而这种发展也同于文书纸张取代口头说明的过程,这取决于人对于信息传递媒介的了解与信赖,而这些也都是前文本文所一再强调的。目前,对于许多使用 EDI 的大型公司来说,已经逐渐形成对电子数据的信任,从而有要求贸易伙伴(供货商)必须同步采行 EDI 的现象,换而言之,对于未来的贸易从业人员来说,电子数据反而会是他们熟悉与信任的信息管理与传递媒介。这种现象正与早年纸张的可信赖性超越口头说明的过程相似。

在 Michael Clanchy 的著作[1]所提及,在 1066 到 1307 年间的一个案例中,Canterbury 的枢机主教 Saint Anselm,与英王亨利一世之间发生纠纷,

---

[1] Michael Clanchy, *From Memory to Written Record: England 1066—1307*, Oxford: Blackwell, 1995.

双方是共同派遣代表组团求助于教皇 Paschal 二世。在代表团返乡后，Anselm 的代表大声宣读了教皇所写的信，但亨利一世的代表则反对，认为教皇给他们的口信（oral message）与书面（writing）不符，当时的群众对此看法有分歧，但 Clanchy 则认为："口头证人的可信任程度高于书面证据的原则，应是法律的共识（legal commonplace）"，"因为作成纪录通常意指以口头证人为证而非制作一纸文件。"（To make a record often meant to bear oral witness, not to produce a document）从这个例子事例，我们可以发现，从口头发展到文书，直到今天的电子数据，人们对于它们的信任都是源自于对掌握是些"凭证"的信心；例如，当时的英国人并不熟悉文字，因而宁可相信一个他所信赖者的誓词（oath），如今我们之所以会相信纸上文字，那是因为我们越来越相信，白纸黑字是比人类随时间而遗忘的记忆更为可靠的。其后，随生活中文书使用的普及和阅读技巧的进步，我们对于文字的产生，及其本身的重要性都有相当的信赖，因而有制定法律要求以文书来取代口头形式之举，在这种发展趋势下，我们可以发现，在以文书为交易基础的交易环境中，凡超出文书资料范围的信息，经常都被忽略或被认为并不存在，换而言之，过去常被使用的握手之交（handshake deal）或者口头承诺，也因此丧失了它在法律上的重要性。此时，我们对于合同关系的观察，也逐渐走向了文书纸张上的叙述，而不重视其文书内容之所以会呈现出来的原因。以当前民法在解决债务不履行的纠纷时的经验为例，虽然再三强调当事人真意的认定，而另一方面，书面证据则却已经是证明当事人真意的最主要依据。这种态度完全忽略了文书的制作，不应只被认为是重制交易信息的技术，而是借以发现人们可以据以互动并交换讯息的态度。换而言之，文书的存在固然可用以证明当事人的真意，然而逻辑上却不应当然反推合同关系的存在必须有文书的存在；在解释上，除法律有使用书面的要式规定外，如不动产交易合同，就不应过度强调文书在合同成立生效上所扮演的角色。这样，我们在处理电子合同相关法制时，不应过度强调科技本身所带来的变动，反之，应强调的是科技对于人与人之间在信息交流与交易关系的互动上所彰显的价值。以电子交易为例，我们就应该从交易当事人双方选择数字传递交易模式的原因及过程加以了解，进而厘清其对于电子数据交换所扮演角色的期待；而不是拘泥于电子数据是否等同于文书的思考。① 质言之,早在联合国制定模范法典之前,电子数据在国际贸易间的运用就已经日渐普及,而这也印证了数据本身早在电子缔约过程中已具备了法律地位。

其实,不论最初用笔来书写,或是通过复印机器、传真机和印刷机器的重制,还是当前使用通讯科技的电波、计算机传输的数据,这些也都不过是不同的讯息传递技术而已,会有影响的只是人类的信赖,以及交易当事人在彼此互动过程中所建构出来的价值观。因此,在面对电子贸易时,我们应着重的法律上思考应是当事人互动方式以其期待的内容的改变,而不是其所使用的技术或媒介的变动。基本上,在社会规范的形成过程中,我们实应尝试对于所需规范提出一些评价的机制,以确认法律的运用是正面的。McAdams氏便曾在研究网络的规范问题后,提出一个规范形成的评价理论(Esteem Theory),认为一般的情况下,人们渴求他人的尊重并希望博得好评价的心态,有助于规范的形成,因而产生了以评价为基础的规范。为了进一步说明这个理论,他补充了三个条件:(1)对行为加以评判的舆论;(2)行为人承担被检验的风险;(3)前述的舆论及风险必须是相关群体所熟知的。② 如果我们尝试将网络规范的形成用McAdams的理论加以检验,可以发现网络世界具有"信息流"的特殊属性,讯息流通快速,缩短了人与人之间距离,加速了舆论的形成及有关社群的认知速度,满足了评价理论第一和第三个条件。然而,因网络世界"匿名"性,使用者的身份不一定会被揭露,行为人保有比在实体社会中更多的隐秘,大幅降低了面临检验的风险,限缩了"评价"的拘束力,虽然评价理论并不能完全适用在网络规范的形成,但这些发现却可以用来诠释前文本文所提及诸多法律调整的必要性。

整体而言,网络世界是一个独特而复杂的社会系统,只有从比较网际网络社会和非数字社会的差异处着手,才能真正了解并体会网络规范的复杂性,进而找出合适的理论来解释网络规范的形成。这点对于电子合同法制的发展而言,又岂能容有例外?

---

① 然而,现在大家的思考重点,似乎都在强调是否数字形态储存的信息也符合民法的文书或签章的要求,而忽略了当事人所作选择与安排的意义,及其对当事人真意如何影响。例如在台湾地区的民商法体系下,台湾地区行政院研究会于1999年12月25日提出的"电子签章法草案"虽然能解决签章的真正的法律基础问题,但新修编的保守态度,却都没有就这部分有所研究,显然对于未来电子交易的发展埋下了不确定的因素。就前文所论及美国 U. C. C. 在修正过程中有关 attribution 的概念的提出,正是与台湾地区当前的法制发展上有所不同之处。

② 详参 McAdams, Richard H., "The Origin, Development, and Regulation of Norms", *MICH. L. REV.* 1997, (96): 338, 355—357。

6.2 电子合同法制化之建议

自网际网络被普遍使用以来,电子交易环境正逐步建构,而电子合同法制亦逐步调整,唯如何自网络经济、信息经济或电子商务经济的角度来掌握电子交易的发展过程及趋势,并充分掌握国内外之法律对应调整,进而具体归纳相关问题之重心,以为深入从事体系分析或探讨之依据,应是基本的研究态度。以发展历程言,最早的合同电子化发展系以电子数据交换模式来呈现,这种动力本源于自律的要求,透过私法自治的功能运作,进而促使国际性规范的调整或诞生,来处理不能由合同协议解决之相关问题。然不可讳言者,电子化环境之冲击,已全面性地影响到原有法制结构;以合同之缔结而言,交易当事人并非透过传统的纸和笔,而系经数字信息之交换要约与承诺,基意思表示合致而成立合同关系[①];尤其,在将自动化计算机系统与电子代理应用于电子合同之情形日趋普遍时,更衍生出许多新兴的法律问题;此问题虽在过去针对自动贩卖机之缔约与履行之需要,已肯定为无碍于相关意思表示之成立与效力[②],然随着科技之进步与发展,自动化计算机系统与电子代理之功能已超越"自动"而有"自主"之能力,此时其法律属性为何?又应如何认定其间所传送讯息之法律效果?均生疑义。再就交易内容而言,原本关税贸易总协议或世界贸易组织(GATT/WTO)架构下的发展系着眼于商品之交易而后及于服务,如今随软件与信息本身之交易发展成为跨国交易的重要内容,所谓在线信息授权(licenses of information)交易,带入了所谓第三类型的交易标的,也颠覆了传统买卖合同对缔约行为、缔约过程、履约方式、损害赔偿、纠纷处理等法律规范之要求。与传统书面合同相较,合同之意义与作用虽无产生改变,但形式上却产生了极大的变化,其主要表现在:(1)订立合同之双方是在一个虚拟市场中运作;(2)电子合同是典型的无纸合同,是以可读形式储存在计算机磁性介质上的一组数字信息;(3)表示合同成立生效之传统签字盖章方式,被电子合同的电子签名所取代;(4)电子合同的订立与成立有其自有之特点,如自动化交易系统之应用等。[③] 是以,吾人以为,经由电子、光学或类似方法来缔结合同,应为一种新的缔约方式,而

---

① 周忠海等:《电子商务法新论》,台北:神州出版社2002年版,第46页。
② 参黄茂荣:《电子商务契约的一些法律问题》,载《植根杂志》,2000,16(6):9。
③ 赵金龙、任心婧:《论电子合同》,载《当代法学》2003年第8期,第43—44页。

得赋予其"电子合同"之功能性名称①;唯现有之民事法制尚不足以涵盖并规范所有电子合同关系中所有之法律问题,应如何评价,殊值得加以研究。

针对逐步成型之电子合同概念言,虽联合国贸易法律委员会早于1996年便曾于《联合国贸易法律委员会电子商务模范法》(United Nations Commission on International Trade Law)②中提出"功能等同"(functional-equivalent)之概念③,试图来解决传统民事法中所涉要约与承诺、发出与收受等传统行为概念,因应交易环境电子化之调整问题,但此概念之提出尚不足以解决因自动化计算机交易系统与电子代理普遍应用于电子合同中所新衍生之问题④,盖其已超过前述"功能等同"观念所能涵盖之范围。是以,联合国及国际商会等组织均快速投入电子交易法律之建制,未来国际交易环境亦将无可避免的呈现出从国际到内国的统一化趋势,如本书所特别介绍《藉数据电文缔结或证明之(国际)合同公约草案初稿》,正是国际社会持续因应国际贸易环境变迁过程中所作的重大努力,鉴于两岸业已逐步迈入电子化国家之林,对于此种攸关电子交易法制之新发展,实不容忽视,而掌握其发展方向并预为因应是两岸中国人所不可忽视之重要事项。

电子化交易之发展,对于传统合同法制之影响已然具体浮现,而有待吾等进一步的去调整相关法制以为因应。面对此国际发展趋势,台湾地区如何藉由电子签章立法之初备,探究其与电子合同所赖民事法规间之调和关系,并就电子合同实务中可能面临之民事基础法律问题,参考国际

---

① 其主要特征有:(1)订立合同的双方往往是互不相识、互不见面的。(2)传统合同的口头形式在贸易上常常表现为店堂交易,并将商家所开具的发票作为合同的依据。(3)表示合同生效的传统签字盖章方式被电子签章所代替。(4)传统合同的生效地点一般为合同成立的地点,而采用数据电文形式订立的合同,收件人的主营业地为合同成立的地点;没有主营业地的,其经常居住地为合同成立的地点。许志坤:《浅析电子双方交易与电子合同》,载《河北师范大学学报(哲学社会科学版)》2003年第6期,第38页;李祖全:《电子合同的证据法学之思考》,载《常德师范学院学报(社会科学版)》2003年第3期,第51页;张展赫:《关于电子合同法律属性的讨论》,载《科技情报开发与经济》2003年第3期,第66页。

② Report of the United Nations Commission on International Trade Law, U. N. Commission on International Trade Law, 29th Sess., U. N. Doc. A/51/17 (1996); Uzelac, Alan, "Comparative Theme: UNCITRAL Notes on Organizing Arbitral Proceedings: A Regional View", *CROAT. ARBIT. YEARB.* 1997, (4): 135.

③ http://www.un.or.at/uncitral/texts/electom/english/m1-ec.htm (visited 2003/5/25); http://www.uzp.gov.pl/zagranica/ONZ/UNCITRAL_english.html (visited 2004/8/5)。

④ 如自动化计算机系统与电子代理之应用之问题等;Bellia Jr., Anthony J., "Contracting With Electronic Agents", *Emory L. J.* 2001, (50): 1047。

社会之立法精神及实践经验,以为未来法制调适与因应之需,实有探讨之必要。就电子合同所涉问题而言,本书以当事人、标的及意思表示为主轴的探讨,试图显现出电子化环境所带来的影响。先就当事人部分言,远距的互动首先挑战了人类传统彼此辨识对方的经验,动摇了传统法制所建构出的交易当事人互信基础,从而也带动了电子签章法制的诞生,一方面透过数字签章作为辨认当事人身份之表征,他方面则透过凭证机构来对签章之真正性加以认证,以达保护交易当事人之目的。此外,如何在交易安全之维护与限制行为或无行为能力之保护间权衡的问题,吾等虽能在民法之相关规定中找到一些探讨方向,然较完善之处理方式仍应进一步调适相关民事法规,以为规范。至于,自动化计算机系统与电子代理之应用,乃电子合同缔结过程中使用计算机软硬件之必然结果,而如何跳脱出传统以"人"为基础的代理概念,发展出以预先设计之"自动"系统或具人工智能之"自主"系统为内容,并以之为界定当事人间之权义及责任归属之依据,正是近来国际间法制之重要发展,而值得加以借镜并立法因应者。至于交易标的所涉问题部分,因智慧财产商品异于传统商品及服务之本质,促使传统贸易的外围法制均呈现涵括不足之现象,这其中又以如何满足确认交易标的及当事人间之权益关系界定问题为最;对此,美国司法实务以类同于买卖合同关系来处理计算机软件研发之做法,以及新修统一计算机信息交易法(UCITA)与统一电子交易法(UETA)之提出,除印证了国际社会对如何规范信息交易标的之不确定性外,更提供我们值得借镜之法制调整经验。最后,以意思表示为核心之探讨,所衍生之要约与要约引诱之区别、非对话意思表示之生效时点认定与意思表示合致过程中之撤回与撤销等问题,乃前揭本文所涵括之重点。原则上,本书以为,欲完善之电子合同法制,就重要的基础性问题应透过立法加以规范,除对要约与承诺之成立生效时点之认定外,如何去判断电子讯息的出处或归属?如何评价"再确认"之机制?均有待法律给予更明确的规范。大陆之合同法与台湾地区电子签章法中虽有相关之规定,然容有不足,从而较佳之处理方式仍应就电子合同环境所赖之私法体系,作一较全面的检讨与补充为是。

除了实体法之问题外,由于技术本身的发展性,以及交易发生之欠缺地域性或法域限制性,主权之概念与管制之可能均受到稀释,从而合同本身之拘束力或执行力也同样的受到影响。在这种背景下法律应如何诠释同时存在于虚拟环境与实体社会中之合同行为,将是对于整体执法体系的考验。一如其他发展中之网络法律课题,法规范之发展须依循逻辑推理来探求其与真实世界法规范之兼容性;而在立法努力跟上科技发展脚步的过程中,国际间的趋势、真实世界中的惯例,以及因应新兴科技所衍生的学理论述,都是吾等须小心以对者。以涉外民事管辖权争端解决方案言,如能透过国际合作签订"多边或双边条约"以决定管辖权之归属,当系最佳的解决之道,然国际间尚未有公约定案之提出,故现阶段尚无法透过此途径解决之;唯海牙《民商事管辖权及外国判决之承认与执行公约草案初稿》与《选择法庭协议公约草案》虽尚未定案,但其中已有共识之部分,仍值得吾等加以参考。再者,在决定该法院是否有管辖权时,吾等应就可能据以为管辖之基础参酌学理及国际间相关发展,视实际状况与关连性加以判断,以决定法院是否具备管辖之权限;是以,对于涉外电子合同之民事管辖问题,于两岸除了修法因应外,当前比较实际的做法应是"类推适用现行民事诉讼法"台湾地区亦可参酌消费者保护法①或电子签章法之规定,以决定法院是否享有管辖权;此外,或可参考美国实务之发展将"网址"作为定管辖基础,或承认"网络法院"之运作机制,均有助于管辖问题之解决。最后,本诸自由市场经济原则,在法律变动过程中,尊重当事人的选择空间,则是另一个值得大家尊重的原则,其实这也是本书在论及当前国际社会寻求解决电子合同涉外民事管辖问题过程中,所加以强调者。此可证诸于《海牙公约草案》与《选择法庭协议公约》之规定,在尊重当事人合同自主之精神下,允许缔约当事人得经由合意定管辖法院,此与民事诉讼法规定大致相符②,且于美国计算机信息交易法(U.C.I.T.A.)亦承认当事人得以就管辖法院与准据法加以选择。③ 是以,于当事人利用网络进行交易时,若得民事诉讼法之规定,任当事人得以合意定管辖法院④,此应可以解决大部分管辖法院决定之问题。

综观电子合同之立法趋势言,我们应对一些根本性的问题需加以厘清。首先,我们想提出的质疑,在现行法是否适用于电子交易?有无增修

---

① 马汉宝:《国际私法总论》,台北:作者1997年自版,第180页;刘铁铮:《国际私法论丛》,台北:三民书局2000年版,第276页;林益山:《国际裁判管辖权冲突之研究》,载《中兴法学》,1993(36):7;林益山:《涉外网络契约管辖之探讨》,载《月旦法学杂志》,2001(77):23。

② 冯震宇、陈家骏等:《电子交易法制相关议题之研究》,台北:经建会2002年版,第190—191页。

③ 详参冯震宇:《论电子商务之法律保护与因应策略》,载《月旦法学杂志》,2002(80):180—181。

④ 依大陆《民事诉讼法》第244条规定,涉外合同的当事人,可以用书面协议选择与争议有实际联系的地点的法律管辖。依台湾地区《民事诉讼法》第24条之规定,亦得以当事人之合意约定管辖。

之必要?虽有论者以为,电子合同所涉之法律问题,并非电子环境所特有的,而系传统合同关系中都会遭遇的问题,故对电子合同提出新规范产生质疑。① 吾人以为,工业时代机械式、系统化、结构化的法规范,已不足以涵盖于动态、随机、成长的电子交易环境,唯电子交易环境对合同法制所生之影响并非全面抑或绝对地,故就电子合同所涉之问题应可区别为:(1)合同之一般问题(如签章与书面形式等问题)与(2)电子化之特殊问题(如电子代理与自动计算机系统之应用等问题),针对前者我们或可透过适用、类推适用或解释之方法加以解决,对于后者我们则需透过增修现行法或另立新法,加以因应。此可证诸于联合国国际贸易法律发展委员会之立法历程,其于1996年提出《电子商务模范法》,试图以"功能等同"之概念,来解决合同之一般问题,然随科技的发展与实际交易经验中,发现此不足以涵括所有新兴之法律问题,是以,拟提出新公约以解决因新的缔约方式所新生之法律问题。

  面对现有之民事法制尚不足以涵盖并规范电子交易之问题,我们是否应增修现行法律?抑或另立专法?国际间之发展趋势正逐步影响各国之立法态度,从目前各国立法现状来看,有两种立法模式,一种是制定专门的电子商务法律,如美国、欧盟、新加坡、印度、巴西等国都对电子商务有专门的立法。另一种就是增修现有规范:大陆系就原有的合同法律制度进行扩大化解释,以使电子合同纳入原有的法律调整的范围②;台湾地区则是通过消费者保护法之增修。是以,大陆于《合同法》中针对电子化之问题设有部分规定,此具预见性的立法对电子商务之发展,虽已起一定之作用。③ 至于是否尚需制定专法,以为因应?有论者以为,可先采用司法解释的方式解决或补充现有合同法的内容④,使其具有适用性;唯有论者以为应直接进行电子商务综合立法。⑤ 对此,台湾地区之因应,虽于《消

---

① United Nations Commission on International Trade Law Working Group on Electronic Commerce, Thirty-ninth session, A/CN.9/WG.IV/WP.96. (2002).
② 朱萍:《电子合同法律调整:模式与框架的探讨》,载《武汉大学学报(社会科学版)》2002年第5期,第568页。
③ 朱宁先、朱成化、朱顺先:《电子商务的电子合同及其法律思考》,载《管理科学》2003年第5期,第96页。
④ 张巍:《网络立法悠着点》,载《检察日报》,1999年4月7日;张娜:《中国法学会民法经济法研究会2000年年会综述》,载《人民法院报》,2000年10月21日。
⑤ 张楚:《关于我国电子商务立法问题的思考》,见中国政法大学民商法教研室:《江平教授七十华诞祝贺文集》,中国法制出版社2000年版,第468页;孙在友、苏哲:《论电子合同的法律效力》,载《天津工业大学学报》2002年第6期,第48页;吴楠:《电子合同中若干法律问题探析及应用建议》,载《学术界》2003年第2期,第224页。

费者保护法》中将网际网络之交易纳入访问买卖之类型[①],并于《电子签章法》设有部分规定外,然就本文所提出之部分问题,虽或可类推适用相关民事法规,尚难获得周延且全面的解决。[②]

承上,若我们认为应另立专法,以为因应。究应针对电子合同此特定议题制定专法? 抑或先就电子交易行为统一立法? 以各国之立法现况言,美国曾就网络银行之议题,制定电子资金移转法、为信息流通之促进,制定信息自由法、英国亦曾针对反社会行为之防治,制定计算机滥用法;至于涉及电子合同之议题,美国更有 UCC2B、UCITA、UETA(Uniform Electronic Transaction Act)与 E-SIGN 等专法之制定。相对于此,而德国则有《多元媒体法》之制定、新加坡则有《电子商务法》之制定。对此,虽有论者以为,以单独制订一部以合同为核心、兼顾其他法律规范的电子商务法为较好的选择[③];但在进程上理论界可以有两种不同的观点:(1) 先就电子商务出现的具体法律问题,先行制定单行规则或修订传统法律,形成统一思路后,再制定电子商务基本法;(2) 先制定电子商务基本法,以此为指导思想,就各个具体问题制定单行规则或修定传统法律。[④] 中国在第九届人大第三次会议上,虽已有代表就专门电子商务立法提交议案,但有几种不同的看法[⑤]:(1) 电子商务立法的时机不成熟说;(2) 电子商务立法的市场自身调节说;(3) 电子商务立法的已有法律涵盖说;(4) 电子商务立法的地方立法说;(5) 电子商务立法的技术万能说。故专家们认为,在立法模式上,可以采取的模式有二:其一为分两步走的方式,从个别法规入手,待时机成熟在统一起草电子商务法;另一种则是由点到面的方式,先透过修改相关部门之法规,再不断实践中逐步开发连点成面的统一立法。[⑥] 而在立法政策上,有建议采行双轨制,在立法的基本框架和原则下,

---

① 详参台湾地区《消费者保护法》第 2 条第 1 项第 10 款之规定。
② 如自动化计算机系统与电子代理之应用问题、以计算机软件为电子合同交易标的之问题、非对话意思表示之生效时点认定等。
③ 刘俊臣:《略论电子合同的法律调整》,载《中国工商管理研究》2002 年第 2 期,第 10 页;张平:《我国电子商务立法的误区》,载《网络法律评论》,法律出版社 2001 年版,第 13 页。
④ 韩勇、王静等:《电子商务立法的实践与探索》,见第七届中国国际电子商务大会:《中国电子商务政策法律论坛论文集》,政策法律论坛组委会 2003 年版,第 4 页。
⑤ 阿拉木斯:《关于中国电子商务立法的五种说法》,载《信息网络与高新技术法律前沿》,法律出版社 2003 年版,第 263 页。
⑥ 杜颖:《电子合同法》,湖南大学出版社 2002 年版,第 91 页。

允许行业与企业发展自治规则。① 至于中国制定《电子商务法》应采取什么样的架构,学者主要有两种看法:一种认为,应以《模范法》为模本,进行本土化移植;另一种观点认为,依照中国的立法习惯和中国人的思维方式,宜采取"总则+分则"模式。② 而立法的核心法律问题,应当包括立法的总则、数字化信息的法律地位和网络合同的法律效力以及网络服务提供者的责任这四个方面。③ 对此立法模式之考量,吾人以为,面对此一新兴科技法律争议,立法者与执法者虽不宜采取冒进的激进行为,或可利用"停看听(wait and see)"的策略,只要不是太大的社会伤害,何妨停一下、看一下,给其他的解决方案有解决的机会,让新的科技法制有反应新文化、新价值观的机会④;同时,藉由停看听,能将国际之规范内国化,藉以达到建构完善法律制度之基础。以目前大陆涉及电子交易之主要立法而言,除已于合同法中作部分条文修改以因应电子化之问题外,另已有电子签章法草案之拟定并送审查外,企业及行业协会亦提出的电子商务立法建议方案及相关自律规则;相对于此,台湾地区于法制之建构方面,并未就传统民法为修正,除于消费者保护法中将网际网络交易列入访问买卖之类型中,试图解决B2C交易之部分问题外,另有电子签章法之制定以解决电子交易中电子签章、电子文书与认证机构之根本问题,更通过政府之措施(如电子商务消费者保护纲领等)与民间之运作(如自律公约与信赖标章之提出)以健全电子交易法制环境。整体言之,两岸电子商务法制显然正朝向"促进具社会容许性之行为"(the promotion of socially acceptable behavior)的方向发展⑤,这种发展特色所呈现出者,将是人类互信与多元价值的尊重,系基道德规范所呈现出之共识⑥,值得我们持续观察之。

---

① 并于立法程序上,鼓励企业与行业动议立法并提出议案,从商业实践中提炼法律规则,更鼓励行业协会发展自治规范,使行业协会真正成为联系企业、学术与政府的桥梁;高富平:"确立自治规范与立法规范双轨制,营造安全有效的电子商务法律环境",见第七届中国国际电子商务大会:《中国电子商务政策法律论坛论文集》,政策法律论坛组委会2003年版,第14页。
② 在拟定《电子商务法(模范法)》的时候,应采取"总则+分则"模式,其中"总则"部分主要以《联合国电子商务模范法》的模本,确定一些原则,"分则"部分则可以分门别类作具体规定;刘俊臣:《略论电子合同的法律调整》,载《中国工商管理研究》,2002年第2期,第10页。
③ 郑成思、薛虹:《我国电子商务立法的核心问题》,载《互联网世界》2000年第10期,第10页。
④ 范建得:《新工业革命时代的科技法制》,收录于《知识经济与法制改造研讨会专辑》,台北:元照出版社2002年版,第50—52页。
⑤ Denning Dorothy E & Lin Herbert S eds., *Rights and Responsibilities of Participants in Networked Communities*, Washington: National Research Council National Academy Press 1994, pp.25—30.
⑥ Casey, Timothy D. & Magenau, Jeff, "A Hybrid Model of Self-Regulation and Governmental Regulation of Electronic Commerce Timothy", *Santa Clara Computer & High Tech. L. J.* 2002, (19): 1.

致 谢

伴随着两岸开放的步伐，抱着诚惶诚恐的心情，我踏上了这片一向只存在于台湾地区历史、地理教科书中的神州大陆，也迈向了一个习法的新里程。犹记得刚踏入政法大学研究生院之际，对于这片土地充满了复杂的情绪，几分敬畏、几分浪漫、几分不安，就这样我历经了在北京这伟大城市的四个寒暑。回首来时路，虽少了些傅斯年的憧憬，也没有徐志摩的诗意，但整个北京城所带给世人的文化深度及活在其中的芸芸众生对传统的执著，让我从中发现到前所未见的华人价值观，更开启了在学习与国际同步之法律过程中的另一扇门。在政法的四年，恩师们浩瀚学养的洗礼，逐渐引领我体会到神州大陆对法律人之期许，更对于法律在引领社会与人类文明成长上所能扮演之积极角色有了更深层的体认。

对于一个台湾地区法律学者而言，21世纪的到来有两项必须加以重视的发展：其一为全球科技之快速发展对三百多年来传统法制之影响；其二为在两岸互动关系混沌不明之前提下，大陆法律制度之演变发展及其与台湾地区之互动。而如何在全球相关法制发展的背景中，以台湾地区既有较能衔接资本市场观点的法律研究为基础，进行与大陆现行充分与国际接轨之发展原则下的科技法制加以比较研究，进而厘清台湾地区未来研究大陆新兴法制时之诠释理念，并将此种观点发展成为具国际学术研究价值的课题，应是吾等责无旁贷之任务。是以，个人尝试申请到中国社会科学院法学研究所从事法学博士后研究工作，以知识经济下电子合同之变革与发展为例，探究中国信息社会法制化之发展趋势。

在这两年中，感谢郑成思教授给了我机会，协助我开启智慧之门，更谢谢郑教授在这段期间以其雍容大度的学者风范，引领我攀登更高深学术殿堂，毕竟，能跳脱字里行间的法律形式而一窥法理堂奥，乃法学追求者的终身职志。其次在社科院的这两年中，李明德教授费心引领我厘清研究方向并给予生活上的辅导，更是令我铭记在心；而李顺德教授及其他社科院的老师们，也都是不吝协助我一尝法理探索夙愿的恩师。

在这一切的心灵成长历程中，师恩浩荡无法言喻，个人何其有幸能同受两岸法律学府之栽培,一样是深感于心,对受业恩师们亦师亦父的提携,受益之处又岂仅在于智识之成长,除了感谢外,当是一辈子的感激。良师之外,益友同样对于自己学位论文的完成,有着不容抹灭之助益,其中个人并要特别谢谢继明师兄、爱民、子聿及明怡的大力协助,谢谢你们。

参 考 文 献

一、中文参考资料

（一）期刊

1. 于海防、韩冰:《电子合同订立过程中的若干问题研究》,载《烟台大学学报》(哲学社会科学版)2002年第2期。
2. 于静:《电子合同若干法律问题初探》,载《政法论坛》1997年第6期。
3. 王江雨:《买卖合同成立的一般规则与国际贸易中的格式之战》,载《民商法论丛》1997年第8卷。
4. 王德全:《试论Internet案件的司法管辖》,载《中外法学》1998年第2期。
5. 冯大同:《国际贸易中应用电子数据交换所遇到的法律问题》,载《中国法学》1993年第5期。
6. 冯震宇:《电子商务法律问题何其多》,载《能力杂志》1998年第11期。
7. 冯震宇:《论电子商务之法律保护与因应策略》,载《月旦法学杂志》2002年第80期。
8. 冯震宇:《论网络商业化所面临的管辖问题(上)》,载《信息法务透析》1997年第9期。
9. 冯震宇:《论网际网络与消费者保护问题(下)》,载《信息法务透析》1998年第7期。
10. 刘俊臣:《略论电子合同的法律调整》,载《中国工商管理研究》2002年第2期。
11. 冯震宇:《论网络商业化所面临的管辖问题(下)》,载《信息法务透析》1997年第10期。
12. 刘晓红:《论合同之债法律冲突解决方法及最新发展——兼论〈国际商事合同通则〉的效力与适用》,载《国际法学》2000年第1期。
13. 刘满达:《网络商务案件管辖权的实证论析》,载《法学》2000年第2期。
14. 刘颖、骆文怡、伍艳:《论电子合同中的书面形式问题及其解决》,载《经济师》2003年第2期。
15. 刘毓骅:《国际贸易中EDI应用的举证、签字和书面要求》,载《国际贸易》1994年第9期。
16. 吕国民:《电子合同订立的若干问题探析》,载《财经问题研究》2002年第5期。
17. 孙在友、苏哲:《论电子合同的法律效力》,载《天津工业大学学报》2002年第6期。
18. 朱宁先、朱成化、朱顺先:《电子商务的电子合同及其法律思考》,载《管理科学》

2003年第5期。

19. 朱萍:《电子合同法律调整:模式与框架的探讨》,载《武汉大学学报(社会科学版)》2002年第5期。
20. 许志坤:《浅析电子双方交易与电子合同》,载《河北师范大学学报(哲学社会科学版)》2003年第6期。
21. 齐爱民:《电子合同典型法律规则研究》,载《武汉大学学报(社会科学版)》2002年第2期。
22. 吴楠:《电子合同中若干法律问题探析及应用建议》,载《学术界》2003年第2期。
23. 吴瑾瑜:《网络中无体商品之民法相关问题——以在线递送付费商业计算机软件为例》,载《政大法学评论》2003年第74期。
24. 张展赫:《关于电子合同法律属性的讨论》,载《科技情报开发与经济》2003年第3期。
25. 李祖全:《电子合同的证据法学之思考》,载《常德师范学院学报(社会科学版)》2003年第3期。
26. 杜维武:《美国关于信息授权与管辖权相关问题(下)》,载《法令月刊》1999,50(4)。
27. 杨芳贤:《电子商务契约及其付款之问题》,载《中原财经法学》2000年第5期。
28. 杨佳政:《电子交易中数字签章与电子文件之法律效力浅析》,载《信息法务透析》1998年第2期。
29. 杨桢:《论电子商务与英美契约法》,载《东吴法律学报》2003,15(1)。
30. 卓小苏:《电子合同形式论》,载《法商研究——中南财经政法大学学报(法学版)》2002年第2期。
31. 林益山:《国际裁判管辖权冲突之研究》,载《中兴法学》1993年第36期。
32. 林益山:《涉外网络契约管辖之探讨》,载《月旦法学杂志》2001年第77期。
33. 林瑞珠:《当前贸易电子化所面临之法律新课题——以两岸法律因应为例》,载《万国法律》2002年第123期。
34. 果芸:《企业如何运用电子商务赚钱》,载《信息与计算机》1999年第4期。
35. 郑成思、薛虹:《台湾地区电子商务立法的核心问题》,载《互联网世界》2000年第10期。
36. 郑远民、易志斌:《试论公证在电子合同中的应用价值》,载《北京理工大学学报(社会科学版)》2002年第2期。
37. 洪淑芬:《数字签字——公开金钥认证机构介绍》,载《信息法务透析》1996年第11期。
38. 赵金龙、任学婧:《论电子合同》,载《当代法学》2003年第8期。
39. 赵骏:《商业EDI活动的法律调整》,载《政治与法律》1998年第1期。
40. 陶岚、王芳:《试论电子合同的法律效力》,载《南昌高专学报》2003年第3期。
41. 高云:《电子合同中电子邮件应用的法律问题研究》,载《电子知识产权》2002年第

3期。
42. 章宏友:《关于电子合同若干问题的法律思考》,载《武汉冶金管理干部学院学报》2003年第1期。
43. 黄茂荣:《电子商务契约的一些法律问题》,载《植根杂志》2000,16(6)。
44. 廖纬民:《论信息时代的隐私权保障——以信息隐私权为中心》,载《信息法务透析》1996年第11期。
45. 樊国桢:《型式认证在台湾地区社会可信赖的信息使用环境中所面临的问题与挑战》,载《信息法务透析》1998年第5期。
46. 薛德明:《国际贸易中EDI的若干法律问题探讨》,载《法律科学》1994年第3期。

(二) 专著

1. Kalakota & Whinston:《电子商务概论(Frontiers of Electronic Commerce)》,查修杰、连丽真、陈雪美译,跨世纪电子商务出版社1999年版。
2. Nicholas Negroponte:《数位革命》,齐若兰译,台北:天下出版社1995年版。
3. 中兴大学法律研究所译:《美国统一商法典及其译注》(上册),台北:台湾地区银行经济研究室编印1986年版。
4. 王伟:《论在线履行数字电子合同的履行地确认机制》,载《政法论丛》2003年第4期。
5. 王传丽:《国际贸易法——国际货物贸易法》,中国政法大学出版社1999年版。
6. 王泽鉴:《民法总则》,台北:三民书局2001年版。
7. 丘联恭:《司法之现代化与程序法》,台北:三民书局1992年版。
8. "司法院":《民事法律专题研究》(四),"司法院"司法业务研究会第5期及第9期研究专题,台北:司法周刊杂志社1987年印行。
9. 台湾地区"经济部"商业司编:《1999中华台北电子商务年鉴》,台北:"经济部"2000年版。
10. 台湾地区"经济部"国际贸易局:"参与国际经贸事务项目小组电子商务工作分组"1999年度第2次会议,会议资料。
11. 石志泉:《民事诉讼法释义》,台北:三民书局1987年版。
12. 李双元:《国际经济贸易法律与实务新论》(第12版),湖南大学出版社1996年版。
13. 杜颖:《电子合同法》,湖南大学出版社2002年版。
14. 汪涛主编:《EDI:国际贸易新手段》,中国经济出版社1997年版。
15. 周忠海:《电子商务导论》,北京邮电大学出版社2000年8月版。
16. 周忠海等:《电子商务法新论》,台北:神州出版社2002年版。
17. 林季红、李蓉:《信用状实务指南》,台北:世界文库1997年版。
18. 林诚二:《民法债编各论》,台北:瑞兴图书股份有限公司1994年版。
19. 林诚二:《民法总则讲义》(上册),台北:瑞兴图书股份有限公司1995年版。
20. 阿拉木斯:《关于中国电子商务立法的五种说法》,载寿步主编:《信息网络与高新技术法律前沿》,法律出版社2003年版。

21. 姚瑞光:《民事诉讼法论》,台北:大中国 1991 年版。
22. 施米托夫:《国际贸易法文选》(第 12 版),中国大百科全书出版社 1993 年版。
23. 施启扬:《民法总则》,台北:三民书局 2000 年版。
24. 范建得:《新工业革命时代的科技法制》,载台湾法学会主编:《知识经济与法制改造研讨会专辑》(第 11 版),台北:元照出版社 2002 年版。
25. 高富平:《确立自治规范与立法规范双轨制,营造安全有效的电子商务法律环境》,载《第七届中国国际电子商务大会·中国电子商务政策法律论坛论文集》,北京:政策法律论坛组委会 2003 年。
26. 常怡主编:《民事诉讼法学》,中国政法大学出版社 1994 年版。
27. 曹伟修:《民事诉讼法释论》,台北:曹游龙 1984 年版。
28. 梁慧星主编:《民商法论丛》(第 4 卷),法律出版社 1996 年版。
29. 郭瑜:《国际货物买卖法》,人民法院出版社 1999 年版。
30. 郭豫珍:《涉外民事之国际管辖权的确定》,"国立"政治大学法律研究所硕士论文,1994 年。
31. 彭万林主编:《民法学》,中国政法大学出版社 1996 年版。
32. 董炳和、李振瑞:《国际商务法律与惯例》,山东人民出版社 1996 年版。
33. 董新民:《国际商务法律》,中国审计出版社 1996 年版。
34. 蔡馥如:《网络管辖之研究》,台北:"国立"台北大学法律硕士班硕士论文,1999 年。
35. 冯大同:《国际货物买卖法》,北京大学出版社 1995 年版。
36. 冯震宇:《网络法基本问题》(一),台北:学林出版社 1999 年版。
37. 冯震宇、陈家骏等:《电子交易法制相关议题之研究》,台北:"经建会" 2002 年版。
38. 刘铁铮:《国际私法论丛》,台北:三民书局 2000 年版。
39. 单文华:《电子贸易的法律问题》,载梁慧星主编:《民商法论丛》(第 10 卷),法律出版社 1998 年版。
40. 吴明轩:《民事诉讼法》,台北:作者 1981 年自版。
41. 吴嘉生:《电子商务法导论》,台北:学林文化 2003 年版。
42. 吴兴光:《国际商法》,中山大学出版社 1997 年版。
43. 孙森焱:《民法债编总论》(上册),台北:三民书局 2001 年版。
44. 孙铁成:《计算器与法律》,法律出版社 1998 年版。
45. 张平:《我国电子商务立法的误区》,载《网络法律评论》,法律出版社 2001 年版。
46. 张圣翠:《国际商法》,上海财经大学出版社 1997 年版。
47. 张勇:《国际货物买卖法》,南开大学出版社 1997 年版。
48. 张楚:《关于我国电子商务立法问题的思考》,见中国政法大学民商法教研室:《江平教授七十华诞祝贺文集》,中国法制出版社 2000 年版。
49. 张学尧:《民事诉讼法论》,台北:三民书局 1970 年版。
50. 杨建华等:《民事诉讼法新论》(第 11 版),台北:三民书局 2000 年版。

51. 杨建华:《问题研析——民事诉讼法》(四),台北:作者1995年自版。
52. 《电子商务概述》,台北:"经济部"国际贸易局1997年版。
53. 苏健华:《科技未来与人类社会——从cyborg概念出发》,南华大学社会学研究所2003年版。
54. 赵威:《国际商事合同法理论与实务》,中国政法大学出版社1995年版。
55. 邓建华:《国际商法》,中国金融出版社1995年版。
56. 郑玉波:《民法总则》,台北:三民书局1998年版。
57. 陈汝吟:《论因特网上电子契约之法规范暨消费者保护》,台北大学法律学研究所硕士论文,1998年。
58. 韩勇、王静等:《电子商务立法的实践与探索》,载《第七届中国国际电子商务大会·中国电子商务政策法律论坛论文集》,政策法律论坛组委会,2003年。
59. 马琳:《略论电子合同形式的合法性》,载《中国工商管理研究》,2003年第11期。
60. 马汉宝:《国际私法总论》,台北:作者1997年自版。
61. 骆永家:《民事诉讼法Ⅰ》,台北:三民书局1999年版。

二、英文参考资料

1. A/51/17 (1996).
2. A/CN.9/333 (1990).
3. A/CN.9/350 (1991).
4. A/CN.9/426 (1996).
5. A/CN.9/484 (2001).
6. A/CN.9/548 (2004).
7. A/CN.9/WG.IV/WP.95. (2002).
8. A/CN.9/WG.IV/WP.95. (2002).
9. A/CN.9/WG.IV/WP.108 (2004).
10. A/CN.9/WG.IV/WP.53 (1991).
11. A/CN.9/WG.IV/WP.94 (2002).
12. A/CN.9/WG.IV/WP.96. (2002).
13. Amelia H. Rose, "Electronic Commerce and The Symbolic Relationship between International and Domestic Law Reform", *Tul L. Rev.* 1998, (72): 1931.
14. Bellia Jr., Anthony J., "Contracting With Electronic Agents", *Emory L. J.* 2001, (50): 1047.
15. Berman, Andrew B., "International Divergence: The 'Keys' to Signing on the Digital Line—The Cross-Border Recognition of Electronic Contracts and Digital Signatures", Syracuse J. *Int'l L. & Com.* 2001, (28): 125.
16. Biddle, C. Bradford, "Misplaced Priorities: The Utah Digital Signature Act and Liability Allocation in a Public Key Infrastructure", *SAN DIEGO L. REV.* 1996,

(33): 1143.
17. Bonell, Michael Joachim, "The UNIDROIT Principles of International Commercial Contracts: Why? What? How?", *Tul. L. Rev.* 1995, (69): 1121.
18. Boss, Amelia H., "Current Issues In Electronic Data Interchange: Electronic Data Interchange Agreements: Private Contracting Toward A Global Environment", *J. INTL. L. BUS.* 1992, (13): 31.
19. Boss, Amelia H., "The International Commercial Use of Electronic Data Interchange and Electronic Communications Technologies", *BUS. LAW* 1991, (48): 1787.
20. Breen, Michele N., "Personal Jurisdiction And The Internet: 'Shoehorning' Cyberspace Into International Shoe", Seton Hall Const. *L. J.* 1998, (8): 763.
21. Byasse, William S, "Jurisdiction of Cyberspace: Applying Real World Precedent To The Virtual Community", *Wake Forest L. Rev.* pp.1995, (30): 197.
22. "CASENOTE: Bensusan Restaurant Corp. v. King: An Erroneous Application of Personal Jurisdiction Law to Internet-based Contacts (Using the Reasonableness Test to Ensure Fair Assertions of Personal Jurisdiction Based on Cyberspace Contacts)", *Pace L. Rev.* 1998, (19): 149.
23. Cate, Fred H., "Data Protection Law And The European Union's Directive: The Challenge For The United States: The Eu Data Protection Directive, Information Privacy and the Public Interest", *Iowa L. Rev.* 1995, (80): 431.
24. Cheng, Chia-jui, *Basic Documents on International Trade Law*, Boston: Hingham, 1986.
25. Committee On The Uniform Commercial Code, An Appraisal Of The March 1, 1990, Preliminary Report Of The Uniform Commercial Code Article 2 Study Group., Prepared By A Task Force Of The A.B.A. Subcommittee On General Provisions, Sales, Bulk Transfers, And Documents Of Title, Delaware Law School of Widener University, Inc.. *Del. J. Corp. L..* 1991 (16): 981.
26. D. Casey, Jeff Magenau, "A Hybrid Model of Self-Regulation and Governmental Regulation of Electronic Commerce Timothy", *Santa Clara Computer & High Tech. L. J.* 2002, (19): 1.
27. Denning Dorothy E & Lin Herbert S eds., *Rights and Responsibilities of Participants in Networked Communities*, Washington: National Research Council National Academy Press 1994.
28. Dube, Jocelyn, "Second Place Canadian Perspectives on the Impact of the CMI Rules for Electronic Bills of Lading on the Liability of the Carrier Towards the Endorsee", *TRANSP. L. J.* 1998, (26): 107.
29. Epstein, Julian, "Cleaning up a mess on the web: a comparison of federal and state digital signature laws", *N.Y.U. J. Legis. & Pub. Pol'y* 2001/2002, (5): 491.

30. Eric Schneiderman & Ronald Kornreich, "Personal Jurisdiction and Internet Commerce", *The New York Law Journal*, 1997.
31. Etienne-Cummings, Shamita, "CASENOTE: Vanishing Boundaries: Extending The Long-Arm Statute Into Cyberspace CompuServe Incorporated v. Patterson", 89 F. 3d 1257 (6th Cir. 1996), *S. Ill. U. L. J.* 1997, (22): 217.
32. Farber, Daniel A. & Matheson, John H., "Beyond Promissory Estoppel: Contract Law and the Invisible Handshake", *U. Chi. L. Rev.* 1985, (52): 903.
33. Fischer, John P., "Computers As Agent: A Proposed Approach to Revised U. C. C. Article 2", *Ind. L. J.*. 1997 (72): 545.
34. Gilmore, Grant, *The Death of Contract*, Columbus: Ohio State University Press, 1995.
35. Gray, Tricia Leigh, "Minimum Contacts in Cyberspace: The Classic Jurisdiction Analysis in a New Setting", *J. High Tech. L.* 2002, (1): 85.
36. Huey, Nathan A., "Do E-Sign and UETA Really Matter?", *Iowa L. Rev.*, 2003, (88): 681.
37. Johnson, David R, & Post, David G, "Law and Borders—The Risk of Law in Cyberspace", *Stanford L. Rev.* 1996, (48): 1367.
38. Jonathan Rosenoer, *CyberLaw The Law of The Internet*, New York: Springer Verlag, 1996.
39. Kelly, Richard Brett, "The Cmi Charts A Course on the Sea Of Electronic Data Interchange: Rules for Electronic Bills Of Lading", *MAR. LAW. J.* 1992, (16): 349.
40. Kerr, Ian R., "Spirits in the Material World: Intelligent Agents as Intermediaries in Electronic Commerce", *Dalhousie L. J.* 1999, (22): 190.
41. Kidd, Donnie L. & Daughtrey William H., Jr., "Adapting Contract Law to Accommodate Electronic Contracts", *Rutgers Computer & Tech. L. J.* 2000, (26): 215.
42. Kotch, Kevin J., "Addressing the Legal Problems of International Electronic Data Interchange: The Use of Computer Records as Evidence in Different Legal Systems", *Temp. Int'l & Comp. L. J.* 1993, (6): 451.
43. Lerouge, Jean-Francois, "The Use of Electronic Agents Questioned Under Contractual Law: Suggested Solutions on a European and American Level", *J. Marshall J. Computer & Info. L.* 1999, (18): 403.
44. Lewis, Mark, "E-COMMERCE: Digital Signatures: Meeting the Traditional Requirements Electronically: A Canadian Perspective", *Asper Rev. Int'l Bus. & Trade L.*, 2002 (2): 63.
45. Livermore, John & Euarjai, Krailerk, "Electronic Bills Of Lading: A Progress Report", *J. MAR. L. & COM.* 1997, (28): 55.
46. Lupton, W. Everett, "The Digital Signature: Your Identity by the Numbers", *Rich. J. L. & Tech.* 1999 (6): 10.

47. Major, April Mara, "Norm Origin and Development in Cyberspace: Models of Cybernorm Evolution", *Wash. U. L. Q.* 2000, (78): 59.
48. Mann, Catherine L., "Symposium on intellectual property, digital technology & electronic commerce: the uniform computer information transactions act and electronic commerce: Balancing Issues and Overlapping Jurisdictions in the Global Electronic Marketplace: The Ucita Example", *Wash. U. J. L. & Pol'y* 2002, (8): 215.
49. McAdams, Richard H., "The Origin, Development, and Regulation of Norms", *MICH. L. REV.* 1997, (96): 338.
50. Meyer, Christoper W., "World Web Advertising: Personal Jurisdiction Around The Whole Wild World", *Wash & Lee L. Rev.* 1997, (54): 1269.
51. Michael Clanchy, *From Memory to Written Record: England 1066—1307*, Oxford: Blackwell, 1995.
52. Mohammad Nsour, "Articlefundamental Facets of the United States-Jordan Free Trade Agreement: E-commerce, Dispute Resolution, and Beyond", *Wash. U. J. L. & Pol'y* 2004 (27): 742.
53. Nahid Jilovec, *The A To Z of EDI and Its Role in E-Commerce 2nd edition*, Loveland: 29th Street Press, 1998.
54. Nelson, "Bolero-An Innovative Legal Concept", *Computers & L.* 1995, (6): 17.
55. Pisciotta, Aileen A. & Barker, James H., "Current Issues in Electronic Data Interchange: Telecommunications Regulatory Implications for International EDI Transactions", *J. INTL. L. BUS.* 1992, (13): 71.
56. Pompian, Shawn, "Is the statute of Frauds Ready for Electronic Contracting?", *Va. L. Rev.* 1999, (85): 1447.
57. Ponte, Lucille M., "Boosting Consumer Confidence in E-business: Recommendations for Establishing Fair and Effective Dispute Resolution Programs for B2C Online Transactions", *Alb. L. J. Sci. & Tech.* 2002, (12): 441.
58. Raymond T. Nimmer, "The Uniform Commercial Code Proposed Article 2b Symposium: Article 2b: An Introduction", *J. Marshall J. Computer & Info. L.* 1997, (16): 211.
59. Raz, Joseph, "Promises in Morality and Law", *HARV. L. REV.* 1982, (95): 916.
60. Raz, Joseph, "The Morality of Freedom", New York: Clarendon Press, 1986.
61. Ritter, Jeffrey B., "Current Issues in Electronic Data Interchange: Defining International Electronic Commerce", *J. INTL. L. BUS.* 1992, (13): 3.
62. Rubin, Edward L., "Consumer Protection And The Uniform Commercial Code: The Code, The Consumer, And The Institutional Structure Of The Common Law", *Wash. U. L. Q.*. 1997 (75): 11.
63. Shaw, Paul D., *Managing Legal and Security Risks in Computing and Communica-*

tions, Oxford: Butterworth-Heinemann, 1998.
64. Smedinghoff, Thomas J F\Et Al, Eds., *Online Law: The SPA'S Legal Guide to Doing Business on the Internet*, 3rd ed. Boston: Addsion Wesley Developers Press, 1997.
65. Solum, Lawrence B., "Legal Personhood for Artificial Intelligences", *N. C. L. REV.* 1992, (70): 1231.
66. Sturley, Michael F., "Proposed Amendments to the Carriage of Goods by Sea Act", *HOUS. J. INT'L Lp.* 1996, (18): 609.
67. TD/WP. 4/GE. 2/R. 123 (1978).
68. Tomaszewski, John P., "The Pandora's Box of Cyberspace: State Regulation of Digital Signatures and the Dormant Commerce Clause", *Gonz. L. Rev.* 1997/1998, (33): 417.
69. Uzelac, Alan, "Comparative Theme: UNCITRAL Notes on Organizing Arbitral Proceedings: A Regional View", *CROAT. ARBIT. YEARB.* 1997, (4): 135.
70. Yacobozzi, Ruth J., "Integrating Computer Information Transactions into Commercial Law in a Global Economy: Why UCITA is a Good Approach, but Ultimately Inadequate, and the Treaty Solution", *Syracuse L. & Tech. J.* 2003, (2003): 4.
71. Zekos, Georgios I., "The Contractual Role of Documents Issued under the Cmi Draft Instrument on Transport Law 2001", *Mar. L. & Com.* 2004, (35): 99.

三、日文参考资料

1. 内贵田:《契约法の现代化》,1996（NBL584）。
2. 早川武夫:"电子取引と书式の斗い(1)(英文契约解释とドラフティソグ74)",《国际商事法务》,1996.12, 24 (12)。
3. 牧野和夫:"电子商务取引法（EC LAW)之现状",《国际商事法务》,1988, 26 (7)。
4. 牧野和夫:"电子商取引法（EC LAW)の现状について(1)～总论および电子契约法〔上〕"~《国际商事法务》,1988, 26 (7)。
5. 室町正实:"EDI 合同の实务上の留意点(中)",《EDI(电子的データ交换)と法》,1996（NBL585）。
6. 室町正实:"EDI 契约の实务上の留意点(上)",《EDI(电子的データ交换)と法》,1996（NBL584）。
7. 野村丰弘:《受癸注のEDI 化の法的诸题の概要》,法とコンビュータ,1995 (13)。
8. 朝冈良平、伊东健治、鹿岛诚之助、菅又久直:《图解よくわかるEDI》,东京:日刊工业新闻社 1998 年版。
9. 电子取引法制に关すゐ研究会(制度关系小委员会)报告书 ヅュリスト(特集・电子取引法制のあり方),1998 (7)。
10. 管知之:《电子商取引に关おる诸问题》(特集 グローバルネットワークの法的课题)(第 21 回法とコソビュータ学会研究报告),法とコソビュタ,1997 (15)。

四、参考网站

1. http://202.130.245.40
2. http://202.84.17.11
3. http://be1.udnnews.com
4. http://daccess-ods.un.org
5. http://europa.eu.int
6. http://hirecruit.nat.gov.tw
7. http://it.sohu.com
8. http://npl.ly.gov.tw/index.jsp
9. http://proj.moeaidb.gov.tw
10. http://sc.info.gov.hk
11. http://stlc.iii.org.tw
12. http://tech.sina.com.cn
13. http://tech.taiwan.com
14. http://w3.abanet.org/home.cfm
15. http://www.2bguide.com
16. http://www.5ipda.com
17. http://www.bolero.net
18. http://www.chinatax.gov.cn
19. http://www.cnc.ac.cn
20. http://www.cnnic.com.cn
21. http://www.comitemaritime.org
22. http://www.cpc.gov.tw
23. http://www.ctiforum.com
24. http://www.dgt.gov.tw
25. http://www.doj.gov.hk
26. http://www.e21times.com
27. http://www.ec.org.cn
28. http://www.ec.org.tw
29. http://www.ecpress.com.tw
30. http://www.find.org.tw
31. http://www.firstmonday.dk
32. http://www.iccwbo.org
33. http://www.ipeclaw.com.tw
34. http://www.juns.com.cn
35. http://www.moea.gov.tw

36. http://www.new54.com
37. http://www.people.com.cn
38. http://www.psd.111.org.tw
39. http://www.sipo.gov.cn
40. http://www.sosa.org.tw/index.asp
41. http://www.tipo.gov.tw
42. http://www.twnic.net.tw
43. http://www.ucitaonline.com
44. http://www.un.or.at
45. http://www.uncitral.org
46. http://www.unctad.org
47. http://www.unidroit.org
48. http://www.uzp.gov.pl
49. http://www.whitehouse.gov
50. http://wwwdoc.trade.gov.tw

附录

1. 两岸电子商务合同法制对照表

电子合同疑义		现行法令依据（大陆地区）	现行法令依据（台湾地区）	备注
书面形式问题		《合同法》第11条 《电子签名法》第4条	《电子签章法》第4条	
签章之问题	中央	《电子签名法》第2条及第14条	1. 台湾地区民法第3条 2. 《电子签章法》第9条	
	地方	1. 上海市《国际经贸电子数据交换管理规定》第7条 2. 广东省《电子交易条例》第6条至第9条		
证据法之问题	中央	1. 《电子签名法》第7条 2. 《民事诉讼法》第63条及69条之规定 3. 《电子签名法》第3条、第7条及第8条	《民事诉讼法》第363条	1. 原件判断产生困难 2. 另立新法
	地方	广东省：《电子交易条例》第8条及第9条		
当事人身份之确认问题		《电子签名法》第9条、13条、第16条及第20条	1. 《电子签章法》第9条 2. 《电子签章法》第11条	
当事人行为能力之欠缺问题		《合同法》第9条	1. 台湾地区民法第75条以下 2. 《邮政法》第12条 3. 《电信法》第9条	1. 适用民法之规定 2. 另立新法
电子代理之应用		1. 非《民法通则》第9条之民事权利能力主体 2. 自无《合同法》第63条规范以下之适用	1. 非权利主体（台湾地区民法第6条） 2. 无台湾地区《民法》第103条之适用	1. 本人之物或代理 2. 制订特别法或统一立法
计算机软件下载合同		非属买卖合同（《合同法》第130条）	非属买卖合同（台湾地区《民法》第345条）	1. 仅生授权之效果 2. 不符完全交付原则 3. 制订特别法或统一立法

要约与要约引诱之区别	《合同法》第14条及第15条	台湾地区《民法》第154条第2项	1. 适用民法之规定 2. 另立新法
要约之方法	《合同法》第10条	未设有相关规定	1. 适用民法之规定 2. 另立新法
要约之生效时点	1.《合同法》第16条第2款 2.《电子签名法》第10条及第11条	《电子签章法》第7条	已立法
意思实现	《合同法》第26条	台湾地区《民法》第169条	1. 适用民法之规定 2. 另立新法
迟到之承诺	《合同法》第29条	台湾地区《民法》第159条	1. 适用民法之规定 2. 另立新法
承诺之生效	1.《合同法》第26条 2.《合同法》第16条 3.《电子签名法》第10、11条	《电子签章法》第7条	已立法
再确认机制	无相关规范	无相关规范	另立新法
意思表示之撤回	1.《合同法》第16条至第18条 2.《合同法》第27条 3.《电子签名法》第11条	1. 台湾地区《民法》第95条、第162条及第163条 2.《电子签章法》第7条	已立法
意思表示之瑕疵	回归私法之规定,《民法通则》第58条及59条	回归私法之规定,台湾地区《民法》第88条以下	1. 解释或类推适用 2. 制订特别法或统一法之方式处理
民事管辖基础	《民事诉讼法》第25条	1.《民事诉讼法》第24条 2.《消费者保护法》第47条	
被告之主营业所或主事务所所在地之法院	1. 近似规范:《民事诉讼法》第22条 2.《电子签名法》第12条	近似规范:《民事诉讼法》第2条	1. 私法自治 2. 解释或类推适用 3. 制订特别法或统一立法
被告可扣押之财产或请求标的所在地法院	无相关规范	近似规范:《民事诉讼法》第3条	大陆: 1. 私法自治 2. 制订特别法或统一立法 台湾地区: 1. 私法自治 2. 解释或类推适用 3. 制订特别法或统一立法
债务履行地之法院	近似规范:《民事诉讼法》第24条	近似规范:《民事诉讼法》第12条	1. 私法自治 2. 解释或类推适用 3. 制订特别法或统一立法

2. A/CN.9/WG.IV/WP.108

United Nations
General Assembly
Limited

Distr.:
18 December 2003
Original: English
V.03-90766(E)

United Nations Commission on International Trade Law
Working Group IV (Electronic Commerce)
Forty-third session
New York, 15—19 March 2004
Legal aspects of electronic commerce
Electronic contracting: provisions for a draft convention
Note by the Secretariat

1. The Working Group began its deliberations on electronic contracting at its thirty-ninth session (New York, 11—15 March 2002), when it considered a note by the Secretariat on selected issues relating to electronic contracting (A/CN.9/WG.IV/WP.95). That note also contained an initial draft tentatively entitled "Preliminary draft convention on [international] contracts concluded or evidenced by data messages" (A/CN.9/WG.IV/WP.95, annex I).

2. At that time, the Working Group held a general exchange of views on the form and scope of the instrument, but agreed to postpone discussion on exclusions from the draft convention until it had had an opportunity to consider the provisions related to the location of the parties and contract formation (see

A/CN. 9/509, paras. 18—40). The Working Group then took up articles 7 and 14, both of which dealt with issues related to the location of the parties (see A/CN. 9/509, paras. 41—65). After it had completed its initial review of those provisions, the Working Group proceeded to consider the provisions dealing with contract formation in articles 8—13 (see A/CN. 9/509, paras. 66—121). The Working Group concluded its deliberations on the draft convention at that session with a discussion of draft article 15 on availability of contract terms (see A/CN. 9/509, paras. 122—125). The Working Group agreed, at that time, that it should consider articles 2—4, dealing with the sphere of application of the draft convention and articles 5 (Definitions) and 6 (Interpretation), at its fortieth session (see A/CN. 9/509, para. 15).

3. The Working Group resumed its deliberations on the preliminary draft convention at its fortieth session (Vienna, 14—18 October 2002). The Working Group began its deliberations by a general discussion on the scope of the preliminary draft convention (see A/CN. 9/527, paras. 72—81). The Working Group proceeded to consider articles 2—4, dealing with the sphere of application of the draft convention and articles 5 (Definitions) and 6 (Interpretation) (see A/CN. 9/527, paras. 82—126).

4. The Secretariat thereafter prepared a revised version of the preliminary draft convention (A/CN. 9/WG. IV/WP. 100, annex I). The Working Group, at its forty-first session (New York, 5—9 May 2003), reviewed articles 1—11 of the revised preliminary draft convention (see A/CN. 9/528, paras. 26—151). The Secretariat was requested to prepare a further revised version of the preliminary draft convention, for consideration by the Working Group at its forty-second session.

5. At its forty-second session (Vienna, 17—21 November 2003), the Working Group held a general discussion on the scope of the preliminary draft convention (see A/CN. 9/546, paras. 33—38). The Working Group noted that a task force had been established by the International Chamber of Commerce to develop contractual rules and guidance on legal issues related to electronic commerce, tentatively called "E-terms 2004". The Working Group considered the work being undertaken by that task force as a useful complement to the work being undertaken by the Working Group to develop an international convention. The Working Group proceeded to consider the revised text of the

preliminary draft convention (A/CN. 9/WG. IV/WP. 103, annex I). The Working Group reviewed articles 8—15 and requested a number of changes in connection therewith (see A/CN. 9/546, paras. 39—135).

6. The annex to the present note contains the newly revised version of the preliminary draft convention, which reflects the deliberations and decisions of the Working Group at its previous sessions. **Annex①Preliminary draft convention② on the use of data messages in [international trade] [the context of international contracts]**

CHAPTER I. SPHERE OF APPLICATION

Article 1. Scope of application

1. This Convention applies to the use of data messages in connection with an existing or contemplated contract between parties whose places of business are in different States:

Variant A③

(a) When the States are Contracting States;

(b) When the rules of private international law lead to the application of the law of a Contracting State; or④

---

① The numbers in square brackets after the article numbers indicate the corresponding numbers in the previous version of the draft convention (A/CN. 9/WG. IV/WP. 103, annex).

② The form of a convention represents a working assumption only (see A/CN. 9/484, para. 124) and is without prejudice to a final decision by the Working Group as to the nature of the instrument.

③ This variant reflects the scope of application of the draft convention essentially as contained in earlier versions. By combining this variant with variant A of draft article Y, a contracting State would make it clear that the provisions of the draft convention apply to messages exchanged under any of the international conventions referred to therein, while preserving the possibility of excluding particular instruments, or adding other instruments as it sees fit.

④ This paragraph reproduces a rule that is contained in the provisions on the sphere of application of other UNCITRAL instruments. There have been objections to this rule on the grounds that such an expansion of the convention's field of application would significantly reduce certainty at the time of contracting owing to its inherent ex post facto nature (see A/CN. 9/509, para. 38). At its forty-first session, the Working Group agreed to retain the subparagraph (see A/CN. 9/528, para. 42). If the draft paragraph is retained, the Working Group would still need to consider whether reservations to this rule should be permitted, as was suggested at its forty-second session (see A/CN. 9/528, para. 42). See also draft article X, paragraph 1.

(c) When the parties have agreed that it applies. ⑤

Variant B⑥

... when these States are parties to this Convention and the data messages are used in connection with an existing or contemplated contract to which, pursuant to the law of these States Parties, one of the following international conventions is to be applied:

Convention on the Limitation Period in the International Sale of Goods (New York, 14 June 1974) and Protocol thereto (Vienna, 11 April 1980)

United Nations Convention on Contracts for the International Sale of Goods (Vienna, 11 April 1980)

United Nations Convention on the Liability of Operators of Transport Terminals in International Trade (Vienna, 17 April 1991)

United Nations Convention on Independent Guarantees and Stand-by Letters of Credit (New York, 11 December 1995)

United Nations Convention on the Assignment of Receivables in International Trade (New York, 12 December 2001).

2. The fact that the parties have their places of business in different States is to be disregarded whenever this fact does not appear either from the contract or from any dealings between the parties or from information disclosed by the parties at any time before or at the conclusion of the contract.

3. Neither the nationality of the parties nor the civil or commercial character of the parties or of the contract is to be taken into consideration in determining the application of this Convention.

---

⑤ This possibility is provided, for instance, in article 1, paragraph 2, of the United Nations Convention on Independent Guarantees and Stand-by Letters of Credit. The Working Group postponed a decision on this subparagraph until it had considered the operative provisions of the draft convention (see A/CN.9/528, paras. 43 and 44). The Working Group may wish to consider whether it should be possible for contracting States to exclude this provision through a declaration made pursuant to draft article X, paragraph 1.

⑥ This variant reflects variant 1 of a proposal that was submitted by Germany to the Working Group at its forty-second session (A/CN.9/WG.IV/XLII/CRP.2). Its practical effect would be to limit the applicability of the draft convention only to messages exchanged under the abovementioned conventions, with the possibility of individual exclusions by contracting States under variant C of draft article Y.

Article 2. Exclusions⁷

This Convention does not apply to the use of data messages [in connection with the following contracts, whether existing or contemplated] [in the context of the formation or performance of the following contracts]:

(a) Contracts concluded for personal, family or household purposes [unless the party offering the goods or services, at any time before or at the conclusion of the contract, neither knew nor ought to have known that they were intended for any such use];⑧

[(b) Contracts for the grant of limited use of intellectual property rights;]⑨

---

⑦ The last version of this draft article contained two variants reflecting alternative approaches for the treatment of consumer contracts. Variant A excluded consumer contracts by using the same technique that is used in article 2, subparagraph (a), of the United Nations Convention on Contracts for the International Sale of Goods (the "United Nations Sales Convention"). Variant B deferred to domestic law on consumer protection issues, without excluding consumer transactions from the draft convention (see A/CN. 9/527, para. 89; see also A/CN. 9/528, paras. 51—54). The present version of the draft article retains only the former variant A. The former variant B has been incorporated into draft article 3, as its content is more akin to that article, in its current formulation. The Working Group may wish to bear in mind that the entire draft article may become redundant if the Working Group chooses to define the scope of application of the draft convention along the lines of variant C of draft article 1, since the draft convention would then apply only to the exchange of data messages falling within the scope of those international conventions in accordance with their own rules on their scope of application.

⑧ The last phrase is in square brackets, since there was some support at the forty-first session of the Working Group to the suggestion that all the words after "household purposes" should be deleted (see A/CN. 9/528, para. 52).

⑨ This exclusion is in square brackets as the Working Group has not yet reached an agreement on the matter (see A/CN. 9/527, paras. 90—93, and A/CN. 9/528, paras. 55—60). The Working Group may wish to note that the International Bureau of the World Intellectual Property Organization sees no need for an exclusion clause with regard to contracts involving intellectual property rights (see A/CN. 9/WG. IV/WP. 106, para. 2).

(c) [Other exclusions that the Working Group may decide to add.]⑩
[Other matters identified by a Contracting State under a declaration made in accordance with article X]. ⑪

Article 3. Matters not governed by this Convention⑫

This Convention does not affect or override⑬ any rule of law relating to:

[(a) The protection of consumers;]⑭

(b) The validity of the contract or of any of its provisions or of any usage [except as otherwise provided in articles [...]]; ⑮

---

⑩ This draft article might contain additional exclusions, as may be decided by the Working Group. Annex II of the initial draft (A/CN. 9/WG. IV/WP. 95) reproduced, for illustrative purposes and without the intention of being exhaustive, exclusions typically found in domestic laws on electronic commerce. Additional exclusions that had been proposed at the fortieth session of the Working Group and reiterated at the forty-first session, related to certain existing financial services markets with well-established rules resulting from specific regulations, standard agreements and practices, system rules or otherwise. Those exclusions included payment systems, negotiable instruments, derivatives, swaps, repurchase agreements (repos), foreign exchange, securities and bond markets, while possibly including general procurement activities of banks and loan activities (see A/CN. 9/527, para. 95, and A/CN. 9/528, para. 61). Additional exclusions proposed at the forty-first session included "real estate transactions, as well as contracts involving courts or public authorities, family law and the law of succession" (see A/CN. 9/528, para. 63). The Working Group may wish to note, in that connection, that the United Nations Commission on International Trade Law (UNCITRAL), at its thirty-sixth session, decided to undertake work in the area of public procurement, including procurement by electronic means (see A/58/17, paras. 225—230). This may render an open-ended exclusion of "contracts involving courts or public authorities" inappropriate.

⑪ This phrase is an alternative formulation that would obviate the need for a common list of exclusions (see A/CN. 9/527, para. 96).

⑫ The Working Group may wish to bear in mind that the entire draft article may become redundant, if the Working Group chooses to define the scope of application of the draft convention along the lines of variant C of draft article 1, since the draft convention would then apply only to the exchange of data messages falling within the scope of those international conventions in accordance with their own rules on their field of application.

⑬ This formulation has been used following a suggestion at the forty-first session of the Working Group that the words previously used ("This Convention is not concerned with") were inaccurate (see A/CN. 9/528, para. 67).

⑭ Draft subparagraph (a) appears within square brackets, as it represents in some respects an alternative to draft article 2, subparagraph (a) (see A/CN. 9/528, para. 52). Under this rule, consumer transactions would not be automatically excluded from the scope of the draft convention, but the provisions of the draft convention would not supersede or affect rules on consumer protection.

⑮ Draft subparagraph (b) is derived from article 4, subparagraph (a), of the United Nations Sales Convention. The Working Group may wish to consider the relationship between the general exclusions under the draft article and other provisions that, for instance, affirm the validity of data messages, such as draft articles 8, 9 and 12 (see A/CN. 9/527, para. 103).

(c) The rights and obligations of the parties arising out of the contract or of any of its provisions or of any usage;⑯ or

(d) The effect, which the contract may have on, the ownership of rights created or transferred by the contract. ⑰

Article 4. Party autonomy

The parties may exclude the application of this Convention or derogate from or vary the effect of any of its provisions [except for the following: ...]. ⑱

CHAPTER II. GENERAL PROVISIONS

*Article 5. Definitions*⑲

For the purposes of this Convention:

(a) "Data message" means information generated, sent, received or stored by electronic, optical or similar means including, but not limited to, electronic data interchange (EDI), electronic mail, telegram, telex or telecopy;

(b) "Electronic data interchange (EDI)" means the electronic transfer

---

⑯ The preliminary draft convention is not concerned with substantive issues arising out of the contract, which, for all other purposes, remains subject to its governing law (see A/CN.9/527, paras. 10—12). The Working Group may wish to consider whether this provision is still required, since the rule contained in the subparagraph might nevertheless be evident from the limited scope of the draft convention.

⑰ Draft subparagraph (d) is based, mutatis mutandis, on article 4, subparagraph (b), of the United Nations Sales Convention. Regardless of its final decision on draft articles 1 and Y, the Working Group may wish to consider whether this provision is still required, since the rule contained in the subparagraph might nevertheless be evident from the limited scope of the draft convention.

⑱ The Working Group has yet to consider whether some limitation to the principle of party autonomy is appropriate or desirable in the context of the preliminary draft convention, in particular in the light of provisions such as draft articles 9, paragraph 3, 11 and 15 (see A/CN.9/527, para.109; see also A/CN.9/528, paras.71—75). The earlier version of this article contained a second paragraph dealing with the agreement of the parties to the use of data messages in a contractual context. That provision has now been combined with draft article 8.

⑲ The definitions contained in draft paragraphs (a) to (e) are derived from article 2 of the UNCITRAL Model Law on Electronic Commerce. The definition of "electronic signature" corresponds to the definition of the same expression in article 2 of the UNCITRAL Model Law on Electronic Signatures. The definitions of "offeror" and "offeree" have been deleted, although the Working Group had tentatively retained them (see A/CN.9/527, para.115). The Secretariat submits that those words have become superfluous in view of the reformulation of draft articles 8 and 13 (see A/CN.9/528, para.106).

from computer to computer of information using an agreed standard to structure the information;

(c) "Originator" of a data message means a person by whom, or on whose behalf, the data message purports to[20] have been sent or generated prior to storage, if any, but it does not include a person acting as an intermediary with respect to that data message;

(d) "Addressee" of a data message means a person who is intended by the originator to receive the data message, but does not include a person acting as an intermediary with respect to that data message;

(e) "Information system" means a system for generating, sending, receiving, storing or otherwise processing data messages;[21]

(f) "Automated information system" means a computer program or an electronic or other automated means used to initiate an action or respond to data messages or performances in whole or in part, without review or intervention by a natural person each time an action is initiated or a response is generated by the system;[22]

[(g) "Electronic signature" means data in electronic form in, affixed to, or logically associated with, a data message, which may be used to identify the person holding the signature creation data in relation to the data message and indicate that person's approval of the information contained in the data message;[23]

---

[20] The wording of this definition is taken from article 2, subparagraph (c), of the UNCITRAL Model Law on Electronic Commerce. It has been suggested to the Secretariat that it might be preferable to delete the words "purports to have been sent" and use instead the words "has been sent".

[21] The Working Group may wish to consider whether this definition needs further clarification, in view of the questions that have been raised in connection with paragraph 2 of the former article 11 (currently article 10) (see A/CN.9/528, paras.148 and 149, and A/CN.9/546, paras.59—80).

[22] This definition is based on the definition of "electronic agent" contained in section 2, paragraph 6, of the Uniform Electronic Transactions Act of the United States of America; a similar definition is also used in section 19 of the Uniform Electronic Commerce Act of Canada. This definition was included in view of the contents of draft article 14.

[23] The initial draft contained in document A/CN.9/WG.IV/WP.95 included, as a variant to this provision, a general definition of "signature". Although the Working Group tentatively agreed on retaining both variants, the Secretariat suggests that it might be more appropriate, given the limited scope of the draft convention, to define only "electronic signatures", leaving a definition of "signature" for the otherwise applicable law, as had been suggested at the fortieth session of the Working Group (see A/CN.9/527, paras.116—119).

[(h) "Place of business"㉔ means [any place of operations where a person carries out a non-transitory activity with human means and goods or services;]㉕[the place where a party maintains a stable establishment to pursue an economic activity other than the temporary provision of goods or services out of a specific location;]㉖]

[(i) "Person" and "party" include natural persons and legal entities;]㉗

[(j) Other definitions that the Working Group may wish to add.]㉘

Article 6. Interpretation

1. In the interpretation of this Convention, regard is to be had to its international character and to the need to promote uniformity in its application and the observance of good faith in international trade.

2. Questions concerning matters governed by this Convention which are

---

㉔ The proposed definition appears within square brackets since the Commission has not thus far defined "place of business" (see A/CN. 9/527, paras. 120—122). At the thirty-ninth session of the Working Group, it was suggested that the rules on the location of the parties should be expanded to include elements such as the place of an entity's organization or incorporation (see A/CN. 9/509, para. 53). The Working Group decided that it could consider the desirability of using supplementary elements to the criteria used to define the location of the parties by expanding the definition of place of business (see A/CN. 9/509, para. 54). The Working Group may wish to consider whether the proposed additional notions and any other new elements should be provided as an alternative to the elements currently used or only as a default rule for those entities without an "establishment". Additional cases that might deserve consideration by the Working Group might include situations where the most significant component of human means or goods or services used for a particular business are located in a place bearing little relationship to the actual centre of a company's affairs, such as when the only equipment and personnel used by a so-called "virtual business" located in one country consists of leased space in a third-party server located elsewhere.

㉕ This alternative reflects the essential elements of the notions of "place of business", as understood in international commercial practice, and "establishment", as used in article 2, subparagraph (f), of the UNCITRAL Model Law on Cross-Border Insolvency.

㉖ This alternative follows the understanding of the concept of "place of business" in the European Union (see para. 19 of the preamble to Directive 2000/31/EC of the European Union).

㉗ During the preparation of the UNCITRAL Model Law on Electronic Commerce, it was felt that such a definition did not belong in the text of the instrument, but in its guide to enactment. As a convention would not normally be accompanied by extensive comments, the proposed definition has been included in the form of a provision, should the Working Group find such a definition necessary, particularly in view of provisions such as draft article 9, variant B, subparagraph 4 (b).

㉘ The Working Group may wish to consider whether definitions of other terms should be included, such as "signatory" (if variant B of draft article 10 (formerly 14) is adopted), "interactive applications", "electronic mail" or "domain name".

not expressly settled in it are to be settled in conformity with the general principles on which it is based or, in the absence of such principles, in conformity with the law applicable [by virtue of the rules of private international law]. ㉙

Article 7. Location of the parties㉚

1. For the purposes of this Convention, a person's place of business is presumed to be the location indicated by that person, [unless the person does not have a place of business at such location [[and] such indication is made solely to trigger or avoid the application of this Convention]].

2. If a person [has not indicated a place of business or, subject to paragraph 1 of this article, a person]㉛ has more than one place of business, the place of business for the purposes of this Convention is that which has the closest relationship to the relevant contract and its performance, having regard to the circumstances known to or contemplated by the parties at any time before or at the conclusion of the contract.

3. If a person does not have a place of business, reference is to be made to the person's habitual residence.

4. The place of location of the equipment and technology supporting an information system used by a person in connection with the formation of a contract or the place from which such information system may be accessed by other persons, in and of themselves, do not constitute a place of business, [unless

---

㉙ The closing phrase has been placed in square brackets at the request of the Working Group. Similar formulations in other instruments had been incorrectly understood as allowing immediate referral to the applicable law pursuant to the rules on conflict of laws of the forum State for the interpretation of a convention without regard to the conflict of laws rules contained in the convention itself (see A/CN. 9/527, paras. 125 and 126).

㉚ The draft paragraph is not intended to create a new concept of "place of business" for the on-line world. The phrase in square brackets aims to prevent a party from benefiting from recklessly inaccurate or untruthful representations (see A/CN. 9/509, para. 49), but not to limit the parties' ability to choose the Convention or otherwise agree on the applicable law. The two variants previously contained in the draft paragraph have been combined as the Working Group preferred the former variant A (see A/CN. 9/528, para. 88). The words "manifest and clear" which the Working Group found to be conducive to legal uncertainty (see A/CN. 9/528, para. 86), have been deleted.

㉛ It has been suggested to the Secretariat that the presumption contemplated in the draft article could also apply in the event that a party does not indicate its place of business. This suggestion has been inserted in square brackets, since the presumption contemplated in the draft article has been used in other UNCITRAL instruments only in connection with multiple places of business.

such legal entity does not have a place of business [within the meaning of article 5 (h)]].㉜

5. The sole fact that a person makes use of a domain name or electronic mail address connected to a specific country does not create a presumption that its place of business is located in such country.㉝

Article 7 bis [11]. *Information requirements*

Nothing in this Convention affects the application of any rule of law that may require the parties to disclose their identities, places of business or other information, or relieves a party from the legal consequences of making inaccurate or false statements in that regard.

CHAPTER III. USE OF DATA MESSAGES IN INTERNATIONAL CONTRACTS

Article 8. Legal recognition of data messages

1. Where a communication, declaration, demand, notice or request that the parties are required to make or choose to make in connection with an existing or contemplated contract, including an offer and the acceptance of an of-

---

㉜ The draft paragraph reflects the principle that rules on location should not result in any given party being considered as having its place of business in one country when contracting electronically and in another country when contracting by more traditional means (see A/CN.9/484, para.103). The draft paragraph follows the solution proposed in paragraph 19 of the preamble to Directive 2000/31/EC of the European Union (see also the overview of issues related to the location of information systems in A/CN.9/WG.IV/WP.104, paras.9—17). The phrase within square brackets is only intended to deal with so-called "virtual companies" and not with natural persons, who are covered by the rule contained in draft paragraph 3. The Working Group may wish to consider whether draft paragraphs 4 and 5, which the Working Group agreed to retain for further consideration, should be combined in one provision (see A/CN.9/509, para.59).

㉝ The current system for assignment of domain names was not originally conceived in geographical terms. Therefore, the apparent connection between a domain name and a country is often insufficient to conclude that there is a genuine and permanent link between the domain name user and the country (see A/CN.9/509, paras.44—46; see also A/CN.9/WG.IV/WP.104, paras.18—20). However, in some countries the assignment of domain names is only made after verification of the accuracy of the information provided by the applicant, including its location in the country to which the relevant domain name relates. For those countries, it might be appropriate to rely, at least in part, on domain names for the purpose of article 7, contrary to what is suggested in the draft paragraph (see A/CN.9/509, para.58). The Working Group may wish to consider whether the proposed rules should be expanded to deal with those situations.

fer, is conveyed by means of data messages, such communication, declaration, demand, notice or request shall not be denied validity or enforceability on the sole ground that data messages were used for that purpose.

[2. Nothing in this Convention requires a person to use or accept information in the form of data messages, but a person's agreement to use or accept information in the form of data messages may be inferred from the person's conduct.]㉞

Article 9. Form requirements

[1. Nothing in this Convention requires a contract or any other communication, declaration, demand, notice or request that the parties are required to make or choose to make in connection with an existing or contemplated contract to be made or evidenced in any particular form.]㉟

2. Where the law requires that a contract or any other communication, declaration, demand, notice or request that the parties are required to make or choose to make in connection with a contract should be in writing, that requirement is met by a data message if the information contained therein is accessible so as to be usable for subsequent reference.㊱

3. Where the law requires that a contract or any other communication, declaration, demand, notice or request that the parties are required to make or choose to make in connection with a contract should be signed, or provides

---

㉞ The provision reflects the idea that parties should not be forced to accept contractual offers or acts of acceptance by electronic means if they do not want to do so (see A/CN. 9/527, para. 108). However, since the provision is not intended to require that the parties should always agree beforehand on the use of data messages, the second phrase provides that a party's agreement to transact electronically may be inferred from its conduct. The reference to "consent" has been replaced with the phrase "a person's agreement to use or accept information in the form of data messages" so as to avoid the erroneous impression that the draft paragraph refers to consent to the underlying transaction (see A/CN. 9/546, para. 43).

㉟ This provision incorporates the general principle of freedom of form contained in article 11 of the United Nations Sales Convention, in the manner suggested at the forty-second session of the Working Group (see A/CN. 9/546, para. 49).

㊱ This provision sets forth the criteria for the functional equivalence between data messages and paper documents, in the same manner as article 6 of the UNCITRAL Model Law on Electronic Commerce. The Working Group may wish to consider the meaning of the words "the law" and "writing" and whether there would be a need for including definitions of those terms (see A/CN. 9/509, paras. 116 and 117).

consequences for the absence of a signature, that requirement is met in relation to a data message if:

(a) A method is used to identify that person and to indicate that person's approval of the information contained in the data message; and

(b) That method is as reliable as appropriate to the purpose for which the data message was generated or communicated, in the light of all the circumstances, including any relevant agreement. ㊲

Article 10. *Time and place of dispatch and receipt of data messages*㊳

1. The time of dispatch of a data message is the time when the data message [enters an information system outside the control of the originator or of the person who sent the data message on behalf of the originator] [leaves an information system under the control of the originator or of the person who sent the data message on behalf of the originator], or, if the message had not [entered an information system outside the control of the originator or of the person who sent the data message on behalf of the originator] [left an information system under the control of the originator or of the person who sent the data message on behalf of the originator], at the time when the message is received.

2. The time of receipt of a data message is the time when the data message becomes capable of being retrieved by the addressee or by any other person named by the addressee. A data message is presumed to be capable of being retrieved by the addressee when the data message enters an information system of the addressee unless it was unreasonable for the originator to have chosen that particular information system for sending the data message, having regard to the circumstances of the case and the content of the data message.

3. A data message is deemed to be dispatched at the place where the o-

㊲ The draft paragraph recites the general criteria for the functional equivalence between handwritten signatures and electronic identification methods referred to in article 7 of the UNCITRAL Model Law on Electronic Commerce.

㊳ Earlier versions of the draft article followed more closely the formulation of article 15 of the UNCITRAL Model Law on Electronic Commerce, with some adjustments to harmonize the style of the individual provisions with the style used elsewhere in the draft convention. The current formulation reflects the deliberations of the Working Group at its forty-second session (see A/CN. 9/546, paras. 59—86). The Working Group may wish to review the new formulation, in particular draft paragraph 2, with a view to ensuring that it is consistent in result with article 15 of the Model Law.

riginator has its place of business and is deemed to be received at the place where the addressee has its place of business, as determined in accordance with article 7.

4. Paragraph 2 of this article applies notwithstanding that the place where the information system is located may be different from the place where the data message is deemed to be received under paragraph 3 of this article.

Article 11 [12]. *Invitations to make offers*㊴

A proposal to conclude a contract made through one or more data messages which is not addressed to one or more specific persons, but is generally accessible to parties making use of information systems, including proposals that make use of interactive applications㊵ for the placement of orders through such information system, is to be considered as an invitation to make offers, unless it clearly indicates the intention of the person making the proposal to be bound in case of acceptance.

㊴ This provision deals with an issue that has given rise to extensive debate. At the forty-first session of the Working Group, it was noted that "there was currently no standard business practice in that area" (see A/CN.9/528, para.117). The current text is inspired by article 14, paragraph 1, of the United Nations Sales Convention and affirms the principle that proposals to conclude a contract that are addressed to an unlimited number of persons are not binding offers, even if they involve the use of interactive applications. The Working Group may wish to consider, however, whether specific rules should be formulated to deal with offers of goods through Internet auction platforms and similar transactions, which in many legal systems have been regarded as binding offers to sell the goods to the highest bidder.

㊵ At its forty-second session, the Working Group noted that the expression "automated information system", which had been used in earlier versions of the draft article, did not offer meaningful guidance since the party that placed an order might have no means of knowing how the order would be processed and to what extent the information system was automated. The notion of "interactive applications", in turn, was considered to be an objective term that better described a situation apparent to any person accessing the system, namely that it was prompted to exchange information through that system by means of immediate actions and responses having an appearance of automaticity. It was noted that the term was not a legal term but rather a term of art highlighting that the provision focused on what was apparent to the party activating the system rather than on how the system functioned internally. On that basis, the Working Group agreed that the term "interactive applications" could be retained (see A/CN.9/546, para. 114).

Article 12 [14]. *Use of automated information systems for contract formation*[41]

A contract formed by the interaction of an automated information system and a person, or by the interaction of automated information systems, shall not be denied validity or enforceability on the sole ground that no person reviewed each of the individual actions carried out by such systems or the resulting agreement.

Article 13 [15]. *Availability of contract terms*

[Variant A[42]

Nothing in this convention affects the application of any rule of law that may require a party that negotiates a contract through the exchange of data messages to make available to the other contracting party the data messages that contain the contractual terms in a particular manner, or relieves a party from the legal consequences of its failure to do so.]

[Variant B[43]

A party offering goods or services through an information system that is generally accessible to persons making use of information systems[44] shall make

---

[41] This article has been redrafted as a non-discrimination rule, as requested by the Working Group at its forty-second session (see A/CN.9/546, paras. 128 and 129). The Working Group may wish to consider whether the provision should be supplemented by a general provision on attribution of data messages, including attribution of data messages exchanged by automated information systems (see A/CN.9/546, paras. 85, 86 and 125—127).

[42] This variant has been added pursuant to a request by the Working Group in view of the controversy around the draft article (see A/CN.9/546, paras. 130—135). If this variant alone is retained, the Working Group may wish to consider placing the draft article in chapter I or II of the draft convention or even combining it with the current draft article 3.

[43] This variant, which is based on article 10, paragraph 3, of Directive 2000/31/EC of the European Union, appears in square brackets, as there was no consensus on the need for the provision within the Working Group (see A/CN.9/509, paras. 123—125, and A/CN.9/546, paras. 130—135). If the provision is retained, the Working Group may wish to consider whether the draft article should provide consequences for the failure by a party to make available the contract terms and what consequences would be appropriate. In some legal systems the consequences might be that a contractual term that has not been made available to the other party cannot be enforced against it.

[44] The Working Group may wish to consider whether these words adequately describe the types of situations that the Working Group intends to address in the draft article.

the data message or messages which contain the contract terms⁴⁵ available to the other party [for a reasonable period of time] in a way that allows for its or their storage and reproduction.]

Article 14 [16]. *Error in electronic communications*

Variant A⁴⁶

correcting errors and by contemplating only private law consequences for the absence of such means.

[Unless otherwise [expressly] agreed by the parties,]⁴⁷ a contract concluded by a person that accesses an automated information system of another party has no legal effect and is not enforceable if the person made an error in a data message and:⁴⁸

(a) The automated information system did not provide the person with an opportunity to prevent or correct the error;

(b) The person notifies the other party of the error as soon as practicable

---

④⑤ The words "and general conditions" have been deleted as they appeared to be redundant. The Working Group may, however, wish to consider whether the provision should be made more explicit as to the version of the contract terms that needs to be retained.

④⑥ This draft paragraph deals with the issue of errors in automated transactions (see A/CN. 9/ WG. IV/WP. 95, paras. 74—79). Earlier versions of the draft article contained, in paragraph 1 of variant A, a rule based on article 11, paragraph 2, of Directive 2000/31/EC of the European Union, which creates an obligation for persons offering goods or services through automated information systems to offer means for correcting input errors, and required such means to be "appropriate, effective and accessible". The draft article was the subject of essentially two types of objections: one objection was that the draft convention should not deal with a complex substantive issue such as error and mistake, a matter on which the Working Group has not yet reached a final decision; another objection was that the obligations contemplated in article 14, paragraph 2, of the first version of the draft convention (as contained in A/ CN. 9/WG. IV/WP. 95) were regarded as being of a regulatory or public law nature (see A/CN. 9/509, para. 108). The Working Group may wish to consider whether the latter objection could be addressed by deleting the reference to an obligation to provide means for.

④⑦ The Working Group may wish to consider whether the possibility of derogation by agreement needs to be expressly made or can result from tacit agreement, for instance when a party proceeds to place an order through the seller's automated information system even though it is apparent to such party that the system does not provide an opportunity to correct input errors.

④⑧ This provision deals with the legal effects of errors made by a natural person communicating with an automated information system. The draft provision is inspired by section 22 of the Uniform Electronic Commerce Act of Canada. At the thirty-ninth session of the Working Group it was suggested that such provisions might not be appropriate in the context of commercial (that is, nonconsumer transactions, since the right to repudiate a contract in case of material error may not always be provided under general contract law. The Working Group nevertheless decided to retain it for further consideration (see A/CN. 9/509, paras. 110 and 111).

when the person making the error learns of it and indicates that he or she made an error in the data message;

[(c) The person takes reasonable steps, including steps that conform to the other party's instructions, to return the goods or services received, if any, as a result of the error or, if instructed to do so, to destroy such goods or services; and

[(d) The person has not used or received any material benefit or value from the goods or services, if any, received from the other party.] ㊾

Variant B

1. [Unless otherwise [expressly] agreed by the parties,] ㊿ a contract concluded by a person that accesses an automated information system of another party has no legal effect and is not enforceable if the person made an error in a data message and the automated information system did not provide the person with an opportunity to prevent or correct the error. The person invoking the error must notify the other party of the error as soon as practicable and indicate that he or she made an error in the data message. (51)

[2. A person is not entitled to invoke an error under paragraph 1:

(a) If the person fails to take reasonable steps, including steps that conform to the other party's instructions, to return the goods or services received, if any, as a result of the error or, if instructed to do so, to destroy such goods or services; or

(b) If the person has used or received any material benefit or value from the goods or services, if any, received from the other party.] (52)

㊾ Subparagraphs (c) and (d) appear within square brackets since it was suggested, at the thirty ninth session of the Working Group, that the matters dealt with therein went beyond matters of contract formation and departed from the consequences of avoidance of contracts under some legal systems (see A/CN.9/509, para. 110).

㊿ See note 47.

(51) This variant combines in two paragraphs the various elements contained in paragraphs 2 and 3 and subparagraphs (a)—(d) of the first version of the draft article (see A/CN.9/WG.IV/WP.95), as requested by the Working Group (see A/CN.9/509, para. 111).

(52) See footnote 49.

[*Other substantive provisions that the Working Group may wish to include.*](53)

CHAPTER IV. FINAL PROVISIONS

[*Article X. Declarations on exclusions*(54)

1. Any State may declare at the time of the deposit of its instrument of ratification, acceptance, approval or accession that it will not be bound by subparagraph 1 (b) of article 1 of this Convention.](55)

2. Any State may declare at the time of the deposit of its instrument of ratification, acceptance, approval or accession that it will not apply this Convention to the matters specified in its declaration.

3. Any declaration made pursuant to paragraphs 1 and 2 of this article shall take effect on the first day of the month following the expiration of [six] months after the date of its receipt by the depositary.]

Article Y. Communications exchanged under other international conventions(56)

---

(53) Such additional provisions might include, beyond consequences for a person's failure to comply with draft articles 11, 15 and 16, an issue that the Working Group has not yet considered (see A/CN. 9/527, para. 103), other issues dealt with in electronic commerce legislation, such as liability of information services providers for loss or delay in the delivery of data messages.

(54) The Working Group has not yet concluded its deliberations on possible exclusions to the preliminary draft convention under draft article 2 (see A/CN. 9/527, paras. 83—98). The draft article has been added as a possible alternative, in the event that consensus is not achieved on possible exclusions to the preliminary draft convention.

(55) At its forty-first session, the Working Group agreed to consider, at a later stage, a provision allowing contracting States to exclude the application of subparagraph (b) of article 1, paragraph 1, along the lines of article 95 of the United Nations Sales Convention (see A/CN. 9/528, para. 42).

(56) The draft article is intended to offer a possible common solution for some of the legal obstacles to electronic commerce under existing international instruments, which had been the object of a survey contained in an earlier note by the Secretariat (see A/CN. 9/WG. IV/WP. 94). At the fortieth session of the Working Group, there was general agreement to proceed in that manner, to the extent that the issues were common, which was the case at least with regard to most issues raised under the instruments listed in variant A (see A/CN. 9/527, paras. 3—48). If either variant B or variant C is adopted, the title of the draft article would need to be changed to "reservations".

Variant A[57]

1. Except as otherwise stated in a declaration made in accordance with paragraph 2 of this article, a State Party to this Convention [may declare at any time that it][58] undertakes to apply the provisions of [article 7 and] chapter III[59] of this Convention to the exchange [by means of data messages] of any communications, declarations, demands, notices or requests, [including an offer and acceptance of an offer], that the parties are required to make or choose to make in connection with or under any of the following international agreements or conventions to which the State is or may become a Contracting State:

Convention on the Limitation Period in the International Sale of Goods (New York, 14 June 1974) and Protocol thereto (Vienna, 11 April 1980)

United Nations Convention on Contracts for the International Sale of Goods (Vienna, 11 April 1980)

United Nations Convention on the Liability of Operators of Transport Terminals in International Trade (Vienna, 17 April 1991)

United Nations Convention on Independent Guarantees and Stand-by Letters of Credit (New York, 11 December 1995)

United Nations Convention on the Assignment of Receivables in International Trade (New York, 12 December 2001).

[2. Any State may declare at the time of the deposit of its instrument of

---

[57] This variant is intended to remove doubts as to the relationship between the rules contained in the draft convention and rules contained in other international conventions. It is not the purpose of this variant effectively to amend or otherwise affect the application of any other international convention. In practice, the draft article would have the effect of an undertaking by a contracting State to use the provisions of the draft convention to remove possible legal obstacles to electronic commerce that might arise under those conventions and to facilitate their application in cases where the parties conduct their transactions through electronic means.

[58] The language in square brackets is intended to give more flexibility in the application of the draft article, since, without such clarification, the provision might be read to the effect that an undertaking pursuant to the draft article needed to be assumed upon signature, ratification or accession and could not be expanded at a later stage. If these words are retained, a provision along the lines of paragraph 3 of draft article X may be needed also in draft article Y.

[59] The specific reference to the substantive provisions of the draft convention contained in chapter III is intended to avoid the impression that the provisions on the scope of application of the draft convention would affect the definition of the scope of application of other international conventions. The Working Group may wish to consider whether the provisions of draft article 7, to which reference is made in square brackets, are also suitable for subsidiary (interpretative) application in the context of other international conventions, or whether they might interfere with the existing interpretation of those conventions.

ratification, acceptance, approval or accession that it will also apply this Convention to the exchange by means of data messages of any communications, declarations, demands, notices or requests under any other international agreement or convention on private commercial law matters to which the State is a Contracting State and which are identified in that State's declaration.] [60]

3. Any State may declare at any time that it will not apply this Convention [or any specific provision thereof] to international contracts falling within the scope of [any of the above conventions.] [one or more international agreements, treaties or conventions to which the State is a Contracting Party and which are identified in that State's declaration.]

4. Any declaration made pursuant to paragraphs 1 and 2 of this article shall take effect on the first day of the month following the expiration of [six] months after the date of its receipt by the depositary.

Variant B[61]

1. Any State may at any time make a reservation to the effect that it shall apply this Convention [or any specific provision thereof] only to data messages in connection with an existing or contemplated contract to which, pursuant to the law of that State, a specific international convention clearly identified in the reservation made by that State is to be applied.

2. Any declaration made pursuant to paragraph 1 of this article shall take effect on the first day of the month following the expiration of [six] months after the date of its receipt by the depositary.

Variant C[62]

1. Any State may declare at any time that it will not apply this Convention

---

[60] Paragraph 1 of variant A is intended to make it clear that the provisions of the draft convention apply also to messages exchanged under any of the international conventions referred to therein. Paragraph 2 contemplates the possibility for a contracting State to extend the application of the new instrument to the use of data messages in the context of other international conventions.

[61] This variant reflects variant 2 of a proposal that was submitted by Germany at the forty-second session of the Working Group (see A/CN.9/WG.IV/XLII/CRP.2). It is logically related to variant A of draft article 1. Its practical effect would be to limit the applicability of the draft convention only to messages exchanged under conventions specifically identified by contracting States.

[62] This variant reflects variant 1 of a proposal that was submitted by Germany at the forty-second session of the Working Group (see A/CN.9/WG.IV/XLII/CRP.2). It is included in the event that the Working Group chooses variant B of draft article 1, so as to give the contracting States the possibility to exclude the application of the draft convention in respect of certain specific conventions.

[or any specific provision thereof] to data messages in connection with an existing or contemplated contract to which one or more of the international conventions referred to in article 1, paragraph 1, are to be applied, provided that the relevant conventions shall be clearly identified in the declaration made by that State.

2. Any declaration made pursuant to paragraph 1 of this article shall take effect on the first day of the month following the expiration of [six] months after the date of its receipt by the depositary.

[*Customary and other final clauses that the Working Group may wish to include.*]

3. UNIDROIT PRINCIPLES OF INTERNATIONAL COMMERCIAL CONTRACTS 2004①

PREAMBLE

(*Purpose of the Principles*)

These Principles set forth general rules for international commercial contracts.

They shall be applied when the parties have agreed that their contract be governed by them. *

They may be applied when the parties have agreed that their contract be governed by general principles of law, the *lex mercatoria* or the like.

They may be applied when the parties have not chosen any law to govern their contract.

They may be used to interpret or supplement international uniform law instruments.

They may be used to interpret or supplement domestic law.

---

① The reader is reminded that the complete version of the UNIDROIT Principles contains not only the black-letter rules reproduced hereunder, but also detailed comments on each article and, where appropriate, illustrations. The volume may be ordered from UNIDROIT at ⟨http://www.unidroit.org⟩.

For an update of international case law and bibliography relating to the Principles see ⟨http://www.unilex.info⟩.

* Parties wishing to provide that their agreement be governed by the Principles might use the following words, adding any desired exceptions or modifications:

"This contract shall be governed by the UNIDROIT Principles (2004) [except as to Articles ...]".

Parties wishing to provide in addition for the application of the law of a particular jurisdiction might use the following words:

"This contract shall be governed by the UNIDROIT Principles (2004) [except as to Articles ...], supplemented when necessary by the law of [jurisdiction X]".

They may serve as a model for national and international legislators.

CHAPTER 1—GENERAL PROVISIONS

ARTICLE 1.1　(*Freedom of contract*)

The parties are free to enter into a contract and to determine its content.

ARTICLE 1.2　(*No form required*)

Nothing in these Principles requires a contract, statement or any other act to be made in or evidenced by a particular form. It may be proved by any means, including witnesses.

ARTICLE 1.3　(*Binding character of contract*)

A contract validly entered into is binding upon the parties. It can only be modified or terminated in accordance with its terms or by agreement or as otherwise provided in these Principles.

ARTICLE 1.4　(*Mandatory rules*)

Nothing in these Principles shall restrict the application of mandatory rules, whether of national, international or supranational origin, which are applicable in accordance with the relevant rules of private international law.

ARTICLE 1.5　(*Exclusion or modification by the parties*)

The parties may exclude the application of these Principles or derogate from or vary the effect of any of their provisions, except as otherwise provided in the Principles.

ARTICLE 1.6　(*Interpretation and supplementation of the Principles*)

(1) In the interpretation of these Principles, regard is to be had to their international character and to their purposes including the need to promote uniformity in their application.

(2) Issues within the scope of these Principles but not expressly settled by them are as far as possible to be settled in accordance with their underlying general principles.

ARTICLE 1.7　(*Good faith and fair dealing*)

(1) Each party must act in accordance with good faith and fair dealing in international trade.

(2) The parties may not exclude or limit this duty.

ARTICLE 1.8　(*Inconsistent Behaviour*)

A party cannot act inconsistently with an understanding it has caused the other party to have and upon which that other party reasonably has acted in reliance to its detriment.

ARTICLE 1.9 (*Usages and practices*)

(1) The parties are bound by any usage to which they have agreed and by any practices which they have established between themselves.

(2) The parties are bound by a usage that is widely known to and regularly observed in international trade by parties in the particular trade concerned except where the application of such a usage would be unreasonable.

ARTICLE 1.10 (*Notice*)

(1) Where notice is required it may be given by any means appropriate to the circumstances.

(2) A notice is effective when it reaches the person to whom it is given.

(3) For the purpose of paragraph (2) a notice "reaches" a person when given to that person orally or delivered at that person's place of business or mailing address.

(4) For the purpose of this article "notice" includes a declaration, demand, request or any other communication of intention.

ARTICLE 1.11 (*Definitions*)

In these Principles

— "court" includes an arbitral tribunal;

— where a party has more than one place of business the relevant "place of business" is that which has the closest relationship to the contract and its performance, having regard to the circumstances known to or contemplated by the parties at any time before or at the conclusion of the contract;

— "obligor" refers to the party who is to perform an obligation and "obligee" refers to the party who is entitled to performance of that obligation.

— "writing" means any mode of communication that preserves a record of the information contained therein and is capable of being reproduced in tangible form.

ARTICLE 1.12 (*Computation of time set by parties*)

(1) Official holidays or non-business days occurring during a period set by parties for an act to be performed are included in calculating the period.

(2) However, if the last day of the period is an official holiday or a non-business day at the place of business of the party to perform the act, the period

is extended until the first business day which follows, unless the circumstances indicate otherwise.

(3) The relevant time zone is that of the place of business of the party setting the time, unless the circumstances indicate otherwise.

CHAPTER 2—FORMATION AND AUTHORITY OF AGENTS

SECTION 1: FORMATION

ARTICLE 2.1.1　(*Manner of formation*)

A contract may be concluded either by the acceptance of an offer or by conduct of the parties that is sufficient to show agreement.

ARTICLE 2.1.2　(*Definition of offer*)

A proposal for concluding a contract constitutes an offer if it is sufficiently definite and indicates the intention of the offeror to be bound in case of acceptance. 4

ARTICLE 2.1.3　(*Withdrawal of offer*)

(1) An offer becomes effective when it reaches the offeree.

(2) An offer, even if it is irrevocable, may be withdrawn if the withdrawal reaches the offeree before or at the same time as the offer.

ARTICLE 2.1.4　(*Revocation of offer*)

(1) Until a contract is concluded an offer may be revoked if the revocation reaches the offeree before it has dispatched an acceptance.

(2) However, an offer cannot be revoked

(a) if it indicates, whether by stating a fixed time for acceptance or otherwise, that it is irrevocable; or

(b) if it was reasonable for the offeree to rely on the offer as being irrevocable and the offeree has acted in reliance on the offer.

ARTICLE 2.1.5　(*Rejection of offer*)

An offer is terminated when a rejection reaches the offeror.

ARTICLE 2.1.6　(*Mode of acceptance*)

(1) A statement made by or other conduct of the offeree indicating assent to an offer is an acceptance. Silence or inactivity does not in itself amount to acceptance.

(2) An acceptance of an offer becomes effective when the indication of

assent reaches the offeror.

(3) However, if, by virtue of the offer or as a result of practices which the parties have established between themselves or of usage, the offeree may indicate assent by performing an act without notice to the offeror, the acceptance is effective when the act is performed.

ARTICLE 2.1.7   (*Time of acceptance*)

An offer must be accepted within the time the offeror has fixed or, if no time is fixed, within a reasonable time having regard to the circumstances, including the rapidity of the means of communication employed by the offeror. An oral offer must be accepted immediately unless the circumstances indicate otherwise.

ARTICLE 2.1.8   (*Acceptance within a fixed period of time*)

A period of acceptance fixed by the offeror begins to run from the time that the offer is dispatched. A time indicated in the offer is deemed to be the time of dispatch unless the circumstances indicate otherwise.

ARTICLE 2.1.9   (*Late acceptance. Delay in transmission*)

(1) A late acceptance is nevertheless effective as an acceptance if without undue delay the offeror so informs the offeree or gives notice to that effect.

(2) If a communication containing a late acceptance shows that it has been sent in such circumstances that if its transmission had been normal it would have reached the offeror in due time, the late acceptance is effective as an acceptance unless, without undue delay, the offeror informs the offeree that it considers the offer as having lapsed.

ARTICLE 2.1.10   (*Withdrawal of acceptance*)

An acceptance may be withdrawn if the withdrawal reaches the offeror before or at the same time as the acceptance would have become effective.

ARTICLE 2.1.11   (*Modified acceptance*)

(1) A reply to an offer which purports to be an acceptance but contains additions, limitations or other modifications is a rejection of the offer and constitutes a counter-offer.

(2) However, a reply to an offer which purports to be an acceptance but contains additional or different terms which do not materially alter the terms of the offer constitutes an acceptance, unless the offeror, without undue delay, objects to the discrepancy. If the offeror does not object, the terms of the con-

tract are the terms of the offer with the modifications contained in the acceptance.

ARTICLE 2.1.12 (*Writings in confirmation*)

If a writing which is sent within a reasonable time after the conclusion of the contract and which purports to be a confirmation of the contract contains additional or different terms, such terms become part of the contract, unless they materially alter the contract or the recipient, without undue delay, objects to the discrepancy.

ARTICLE 2.1.13 (*Conclusion of contract dependent on agreement on specific matters or in a particular form*)

Where in the course of negotiations one of the parties insists that the contract is not concluded until there is agreement on specific matters or in a particular form, no contract is concluded before agreement is reached on those matters or in that form.

ARTICLE 2.1.14 (*Contract with terms deliberately left open*)

(1) If the parties intend to conclude a contract, the fact that they intentionally leave a term to be agreed upon in further negotiations or to be determined by a third person does not prevent a contract from coming into existence.

(2) The existence of the contract is not affected by the fact that subsequently

(a) the parties reach no agreement on the term; or

(b) the third person does not determine the term,

provided that there is an alternative means of rendering the term definite that is reasonable in the circumstances, having regard to the intention of the parties.

ARTICLE 2.1.15 (*Negotiations in bad faith*)

(1) A party is free to negotiate and is not liable for failure to reach an agreement.

(2) However, a party who negotiates or breaks off negotiations in bad faith is liable for the losses caused to the other party.

(3) It is bad faith, in particular, for a party to enter into or continue negotiations when intending not to reach an agreement with the other party.

ARTICLE 2.1.16 (*Duty of confidentiality*)

Where information is given as confidential by one party in the course of negotiations, the other party is under a duty not to disclose that information or to use it improperly for its own purposes, whether or not a contract is subsequently concluded. Where appropriate, the remedy for breach of that duty may include compensation based on the benefit received by the other party.

ARTICLE 2.1.17 (*Merger clauses*)

A contract in writing which contains a clause indicating that the writing completely embodies the terms on which the parties have agreed cannot be contradicted or supplemented by evidence of prior statements or agreements. However, such statements or agreements may be used to interpret the writing.

ARTICLE 2.1.18 (*Modification in a particular form*)

A contract in writing which contains a clause requiring any modification or termination by agreement to be in a particular form may not be otherwise modified or terminated. However, a party may be precluded by its conduct from asserting such a clause to the extent that the other party has reasonably acted in reliance on that conduct.

ARTICLE 2.1.19 (*Contracting under standard terms*)

(1) Where one party or both parties use standard terms in concluding a contract, the general rules on formation apply, subject to Articles 2.1.20 — 2.1.22.

(2) Standard terms are provisions which are prepared in advance for general and repeated use by one party and which are actually used without negotiation with the other party.

ARTICLE 2.1.20 (*Surprising terms*)

(1) No term contained in standard terms which is of such a character that the other party could not reasonably have expected it, is effective unless it has been expressly accepted by that party.

(2) In determining whether a term is of such a character regard shall be had to its content, language and presentation.

ARTICLE 2.1.21 (*Conflict between standard terms and non-standard terms*)

In case of conflict between a standard term and a term which is not a standard term the latter prevails.

ARTICLE 2.1.22　(*Battle of forms*)

Where both parties use standard terms and reach agreement except on those terms, a contract is concluded on the basis of the agreed terms and of any standard terms which are common in substance unless one party clearly indicates in advance, or later and without undue delay informs the other party, that it does not intend to be bound by such a contract.

SECTION 2: AUTHORITY OF AGENTS

ARTICLE 2.2.1　(*Scope of the Section*)

(1) This Section governs the authority of a person ("the agent"), to affect the legal relations of another person ("the principal"), by or with respect to a contract with a third party, whether the agent acts in its own name or in that of the principal.

(2) It governs only the relations between the principal or the agent on the one hand, and the third party on the other.

(3) It does not govern an agent's authority conferred by law or the authority of an agent appointed by a public or judicial authority.

ARTICLE 2.2.2　(*Establishment and scope of the authority of the agent*)

(1) The principal's grant of authority to an agent may be express or implied.

(2) The agent has authority to perform all acts necessary in the circumstances to achieve the purposes for which the authority was granted.

ARTICLE 2.2.3　(*Agency disclosed*)

(1) Where an agent acts within the scope of its authority and the third party knew or ought to have known that the agent was acting as an agent, the acts of the agent shall directly affect the legal relations between the principal and the third party and no legal relation is created between the agent and the third party.

(2) However, the acts of the agent shall affect only the relations between the agent and the third party, where the agent with the consent of the principal undertakes to become the party to the contract.

ARTICLE 2.2.4　(*Agency undisclosed*)

(1) Where an agent acts within the scope of its authority and the third party neither knew nor ought to have known that the agent was acting as an a-

gent, the acts of the agent shall affect only the relations between the agent and the third party.

(2) However, where such an agent, when contracting with the third party on behalf of a business, represents itself to be the owner of that business, the third party, upon discovery of the real owner of the business, may exercise also against the latter the rights it has against the agent.

ARTICLE 2.2.5　(*Agent acting without or exceeding its authority*)

(1) Where an agent acts without authority or exceeds its authority, its acts do not affect the legal relations between the principal and the third party.

(2) However, where the principal causes the third party reasonably to believe that the agent has authority to act on behalf of the principal and that the agent is acting within the scope of that authority, the principal may not invoke against the third party the lack of authority of the agent.

ARTICLE 2.2.6　(*Liability of agent acting without or exceeding its authority*)

(1) An agent that acts without authority or exceeds its authority is, failing ratification by the principal, liable for damages that will place the third party in the same position as if the agent had acted with authority and not exceeded its authority.

(2) However, the agent is not liable if the third party knew or ought to have known that the agent had no authority or was exceeding its authority.

ARTICLE 2.2.7　(*Conflict of interests*)

(1) If a contract concluded by an agent involves the agent in a conflict of interests with the principal of which the third party knew or ought to have known, the principal may avoid the contract. The right to avoid is subject to Articles 3.12 and 3.14 to 3.17.

(2) However, the principal may not avoid the contract

(a) if the principal had consented to, or knew or ought to have known of, the agent's involvement in the conflict of interests; or

(b) if the agent had disclosed the conflict of interests to the principal and the latter had not objected within a reasonable time.

ARTICLE 2.2.8　(*Sub-agency*)

An agent has implied authority to appoint a sub-agent to perform acts which it is not reasonable to expect the agent to perform itself. The rules of this

Section apply to the sub-agency.

ARTICLE 2.2.9 (*Ratification*)

(1) An act by an agent that acts without authority or exceeds its authority may be ratified by the principal. On ratification the act produces the same effects as if it had initially been carried out with authority.

(2) The third party may by notice to the principal specify a reasonable period of time for ratification. If the principal does not ratify within that period of time it can no longer do so.

(3) If, at the time of the agent's act, the third party neither knew nor ought to have known of the lack of authority, it may, at any time before ratification, by notice to the principal indicate its refusal to become bound by a ratification.

ARTICLE 2.2.10 (*Termination of authority*)

(1) Termination of authority is not effective in relation to the third party unless the third party knew or ought to have known of it.

(2) Notwithstanding the termination of its authority, an agent remains authorized to perform the acts that are necessary to prevent harm to the principal's interests.

CHAPTER 3—VALIDITY

ARTICLE 3.1 (*Matters not covered*)

These Principles do not deal with invalidity arising from

(a) lack of capacity;

(b) immorality or illegality.

ARTICLE 3.2 (*Validity of mere agreement*)

A contract is concluded, modified or terminated by the mere agreement of the parties, without any further requirement.

ARTICLE 3.3 (*Initial impossibility*)

(1) The mere fact that at the time of the conclusion of the contract the performance of the obligation assumed was impossible does not affect the validity of the contract.

(2) The mere fact that at the time of the conclusion of the contract a party was not entitled to dispose of the assets to which the contract relates does not affect the validity of the contract.

ARTICLE 3.4　(*Definition of mistake*)

Mistake is an erroneous assumption relating to facts or to law existing when the contract was concluded.

ARTICLE 3.5　(*Relevant mistake*)

(1) A party may only avoid the contract for mistake if, when the contract was concluded, the mistake was of such importance that a reasonable person in the same situation as the party in error would only have concluded the contract on materially different terms or would not have concluded it at all if the true state of affairs had been known, and

(a) the other party made the same mistake, or caused the mistake, or knew or ought to have known of the mistake and it was contrary to reasonable commercial standards of fair dealing to leave the mistaken party in error; or

(b) the other party had not at the time of avoidance reasonably acted in reliance on the contract.

(2) However, a party may not avoid the contract if

(a) it was grossly negligent in committing the mistake; or

(b) the mistake relates to a matter in regard to which the risk of mistake was assumed or, having regard to the circumstances, should be borne by the mistaken party.

ARTICLE 3.6　(*Error in expression or transmission*)

An error occurring in the expression or transmission of a declaration is considered to be a mistake of the person from whom the declaration emanated.

ARTICLE 3.7　(*Remedies for non-performance*)

A party is not entitled to avoid the contract on the ground of mistake if the circumstances on which that party relies afford, or could have afforded, a remedy for non-performance.

ARTICLE 3.8　(*Fraud*)

A party may avoid the contract when it has been led to conclude the contract by the other party's fraudulent representation, including language or practices, or fraudulent non-disclosure of circumstances which, according to reasonable commercial standards of fair dealing, the latter party should have disclosed.

ARTICLE 3.9　(*Threat*)

A party may avoid the contract when it has been led to conclude the contract by the other party's unjustified threat which, having regard to the circumstances, is so imminent and serious as to leave the first party no reasonable alternative. In particular, a threat is unjustified if the act or omission with which a party has been threatened is wrongful in itself, or it is wrongful to use it as a means to obtain the conclusion of the contract.

ARTICLE 3.10　(*Gross disparity*)

(1) A party may avoid the contract or an individual term of it if, at the time of the conclusion of the contract, the contract or term unjustifiably gave the other party an excessive advantage. Regard is to be had, among other factors, to

(a) the fact that the other party has taken unfair advantage of the first party's dependence, economic distress or urgent needs, or of its improvidence, ignorance, inexperience or lack of bargaining skill, and

(b) the nature and purpose of the contract.

(2) Upon the request of the party entitled to avoidance, a court may adapt the contract or term in order to make it accord with reasonable commercial standards of fair dealing.

(3) A court may also adapt the contract or term upon the request of the party receiving notice of avoidance, provided that that party informs the other party of its request promptly after receiving such notice and before the other party has reasonably acted in reliance on it. The provisions of Article 3.13(2) apply accordingly.

ARTICLE 3.11　(*Third persons*)

(1) Where fraud, threat, gross disparity or a party's mistake is imputable to, or is known or ought to be known by, a third person for whose acts the other party is responsible, the contract may be avoided under the same conditions as if the behaviour or knowledge had been that of the party itself.

(2) Where fraud, threat or gross disparity is imputable to a third person for whose acts the other party is not responsible, the contract may be avoided if that party knew or ought to have known of the fraud, threat or disparity, or has not at the time of avoidance reasonably acted in reliance on the contract.

ARTICLE 3.12　(*Confirmation*)

If the party entitled to avoid the contract expressly or impliedly confirms the contract after the period of time for giving notice of avoidance has begun to run, avoidance of the contract is excluded.

ARTICLE 3.13 (*Loss of right to avoid*)

(1) If a party is entitled to avoid the contract for mistake but the other party declares itself willing to perform or performs the contract as it was understood by the party entitled to avoidance, the contract is considered to have been concluded as the latter party understood it. The other party must make such a declaration or render such performance promptly after having been informed of the manner in which the party entitled to avoidance had understood the contract and before that party has reasonably acted in reliance on a notice of avoidance.

(2) After such a declaration or performance the right to avoidance is lost and any earlier notice of avoidance is ineffective.

ARTICLE 3.14 (*Notice of avoidance*)

The right of a party to avoid the contract is exercised by notice to the other party.

ARTICLE 3.15 (*Time limits*)

(1) Notice of avoidance shall be given within a reasonable time, having regard to the circumstances, after the avoiding party knew or could not have been unaware of the relevant facts or became capable of acting freely.

(2) Where an individual term of the contract may be avoided by a party under Article 3.10, the period of time for giving notice of avoidance begins to run when that term is asserted by the other party.

ARTICLE 3.16 (*Partial avoidance*)

Where a ground of avoidance affects only individual terms of the contract, the effect of avoidance is limited to those terms unless, having regard to the circumstances, it is unreasonable to uphold the remaining contract.

ARTICLE 3.17 (*Retroactive effect of avoidance*)

(1) Avoidance takes effect retroactively.

(2) On avoidance either party may claim restitution of whatever it has supplied under the contract or the part of it avoided, provided that it concurrently makes restitution of whatever it has received under the contract or the part of it avoided or, if it cannot make restitution in kind, it makes an allowance for what it has received.

ARTICLE 3.18 (*Damages*)

Irrespective of whether or not the contract has been avoided, the party who knew or ought to have known of the ground for avoidance is liable for damages so as to put the other party in the same position in which it would have been if it had not concluded the contract.

ARTICLE 3.19 (*Mandatory character of the provisions*)

The provisions of this Chapter are mandatory, except insofar as they relate to the binding force of mere agreement, initial impossibility or mistake.

ARTICLE 3.20 (*Unilateral declarations*)

The provisions of this Chapter apply with appropriate adaptations to any communication of intention addressed by one party to the other.

CHAPTER 4—INTERPRETATION

ARTICLE 4.1 (*Intention of the parties*)

(1) A contract shall be interpreted according to the common intention of the parties.

(2) If such an intention cannot be established, the contract shall be interpreted according to the meaning that reasonable persons of the same kind as the parties would give to it in the same circumstances.

ARTICLE 4.2 (*Interpretation of statements and other conduct*)

(1) The statements and other conduct of a party shall be interpreted according to that party's intention if the other party knew or could not have been unaware of that intention.

(2) If the preceding paragraph is not applicable, such statements and other conduct shall be interpreted according to the meaning that a reasonable person of the same kind as the other party would give to it in the same circumstances.

ARTICLE 4.3 (*Relevant circumstances*)

In applying Articles 4.1 and 4.2, regard shall be had to all the circumstances, including

(a) preliminary negotiations between the parties;

(b) practices which the parties have established between themselves;

(c) the conduct of the parties subsequent to the conclusion of the contract;

(d) the nature and purpose of the contract;

(e) the meaning commonly given to terms and expressions in the trade concerned;

(f) usages.

ARTICLE 4.4　(*Reference to contract or statement as a whole*)

Terms and expressions shall be interpreted in the light of the whole contract or statement in which they appear.

ARTICLE 4.5　(*All terms to be given effect*)

Contract terms shall be interpreted so as to give effect to all the terms rather than to deprive some of them of effect.

ARTICLE 4.6　(*Contra proferentem rule*)

If contract terms supplied by one party are unclear, an interpretation against that party is preferred.

ARTICLE 4.7　(*Linguistic discrepancies*)

Where a contract is drawn up in two or more language versions which are equally authoritative there is, in case of discrepancy between the versions, a preference for the interpretation according to a version in which the contract was originally drawn up.

ARTICLE 4.8　(*Supplying an omitted term*)

(1) Where the parties to a contract have not agreed with respect to a term which is important for a determination of their rights and duties, a term which is appropriate in the circumstances shall be supplied.

(2) In determining what is an appropriate term regard shall be had, among other factors, to

(a) the intention of the parties;

(b) the nature and purpose of the contract;

(c) good faith and fair dealing;

(d) reasonableness.

CHAPTER 5—CONTENT AND THIRD PARTY RIGHTS

SECTION 1: CONTENT

ARTICLE 5.1.1　(*Express and implied obligations*)

The contractual obligations of the parties may be express or implied.

ARTICLE 5.1.2 (*Implied obligations*)

Implied obligations stem from

(a) the nature and purpose of the contract;

(b) practices established between the parties and usages;

(c) good faith and fair dealing;

(d) reasonableness.

ARTICLE 5.1.3 (*Co-operation between the parties*)

Each party shall cooperate with the other party when such co-operation may reasonably be expected for the performance of that party's obligations.

ARTICLE 5.1.4 (*Duty to achieve a specific result. Duty of best efforts*)

(1) To the extent that an obligation of a party involves a duty to achieve a specific result, that party is bound to achieve that result.

(2) To the extent that an obligation of a party involves a duty of best efforts in the performance of an activity, that party is bound to make such efforts as would be made by a reasonable person of the same kind in the same circumstances.

ARTICLE 5.1.5 (*Determination of kind of duty involved*)

In determining the extent to which an obligation of a party involves a duty of best efforts in the performance of an activity or a duty to achieve a specific result, regard shall be had, among other factors, to

(a) the way in which the obligation is expressed in the contract;

(b) the contractual price and other terms of the contract;

(c) the degree of risk normally involved in achieving the expected result;

(d) the ability of the other party to influence the performance of the obligation.

ARTICLE 5.1.6 (*Determination of quality of performance*)

Where the quality of performance is neither fixed by, nor determinable from, the contract a party is bound to render a performance of a quality that is reasonable and not less than average in the circumstances.

ARTICLE 5.1.7 (*Price determination*)

(1) Where a contract does not fix or make provision for determining the price, the parties are considered, in the absence of any indication to the contrary, to have made reference to the price generally charged at the time of the conclusion of the contract for such performance in comparable circumstances in

the trade concerned or, if no such price is available, to a reasonable price.

(2) Where the price is to be determined by one party and that determination is manifestly unreasonable, a reasonable price shall be substituted notwithstanding any contract term to the contrary.

(3) Where the price is to be fixed by a third person, and that person cannot or will not do so, the price shall be a reasonable price.

(4) Where the price is to be fixed by reference to factors which do not exist or have ceased to exist or to be accessible, the nearest equivalent factor shall be treated as a substitute.

ARTICLE 5.1.8 (*Contract for an indefinite period*)

A contract for an indefinite period may be ended by either party by giving notice a reasonable time in advance.

ARTICLE 5.1.9 (*Release by agreement*)

(1) An obligee may release its right by agreement with the obligor.

(2) An offer to release a right gratuitously shall be deemed accepted if the obligor does not reject the offer without delay after having become aware of it.

SECTION 2: THIRD PARTY RIGHTS

ARTICLE 5.2.1 (*Contracts in favour of third parties*)

(1) The parties (the "promisor" and the "promisee") may confer by express or implied agreement a right on a third party (the "beneficiary").

(2) The existence and content of the beneficiary's right against the promisor are determined by the agreement of the parties and are subject to any conditions or other limitations under the agreement.

ARTICLE 5.2.2 (*Third party identifiable*)

The beneficiary must be identifiable with adequate certainty by the contract but need not be in existence at the time the contract is made.

ARTICLE 5.2.3 (*Exclusion and limitation clauses*)

The conferment of rights in the beneficiary includes the right to invoke a clause in the contract which excludes or limits the liability of the beneficiary.

ARTICLE 5.2.4 (*Defences*)

The promisor may assert against the beneficiary all defences which the promisor could assert against the promisee.

ARTICLE 5.2.5　(*Revocation*)

The parties may modify or revoke the rights conferred by the contract on the beneficiary until the beneficiary has accepted them or reasonably acted in reliance on them.

ARTICLE 5.2.6　(*Renunciation*)

The beneficiary may renounce a right conferred on it.

CHAPTER 6—PERFORMANCE

SECTION 1: PERFORMANCE IN GENERAL

ARTICLE 6.1.1　(*Time of performance*)

A party must perform its obligations:

(a) if a time is fixed by or determinable from the contract, at that time;

(b) if a period of time is fixed by or determinable from the contract, at any time within that period unless circumstances indicate that the other party is to choose a time;

(c) in any other case, within a reasonable time after the conclusion of the contract.

ARTICLE 6.1.2　(*Performance at one time or in installments*)

In cases under Article 6.1.1(b) or (c), a party must perform its obligations at one time if that performance can be rendered at one time and the circumstances do not indicate otherwise.

ARTICLE 6.1.3　(*Partial performance*)

(1) The obligee may reject an offer to perform in part at the time performance is due, whether or not such offer is coupled with an assurance as to the balance of the performance, unless the obligee has no legitimate interest in so doing.

(2) Additional expenses caused to the obligee by partial performance are to be borne by the obligor without prejudice to any other remedy.

ARTICLE 6.1.4　(*Order of performance*)

(1) To the extent that the performances of the parties can be rendered simultaneously, the parties are bound to render them simultaneously unless the circumstances indicate otherwise.

(2) To the extent that the performance of only one party requires a period

of time, that party is bound to render its performance first, unless the circumstances indicate otherwise.

ARTICLE 6.1.5 (*Earlier performance*)

(1) The obligee may reject an earlier performance unless it has no legitimate interest in so doing.

(2) Acceptance by a party of an earlier performance does not affect the time for the performance of its own obligations if that time has been fixed irrespective of the performance of the other party's obligations.

(3) Additional expenses caused to the obligee by earlier performance are to be borne by the obligor, without prejudice to any other remedy.

ARTICLE 6.1.6 (*Place of performance*)

(1) If the place of performance is neither fixed by, nor determinable from, the contract, a party is to perform:

(a) a monetary obligation, at the obligee's place of business;

(b) any other obligation, at its own place of business.

(2) A party must bear any increase in the expenses incidental to performance which is caused by a change in its place of business subsequent to the conclusion of the contract.

ARTICLE 6.1.7 (*Payment by cheque or other instrument*)

(1) Payment may be made in any form used in the ordinary course of business at the place for payment.

(2) However, an obligee who accepts, either by virtue of paragraph (1) or voluntarily, a cheque, any other order to pay or a promise to pay, is presumed to do so only on condition that it will be honoured.

ARTICLE 6.1.8 (*Payment by funds transfer*)

(1) Unless the obligee has indicated a particular account, payment may be made by a transfer to any of the financial institutions in which the obligee has made it known that it has an account.

(2) In case of payment by a transfer the obligation of the obligor is discharged when the transfer to the obligee's financial institution becomes effective.

ARTICLE 6.1.9 (*Currency of payment*)

(1) If a monetary obligation is expressed in a currency other than that of the place for payment, it may be paid by the obligor in the currency of the

place for payment unless

(a) that currency is not freely convertible; or

(b) the parties have agreed that payment should be made only in the currency in which the monetary obligation is expressed.

(2) If it is impossible for the obligor to make payment in the currency in which the monetary obligation is expressed, the obligee may require payment in the currency of the place for payment, even in the case referred to in paragraph (1)(b).

(3) Payment in the currency of the place for payment is to be made according to the applicable rate of exchange prevailing there when payment is due.

(4) However, if the obligor has not paid at the time when payment is due, the obligee may require payment according to the applicable rate of exchange prevailing either when payment is due or at the time of actual payment.

ARTICLE 6.1.10 (*Currency not expressed*)

Where a monetary obligation is not expressed in a particular currency, payment must be made in the currency of the place where payment is to be made.

ARTICLE 6.1.11 (*Costs of performance*)

Each party shall bear the costs of performance of its obligations.

ARTICLE 6.1.12 (*Imputation of payments*)

(1) An obligor owing several monetary obligations to the same obligee may specify at the time of payment the debt to which it intends the payment to be applied. However, the payment discharges first any expenses, then interest due and finally the principal.

(2) If the obligor makes no such specification, the obligee may, within a reasonable time after payment, declare to the obligor the obligation to which it imputes the payment, provided that the obligation is due and undisputed.

(3) In the absence of imputation under paragraphs (1) or (2), payment is imputed to that obligation which satisfies one of the following criteria in the order indicated:

(a) an obligation which is due or which is the first to fall due;

(b) the obligation for which the obligee has least security;

(c) the obligation which is the most burdensome for the obligor;

(d) the obligation which has arisen first.

If none of the preceding criteria applies, payment is imputed to all the obligations proportionally.

ARTICLE 6.1.13　(*Imputation of non-monetary obligations*)

Article 6.1.12 applies with appropriate adaptations to the imputation of performance of non-monetary obligations.

ARTICLE 6.1.14　(*Application for public permission*)

Where the law of a State requires a public permission affecting the validity of the contract or its performance and neither that law nor the circumstances indicate otherwise

(a) if only one party has its place of business in that State, that party shall take the measures necessary to obtain the permission;

(b) in any other case the party whose performance requires permission shall take the necessary measures.

ARTICLE 6.1.15　(*Procedure in applying for permission*)

(1) The party required to take the measures necessary to obtain the permission shall do so without undue delay and shall bear any expenses incurred.

(2) That party shall whenever appropriate give the other party notice of the grant or refusal of such permission without undue delay.

ARTICLE 6.1.16　(*Permission neither granted nor refused*)

(1) If, notwithstanding the fact that the party responsible has taken all measures required, permission is neither granted nor refused within an agreed period or, where no period has been agreed, within a reasonable time from the conclusion of the contract, either party is entitled to terminate the contract.

(2) Where the permission affects some terms only, paragraph (1) does not apply if, having regard to the circumstances, it is reasonable to uphold the remaining contract even if the permission is refused.

ARTICLE 6.1.17　(*Permission refused*)

(1) The refusal of a permission affecting the validity of the contract renders the contract void. If the refusal affects the validity of some terms only, only such terms are void if, having regard to the circumstances, it is reasonable to uphold the remaining contract.

(2) Where the refusal of a permission renders the performance of the contract impossible in whole or in part, the rules on non-performance apply.

SECTION 2: HARDSHIP

ARTICLE 6.2.1 (*Contract to be observed*)

Where the performance of a contract becomes more onerous for one of the parties, that party is nevertheless bound to perform its obligations subject to the following provisions on hardship.

ARTICLE 6.2.2 (*Definition of hardship*)

There is hardship where the occurrence of events fundamentally alters the equilibrium of the contract either because the cost of a party's performance has increased or because the value of the performance a party receives has diminished, and

(a) the events occur or become known to the disadvantaged party after the conclusion of the contract;

(b) the events could not reasonably have been taken into account by the disadvantaged party at the time of the conclusion of the contract;

(c) the events are beyond the control of the disadvantaged party; and

(d) the risk of the events was not assumed by the disadvantaged party.

ARTICLE 6.2.3 (*Effects of hardship*)

(1) In case of hardship the disadvantaged party is entitled to request renegotiations. The request shall be made without undue delay and shall indicate the grounds on which it is based.

(2) The request for renegotiation does not in itself entitle the disadvantaged party to withhold performance.

(3) Upon failure to reach agreement within a reasonable time either party may resort to the court.

(4) If the court finds hardship it may, if reasonable,

(a) terminate the contract at a date and on terms to be fixed, or

(b) adapt the contract with a view to restoring its equilibrium.

CHAPTER 7—NON-PERFORMANCE

SECTION 1: NON-PERFORMANCE IN GENERAL

ARTICLE 7.1.1 (*Non-performance defined*)

Non-performance is failure by a party to perform any of its obligations under the contract, including defective performance or late performance.

ARTICLE 7.1.2　(*Interference by the other party*)

A party may not rely on the non-performance of the other party to the extent that such non-performance was caused by the first party's act or omission or by another event as to which the first party bears the risk.

ARTICLE 7.1.3　(*Withholding performance*)

(1) Where the parties are to perform simultaneously, either party may withhold performance until the other party tenders its performance.

(2) Where the parties are to perform consecutively, the party that is to perform later may withhold its performance until the first party has performed.

ARTICLE 7.1.4　(*Cure by non-performing party*)

(1) The non-performing party may, at its own expense, cure any nonperformance, provided that

(a) without undue delay, it gives notice indicating the proposed manner and timing of the cure;

(b) cure is appropriate in the circumstances;

(c) the aggrieved party has no legitimate interest in refusing cure; and

(d) cure is effected promptly.

(2) The right to cure is not precluded by notice of termination.

(3) Upon effective notice of cure, rights of the aggrieved party that are inconsistent with the non-performing party's performance are suspended until the time for cure has expired.

(4) The aggrieved party may withhold performance pending cure.

(5) Notwithstanding cure, the aggrieved party retains the right to claim damages for delay as well as for any harm caused or not prevented by the cure.

ARTICLE 7.1.5　(*Additional period for performance*)

(1) In a case of non-performance the aggrieved party may by notice to the other party allow an additional period of time for performance.

(2) During the additional period the aggrieved party may withhold performance of its own reciprocal obligations and may claim damages but may not resort to any other remedy. If it receives notice from the other party that the latter will not perform within that period, or if upon expiry of that period due performance has not been made, the aggrieved party may resort to any of the remedies that may be available under this Chapter.

(3) Where in a case of delay in performance which is not fundamental the aggrieved party has given notice allowing an additional period of time of reasonable length, it may terminate the contract at the end of that period. If the additional period allowed is not of reasonable length it shall be extended to a reasonable length. The aggrieved party may in its notice provide that if the other party fails to perform within the period allowed by the notice the contract shall automatically terminate.

(4) Paragraph (3) does not apply where the obligation which has not been performed is only a minor part of the contractual obligation of the non-performing party.

ARTICLE 7.1.6　(*Exemption clauses*)

A clause which limits or excludes one party's liability for non-performance or which permits one party to render performance substantially different from what the other party reasonably expected may not be invoked if it would be grossly unfair to do so, having regard to the purpose of the contract.

ARTICLE 7.1.7　(*Force majeure*)

(1) Non-performance by a party is excused if that party proves that the nonperformance was due to an impediment beyond its control and that it could not reasonably be expected to have taken the impediment into account at the time of the conclusion of the contract or to have avoided or overcome it or its consequences.

(2) When the impediment is only temporary, the excuse shall have effect for such period as is reasonable having regard to the effect of the impediment on the performance of the contract.

(3) The party who fails to perform must give notice to the other party of the impediment and its effect on its ability to perform. If the notice is not received by the other party within a reasonable time after the party who fails to perform knew or ought to have known of the impediment, it is liable for damages resulting from such nonreceipt.

(4) Nothing in this article prevents a party from exercising a right to terminate the contract or to withhold performance or request interest on money due.

SECTION 2: RIGHT TO PERFORMANCE

ARTICLE 7.2.1 (*Performance of monetary obligation*)

Where a party who is obliged to pay money does not do so, the other party may require payment.

ARTICLE 7.2.2 (*Performance of non-monetary obligation*)

Where a party who owes an obligation other than one to pay money does not perform, the other party may require performance, unless

(a) performance is impossible in law or in fact;

(b) performance or, where relevant, enforcement is unreasonably burdensome or expensive;

(c) the party entitled to performance may reasonably obtain performance from another source;

(d) performance is of an exclusively personal character; or

(e) the party entitled to performance does not require performance within a reasonable time after it has, or ought to have, become aware of the non-performance.

ARTICLE 7.2.3 (*Repair and replacement of defective performance*)

The right to performance includes in appropriate cases the right to require repair, replacement, or other cure of defective performance. The provisions of Articles 7.2.1 and 7.2.2 apply accordingly.

ARTICLE 7.2.4 (*Judicial penalty*)

(1) Where the court orders a party to perform, it may also direct that this party pay a penalty if it does not comply with the order.

(2) The penalty shall be paid to the aggrieved party unless mandatory provisions of the law of the forum provide otherwise. Payment of the penalty to the aggrieved party does not exclude any claim for damages.

ARTICLE 7.2.5 (*Change of remedy*)

(1) An aggrieved party who has required performance of a non-monetary obligation and who has not received performance within a period fixed or otherwise within a reasonable period of time may invoke any other remedy.

(2) Where the decision of a court for performance of a non-monetary obligation cannot be enforced, the aggrieved party may invoke any other remedy.

SECTION 3: TERMINATION

ARTICLE 7.3.1 (*Right to terminate the contract*)

(1) A party may terminate the contract where the failure of the other party to perform an obligation under the contract amounts to a fundamental non-performance.

(2) In determining whether a failure to perform an obligation amounts to a fundamental non-performance regard shall be had, in particular, to whether

(a) the non-performance substantially deprives the aggrieved party of what it was entitled to expect under the contract unless the other party did not foresee and could not reasonably have foreseen such result;

(b) strict compliance with the obligation which has not been performed is of essence under the contract;

(c) the non-performance is intentional or reckless;

(d) the non-performance gives the aggrieved party reason to believe that it cannot rely on the other party's future performance;

(e) the non-performing party will suffer disproportionate loss as a result of the preparation or performance if the contract is terminated.

(3) In the case of delay the aggrieved party may also terminate the contract if the other party fails to perform before the time allowed it under Article 7.1.5 has expired.

ARTICLE 7.3.2 (*Notice of termination*)

(1) The right of a party to terminate the contract is exercised by notice to the other party.

(2) If performance has been offered late or otherwise does not conform to the contract the aggrieved party will lose its right to terminate the contract unless it gives notice to the other party within a reasonable time after it has or ought to have become aware of the offer or of the non-conforming performance.

ARTICLE 7.3.3 (*Anticipatory non-performance*)

Where prior to the date for performance by one of the parties it is clear that there will be a fundamental non-performance by that party, the other party may terminate the contract.

ARTICLE 7.3.4 (*Adequate assurance of due performance*)

A party who reasonably believes that there will be a fundamental non-performance by the other party may demand adequate assurance of due performance and may meanwhile withhold its own performance. Where this assurance is not provided within a reasonable time the party demanding it may terminate the contract.

ARTICLE 7.3.5 (*Effects of termination in general*)

(1) Termination of the contract releases both parties from their obligation to effect and to receive future performance.

(2) Termination does not preclude a claim for damages for non-performance.

(3) Termination does not affect any provision in the contract for the settlement of disputes or any other term of the contract which is to operate even after termination.

ARTICLE 7.3.6 (*Restitution*)

(1) On termination of the contract either party may claim restitution of whatever it has supplied, provided that such party concurrently makes restitution of whatever it has received. If restitution in kind is not possible or appropriate allowance should be made in money whenever reasonable.

(2) However, if performance of the contract has extended over a period of time and the contract is divisible, such restitution can only be claimed for the period after termination has taken effect.

SECTION 4: DAMAGES

ARTICLE 7.4.1 (*Right to damages*)

Any non-performance gives the aggrieved party a right to damages either exclusively or in conjunction with any other remedies except where the non-performance is excused under these Principles.

ARTICLE 7.4.2 (*Full compensation*)

(1) The aggrieved party is entitled to full compensation for harm sustained as a result of the non-performance. Such harm includes both any loss which it suffered and any gain of which it was deprived, taking into account any gain to the aggrieved party resulting from its avoidance of cost or harm.

(2) Such harm may be non-pecuniary and includes, for instance, physical suffering or emotional distress.

ARTICLE 7.4.3　(*Certainty of harm*)

(1) Compensation is due only for harm, including future harm, that is established with a reasonable degree of certainty.

(2) Compensation may be due for the loss of a chance in proportion to the probability of its occurrence.

(3) Where the amount of damages cannot be established with a sufficient degree of certainty, the assessment is at the discretion of the court.

ARTICLE 7.4.4　(*Foreseeability of harm*)

The non-performing party is liable only for harm which it foresaw or could reasonably have foreseen at the time of the conclusion of the contract as being likely to result from its non-performance.

ARTICLE 7.4.5　(*Proof of harm in case of replacement transaction*)

Where the aggrieved party has terminated the contract and has made a replacement transaction within a reasonable time and in a reasonable manner it may recover the difference between the contract price and the price of the replacement transaction as well as damages for any further harm.

ARTICLE 7.4.6　(*Proof of harm by current price*)

(1) Where the aggrieved party has terminated the contract and has not made a replacement transaction but there is a current price for the performance contracted for, it may recover the difference between the contract price and the price current at the time the contract is terminated as well as damages for any further harm.

(2) Current price is the price generally charged for goods delivered or services rendered in comparable circumstances at the place where the contract should have been performed or, if there is no current price at that place, the current price at such other place that appears reasonable to take as a reference.

ARTICLE 7.4.7　(*Harm due in part to aggrieved party*)

Where the harm is due in part to an act or omission of the aggrieved party or to another event as to which that party bears the risk, the amount of damages shall be reduced to the extent that these factors have contributed to the harm, having regard to the conduct of each of the parties.

ARTICLE 7.4.8　(*Mitigation of harm*)

(1) The non-performing party is not liable for harm suffered by the ag-

grieved party to the extent that the harm could have been reduced by the latter party's taking reasonable steps.

(2) The aggrieved party is entitled to recover any expenses reasonably incurred in attempting to reduce the harm.

ARTICLE 7.4.9 (*Interest for failure to pay money*)

(1) If a party does not pay a sum of money when it falls due the aggrieved party is entitled to interest upon that sum from the time when payment is due to the time of payment whether or not the non-payment is excused.

(2) The rate of interest shall be the average bank short-term lending rate to prime borrowers prevailing for the currency of payment at the place for payment, or where no such rate exists at that place, then the same rate in the State of the currency of payment. In the absence of such a rate at either place the rate of interest shall be the appropriate rate fixed by the law of the State of the currency of payment.

(3) The aggrieved party is entitled to additional damages if the non-payment caused it a greater harm.

ARTICLE 7.4.10 (*Interest on damages*)

Unless otherwise agreed, interest on damages for non-performance of non-monetary obligations accrues as from the time of non-performance.

ARTICLE 7.4.11 (*Manner of monetary redress*)

(1) Damages are to be paid in a lump sum. However, they may be payable in installments where the nature of the harm makes this appropriate.

(2) Damages to be paid in installments may be indexed.

ARTICLE 7.4.12 (*Currency in which to assess damages*)

Damages are to be assessed either in the currency in which the monetary obligation was expressed or in the currency in which the harm was suffered, whichever is more appropriate.

ARTICLE 7.4.13 (*Agreed payment for non-performance*)

(1) Where the contract provides that a party who does not perform is to pay a specified sum to the aggrieved party for such non-performance, the aggrieved party is entitled to that sum irrespective of its actual harm.

(2) However, notwithstanding any agreement to the contrary the specified sum may be reduced to a reasonable amount where it is grossly excessive in relation to the harm resulting from the non-performance and to the other cir-

cumstances.

CHAPTER 8—SET-OFF

ARTICLE 8.1   (*Conditions of set-off*)

(1) Where two parties owe each other money or other performances of the same kind, either of them ("the first party") may set off its obligation against that of its obligee ("the other party") if at the time of set-off,

(a) the first party is entitled to perform its obligation;

(b) the other party's obligation is ascertained as to its existence and amount and performance is due.

(2) If the obligations of both parties arise from the same contract, the first party may also set off its obligation against an obligation of the other party which is not ascertained as to its existence or to its amount.

ARTICLE 8.2   (*Foreign currency set-off*)

Where the obligations are to pay money in different currencies, the right of set-off may be exercised, provided that both currencies are freely convertible and the parties have not agreed that the first party shall pay only in a specified currency.

ARTICLE 8.3   (*Set-off by notice*)

The right of set-off is exercised by notice to the other party.

ARTICLE 8.4   (*Content of notice*)

(1) The notice must specify the obligations to which it relates.

(2) If the notice does not specify the obligation against which set-off is exercised, the other party may, within a reasonable time, declare to the first party the obligation to which set-off relates. If no such declaration is made, the set-off will relate to all the obligations proportionally.

ARTICLE 8.5   (*Effect of set-off*)

(1) Set-off discharges the obligations.

(2) If obligations differ in amount, set-off discharges the obligations up to the amount of the lesser obligation.

(3) Set-off takes effect as from the time of notice.

CHAPTER 9—ASSIGNMENT OF RIGHTS, TRANSFER OF OBLIGATIONS, ASSIGNMENT OF CONTRACTS

SECTION 1: ASSIGNMENT OF RIGHTS

ARTICLE 9.1.1 (*Definitions*)

"Assignment of a right" means the transfer by agreement from one person (the "assignor") to another person (the "assignee"), including transfer by way of security, of the assignor's right to payment of a monetary sum or other performance from a third person ("the obligor").

ARTICLE 9.1.2 (*Exclusions*)

This Section does not apply to transfers made under the special rules governing the transfers:

(a) of instruments such as negotiable instruments, documents of title or financial instruments, or

(b) of rights in the course of transferring a business.

ARTICLE 9.1.3 (*Assignability of non-monetary rights*)

A right to non-monetary performance may be assigned only if the assignment does not render the obligation significantly more burdensome.

ARTICLE 9.1.4 (*Partial assignment*)

(1) A right to the payment of a monetary sum may be assigned partially.

(2) A right to other performance may be assigned partially only if it is divisible, and the assignment does not render the obligation significantly more burdensome.

ARTICLE 9.1.5 (*Future rights*)

A future right is deemed to be transferred at the time of the agreement, provided the right, when it comes into existence, can be identified as the right to which the assignment relates.

ARTICLE 9.1.6 (*Rights assigned without individual specification*)

A number of rights may be assigned without individual specification, provided such rights can be identified as rights to which the assignment relates at the time of the assignment or when they come into existence.

ARTICLE 9.1.7 (*Agreement between assignor and assignee sufficient*)

(1) A right is assigned by mere agreement between the assignor and the assignee, without notice to the obligor.

(2) The consent of the obligor is not required unless the obligation in the circumstances is of an essentially personal character.

ARTICLE 9.1.8　(*Obligor's additional costs*)

The obligor has a right to be compensated by the assignor or the assignee for any additional costs caused by the assignment.

ARTICLE 9.1.9　(*Non-assignment clauses*)

(1) The assignment of a right to the payment of a monetary sum is effective notwithstanding an agreement between the assignor and the obligor limiting or prohibiting such an assignment. However, the assignor may be liable to the obligor for breach of contract.

(2) The assignment of a right to other performance is ineffective if it is contrary to an agreement between the assignor and the obligor limiting or prohibiting the assignment. Nevertheless, the assignment is effective if the assignee, at the time of the assignment, neither knew nor ought to have known of the agreement. The assignor may then be liable to the obligor for breach of contract.

ARTICLE 9.1.10　(*Notice to the obligor*)

(1) Until the obligor receives a notice of the assignment from either the assignor or the assignee, it is discharged by paying the assignor.

(2) After the obligor receives such a notice, it is discharged only by paying the assignee.

ARTICLE 9.1.11　(*Successive assignments*)

If the same right has been assigned by the same assignor to two or more successive assignees, the obligor is discharged by paying according to the order in which the notices were received.

ARTICLE 9.1.12　(*Adequate proof of assignment*)

(1) If notice of the assignment is given by the assignee, the obligor may request the assignee to provide within a reasonable time adequate proof that the assignment has been made.

(2) Until adequate proof is provided, the obligor may withhold payment.

(3) Unless adequate proof is provided, notice is not effective.

(4) Adequate proof includes, but is not limited to, any writing emanating from the assignor and indicating that the assignment has taken place.

ARTICLE 9.1.13   (*Defences and rights of set-off*)

(1) The obligor may assert against the assignee all defences that the obligor could assert against the assignor.

(2) The obligor may exercise against the assignee any right of set-off available to the obligor against the assignor up to the time notice of assignment was received.

ARTICLE 9.1.14   (*Rights related to the right assigned*)

The assignment of a right transfers to the assignee:

(a) all the assignor's rights to payment or other performance under the contract in respect of the right assigned, and

(b) all rights securing performance of the right assigned.

ARTICLE 9.1.15   (*Undertakings of the assignor*)

The assignor undertakes towards the assignee, except as otherwise disclosed to the assignee, that:

(a) the assigned right exists at the time of the assignment, unless the right is a future right;

(b) the assignor is entitled to assign the right;

(c) the right has not been previously assigned to another assignee, and it is free from any right or claim from a third party;

(d) the obligor does not have any defences;

(e) neither the obligor nor the assignor has given notice of set-off concerning the assigned right and will not give any such notice;

(f) the assignor will reimburse the assignee for any payment received from the obligor before notice of the assignment was given.

SECTION 2: TRANSFER OF OBLIGATIONS

ARTICLE 9.2.1   (*Modes of transfer*)

An obligation to pay money or render other performance may be transferred from one person (the "original obligor") to another person (the "new obligor") either

a) by an agreement between the original obligor and the new obligor subject to Article 9.2.3, or

b) by an agreement between the obligee and the new obligor, by which the new obligor assumes the obligation.

ARTICLE 9.2.2 (*Exclusion*)

This Section does not apply to transfers of obligations made under the special rules governing transfers of obligations in the course of transferring a business.

ARTICLE 9.2.3 (*Requirement of obligee's consent to transfer*)

The transfer of an obligation by an agreement between the original obligor and the new obligor requires the consent of the obligee.

ARTICLE 9.2.4 (*Advance consent of obligee*)

(1) The obligee may give its consent in advance.

(2) If the obligee has given its consent in advance, the transfer of the obligation becomes effective when a notice of the transfer is given to the obligee or when the obligee acknowledges it.

ARTICLE 9.2.5 (*Discharge of original obligor*)

(1) The obligee may discharge the original obligor.

(2) The obligee may also retain the original obligor as an obligor in case the new obligor does not perform properly.

(3) Otherwise the original obligor and the new obligor are jointly and severally liable.

ARTICLE 9.2.6 (*Third party performance*)

(1) Without the obligee's consent, the obligor may contract with another person that this person will perform the obligation in place of the obligor, unless the obligation in the circumstances has an essentially personal character.

(2) The obligee retains its claim against the obligor.

ARTICLE 9.2.7 (*Defences and rights of set-off*)

(1) The new obligor may assert against the obligee all defences which the original obligor could assert against the obligee.

(2) The new obligor may not exercise against the obligee any right of set-off available to the original obligor against the obligee.

ARTICLE 9.2.8 (*Rights related to the obligation transferred*)

(1) The obligee may assert against the new obligor all its rights to payment or other performance under the contract in respect of the obligation transferred.

(2) If the original obligor is discharged under Article 9.2.5(1), a security granted by any person other than the new obligor for the performance of the

obligation is discharged, unless that other person agrees that it should continue to be available to the obligee.

(3) Discharge of the original obligor also extends to any security of the original obligor given to the obligee for the performance of the obligation, unless the security is over an asset which is transferred as part of a transaction between the original obligor and the new obligor.

SECTION 3: ASSIGNMENT OF CONTRACTS

ARTICLE 9.3.1　(*Definitions*)

"Assignment of a contract" means the transfer by agreement from one person (the "assignor") to another person (the "assignee") of the assignor's rights and obligations arising out of a contract with another person (the "other party").

ARTICLE 9.3.2　(*Exclusion*)

This Section does not apply to the assignment of contracts made under the special rules governing transfers of contracts in the course of transferring a business.

ARTICLE 9.3.3　(*Requirement of consent of the other party*)

The assignment of a contract requires the consent of the other party.

ARTICLE 9.3.4　(*Advance consent of the other party*)

(1) The other party may give its consent in advance.

(2) If the other party has given its consent in advance, the assignment of the contract becomes effective when a notice of the assignment is given to the other party or when the other party acknowledges it.

ARTICLE 9.3.5　(*Discharge of the assignor*)

(1) The other party may discharge the assignor.

(2) The other party may also retain the assignor as an obligor in case the assignee does not perform properly.

(3) Otherwise the assignor and the assignee are jointly and severally liable.

ARTICLE 9.3.6　(*Defences and rights of set-off*)

(1) To the extent that the assignment of a contract involves an assignment of rights, Article 9.1.13 applies accordingly.

(2) To the extent that the assignment of a contract involves a transfer of

obligations, Article 9.2.7 applies accordingly.

ARTICLE 9.3.7 (*Rights transferred with the contract*)

(1) To the extent that the assignment of a contract involves an assignment of rights, Article 9.1.14 applies accordingly.

(2) To the extent that the assignment of a contract involves a transfer of obligations, Article 9.2.8 applies accordingly.

CHAPTER 10—LIMITATION PERIODS

ARTICLE 10.1 (*Scope of the Chapter*)

(1) The exercise of rights governed by these Principles is barred by the expiration of a period of time, referred to as "limitation period", according to the rules of this Chapter.

(2) This Chapter does not govern the time within which one party is required under these Principles, as a condition for the acquisition or exercise of its right, to give notice to the other party or to perform any act other than the institution of legal proceedings.

ARTICLE 10.2 (*Limitation periods*)

(1) The general limitation period is three years beginning on the day after the day the obligee knows or ought to know the facts as a result of which the obligee's right can be exercised.

(2) In any event, the maximum limitation period is ten years beginning on the day after the day the right can be exercised.

ARTICLE 10.3 (*Modification of limitation periods by the parties*)

(1) The parties may modify the limitation periods.

(2) However they may not

(a) shorten the general limitation period to less than one year;

(b) shorten the maximum limitation period to less than four years;

(c) extend the maximum limitation period to more than fifteen years.

ARTICLE 10.4 (*New limitation period by acknowledgement*)

(1) Where the obligor before the expiration of the general limitation period acknowledges the right of the obligee, a new general limitation period begins on the day after the day of the acknowledgement.

(2) The maximum limitation period does not begin to run again, but may be exceeded by the beginning of a new general limitation period under Art.

10.2(1).

ARTICLE 10.5 (*Suspension by judicial proceedings*)

(1) The running of the limitation period is suspended

(a) when the obligee performs any act, by commencing judicial proceedings or in judicial proceedings already instituted, that is recognised by the law of the court as asserting the obligee's right against the obligor;

(b) in the case of the obligor's insolvency when the obligee has asserted its rights in the insolvency proceedings; or

(c) in the case of proceedings for dissolution of the entity which is the obligor when the obligee has asserted its rights in the dissolution proceedings.

(2) Suspension lasts until a final decision has been issued or until the proceedings have been otherwise terminated.

ARTICLE 10.6 (*Suspension by arbitral proceedings*)

(1) The running of the limitation period is suspended when the obligee performs any act, by commencing arbitral proceedings or in arbitral proceedings already instituted, that is recognised by the law of the arbitral tribunal as asserting the obligee's right against the obligor. In the absence of regulations for arbitral proceedings or provisions determining the exact date of the commencement of arbitral proceedings, the proceedings are deemed to commence on the date on which a request that the right in dispute should be adjudicated reaches the obligor.

(2) Suspension lasts until a binding decision has been issued or until the proceedings have been otherwise terminated.

ARTICLE 10.7 (*Alternative dispute resolution*)

The provisions of Articles 10.5 and 10.6 apply with appropriate modifications to other proceedings whereby the parties request a third person to assist them in their attempt to reach an amicable settlement of their dispute.

ARTICLE 10.8 (*Suspension in case of force majeure, death or incapacity*)

(1) Where the obligee has been prevented by an impediment that is beyond its control and that it could neither avoid nor overcome, from causing a limitation period to cease to run under the preceding articles, the general limitation period is suspended so as not to expire before one year after the relevant impediment has ceased to exist.

(2) Where the impediment consists of the incapacity or death of the obligee or obligor, suspension ceases when a representative for the incapacitated or deceased party or its estate has been appointed or a successor has inherited the respective party's position. The additional one-year period under paragraph (1) applies accordingly.

ARTICLE 10.9 (*The effects of expiration of limitation period*)

(1) The expiration of the limitation period does not extinguish the right.

(2) For the expiration of the limitation period to have effect, the obligor must assert it as a defence.

(3) A right may still be relied on as a defence even though the expiration of the limitation period for that right has been asserted.

ARTICLE 10.10 (*Right of set-off*)

The obligee may exercise the right of set-off until the obligor has asserted the expiration of the limitation period.

ARTICLE 10.11 (*Restitution*)

Where there has been performance in order to discharge an obligation, there is no right of restitution merely because the limitation period has expired.

4. PRELIMINARY DRAFT CONVENTION ON EXCLUSIVE CHOICE OF COURT AGREEMENTS

AVANT-PROJET DE CONVENTION SUR LES ACCORDS EXCLUSIFS D'ELECTION DE FOR PROJET DE RAPPORT

par Masato Dogauchi et Trevor C. Hartley

* * *

PRELIMINARY DRAFT CONVENTION ON EXCLUSIVE CHOICE OF COURT AGREEMENTS DRAFT REPORT

drawn up by Masato Dogauchi and Trevor C. Hartley

PREFACE
References to other documents
The following documents are referred to in the abbreviated form set out below:

"**Brussels Convention**": Convention on Jurisdiction and the Enforcement of Judgments in Civil and Commercial Matters. It was opened for signature in Brussels on 27 September 1968. The original parties were the six original Member States of what was then the EEC. As new States have joined the EU, as it is now called, they have become parties to the Brussels Convention. The text has been amended on a number of occasions. An amended text may be found in the *Official Journal of the European Communities* ("O. J."), 1998, Volume 27 of the "L" series, p. 1. Today, it has been largely superseded by the "Brussels Regulation" (below). It now applies only between Denmark and the other EU Member States.

"**Jenard Report**": Report by Mr Jenard on the original Brussels Convention, published in O. J. 1979 C 59, p. 1.

"**Schlosser Report**": Report by Professor Schlosser on the Accession Convention of 9 October 1978, under which Denmark, Ireland and the United Kingdom acceded to the Brussels Convention, published in O. J. 1979 C 59, p. 71. ①

"**Lugano Convention**": *Convention on Jurisdiction and the Enforcement of Judgments in Civil and Commercial Matters.* It was originally opened for signature in Lugano, Switzerland on 16 September 1988. It contains similar provisions to the Brussels Convention, but the two Conventions are not identical. It applies between the EU countries and certain other States in Europe. At the time of writing, these are Iceland, Norway, Poland and Switzerland. The demarcation between the Brussels and Lugano Conventions is laid down in Article 54B of the Lugano Convention. It is based on the principle that the Lugano Convention will not apply to relations among the EU Member States, but will apply where one of the other countries mentioned above is involved. The text may be found in O. J. 1988 L 319, p. 9.

"**Jenard/Möller Report**": Report by Mr Jenard and Mr Möller on the Lugano Convention, published in O. J. 1990 C 189, p. 57.

"**Brussels Regulation**": Council Regulation (EC) No 44/2001 of 22 December 2000 on jurisdiction and the recognition and enforcement of judgments in civil and commercial matters, O. J. 2001 L 12, p. 1. It applies among all the EU Member States except Denmark and replaces the Brussels Convention in the mutual relations between those States to which it applies.

"**Preliminary draft Convention 1999**": Preliminary draft Convention on

---

① There are also reports on the Accession Convention for Spain and Portugal (de Almeida Cruz, Desantes Real and Jenard) O. J. 1990 C 189, p. 35; and on the Accession Convention for Greece (Evrigenis and Kerameus), O. J. 1986 C 298, p. 1.

Jurisdiction and Foreign Judgments in Civil and Commercial Matters of 1999. This was an earlier, much larger version of the present preliminary draft Convention drawn up within the Hague Conference on Private International Law in 1999. It covered much the same ground as the Brussels and Lugano Conventions. Work on it was put on hold when it became apparent that it would be difficult to obtain agreement at that time. Its text, together with a draft Report by the late Professor Peter Nygh and Professor Fausto Pocar, was published by the Permanent Bureau of the Hague Conference in August 2000. ②

"**Nygh/Pocar Report**": Report on the preliminary draft Convention (see footnote No 2).

"**Schulz Report**": Report by Dr Andrea Schulz on the work of the informal working group on the Judgments Project, published by the Permanent Bureau of the Hague Conference in June 2003. ③

Acknowledgements

The authors of the present Report would like to acknowledge their debt to the authors of these earlier reports, especially to the authors of the Nygh/Pocar Report, the late Professor Nygh and Professor Pocar. They would also like to acknowledge the assistance given by Dr Andrea Schulz of the Permanent Bureau and Dr Gottfried Musger, Chairman of the Drafting Committee.

Terminology

The following terminology is used in the Convention:

"**Court of origin**": the court which granted the judgment.

"**State of origin**": the State in which the court of origin is situated.

"**Court addressed**": the court which is asked to recognise or enforce the judgment.

"**Requested State**": the State in which the court addressed is situated. ④

Note: Passages in square brackets will not form part of the final Report.

INTRODUCTION

1. **Objective of the Convention.** The objective of the Convention is to

---

② Preliminary Document No 11, available at ⟨www.hcch.net⟩.
③ Preliminary Document No 22, available at ⟨www.hcch.net⟩.
④ The preliminary draft Convention 1999 uses "State addressed" in the English version instead of "requested State" as used in this Report.

make exclusive choice of court agreements as effective as possible in the context of international business. The hope is that the Convention will do for choice of court agreements what the New York Convention of 1958[5] has done for arbitration agreements.

2. **Three key obligations**. In order to achieve this objective, it is necessary to impose three obligations on the courts of Member States: the chosen court must be obliged to hear the dispute; all other courts must be obliged to decline jurisdiction; and the judgment given by the chosen court must be recognised and enforced by courts in other countries.

3. **Three key provisions**. These obligations are laid down by three key provisions in the Convention, Articles 4, 5 and 7. Article 4, which is addressed to the chosen court, provides that the court designated in an exclusive choice of court agreement has jurisdiction and must exercise it; Article 5, which is addressed to all other courts, provides that courts other than that chosen must suspend or dismiss the proceedings before them; and Article 7, which is addressed to the court in which recognition is sought, provides that a judgment given by the court of a Contracting State designated in an exclusive choice of court agreement must be recognised and enforced.

4. **The original project: a "mixed" convention**. The original project (the preliminary draft Convention 1999) was intended to be a "mixed" convention. This is a convention in which jurisdictional grounds are divided into three categories. There is a "white list", which contains a number of specified grounds of jurisdiction; there is a "black list", which contains other specified grounds of jurisdiction; and there is the socalled "grey area", which consists of all other grounds of jurisdiction under the national law of Contracting States. The idea is that where the court has jurisdiction on a "white" ground, it can hear the case, and the resulting judgment will be recognised and enforced in other Contracting States (provided certain other requirements are satisfied). "Black list" grounds are prohibited: a court of a Contracting State cannot take jurisdiction on these grounds. Courts are permitted to take jurisdiction on the "grey list" grounds, but the resulting judgment will not be recognised under

---

[5] *Convention on the Recognition and Enforcement of Foreign Arbitral Awards of* 10 *June* 1958.

the Convention.⑥

5. As work proceeded on drafting, however, it became apparent that it would not be possible to draw up a satisfactory text for a "mixed" convention within a reasonable period of time. The reasons for this included the wide differences in the existing rules of jurisdiction in different States and the unforeseeable effects of technological developments, including the Internet, on the jurisdictional rules that might be laid down in the Convention. At the end of the First Part of the Nineteenth Session, held in June 2001, it was decided to postpone further work on the draft Convention. In order to find a way forward, the Commission I, meeting in April 2002, decided that the Permanent Bureau, assisted by an informal working group, would prepare a text to be submitted to a Special Commission. It was decided that the starting point for this process would be such core areas as jurisdiction based on choice of court agreements in business-to-business cases, submission, defendant's forum, counterclaims, trusts, physical torts and certain other possible grounds.

6. After three meetings, the informal working group proposed that the objective should be scaled down to a convention on choice of court agreements in business-to-business cases. After receiving positive reactions from the Member States, a meeting of the Special Commission was held in December 2003 to discuss the draft that had been prepared by the Permanent Bureau, assisted by the informal working group. This meeting of the Special Commission produced the draft considered in this Report.⑦

7. The relationship between the original project and the present draft. If we apply the terminology explained in paragraph 4, we can say that the present draft provides for only one jurisdictional ground in the "white" list—an exclusive choice of court agreement. A court of a Contracting State selected in such an agreement must exercise jurisdiction, and other Contracting States must

---

⑥ The European instruments in this area (the Brussels Regulation, the Brussels Convention and the Lugano Convention) are based on a slightly different idea. Where the defendant is domiciled in another State to which the instrument applies, there is no grey area: jurisdiction may be exercised only on the grounds laid down in the instrument. Where the defendant is not domiciled in such a State, however, jurisdiction may, subject to certain exceptions, be exercised on any ground permitted by national law; the resulting judgment must nevertheless be recognised and enforced in the other States.

⑦ The draft on Exclusive Choice of Court Agreements. It is set out in the Annex to this Report.

recognise and enforce the resulting judgment in accordance with the Convention. There is no "black" list in the sense previously explained, though courts of Contracting States other than that selected are not permitted to exercise jurisdiction in a case covered by the agreement. The "grey" area is accordingly very wide. It consists of all cases not covered by an exclusive choice of court agreement. Moreover, a "grey" area exists even where there *is* an exclusive choice of court agreement: since exclusive choice of court agreements concerning consumer contracts and employment contracts are excluded from the scope of the Convention, Contracting States are free to exercise, or not to exercise, jurisdiction in such cases. The courts of other Contracting States are free to recognise, or not to recognise, such judgments.

ARTICLE-BY-ARTICLE COMMENTARY

Article 1   Scope of the Convention

8. **Business-to-business transactions**. The intention, as set out in the Preamble, was to limit the Convention largely to business-to-business transactions.[8] Thus, the Convention does not apply to choice of court agreements between a business and a consumer, or between two consumers.[9] Employment contracts are also excluded.[10]

9. **Exclusive choice of court agreements**. The first paragraph of Article 1 makes clear that the scope of the Convention is limited in two ways: it applies only to exclusive choice of court agreements; and it applies only in civil or commercial matters. There were various reasons for the first limitation. Clearly, Article 5 (which prohibits courts rather than that chosen from hearing the case) could not apply if the choice of court agreement was not exclusive. Moreover, Article 4 (which requires the chosen court to hear the case) could not apply as it stands, since a court other than the chosen court might have been seised first, and it would have been entitled to hear the case if the choice of court agreement was not exclusive. This would have raised issues of *lis pendens* that would have been difficult to resolve in an acceptable way.

10. **Civil or commercial matters**. The second limitation is standard in

---

[8]   The main provision on the scope of the Convention is article 1 (discussed *infra*).
[9]   Article 1(2)(a).
[10] Article 1(2)(b).

international conventions of this kind. It is clearly necessary to exclude public law and criminal law.⑪ The reason for using the word commercial as well as "civil" is that in some legal systems "civil" and "commercial" are regarded as separate and mutually exclusive categories. The use of both terms is necessary for those legal systems.⑫

It does no harm with regard to systems in which commercial proceedings are a sub-category of civil proceedings.⑬ However, certain matters that clearly fall within the class of civil or commercial matters are nevertheless excluded. Thus, proceedings are outside the scope of the Convention when they have as their object one of the following: family law matters, succession, carriage of goods by sea, nuclear liability, rights *in rem* in immovable property, certain questions relating to legal persons (corporations) and the validity of certain intellectual property rights.

11. Article 1(1) of the preliminary draft Convention 1999 contained a further provision expressly stating that the Convention would not apply to revenue, customs or administrative matters. This provision was not included in the current draft because it was thought to be unnecessary: it was considered obvious that such matters could not be civil or commercial. The precise borderline between public-law and private-law matters is mainly a problem when a State or other public-law entity is a party to the contract. It is considered further below.⑭

12. **Consumer contracts.** Article 1(2)(*a*) provides that the Convention does not apply to choice of court agreements between a consumer and a party acting for the purposes of his/its trade or profession, or between two consumers. Many legal systems have mandatory rules to protect consumers, and these systems would not give effect to a choice of court agreement that required proceedings under a consumer contract to be brought in a foreign State. A

---

⑪ However, a civil award of damages—for example, for personal injury—would be a civil matter, even if it was given in the course of criminal proceedings.

⑫ It would not be possible to use "commercial" alone because in some systems it is too vague and in others it is too narrowly defined.

⑬ For further discussion of "civil or commercial matters", see pp. 29—31 of the Nygh/Pocar Report (*supra* footnote No 2).

⑭ See paragraphs 38 *et seq.*

"consumer" is defined as "a natural person acting primarily for personal, family or household purposes". A person who is not acting for the purposes of his trade or profession is not necessarily a consumer. Contracts concluded by a State are covered by the Convention;[15] yet a State does not act for the purposes of its trade or profession. It has no trade or profession in the normal sense of the words. The same is true of at least some public authorities and public corporations.[16] A contract between a State (or other non-commercial entity) and a consumer would, therefore, be covered by the Convention. [**If this is not what is intended, Article 1(2)(a) should say, "to which a natural person acting primarily for personal, family or household purposes (the [a] consumer) is a party".**]

13. **Employment contracts.** Article 1(2)(b) excludes choice of court agreements relating to individual or collective contracts of employment. These are excluded for the same reason as consumer contracts. An individual contract of employment is one between an employer and an individual employee; a collective contract of employment is one between an employer or a group of employers and a group of employees or an organisation such as a trade union (labour union) representing them.

14. **Other excluded matters.** Article 1(3) states that the Convention does not apply to proceedings that have as their object one of the matters listed in sub-paragraphs a) to m).[17] This means that even if the choice of court agreement covers one of these matters, the Convention does not apply to proceedings that have it as their "object".[18] On the other hand, if one of the matters listed in sub-paragraphs a) to m) arises incidentally in proceedings that have some other matter as their object, the Convention will nevertheless apply.

---

[15] Article 1(6).

[16] A charity or a religious organisation likewise has no trade or profession.

[17] This list is partly derived from Article 1(2), combined with Article 22, of the Brussels Regulation, and equivalent provisions in the Brussels and Lugano Conventions.

[18] A terminological problem arises at this point. In French, there is a well understood distinction between proceedings that deal with a given matter *à titre principal* and those that deal with it *à titre incident*. This distinction cannot be expressed so clearly in English. In the English text of article 1(3), the phrase "proceedings that have as their object" is meant to convey the same idea as "*litiges portant à titre principal*" in the French text, while the phrase "arises ... as an incidental question" in the English text of article 1(4) is meant to convey the same idea as "*évoquée à titre incident*" in the French text.

15. Insolvency[19] provides an example. Assume that A and B enter into a contract, under which B owes A a sum of money. The contract contains a choice of court agreement in favour of the courts of State X. B then becomes insolvent. The Convention would apply to any proceedings concerning the question whether B did in fact owe A the money, but it would not apply to proceedings directly concerning the insolvency—for example, where A ranks among B's creditors—even if the choice of court agreement was interpreted as covering them.

16. There are various reasons why the matters referred to in Article 1(3) are excluded. In some cases, the public interest, or the interests of third parties, is involved, so that the parties have no right to dispose of the matter between themselves. In such cases, a particular court will often have exclusive jurisdiction that cannot be ousted by means of a choice of court agreement.

17. **Family law and succession**. Sub-paragraphs a) to d) concern personal and family matters that require special consideration.[20] In sub-paragraph b), "maintenance" includes child support. In sub-paragraph c), "matrimonial property" includes the special rights that a spouse has to the matrimonial home in some jurisdictions; while "similar relationships" covers a relationship between unmarried couples (including those of the same sex), to the extent that it is given legal recognition.[21]

18. **Insolvency**. Sub-paragraph e) excludes insolvency, composition and analogous matters. The term "insolvency" covers the bankruptcy of individuals as well as the winding-up or liquidation of corporations that are insolvent, but does not cover the winding-up or liquidation of corporations for reasons other than insolvency, which is dealt with by sub-paragraph j). The term "composition" refers to procedures whereby the debtor may enter into agreements with creditors in respect of a moratorium on the payment of debts or on the discharge of those debts. The term "analogous matters" covers a broad range of other methods whereby insolvent persons or entities can be assisted to regain

---

[19] Sub-paragraph e); see below paragraph 18.

[20] Some of these matters are dealt with in other Hague Conventions.

[21] These provisions are largely taken from sub-paragraphs a) to d) of article 1(2) of the preliminary draft Convention 1999, and their scope is further examined at pp. 32—34 of the Nygh/Pocar Report.

solvency while continuing to trade, such as Chapter 11 of the US Federal Bankruptcy Code.㉒

19. **Carriage of goods by sea**. Sub-paragraph f) excludes contracts for the carriage of goods by sea. This is because States that are parties to the Hague Rules on Bills of Lading㉓ might be unwilling to accept a choice of court clause in a bill of lading if it granted jurisdiction to the courts of a State that was not a party to the Rules, since this could allow the ship owner to evade the mandatory provisions laid down in the Rules.㉔ A second reason is that this matter forms the subject of a new project by UNCITRAL and the Conference did not want to interfere with that.㉕ [**The question of other maritime matters is still to be resolved. Proceedings, such as the limitation of ship owners' liability or general average that affect the interests of third parties raise special issues.**]

20. **Anti-trust/competition**. Proceedings that have anti-trust/competition matters as their object are excluded by sub-paragraph g). This refers to proceedings of the kind that may be brought under the Sherman and Clayton Acts in the United States, under Articles 81 and 82 (formerly Articles 85 and 86) of the EC Treaty, and under equivalent provisions in other countries. The standard term in the United States is "anti-trust law"; in Europe it is "competition law". It does not cover what Continental lawyers sometimes call "unfair competition" (*concurrence déloyale*).

21 Criminal anti-trust/competition proceedings are not civil or commercial matters; therefore, they are outside the scope of the Convention by virtue of

---

㉒ There is an identical provision in article 1(2)(e) of the preliminary draft Convention 1999, and its scope is further examined at pp. 34—35 of the Nygh/Pocar Report.

㉓ They were adopted in 1924 and were amended by the Brussels Protocol of 1968. They are sometimes called the "Hague-Visby Rules".

㉔ An alternative way of dealing with this problem would be to use article 19 (not yet drafted) to give priority to the Hague Rules as an international agreement governing a particular matter. Such a provision would have to state that, in proceedings having contracts for the carriage of goods by sea as their object, a Contracting State that was a party to the Hague Rules (or any future agreement replacing them) would not be required to give effect to a choice of court agreement in favour of the courts of a State that was not a party to those Rules.

㉕ This could also be dealt with under article 19: see previous footnote.

Article 1(1). [26]

22. However, anti-trust/competition matters can form the object of private-law proceedings. An action in tort for damages for breach of anti-trust/competition law, possible both in the United States and in the European Union, is a prime example. These actions are excluded by Article 1(2)(g) because, though they are between private parties, they nevertheless affect the public interest, since they discourage anti-competitive behaviour.

23. Another example is the rule laid down by the European Court of Justice in *Courage Ltd* v. *Crehan*,[27] under which an economically weak party, who is forced to accept terms in a contract that infringe EC competition law, can claim damages from the other party. The purpose of this rule is twofold: to do justice to the economically weak party and to benefit the public interest. It would be wrong to allow the economically strong party to avoid it by means of a choice-of-law clause in favour of the law of a non-EU State coupled with a choice of court agreement in favour of the courts of that State.

24. On the other hand, if a person sues someone under a contract, and the defendant claims that the contract is void because it infringes anti-trust/competition law; the proceedings are *not* outside the scope of the Convention, since anti-trust/competition matters are not the object of the proceedings: the matters listed in Article 1(3) are excluded only with regard to proceedings that have one of them "as their object".[28] The object of the proceedings is the claim under the contract: the principal issue before the court is whether judgment should be given against the defendant because he or she has committed a breach of contract.

25. **Nuclear liability**. This is the subject of various international conventions, which provide that the State where the nuclear accident takes place has exclusive jurisdiction over actions for damages for liability resulting from the

---

[26] This applies both to criminal proceedings under US anti-trust law and to the quasi-criminal proceedings under Articles 81 and 82 of the EC Treaty.
[27] Case C-453/99, [2001] ECR I-6297; [2001] 3 WLR 1643.
[28] See the "*chapeau*" to paragraph 3. See also paragraph 4.

accident.[29] A "disconnection" clause[30] in the Convention could permit Contracting Parties to the nuclear-liability conventions to give those conventions priority over this Convention. However, there are some States with nuclear power plants that are not Parties to any of the nuclear-liability conventions.[31] Such States would be understandably re luctant to allow legal proceedings to be brought in another State by virtue of a choice of court agreement, since, where the operators of the nuclear power plants benefit from limited liability under the law of the State in question, or where compensation for damage is paid out of public funds, a single collective procedure would be necessary in order to have an uniform solution in respect of liability and an equitable distribution of a limited fund among the victims.

26. In the preliminary draft Convention 1999, there was a special provision on exclusive jurisdiction. It was contained in Article 12, and covered four matters: rights *in rem* in immovable property, legal persons, public registers, and the validity of certain intellectual property rights. Since the current Convention deals only with jurisdiction based on choice of court agreements, it was decided to exclude these matters from the scope of the Convention since choice of court agreements are not normally allowed with respect to them under national, supranational or international law.

27. **Immovable property**. Sub-paragraph i) excludes rights *in rem* in immovable property. This concept should be interpreted as relating only to proceedings concerning ownership or possession of, or other rights *in rem* in, the immovable, not proceedings about immovables which do not have as their object a right *in rem*.[32] It is said that one of the explanations for exclusive jurisdiction in this respect is the territorial sovereignty of the State where the im-

---

[29] The *Paris Convention on Third-Party Liability in the Field of Nuclear Energy* 1960; the Convention Supplementary to the Paris Convention 1964; the Vienna Convention 1963; the Joint Protocol relating to the Application of the Vienna Convention and the Paris Convention 1988.

[30] Article 19 (not yet drafted).

[31] For example, Canada, China, Japan, Korea and the United States.

[32] For the meaning of a similar provision in Article 16(1)(a) of the Brussels Convention, see *Webb* v. *Webb*, C-294/92, [1994] ECR I-1717; *Reichert* v. *Dresdner Bank*, Case C-115/88, [1990] ECR I-27; *Lieber* v. *Göbel*, Case C-292/93, [1994] ECR I-2535; see further Dicey & Morris, *The Conflict of Laws* (13th edn, 2000 by Lawrence Collins and specialist editors, Sweet and Maxwell, London), paragraphs 23-010 to 23-015 (pp. 941—943); Hélène Gaudemet-Tallon, *Compétence et exécution des jugements en Europe* (3rd edn, 2002, LGDJ, Paris) paragraph 102 (p. 74).

movable is situated. Thus, State A cannot allow the courts of State B to decide who is the owner of an immovable within State A's territory. Accordingly, it is natural for the State in which the immovable is situated to have exclusive jurisdiction over proceedings which have as their object rights *in rem* in immovable property: the Convention does not apply to choice of court agreements in such proceedings.

28. **Legal persons**. Sub-paragraph j) excludes the validity, nullity, or dissolution of legal persons, and the validity of decisions of their organs. [33] The reason for this exclusion is similar to that stated above with regard to immovable property. As legal persons are created by the sovereign power of the State, it is natural for the courts of the State where they were established to have exclusive jurisdiction over proceedings which have as their object the matters mentioned above. Accordingly, the Convention does not apply to choice of court agreements in such proceedings.

29. **Intellectual property**. Sub-paragraphs k) and l) deal with intellectual property. [34] They do not exclude intellectual property as such, but only proceedings that have the validity of certain intellectual property rights as their object. The reason for the exclusion is similar to that applicable with regard to immovable property and legal persons. The creation of intellectual property rights could be regarded as an exercise of the sovereign power of the State; so the validity of these rights should be decided solely by the courts of the State in which they were registered or under the law of which they arose.

30. The rights in question fall into two classes. The first class consists of those covered in sub-paragraph k): the validity of patents, trademarks, protected industrial designs, and layout-designs of integrated circuits—rights listed in the TRIPS Agreement. [35] These rights are excluded from the scope of the Convention irrespective of whether or not they are registered. Thus, proceed-

---

[33] This same phrase appears (with purely verbal differences) in article 12(2) of the preliminary draft Convention 1999. The commentary on it in the Nygh/Pocar Report is at pp. 65—66.

[34] Although these matters were also subject to exclusive jurisdiction under article 12 of the preliminary draft Convention 1999, there are significant differences in the present text.

[35] *Agreement on Trade Related Aspects of Intellectual Property Rights* (Annex 1C to the Agreement Establishing the World Trade Organization), signed in Marrakesh/Morocco on 15 April 1994, Part II, Sections 2, 4, 5 and 6.

ings having the validity of an unregistered trademark as their object are outside the scope of the Convention. The second class consists of the rights listed in sub-paragraph l): the validity of other intellectual property rights the validity of which depends on, or arises from, their registration, except copyright. Thus, proceedings concerning the validity of utility model rights under Japanese law, which are registered without examination as to their substance, are excluded by virtue of subparagraph l). Copyright can be, or even has to be, registered in some countries;

nevertheless, it is not excluded from the scope of the Convention even if it is registered. The reference to copyright does not, however, include neighbouring rights. Consequently, proceedings that have the validity of neighbouring rights as their object are excluded from the scope of the Convention if they are subject to registration. [**If this was not what was intended, the words "or neighbouring rights" should be inserted after "copyright".**] [**It is not yet settled whether sub-paragraph l) will be part of the Convention and, if so, what intellectual property rights it will cover.**]

31. **Public registers**. Sub-paragraph m) excludes the validity of entries in public registers.[36] Some people might not regard this as a civil or commercial matter. However, as some international instruments[37] provide for exclusive jurisdiction over proceedings that have the validity of such entries as their object, it was thought better to exclude them explicitly in order to avoid any doubts.

32. **Incidental questions**. Paragraph 4 of Article 1 provides that proceedings are not excluded from the scope of the Convention if a matter referred to in paragraph 3 arises merely as an incidental question. An incidental question is a question that is not the object of the proceedings but is a question that the court has to decide in order to give judgment.[38] For example, the plaintiff may claim a sum of money due under a patentlicensing agreement. The defendant may argue that the sum is not due because the patent is invalid. Then the validity of the patent would be an incidental question: the court would have

---

[36] This same phrase appears (with purely verbal differences) in article 12(3) of the preliminary draft Convention 1999. The commentary on it in the Nygh/Pocar Report is at p. 66.

[37] For instance, Article 22(3) of the Brussels Regulation.

[38] See paragraph 14 *supra*.

to decide it in order to be able to decide the main question (whether the money is due). Another example is an action for breach of contract in which the defendant (who is a natural person, not a corporation) claims that he lacked capacity to enter into the contract: the main question would be whether he was liable for breach of contract; the incidental question would be whether he had capacity.

33. It will be remembered that the "*chaupeau*" to paragraph 3 states that the Convention does not apply to proceedings "that have as their object" any of the matters listed in paragraph 3. This indicates that proceedings are not excluded from the scope of the Convention merely because one of the matters listed arises as an incidental question.[39] This rule is so important that it is reinforced by paragraph 4.

34. In some countries, parties are precluded from re-litigating matters decided as incidental questions in a judgment given in previous proceedings. In the United States, this is known as "issue preclusion" or "collateral estoppel"; in England it is called "issue estoppel". In other countries, such matters can be re-litigated. As we shall see below, however, a ruling on an incidental question does not have to be recognised or enforced under the Convention:[40] recognition is limited to the ruling on the principal question. [**This may be subject to further consideration.**]

35. **Arbitration.** The first sentence of paragraph 5 excludes arbitration and proceedings relating thereto.[41] The purpose of this provision is to ensure that the present Convention does not interfere with existing instruments on arbitration.

36. Paragraph 5 goes on to provide that the Convention does not require a Contracting State to recognise and enforce a judgment if the exercise of juris-

---

[39] The exclusion of a matter from the scope of the Convention does not of course prevent a court of a Contracting State from hearing proceedings that have it as their object, but the resulting judgment will normally be outside the scope of the Convention. The significance of the rule under discussion is that it requires the judgment to be recognised and enforced under the Convention, despite the fact that some excluded matter—for example, the validity of a patent or the capacity of a party—was decided as an incidental question.

[40] See paragraphs 125 *et seq.*

[41] An identical provision is found in article 1(2)(g) of the preliminary draft Convention 1999: the relevant passage in the Nygh/Pocar Report is at p. 35.

diction by the court of origin was contrary to the terms of an arbitration agreement. It is unlikely that the same matter would be subject to both a choice of court agreement and an arbitration agreement, but if it was, a court would not be required under the Convention to recognise the judgment given by the court designated in the choice of court agreement, even if it was given first. It is not, however, precluded from doing so.

37. It is implicit in this provision that the arbitration agreement is valid, operative and capable of being performed. The purpose of the second sentence of Article 1(5) is also to avoid any undermining of arbitration, especially of the New York Convention of 1958. [42] However, if the arbitration agreement is null and void, inoperative or incapable of being performed, there can be no conflict. [43]

38. **Governments**. Article 1(6) provides that proceedings are not excluded from the scope of the Convention by the mere fact that a government, a governmental agency or any person acting for a State is a party thereto. [44] The proceedings will, however, be excluded if they do not concern a civil or commercial matter. As a general rule of thumb, one can say that if a public authority is doing something that an ordinary citizen could do, and is not exercising any special rights or privileges, the case probably involves a civil or commercial matter. [45]

39. Where a government or other public authority is involved, this can

---

[42] *Convention on the Recognition and Enforcement of Foreign Arbitral Awards of* 10 *June* 1958.

[43] See Article II(3) of the New York Convention, under which a court of a State party to the Convention, when seised of an action in a matter in respect of which the parties have made an arbitration agreement, must, at the request of one of the parties, refer the parties to arbitration unless the agreement is "null and void, inoperative or incapable of being performed".

[44] This provision is taken (with only verbal differences) from article 1(3) of the preliminary draft Convention 1999. The commentary on it in the Nygh/Pocar Report is at pp. 35—36.

[45] For the interpretation by the European Court of Justice of a similar provision in Article 1 of the Brussels Convention, see *LTU* v. *Eurocontrol*, Case 29/76, [1976] ECR 1541; [1977] 1 CMLR 88; *Netherlands* v. *Rüffer*, Case 814/79, [1980] ECR 3807 (but see *United States of America* v. *Ivey* (1996) 130 DLR (4th) 674 (Ontario High Court, Canada), affirmed (1998) 139 DLR (4th) 570 (Ontario Court of Appeal)); *Sonntag* v. *Waidmann*, Case C-172/91, [1993] ECR I-1963. See further Dicey & Morris, *The Conflict of Laws* (13th edn, 2000 by Lawrence Collins and specialist editors, Sweet and Maxwell, London), paragraphs 11-013 to 11-016 (pp. 267—269); Hélène Gaudemet-Tallon, *Compétence et exécution des jugements en Europe* (3rd edn, 2002, LGDJ, Paris) paragraph 39 (pp. 26—28).

raise difficult questions, especially in the case of contracts. A contract does not cease to be civil or commercial just because a public authority is a party to it; nevertheless, it will not be civil or commercial if the public authority is exercising any of its public—law powers, or if the contract is closely linked to the exercise of such a power. Thus, where a public authority uses its governmental powers to force a party to enter into a contract, the contract is probably not civil or commercial. For example, if a government authority offers to release an arrested person on condition that he enters into a contract under which he will pay a large sum of money if he does not appear for trial, the contract is probably too closely related to the criminal proceedings to come within the scope of the Convention. ㊻

40. **Immunities of sovereign States**. Article 1(7) provides that nothing in the Convention affects the privileges and immunities of sovereign States or of entities of sovereign States, or of international organisations. ㊼

Article 2　Exclusive choice of court agreements

41. **Definition: four requirements.** As mentioned above, ㊽ the Convention applies only to exclusive choice of court agreements. Article 2(1) gives a definition, which contains the following requirements: first, there must be an agreement between two or more parties; secondly, the formal requirements of paragraph 3 must be satisfied; thirdly, the agreement must designate the courts of one State or one specific court to the exclusion of the jurisdiction of all other courts; and finally, the designation must be for the purpose of deciding disputes which have arisen or may arise in connection with a particular legal relationship.

42. **The first requirement**. A choice of court agreement cannot be laid

---

㊻ See *United States of America* v. *Inkley* [1989] QB 255; [1988] 3 WLR 304; [1988] 3 All ER 144 (Court of Appeal, England). See also *Attorney General for the United Kingdom* v. *Heinemann Publishers Australia Pty Ltd* (1988) 165 CLR 30 (High Court of Australia) (where a claim by the British Government, partly based on breach of contract, to compel the defendant not to reveal intelligence secrets was not enforced in Australia).

㊼ This provision is taken from article 1(4) of the preliminary draft Convention 1999. The commentary on it in the Nygh/Pocar Report is at p. 36.

㊽ Paragraph 9.

down unilaterally: there must be agreement. (49) In interpreting a similar provision in the Brussels Convention, (50) the European Court of Justice has laid down autonomous, Community-law rules as to what constitutes consent for this purpose. (51) The application of autonomous rules may have been correct in the context of the Brussels Convention, but it is not correct with regard to the Hague Convention, under which the law of the State in question must decide whether there is consent: the explicit references in various articles to State law clearly indicate this. (52)

43. **The second requirement**. This concerns the form of the choice of court agreement. The relevant rules are laid down in paragraph 3, discussed below.

44. **The third requirement**. This is that the choice of court agreement must designate the courts of one State or one specific court as having exclusive jurisdiction. This will be discussed below in connection with paragraph 2.

45. **The fourth requirement**. This is that the designation must be for the purpose of deciding disputes which have arisen or may arise in connection with a particular legal relationship. This makes clear that the choice of court agreement can be restricted to, or include, disputes that have already arisen. It can also cover future disputes, provided they relate to a particular legal relationship. It is not limited to claims in contract, but could, for example, cover claims in tort arising out of a particular relationship. Thus, a widely-drafted choice of court clause in a joint-venture agreement could cover an action in tort for patent infringement in connection with the activities carried on under the contract; or a choice of court clause in a contract for the carriage of goods by road could cover a tort action for damage to the goods. Whether this would be

---

(49) For this reason, the Convention does not apply to a choice of court made by a settlor in a trust instrument.

(50) Article 17.

(51) For example, in *Estasis Salotti and Colzani* v. *RüWA*, Case 24/76, [1976] ECR 1831; [1977] 1 CMLR 345, it held that where a person signs a contract written on one side of a sheet of paper, he or she does not consent to a choice of court agreement on the other side, unless there is an explicit reference to it on the side that he signed. This decision was based on Community law, not on the law of any of the Contracting States.

(52) In articles 4(1), 5 a) and 7(1)(a), there is a reference to the law of the State of the chosen court; in article 5 b) to the law of the State of the court seised, and in article 7 b) to the law of the requested State.

so in any particular case would depend on the terms of the agreement.

46. **Agreements deemed exclusive.** Article 2(2) lays down the important rule (foreshadowed by the third requirement in paragraph 1) that a choice of court agreement which designates the courts of one State or one specific court will be deemed to be exclusive unless the parties have expressly provided otherwise.

47. The first element of this is that the choice of court agreement may refer either to the courts of a State in general, or to a specific court. Thus an agreement designating "the courts of France" is regarded as exclusive for the purposes of the Convention, even though it does not specify *which* court in France will hear the proceedings. In such a case, French law will be entitled to decide in which court or courts the action may be brought. [53] Subject to any such rule, the plaintiff can choose the court (in France) in which he brings the action.

48. An agreement referring to a particular court in France—for example, the Commercial Court of Paris—would also be exclusive. [54] Somewhat paradoxically, however, an agreement referring to *two* specific courts in the same State—for example, "either the Commercial Court of Paris or the Commercial Court of Lyon"—would not be an exclusive choice of court agreement for the purpose of the Convention. [**If this is not what was intended, the phrase "the courts of one State or one specific court" in paragraphs 1 and 2 of Article 2 should be amended to read "either the courts of one State or one or more specific courts in one State".**]

49. **One-sided (asymmetric) agreements.** Sometimes a choice of court agreement is drafted to be exclusive as regards proceedings brought by one party but not as regards proceedings brought by the other party. International loan agreements are often drafted in this way. A choice of court clause in such an agreement may provide, "Proceedings by the borrower against the lender may be brought exclusively in the courts of State X; proceedings by the lender against the borrower may be brought in the courts of State X or in the courts of

---

[53] See article 4(3).

[54] The problems that arise where the court designated cannot hear the case under national law are discussed *infra*: see paragraphs 79 *et seq*.

any other State having jurisdiction under their own law." Such an agreement would not be covered by the Convention even when the borrower brought the proceedings: for the purpose of paragraph 1, the agreement must be exclusive irrespective of the party bringing the proceedings. [**To make this clear, it might be desirable to add to Article 2(1) the words, "Such an agreement must be exclusive irrespective of the party bringing the proceedings."**]

50. It might be thought that such an agreement would be covered by the Convention when the proceedings were brought by the borrower, but not when they were brought by the lender. However, this would produce unacceptable results. Assume, in the above example, that the lender brings proceedings in State Y. They would not be covered by the Convention, and the courts of State Y would be entitled to hear them. If the borrower then brought proceedings in State X, those proceedings would be covered; so the courts of State X would have to hear them even though the case was already pending in State Y. Moreover, a judgment given by the courts of State X would have to be recognized under the Convention in State Y, even if the courts of the latter had already given judgment in the proceedings brought by the lender, since there is [so far] no provision in Article 7 regarding conflicting judgments.

51. **Meaning of "State"⑤ in the case of a non-unified legal system.** What does the word "State" mean in relation to a Contracting State in which two or more systems of law apply in different territorial units with regard to a matter dealt with by the Convention—for example, Canada, China, the United Kingdom or the United States? According to Article 18 (discussed below at paragraphs 159 *et seq.*) it can refer either to the State as a whole—for example, Canada, China, the United Kingdom or the United States—or to a territorial unit within that State—for example, Hong Kong, Ontario, Scotland or New Jersey. Consequently, both a clause designating "the courts of the United States" and a clause designating "the courts of New Jersey" are valid, exclu-

---

⑤ In this Report, "state" with a lower-case "s" refers to a territorial unit of a federal State (for example, a USAmerican state); "State" with an upper-case "S" refers to a State in the international sense.

sive choice of court agreements under the Convention.[56]

52. The Convention is not restricted to choice of court agreements in favour of the courts of Contracting States: an agreement in favour of the courts of a non-Contracting State is equally covered by some of its operative provisions—in particular, Articles 2 and 5.

53. Although the Convention is restricted to exclusive choice of court agreements, Article 2(2) provides that an agreement which designates the courts of one State or one specific court is deemed to be exclusive unless the parties expressly provide otherwise. As a result, the following must be regarded as exclusive choice of court agreements:

"The courts of State X shall have jurisdiction to hear proceedings under this contract."

"Proceedings under this contract shall be brought before the courts of State X."

54. The following would not be exclusive:

"The courts of State X shall have non-exclusive jurisdiction to hear proceedings under this contract."

"Proceedings under this contract may be brought before the courts of State X, but this shall not preclude proceedings before the courts of any other State having jurisdiction under its law."

55. **Formal requirements.** The third paragraph deals with formal requirements. These are both necessary and sufficient under the Convention: a choice of court agreement is not covered by the Convention[57] if it does not comply with them, but, if it does, no further requirements of a formal nature may be imposed under national law. Thus, for example, a court of a Contracting State cannot refuse to give effect to a choice of court agreement because:

it is written in a foreign language;

it is not in special bold type;

it is in small type; or

---

[56] A clause designating "the state courts of the state of New Jersey or the federal courts located in that state" would also be a valid, exclusive choice of court agreement.

[57] If it is valid under the law of the State of the chosen court, that court may hear the case, but the courts of other States would not be obliged to apply the Convention with regard to the agreement (article 5) or the resulting judgment (article 7).

it is not signed by the parties separately from the main agreement.①

56 Paragraph 3 provides that the choice of court agreement must be entered into or evidenced either a) "in writing" or b) "by any other means of communication which renders information accessible so as to be usable for subsequent reference".

57. Where the agreement is in writing, its formal validity is not dependent on its being signed, though the lack of a signature might make it more difficult to prove the existence of the agreement. [**If this is not what was intended, the text should be altered.**] The other possible form is intended to cover electronic means of data transmission or storage. This includes all normal possibilities, provided that the data is retrievable so that it can be referred to on future occasions. It covers, for example, e-mail and fax.⑤⑨

58. The agreement must either be concluded in one or other of these forms or it must be *evidenced* in them. In interpreting a similar provision in the Brussels Convention,⑥⓪ the European Court of Justice has held that the "evidenced in writing" requirement is satisfied if the following facts are proved:

there is an oral choice of court agreement;

the agreement is confirmed in writing by one of the parties;

the confirmation is received by the other party; and

the latter raises no objection.⑥①

59. It is not necessary for the party who received the confirmation expressly to accept it: if he or she did, that would constitute a new agreement in writing. The European Court has also held that it does not matter if the party who put the oral agreement into writing was the one who benefited from it—for example, because it was in favour of the courts of his State.⑥② In all cases,

---

① In some legal systems, these might be requirements of national law: see, *e. g.* , *Trasporti Castelletti* v. *Hugo Trumpy*, Case C-159/97, [1999] ECR I-1597.

⑤⑨ The wording of this provision was inspired by Article 6(1) of the *UNCITRAL Model Law on Electronic Commerce* 1996.

⑥⓪ Article 17.

⑥① *Berghoefer* v. *ASA*, Case 221/84, [1985] ECR 2699; [1986] 1 CMLR 13. It was not necessary on the facts of the case for the European Court to consider the position where the written confirmation is not communicated to the other party, but Advocate General Slynn said that this would not be sufficient: [1985] ECR at p. 2702.

⑥② Ibid.

however, there must have been consent by both parties to the original oral agreement. The position would be the same under Article 2(3) of the Convention.

60. Article 2(4) provides that an exclusive choice of court agreement that forms part of a contract must be treated as an agreement independent of the other terms of the contract for the purpose of determining its validity: the validity of the exclusive choice of court agreement cannot be contested solely on the ground that the contract is not valid. The purpose of this provision is to prevent a party from arguing that effect cannot be given to a choice of court agreement because the contract of which it is part is invalid: the validity of the choice of court agreement must be determined independently, according to the criteria set out in the Convention.[63] Thus, it is possible for the designated court to hold the contract invalid without depriving the choice of court agreement of validity. On the other hand, of course, it is also possible for the ground on which the contract is invalid to apply equally to the choice of court agreement: it all depends on the circumstances. This approach is in accordance with that normally adopted with regard to the validity of arbitration agreements.

Article 3   Other definitions

61. "**Judgment**". Article 3 contains two further definitions. The first, in Article 3(1), is of "judgment". This is widely defined so as to cover any decision on the merits, regardless of what it is called. It excludes a procedural ruling, but covers an order as to costs or expenses (even if given by an officer of the court, rather than by a judge) provided it relates to a judgment that may be recognised or enforced under the Convention. It does not cover a decision to grant interim relief (provisional and protective measures), as this is not a decision on the merits.[64]

62. "**Habitual residence**". Article 3(2) defines "habitual residence" with regard to an entity or person other than a natural person. (It was felt unnecessary to define "habitual residence" with regard to a natural person.) The definition is primarily intended to apply to corporations and will be explained

---

[63] See articles 4(1), 5 and 7(1).
[64] On interim relief, see article 6.

on this basis. ⑥

63. The concept of habitual residence plays only a limited role in the Convention: it is used only to determine when a situation is wholly domestic so as to warrant its exclusion from the Convention. ⑥

64. The problem faced by the Special Commission was to reconcile the different conceptions of the common law and civil law countries, as well as those within the civil law countries. ⑥

65. In the common law, the law of the place of incorporation is traditionally regarded as the personal law of the corporation. ⑥ It is the legal system that gives birth to the corporation and endows it with legal personality. For jurisdictional purposes, however, the principal place of business and the place of its central management are also important. ⑥ The latter is the administrative centre of the corporation, the place where the most important decisions are taken. The principal place of business is the centre of its economic activities. Though normally in the same place, these two could be different. For example, a mining company with its headquarters in London (central administration) might carry on its mining activity in Namibia (principal place of business). Since all three concepts are important in the common law, the Convention provides that a corporation is habitually resident in all three places.

66. Although some civil law systems also look to the law of the place of incorporation as the personal law of the company, ⑦ the dominant view favours the law of the "corporate seat" (*siège social*). The place of the corporate seat is also regarded as the domicile of the corporation. However, there are two

---

⑥ A State or a public authority of a State would be habitually resident only in the territory of that State.

⑥ See articles 4(4), 5 f) and 15.

⑥ For a comparative discussion of these matters, see Stephan Rammeloo, *Corporations in Private International Law* (Oxford University Press, Oxford, England, 2001), Chaps 4 and 5.

⑥ For England, see Dicey & Morris, *The Conflict of Laws* (13th edn, 2000 by Lawrence Collins and specialist editors, Sweet and Maxwell, London), Rules 152(1) and 153 (pp. 1101—1109); for the United States, see *Restatement of the Law Second*, *Conflict of Laws*, § § 296—299.

⑥ For English law, see Dicey & Morris, *The Conflict of Laws* (13th edn, 2000 by Lawrence Collins and specialist editors, Sweet and Maxwell, London), Rule 152(2) (p. 1101). For the purpose of diversity jurisdiction in the United States (discussed *infra* at paragraphs 80 *et seq.*), a corporation is a citizen both of the state where it was incorporated and of that in which it has its principal place of business: 28 US Code § 1332(c).

⑦ For example, Japan and the Netherlands.

views as to how the corporate seat is to be determined. According to the first view, one looks to the legal document under which the corporation was constituted (the *statut* of the corporation). This will state where the corporate seat is, and should be regarded as decisive. The corporate seat thus determined is called the *siège statutaire*.

67. The *siège statutaire* may not, however, be the actual corporate headquarters. The second view is that one should look to the place where the company in fact has its central administration, sometimes called the *siège réel*. This corresponds to the common law concept of the place of central administration.

68. To cover all points of view, it was thus necessary to include the *siège statutaire*, which is translated into English as "statutory seat". However, this term does not refer to the corporation's seat as laid down by some statute (legislation)[71] but as laid down by the *statut*, the document containing the constitution of the company—for example, the articles of association. In United Kingdom law, the nearest equivalent is "registered office".[72] In practice, the State where the corporation has its statutory seat will almost always be the State under whose law it was incorporated or formed; while the State where it has its central administration will usually be that in which it has its principal place of business. On the other hand, it is not uncommon for a company to be incorporated in one State—for example, Panama—and to have its central administration and principal place of business in another.

Article 4   Jurisdiction of the chosen court

69. Article 4 is one of the "key provisions" of the Convention. A choice of court agreement would be of little value if the chosen court did not hear the case when proceedings were brought before it. For this reason, Article 4(1) provides that the court designated by an exclusive choice of court agreement has jurisdiction to decide a dispute to which the choice of court agreement applies, unless the agreement is null and void under the law of the State of the court designated.[73]

---

[71] The French for "statute" is "*loi*".
[72] See the Brussels Regulation, Article 60(2).
[73] For another exception that applies in certain cases, see article 14.

70. **Null and void**. The "null and void" provision is the only exception to the rule that the chosen court must hear the case. The question whether the agreement is null and void is decided according to the law of the State of the chosen court. The phrase "law of the State" includes the choice-of-law rules of that State as well as its rules of internal law.[74] Thus, if the chosen court considers that the law of another State should be applied under its choice-of-law rules, it will apply that law.

71. The "null and void" provision is intended to refer primarily to generally recognized grounds of invalidity like fraud, mistake, misrepresentation, duress and lack of capacity.[75]

72. **Declining jurisdiction**. Article 4(2) provides that the chosen court must not decline to exercise jurisdiction on the ground that the dispute should be decided in a court of another State. This provision reinforces the obligation laid down in Article 4(1). However, it applies only with regard to a court in another State, not to a court in the same State. It does not, therefore, affect rules for the transfer of cases between courts in the same State.[76]

73. **Meaning of "State"**. What is meant by "State" in this context? In the case of a State containing a single law-district, there is no problem. Where the State contains a number of territories subject to different systems of law, such as the United States, Canada or the United Kingdom, the question is more difficult. Under Article 18(1)(c) of the Convention, a reference to "the court or courts of a State" means a court or courts of the relevant territori-

---

[74] If this had not been the intention, the text would have used the phrase "internal law of the State".

[75] In articles 5 b) and 7(1)(b), lack of capacity is dealt with separately because it is determined by a different system of law from other grounds of invalidity—that of the court seised, rather than that of the chosen court. In article 4, on the other hand, the court seised *is* the chosen court; so there is no need to deal separately with it.

[76] On this see Schulz, Mechanisms for the Transfer of Cases within Federal Systems, Preliminary Document No 23, October 2003. Where the exclusive choice of court agreement designates a particular court, a judgment given by another court in the same State will not be recognised or enforced under the Convention, even if the case was transferred to that court by the designated court: it will not be "a judgment given by a court of a Contracting State designated in an exclusive choice of court agreement", as required by article 7(1). Where, on the other hand, the choice of court agreement refers in general to the courts of a Contracting State (without designating any particular court), the judgment will be recognised and enforced under the Convention, even if the case was transferred from the court where the proceedings were initiated to another court in the same State.

al unit. From this it follows, that the reference in Article 4(2) to "a court of another State" must be understood as referring to the relevant territorial unit.

74. What is the relevant territorial unit? This could depend on the terms of the choice of court agreement. If it referred to "the courts of England", England would be the relevant territorial unit, and Article 4(2) would preclude a transfer to a court in Scotland. If, on the other hand, the choice of court agreement referred to "the courts of the United Kingdom", the relevant territorial unit would be the United Kingdom, and a court in England would not be precluded by Article 4(2) from transferring the case to a court in Scotland. ⑦

75. In the case of the United States, the position could depend on whether the chosen court was a state court or a federal court. If the choice of court agreement referred to "the courts of the state of New York", a transfer to a court in New Jersey would be precluded. Here, "state" would refer to the state of New York, not to the United States. ⑱ However, if the reference was to "the Federal District Court for the Southern District of New York", Article 4(2) would not necessarily preclude a transfer to a federal district court in a different state of the United States, since the relevant territorial unit would be the United States. ⑲

76. **Forum non conveniens.** There are two legal doctrines on the basis of which a court might consider that the dispute should be decided in a court of another State. ⑳ The first is *forum non conveniens*. This is a doctrine mainly applied by common law countries. ㉑ Its precise formulation varies from country to country, but in general one can say that it permits a court having jurisdiction to stay (suspend) or dismiss the proceedings if it considers that another court

---

⑦ In this case, the Scottish judgment would be entitled to be recognised and enforced under the Convention.

⑱ The same would be true if the agreement referred to "the state courts of New York or the federal courts located in that state".

⑲ The resulting judgment would be entitled to recognition and enforcement under the Convention.

⑳ See J. J. Fawcett (ed.), *Declining Jurisdiction in Private International Law* (Clarendon Press, Oxford, 1995).

㉑ It actually originated in Scotland, a mixed common/civil-law country. It still applies in Scotland today and has also been adopted in civil-law jurisdictions such as Quebec. For the application of this doctrine and other statutory substitutes in the context of choice of court clauses, see Schulz, Mechanisms for the Transfer of Cases within Federal Systems, Preliminary Document No 23, October 2003.

would be a more appropriate forum. ⑫ The granting of a stay or dismissal is discretionary and involves weighing up all relevant factors in the particular case. It applies irrespective of whether or not proceedings have been commenced in the other court (though this is a factor that may be taken into account).

77. **Lis pendens.** The second doctrine is that of *lis pendens*. This is applied mainly by civil law countries. It requires a court to suspend or terminate proceedings if another court has been seised first in proceedings involving the same cause of action between the same parties. ⑬ It is not discretionary, does not involve the weighing up of relevant factors to determine the more appropriate court and applies only when proceedings have already been commenced in the other court.

78. Article 4(2) precludes resort to either of these doctrines if the court in whose favour the proceedings would be stayed or dismissed is in another State, since under either doctrine the court would decline to exercise jurisdiction "on the ground that the dispute should be decided in a court of another State."

79. **Subject-matter jurisdiction.** Article 4(3) provides that Article 4 does not affect national rules on subject-matter jurisdiction or jurisdictional rules based on the value of the claim. The phrase "subject-matter jurisdiction" can have a variety of meanings. Here it refers to the division of jurisdiction among different courts in the same territorial unit on the basis of the subject matter of the dispute. It is not concerned with determining which State's courts will hear the case but with the question what kind of court *within* a State will hear it. For example, specialized courts may exist for matters such as divorce, tax or patents. Thus, a specialized tax court would lack subject-matter jurisdiction to hear an action for breach of contract. So even if the parties concluded an exclusive choice of court agreement designating such a court, it would not be obliged under the Convention to hear the case.

80. In the United States, subject-matter jurisdiction can also refer to the

---

⑫ For the formulation in English law, see Dicey & Morris, *The Conflict of Laws* (13th edn, 2000 by Lawrence Collins and specialist editors, Sweet and Maxwell, London), Rule 31(2) (p.385); for the formulation in the United States see The American Law Institute, *Second Restatement on Conflict of Laws* (The American Law Institute Publishers, St. Paul, Minn., 1971), §84.

⑬ See, for example, Article 27 of the Brussels Regulation.

allocation of jurisdiction between state and federal courts.[84] As a general rule, one can say that state courts have subject-matter jurisdiction in all cases unless there is a specific rule depriving them of jurisdiction. Federal courts, on the other hand, have jurisdiction only if a specific rule grants them jurisdiction. The basic rules on federal jurisdiction are laid down in Article III, section 2 of the United States Constitution. The two most important cases in which federal courts have jurisdiction are cases arising under federal law[85] and cases in which there is diversity of citizenship. Diversity of citizenship arises if one party is a citizen of a different state from another party, or if one party is a citizen of a US state and the other party is a foreign national.[86]

81. The parties cannot waive these rules. If subject-matter jurisdiction does not exist, a federal court cannot hear the case, even if the parties submit to its jurisdiction. Thus, if a Japanese citizen and a German citizen, both habitually resident in their respective countries, enter into a contract for the sale of goods, and the contract contains a choice of court agreement designating "the Federal District Court for the Southern District of New York" as having exclusive jurisdiction to hear disputes arising out of the contract, the chosen court will not be able to hear the case. It will lack subject-matter jurisdiction because federal law will not govern the case[87] and there will be no diversity of citizenship.[88] The Convention will not affect this outcome. The result is that the choice of court agreement will be void: there would be no justification for treating it as referring to the *state* courts of New York. If, on the other hand, the parties designated "the courts of New York" and the plaintiff brought pro-

---

[84] For a detailed discussion of federal jurisdiction in Australia, Canada and the United States, see Schulz, Mechanisms for the Transfer of Cases within Federal Systems, Preliminary Document No 23, October 2003.

[85] Federal law covers the United States Constitution, federal statutes and international treaties concluded by the United States.

[86] There must be complete diversity: no party on one side can be a citizen of the same state as any party on the other side. To be a citizen of a state, a person must be a citizen of the United States (or an alien admitted for permanent residence) and must be resident in a state of the United States. In addition, the value of the claim must be above a specified minimum, at present $ 75,000. See 28 US Code § 1332. For the citizenship of a corporation, see footnote No 69 *supra*.

[87] In general, state law governs most areas of commercial law, such as sale of goods and contracts.

[88] Under US law, there is no diversity if both parties are citizens of foreign States.

ceedings in a federal court in New York, the case could be transferred to a state court in New York, if the law of the United States so provided.

82. In some countries, certain courts have jurisdiction only if the value of the claim is greater, or less, than a specified amount. Since this concerns the internal allocation of jurisdiction within a single State, it is a question of subject-matter jurisdiction as defined above. However, some States do not use this terminology; so Article 4(3) refers specifically to jurisdiction based on the value of the claim. The comments in the previous paragraph on subject-matter jurisdiction apply here as well.

83. [**The last part of Article 4(3) provides that paragraphs 1 and 2 of Article 4 do not "affect the internal allocation of jurisdiction among the courts of a Contracting State [unless the parties designated a specific court].**" **The words in square brackets raise a policy issue. If no specific court is designated by the parties—if, for example, the choice of court agreement refers merely to "the courts of the Netherlands" or "the courts of the state of New Jersey"—there is no reason why the normal rules on the internal allocation of jurisdiction question should not apply.**

84. **What if the parties designate a specific court—for example, "the Federal District Court for the Southern District of New York"? In such a case, it might be thought wrong for the federal court in New York to transfer it to a federal court in Ohio. The parties might have had a special reason for their choice. On the other hand, rules for transferring a case within a court system fulfil a purpose—for example, spreading the workload among different courts—and it would be wrong for the Convention to interfere with that. One possible compromise would be to say that the rules apply but that in deciding whether to transfer the case, foreigners should not be treated differently from local persons.**]

85. Article 4(4) provides that the preceding paragraphs of Article 4 do not apply if all the parties to the agreement are habitually resident in the State of the chosen court. The policy behind this is to exclude the application of Article 4 in entirely internal situations. In such a case, the chosen court would not be obliged under the Convention to hear the case. [**Such a situation is not easy to define. The objection to the reference to "the relationship of the parties and all elements relevant to the dispute" is its vagueness. For**

example, if the parties designated a foreign system of law as the governing law of the contract, would this mean that all elements of the dispute were no longer connected with the same State? A possible compromise would be to exclude it, but to restrict the exception by saying that the parties must be habitually resident *only*[89] in the State in question and that this must be the case both when the agreement is concluded *and* when the proceedings are commenced.]

Article 5   Obligations of a court not chosen

86. Article 5 is the second "key" provision of the Convention. Like other provisions, it applies only if the choice of court agreement is exclusive, though it applies to such agreements even if the chosen court is in a non-Contracting State. It is addressed to courts other than that chosen, and requires them to refrain from hearing the case, even if they have jurisdiction under their national law. This is essential if the exclusive character of the choice of court agreement is to be respected.

87. Article 5 requires the court to suspend or dismiss the "proceedings". It is not stated expressly what proceedings this refers to. However, it is clear from the context that it covers all proceedings inconsistent with the choice of court agreement. To determine what these are, the court must interpret the agreement. Under Article 2(1) of the Convention, the agreement applies to disputes "which have arisen or may arise in connection with a particular legal relationship". In interpreting the agreement, the court must decide what that relationship is, and which disputes the agreement applies to. It must decide, for example, whether a choice of court clause in a loan agreement covers a tort action by the borrower against the lender for enforcing the agreement in an allegedly abusive manner.[90]

88. The most common situation in which Article 5 would apply is where a party brings an action covered by the choice of court agreement in a court other

---

[89] It must be remembered that, under article 3(2), a corporation may be habitually resident in more than one State. Accordingly, if "only" was inserted here, a choice of court agreement between domestic corporation X and corporation Y, which is incorporated domestically but has its central administration at the office of its parent company in a foreign State, would not be covered by paragraph 4.

[90] See *Continental Bank* v. *Aeakos Compania Naviera* [1994] 1 WLR 588; [1994] 2 All ER 540; [1994] 1 Lloyd's Rep. 505 (Court of Appeal, England).

than that designated.

89. Proceedings for an antisuit injunction to prevent one of the parties from suing in the chosen court would be inconsistent with the choice of court agreement. They too would be covered by Article 5.

90. The court must decide whether the party bringing the proceedings is bound by the choice of court agreement. If a person who was not an original party to the contract claims rights under it by virtue of assignment, succession or some other ground,[91] he or she would normally be bound by a choice of court agreement that forms part of it.[92]

91. If the proceedings are covered by Article 5, the court must either suspend or dismiss them, unless one of the exceptions applies. It would be appropriate to suspend the proceedings, if possible,[93] where further developments might occur that would change the situation—for example, if the chosen court has not yet heard the case and it is uncertain whether it will do so.

92. **Six exceptions**. Article 5 lays down six exceptions to the rule that the proceedings must be suspended or dismissed. The first two[94] are fairly standard, but the third and fourth[95] are intended to apply only in the most exceptional circumstances. If they were applied too widely, the whole purpose of the Convention would be undermined.

93. **The first exception: null and void**. The first exception is where the agreement is null and void under the law of the chosen court. This was discussed above.[96]

94. **The second exception: incapacity**. The second exception is where a party lacked capacity to enter into the agreement under the law of the State of the court seised. Here again "law" includes the choice-of-law rules of that

---

[91] For example, a merger between two companies.

[92] See *Russ* v. *Nova* (*The Tilly Russ*), Case 71/83, [1984] ECR 2417 (Court of Justice of the European Communities).

[93] In some countries, the court has only limited powers to stay the proceedings. For example, under the Japanese Code of Civil Procedure, a court can stay the proceedings only where the court is unable to function because of a natural disaster or similar emergency (Article 130), or where a party is, for an indefinite period of time, not in a position to continue the proceedings (Article 131).

[94] In sub-paragraphs a) and b).

[95] In sub-paragraphs c) and d).

[96] At paragraphs 70 *et seq*.

State.[97] In deciding whether the choice of court agreement is null and void, the law of the chosen court must be applied by courts in all the Contracting States. In the case of capacity, however, it was considered too ambitious to lay down a uniform choice-of-law rule for all the Contracting States; accordingly, under Article 5 b) the court seised will apply the law designated by its own choice-of-law rules.[98] Since lack of capacity would also make the agreement null and void in terms of Article 5 a), this could mean that capacity is determined *both* by the law of the chosen court *and* by the law of the court seised.[99] [**This interpretation might be contrary to the rule** "*Lex specialis derogat legi generali*". **Since Article 5 a) is a general rule applying to all grounds on which the agreement might be null and void, and Article 5 b) is a specific rule applying to incapacity, it could be argued that incapacity is covered only by the latter provision. The matter should be clarified. Article 5 a) should say either "the agreement is null and void under the law of the State of the chosen court on any ground, including incapacity" or "the agreement is null and void under the law of the State of the chosen court on some ground other than incapacity".**]

95. **The third exception (first limb): injustice.** The third exception is where giving effect to the agreement would lead to a "very serious injustice" or would be "manifestly contrary to fundamental principles of public policy". In some legal systems, the first phrase would be regarded as covered by the second. Lawyers from those systems would consider it axiomatic that an agreement leading to a very serious injustice would necessarily be contrary to public policy. In the case of such legal systems, the first phrase might be redundant.[100] In other legal systems, however, the concept of public policy refers to general interests—the interests of the public at large—rather than the interests of any particular individual, including a party. It is for this reason that both phrases are necessary.

---

[97] See paragraph 70 *supra*.

[98] In recognition or enforcement proceedings, the court addressed will also apply its own choice-of-law rules when deciding questions of capacity under article 7(1)(b).

[99] See paragraph 71 *supra*.

[100] For lawyers from these legal systems, it would seem natural to insert the word "otherwise" before "be manifestly contrary": see footnote No 2 to the present text of the Convention.

96. The phrase "very serious injustice" would cover the case where one of the parties would not get a fair trial in the foreign State, perhaps because of bias or corruption, or where there were other reasons specific to that party that would preclude him or her from bringing or defending proceedings in the chosen court.

97. **The third exception (second limb): public policy.** The phrase "manifestly contrary to fundamental principles of public policy" would cover situations where the chosen court would not apply some rule or principle that was regarded in the State of the court seised as being manifestly part of its fundamental public policy.

98. **The fourth exception: incapable of performance.** The fourth exception is where for exceptional reasons the agreement cannot reasonably be performed. This is intended to apply to cases where it would not be possible to bring proceedings before the chosen court. It need not be absolutely impossible, but the situation must be exceptional. One example would be where there is a war in the State concerned and its courts are not functioning. Another example would be where the chosen court no longer exists, or has changed to such a fundamental degree that it could no longer be regarded as the same court.[101] This exception could be regarded as an application of the doctrine of frustration (or similar doctrines), under which a contract is discharged if, due to a change of circumstances after its conclusion, it is no longer possible to carry it out.[102]

99. **The fifth exception: case not heard.** The fifth exception is where the chosen court has decided not to hear the case. This could be regarded as covered by the fourth exception, but it is sufficiently different to deserve separate treatment. If the chosen court is in a Contracting State, it will be obliged under Article 4 of the Convention to hear the case unless it considers that the agreement is null and void. If the chosen court is in a non-Contracting State, however, it will be under no such obligation; so it might decide for reasons of its own not to hear it. The exception would be of particular importance in this

---

[101] See *Carvalho* v. *Hull Blyth* [1979] 1 WLR 1228; [1979] 3 All ER 280; [1980] 1 Lloyd's Rep. 172 (Court of Appeal, England).

[102] Under German law, for example, it could be covered by the doctrine of *Wegfall der Geschäftsgrundlage*.

latter case.

100. **The sixth exception: internal matters.** The sixth exception covers the case where all aspects of the matter other than the location of the chosen court are internal to the State of the court seised. In such a case, the Convention does not oblige a Contracting State to permit parties to contract out of the jurisdiction of its courts.[103] This provision mirrors that in Article 4(4), and the comments made above[104] are applicable here too.

Article 6   Interim measures of protection

101. Article 6 provides that nothing in the Convention prevents a court from granting interim measures of protection. This refers primarily to interim (temporary) measures to protect the position of one of the parties, pending judgment by the chosen court,[105] though it could also cover measures granted after judgment that are intended to facilitate its enforcement. An order freezing the defendant's assets is an obvious example. Another example is an interim injunction preventing the defendant from doing something that is alleged to be an infringement of the plaintiff's rights. A third example is an antisuit injunction precluding a party from bringing proceedings in a court other than that chosen.[106] A fourth example would be an order for the production of evidence for use in proceedings before the chosen court. All these measures are intended to support the choice of court agreement by making it more effective. They thus help to achieve the objective of the Convention.

102. Article 6 permits the granting of interim measures only if they are consistent with the choice of court agreement. Thus, an antisuit injunction precluding the bringing of proceedings in the chosen court would not be covered by Article 6.[107]

103. Once the chosen court has given judgment, an interim measure that is inconsistent with the judgment must be rescinded. To allow it to continue in

---

[103]   Article 15 complements this provision by allowing a State to which article 5 f) applies to refuse to recognise or enforce a judgment given by the chosen court, if proceedings are brought there.

[104]   See paragraph 85.

[105]   The measure might be granted either before, or after, proceedings are commenced in the chosen court.

[106]   See paragraph 102 *infra*.

[107]   See paragraph 89 *supra*.

force would conflict with the requirement to recognise the judgment laid down in Article 7. For example, if a court other than that chosen grants an interim injunction to protect a right claimed by the plaintiff, it must lift the injunction if the chosen court rules that the plaintiff has no such right (unless that judgment is not subject to recognition under the Convention). Likewise, an asset-freezing order should be lifted if the chosen court gives judgment for the defendant (unless that judgment is not subject to recognition under the Convention)

104. A court that grants a measure of this kind does so under its own law. The Convention does not require the measure to be granted but it does not preclude the court from granting it. Courts in other Contracting States are not required to recognise or enforce it; however, they are not precluded from doing so. It all depends on national law.

105. It goes without saying that the court designated in the choice of court agreement can grant any interim measure it thinks appropriate. If an interim measure—for example, an injunction—granted by that court is subsequently made permanent, it will be enforceable under the Convention in other Contracting States.[108] If it is merely temporary, it will not constitute a "judgment" as defined by Article 3.[109] In such a case, courts in other Contracting States could enforce it under their national law, but would not be obliged to do so under the Convention.

Article 7　Recognition and enforcement

106. **Reciprocity**. Article 7(1) is the third "key" provision in the Convention. It states that a judgment given by a court in a Contracting State designated in an exclusive choice of court agreement must be recognised and enforced in other Contracting States. Unlike Article 5, therefore, Article 7 operates only in favour of other Contracting States.

107. **Five exceptions**. In addition to laying down the principle of recognition, Article 7(1) also sets out five exceptions to it in sub-paragraphs a) to e). Where these exceptions apply, the court addressed is not obliged to recog-

---

[108]　Article 7(1).
[109]　See paragraph 61 *supra*.

nise or enforce the judgment under the Convention;⑩ nevertheless, it may do so if it wishes.⑪

108. The first exception: null and void. The first two exceptions mirror those in Article 5. Sub-paragraph a) states that recognition or enforcement may be refused if the agreement was null and void under the law of the State of the chosen court.⑫ However, it adds, "unless the chosen court has determined that the agreement is valid", thus indicating that the court addressed may not substitute its judgment for that of the chosen court.⑬ The purpose of this is to avoid conflicting rulings on the validity of the agreement among different Contracting States: they are all required to apply the law of the State of the chosen court, and they must respect any ruling on the point by that court.

109. The second exception: capacity. The second exception, set out in subparagraph b), follows the wording of Article 5 b). In both provisions, capacity is determined by the law of the forum (including its choice-of-law rules). However, the forum is different in the two cases: in Article 5 b) it is a court before which proceedings inconsistent with the agreement are brought; in Article 7(1)(b) it is the court asked to recognise or enforce the judgment of the chosen court. As mentioned previously, it was thought too ambitious to attempt to unify choice-of-law rules on capacity. The point made in paragraph 94, above, applies here too: since lack of capacity would also make the agreement null and void in terms of Article 7(1)(a), this could mean that capacity is determined *both* by the law of the chosen court *and* by the law of the court seised. [**This interpretation might be contrary to the rule "*Lex specialis derogat legi generali*". Since Article 7(1)(a) is a general rule applying to all grounds on which the agreement might be null and void, and Article 7(1)(b) is a specific rule applying to incapacity, it could be argued**

---

⑩ This Report is concerned only with recognition and enforcement under the Convention. It does not deal with recognition or enforcement under national law. The latter always remains a possibility, even when there is a bar to recognition and enforcement under the Convention.

⑪ This is indicated by the use of "may", rather than "shall", in the "*chapeau*" to article 7(1).

⑫ The law of the State of the chosen court includes the choice-of-law rules of that State: see paragraph 70 *supra*.

⑬ The fact that the court of origin gave judgment does not necessarily mean that it considered the choice of court agreement to be valid: it may have taken jurisdiction on some other ground permitted by its national law.

that incapacity is covered only by the latter provision. The matter should be clarified. Article 7(1)(a) should say either "the agreement was null and void under the law of the State of the chosen court **on any ground, including incapacity**, unless the chosen court has determined that the agreement is valid" or "the agreement was null and void under the law of the State of the chosen court **on some ground other than incapacity**, unless the chosen court has determined that the agreement is valid".]

110. **The third exception: notification**. The third exception, set out in subparagraph c), permits non-recognition if the defendant was not properly notified. [**The details of this have not yet been settled. The question is whether the Convention should itself lay down the factual requirements, as is done in the first three lines of the present text,**[114] **or whether reference should be made to the law of the State where notification takes place.**[115] **There was a difference of opinion on this matter. Those who object to the latter formulation point out that service may be invalid for some technical reason under the law of the State where it took place,**[116] **even though the defendant might have known perfectly well what was happening. In such a case, it may be argued, there is no reason why the judgment should not be recognised and enforced. Insistence on full compliance with the law of the State of notification would make the procedure unnecessarily technical and complicated.**

Those who support the words in the first set of square brackets, on the other hand, point out that some States take the view that rules on the notification of foreign proceedings raise issues of sovereignty. Thus, under the Service Convention,[117] **Contracting States may object to the meth-**

---

[114] This reads, "the document which instituted the proceedings or an equivalent document, including the essential elements of the claim, was not notified to the defendant in sufficient time and in such a way as to enable him to arrange for his defence".

[115] See the first passage between square brackets. The words in the second set of square brackets could be added either to the initial (unbracketed) words or to the first passage between square brackets.

[116] For example, the document may not have been translated into the language of the State where notification took place, even though it may have been in a language spoken by the defendant.

[117] Hague Convention of 15 November 1965 on the Service Abroad of Judicial and Extrajudicial Documents in Civil or Commercial Matters.

ods of service provided for in Article 10(1)(a), (b) and (c).⑱ In at least some civil law countries, the service of process is considered a governmental act. Consequently, service of process by judicial officers of a foreign State directly through judicial officers of the State in which service takes place, as envisaged by Article 10 b) of the Service Convention, could be seen as an invasion of sovereignty. If there was no reference in Article 7(1)(c) to the law of the State where notification takes place (including international conventions to which it is a party), that State might be obliged to recognise and enforce foreign judgments resulting from a service of process that infringed its sovereignty. ⑲Non-recognition is the only sanction that State can apply, if the State which granted the judgment overlooked the invasion of sovereignty.

A possible compromise would be to delete the words in the first set of square brackets, but to allow the State in which service took place to refuse recognition and enforcement if it considered that the method of service constituted a violation of its sovereignty.

Another unresolved question is whether it should be possible for defects in the method of notification to be cured if the defendant entered an appearance and presented his case without challenging the service of the writ, assuming such a challenge to be possible under the law of the State of origin. ⑳In many countries, service of a writ in a foreign State in a manner that violates the law of that State would not be regarded as good service; consequently, in such countries, the defendant could have serv-

---

⑱ Argentina, China, Germany, Korea, Norway, Switzerland and others have objected to the methods of service provided for in paragraphs a), b) and c); Finland, Ireland, Israel, Japan, Luxembourg, Sweden and others to those provided for in paragraphs b) and c); and Denmark to that provided for in paragraph c).

⑲ In the judgment of the Japanese Supreme Court of 28 April 1998, Minshu, Vol. 52, No 3, p. 853 (English translation in the Japanese Annual of International Law, No 42, p. 155), it was held that the direct delivery of process by a Japanese lawyer, who was asked to do so by a Hong Kong lawyer, did not comply with the rules provided for in the Service Convention, and it did not satisfy the requirement of Article 118(ii) of the Japanese Code of Civil Procedure. Article 118(ii) provides as follows: "A final and conclusive judgment rendered by a foreign court shall have effect insofar as it satisfies the following conditions: ... (ii) The unsuccessful defendant was served with a summons or an order necessary for the commencement of the procedure other than by service by publication, or has voluntarily appeared without being so served. ..."

⑳ This could be done by entering a special appearance to challenge jurisdiction.

ice set aside if this occurred. The plaintiff would then have to begin the action all over again. However, if the infringement of foreign law was not brought to the court's attention, it could not take steps to put matters right. A cynical defendant might deliberately keep quiet about it, so that he would have a ground for challenging enforcement if he lost the case. It is in order to prevent this that it was proposed to add the words, "unless the defendant entered an appearance and presented his case without contesting notification in the court of origin, provided that the law of the State of origin permitted notification to be contested". On the other hand, it could be argued that the purpose of the rule is to protect the rights of the State in which notification takes place. If this were so, it would follow that that State's rights should not be prejudiced because of the defendant's failure to raise the matter.]

111. **The fourth exception: fraud.** The fourth exception, set out in sub-paragraph d), is that the judgment was obtained by fraud in connection with a matter of procedure. Fraud is deliberate dishonesty or deliberate wrongdoing. Examples would be where the plaintiff deliberately serves the writ, or causes it to be served, on the wrong address; where the plaintiff deliberately gives the defendant wrong information as to the time and place of the hearing; or where either party seeks to corrupt a judge or juror. For the purpose of sub-paragraph d), fraud may be committed by either party or by the court.

112. **The fifth exception: public policy.** The fifth exception, set out in subparagraph e), is that recognition or enforcement would be manifestly incompatible with the public policy of the requested State, in particular if the specific proceedings leading to the judgment were incompatible with fundamental principles of procedural fairness of that State. The first part of this provision simply repeats the public—policy exception normally found in conventions of this kind. The second part is intended to focus attention on serious procedural failings in the particular case at hand, thus discouraging an attack on the general procedural standards of the State that granted the judgment.

113. It will be seen that there is considerable overlap among the last three exceptions, since they all relate, partly or wholly, to procedural fairness. Thus, for example, if, owing to the plaintiff's fraud, the writ was not served on the defendant and he was unaware of the proceedings, the exceptions set

out in sub-paragraphs c), d) and e) could all be invoked. The reason for this emphasis on procedural fairness is that in some countries procedural fairness (also known as due process of law, natural justice or the right to a fair trial) is constitutionally mandated. In such countries, it might be unconstitutional to recognise a foreign judgment obtained in proceedings in which a fundamental breach of this principle occurred.

114. In Europe, some 45 States are parties to the *European Convention on Human Rights*, Article 6 of which grants the right to a fair trial. The European Court of Human Rights has held that this precludes a court in a Contracting State to the ECHR from recognizing a judgment from a non-Contracting State if the proceedings that resulted in the judgment infringed the standard laid down in Article 6.[121] This means that none of these 45 States could recognise a judgment where the court that granted it infringed the right to a fair trial. Similar rights are laid down by the Fifth and Fourteenth Amendments to the United States Constitution and by the constitutions of many other countries.[122] For these reasons, the Convention has to ensure that it does not oblige Contracting States to do something that they are not constitutionally able to do.

115. ***Révision au fond.*** Article 7(2) prohibits review as to the merits of the judgment (though it permits such review as is necessary to apply the provisions of Chapter III of the Convention). This is a standard provision in conventions of this kind. Without it, foreign judgments might in some countries be reviewed by the court addressed as if it were an appellate court hearing an appeal from the court of origin.

116. **Findings of fact.** The second sentence of Article 7(2) provides that the court addressed is bound by the findings of fact on which the court of

---

[121] *Pellegrini* v. *Italy*, judgment of 20 July 2001 (available at ⟨www.echr.coe.int⟩); but see the earlier cases of *Drozd and Janousek* v. *France and Spain*, judgment of 26 June 1992, Series A, No 240; (1992) 14 EHRR 745 (paragraph 110); and *Soering* v. *United Kingdom*, judgment of 7 July 1989, Series A, No 161; (1989) 11 EHRR 439 (paragraph 113), in which the (old) European Court of Human Rights, sitting in plenary session, held that recognition had to be refused only if there was a flagrant breach of the standards laid down in Article 6. See also *Lindberg* v. *Sweden*, admissibility decision of 15 January 2004 (available at ⟨www.echr.coe.int⟩), which, however, concerned a slightly different question.

[122] In the case of Japan, Article 31 of the Constitution provides that "[n]o person shall be deprived of life or liberty, nor shall any other criminal penalty be imposed, except according to procedure established by law."

origin based its jurisdiction, unless the judgment was given by default. In this provision, "jurisdiction" means jurisdiction under the Convention. Since this will be based on the choice of court agreement, the provision applies to findings of fact that relate to the formal or substantive validity of the agreement, including the capacity of the parties to conclude it. It also applies to any findings of fact relevant to determining the scope of the agreement. Thus, when the court addressed is applying Article 7(1)(a) or 7(1)(b), it will have to accept findings of fact made by the court of origin. However, the court addressed will not be bound by the legal evaluation made by the court of origin of the facts it has found. For example, if the court of origin found that the choice of court agreement was entered into by electronic means that satisfy the requirements of Article 2(3)(b), the court addressed may, nevertheless, decide that Article 2(3)(b) was not satisfied because the text was not accessible for subsequent reference.

117. The position is different with regard to the grounds of non-recognition laid down in sub-paragraphs c), d) and e) of Article 7(1). These are not concerned with jurisdiction under the Convention, but with public policy and procedural fairness. Thus, the court addressed must be able to decide for itself whether the defendant was notified; whether there was fraud; or whether there was a fair trial: a finding by the judge of origin that he did not take a bribe, for example, cannot be binding on the court addressed.[123]

118. The same is true with regard to procedural fairness under sub-paragraph e). Assume that the defendant resists recognition and enforcement on the ground that the proceedings were incompatible with the fundamental principles of procedural fairness of the requested State. He claims that he was not able to go to the State of origin to defend the case because he would have been in danger of imprisonment on political grounds. A finding by the court of origin that this was not true cannot be binding on the court addressed. Where matters of procedural fairness are concerned, the court addressed must be able to de-

---

[123] The same applies to a finding by an appeal court that the first instance judge was not guilty of corruption.

cide for itself.⁽¹²⁹⁾

119. The result is as follows: rulings by the court of origin on the merits of the case cannot be reviewed by the court addressed, irrespective of whether they relate to questions of fact or law; rulings by the court of origin on the validity and scope of the choice of court agreement cannot be reviewed in so far as they relate to questions of fact; rulings by the court of origin on the grounds of non-recognition under subparagraphs c), d) and e) are not binding on the court addressed, irrespective of whether they relate to fact or law. [**If this is not what was intended, the Convention should be amended to make this clear. If it is what is intended, it might be better to amend the text to say, "When applying sub-paragraphs a) and b) of paragraph 1 of this article, the court addressed shall be bound by the findings of fact on which the court of origin based its jurisdiction, unless the judgment was given by default."**]

120. **"Recognition" and "enforcement"**. Article 7(3) provides that a judgment will be recognised only if it has effect in the State of origin, and will be enforced only if it is enforceable in the State of origin. This raises the distinction between recognition and enforcement. Recognition means that the court addressed accepts the determination of the legal rights and obligations made by the court of origin. If the court of origin held that the plaintiff had, or did not have, a given right, the court addressed accepts that this is the case. Enforcement means the application of the legal procedures of the court addressed to ensure that the defendant obeys the judgment given by the court of origin. Thus, if the court of origin rules that the defendant must pay the plaintiff 1000 Euros, the court addressed will ensure that the money is handed over to the plaintiff. Since this would be legally indefensible if the defendant did not owe 1000 Euros to the plaintiff, a decision to enforce the judgment must logically be preceded or accompanied by the recognition of the judgment. However, recognition need not be accompanied or followed by enforcement.

⁽¹²⁹⁾ The international and constitutional provisions on the right to a fair trial mentioned above probably require this. In paragraph 40 of its judgment in the Pellegrini case (footnote No 121 supra), the European Court of Human Rights held that the court addressed must "duly satisf[y] [itself] that the relevant proceedings fulfilled the guarantees of Article 6 [of the European Convention on Human Rights]." This would seem to preclude reliance on a finding by the court of origin.

For example, if the court of origin held that the defendant did *not* owe any money to the plaintiff, the court addressed may simply recognise this finding. Therefore, if the plaintiff sues the defendant again on the same claim before the court addressed, the recognition of the foreign judgment will be enough to dispose of the case.

121. In the light of this distinction, it is easy to see why Article 7(3) says that a judgment will be recognised only if it has effect in the State of origin. Having effect means that it is legally valid or operative. If it does not have effect, it will not constitute a valid determination of the parties' rights and obligations. Thus, if it does not have effect in the State of origin, it should not be recognised under the Convention in any other Contracting State. Moreover, if it ceases to have effect in the State of origin, the judgment should not thereafter be recognised under the Convention in other Contracting States. [125]

122. Likewise, if the judgment is not enforceable in the State of origin, it should not be enforced elsewhere under the Convention. It is of course possible that the judgment will be effective in the State of origin without being enforceable there. Enforceability may, for example, be suspended pending an appeal. In such a case, enforcement will be suspended in other Contracting States until the matter is resolved in the State of origin. Moreover, if the judgment ceases to be enforceable in the State of origin, it should not thereafter be enforced in another Contracting State under the Convention. [126]

123. **Judgments subject to review.** Article 7(4) provides that recognition or enforcement may be postponed or refused if the judgment is the subject of review in the State of origin or if the time limit for seeking ordinary review has not expired. [127] This means that the court addressed may delay recognition

---

[125] At the Diplomatic Conference held in June 2001, the following text was inserted, in square brackets, into article 25 of the preliminary draft Convention 1999: "A judgment referred to in paragraph 1 shall be recognized from the time, and for as long as, it produces its effects in the State of origin."

[126] At the Diplomatic Conference held in June 2001, the following text was inserted, in square brackets, into article 25 of the preliminary draft Convention 1999: "A judgment referred to in the preceding paragraphs shall be enforceable from the time, and for as long as, it is enforceable in the State of origin."

[127] This rule will be applied only if enforcement of the judgment has not been suspended in the State of origin by reason of the appeal. If it has been suspended, the rule in article 7(3) will be applicable: see paragraph 122 supra.

or enforcement if the judgment might be set aside or amended by another court in the State of origin. It is not, however, obliged to do this.[128] Some courts might prefer to enforce the judgment. If it is subsequently set aside in the State of origin, the court addressed will rescind the enforcement. The judgment-creditor may be required to provide security to ensure that the judgment-debtor is not prejudiced.

124. If the court addressed does not want to enforce the judgment straight away, Article 7(4) gives it the option of either suspending the enforcement process or refusing to enforce the judgment.[129] It goes on to provide, however, that if the court addressed chooses the latter option, that will not prevent a new application for enforcement once the situation in the State of origin is clarified. Here, therefore, refusal means dismissal without prejudice.

125. **Estoppel and foreign judgments.** When the Convention requires recognition or enforcement of a judgment, all it requires is that the final order by the court of origin should be recognised or enforced. Often a court has to rule on various questions of fact or law as preliminary matters before it can rule on the plaintiff's claim. For example, if the plaintiff claims damages in a personal injury case as a result of a motor accident, the court may have to decide whether the brakes on the defendant's car were defective. Likewise, in a patent infringement case, it might have to rule whether the patent is valid. These are both preliminary rulings. They pave the way for the final judgment, which will be that the defendant is, or is not, liable to pay damages to the plaintiff. All the court addressed has to do is to recognise this final order and, if damages are awarded, to enforce the judgment. It is not required to recognise the rulings on the incidental questions. [**It seems that there is no agreement on this question; it should be considered further in the plenary.**]

126. In the civil law States, a judgment normally has effect only as regards the final ruling—for example, the *Tenor* or *Spruch* in Germany and Austria, and the *dispositif* in France. In the common-law world, however, the doctrine known variously as issue estoppel, collateral estoppel or issue preclu-

---

[128] This assumes that the judgment is still enforceable in the State of origin.

[129] As stated in footnote No 93 supra, in some civil law countries the judge has only limited powers to stay the proceedings.

sion permits a court in a later case to recognise rulings on incidental questions given in an earlier judgment. This can apply both where the original judgment was given by a court in the same State and where it was given by a court in another State.[129] The Convention does not preclude a court from doing this. However, it does not require it. The application of these various forms of estoppel is outside the scope of the Convention. [**It seems that there is no agreement on this question; it should be considered further in the plenary.**]

Article 8   Documents to be produced

127. Article 8(1) lists the documents to be produced by the party seeking recognition or enforcement of a judgment under the Convention.[130] The way in which the documents must be produced depends on the procedural law of the requested State. Article 8(1)(b) requires documentary evidence that the defendant was notified, but this applies only in the case of a default judgment. In other cases, it is assumed that the defendant was notified unless he or she produces evidence to the contrary. The law of the requested State determines the consequences of failure to produce the required documents. Excessive formalism should, however, be avoided: if the judgment-debtor was not prejudiced, the judgment-creditor should be allowed to rectify omissions.

128. The fact that recognition is mentioned in the "*chapeau*" to Article 8 does not mean that there has to be any special procedure. Recognition of a judgment under the Convention can be entirely automatic.[131] However, if the other party disputes it, the party requesting recognition must produce the documents required by Article 8.

129. Article 8(2) provides that the court addressed may require the production of further documents or other evidence where this is necessary in order to establish that the conditions for recognition and enforcement have been satisfied. This makes clear that the list in paragraph 1 is not exhaustive. Production of further documents may be required to the extent that it is necessary to verify that the requirements of Chapter III of the Convention have been satis-

---

[129] On the latter, see Peter Barnett, Res Judicata, Estoppel and Foreign Judgments (Oxford University Press, Oxford, England, 2001).

[130] This provision is virtually identical to sub-paragraphs a) to c) of article 29(1) in the preliminary draft Convention 1999. The commentary on the latter in the Nygh/Pocar Report is at pp. 109—110.

[131] See paragraph 132 infra.

fied. Unnecessary burdens on the parties should be avoided.

130. Article 8(3) provides for the Hague Conference on Private International Law to recommend and publish a form which may be used by a person seeking recognition or enforcement of a judgment under the Convention. The use of such a form will not be obligatory. Information contained in it may be relied on by the court addressed in the absence of challenge. Even if there is no challenge, however, the information is not conclusive: the court addressed can decide the matter in the light of all the evidence before it. The Special Commission expressed the desire that the form should be published in the *Collection of Conventions*, though it also wanted to make it possible to amend it without undue difficulty, to meet new needs or to overcome problems that were not originally foreseen. For this reason, it was decided that the form should not constitute an Annex to the Convention. [**However, another option might be to follow the example of the 1980** *Hague Convention on Access to Justice*, **which provides in Article 30, "The model forms annexed to this Convention may be amended by a decision of a Special Commission convoked by the Secretary General of the Hague Conference to which all Contracting States and all Member States shall be invited. Notice of the proposal to amend the forms shall be included in the agenda for the meeting."**]

131. Article 8(4) provides that the court addressed may require a translation of any document referred to in Article 8. This depends on the rules of procedure of the requested State.

Article 9   Procedure

132. Article 9 provides that the procedure for recognition, declaration of enforceability or registration for enforcement, and the enforcement of the judgment are governed by the law of the requested State unless the Convention provides otherwise.[133] Where there is no special procedure for the recognition of a foreign judgment under the law of the requested State, recognition (as distinct from enforcement) must be granted without any special procedure. In all proceedings covered by Article 9, the court addressed must act expeditiously, though there is no explicit sanction against delay. This means that the court

---

[133] Except for purely verbal alterations, this is the same as article 30 of the preliminary draft Convention 1999. The commentary on this article is at p. 100 of the Nygh/Pocar Report.

must use the most expeditious procedure available to it. Contracting States should consider ways in which provision can be made to ensure that unnecessary delays are avoided.

Article 10 *Damages*

133. Article 10 deals with two issues: non-compensatory damages and excessive damages. The latter may be either compensatory or non-compensatory. The first paragraph applies only to non-compensatory damages. The second (which is concerned with excessive damages) appears to cover both, though the Nygh/Pocar Report states that it applies only to compensatory damages.[134] The third applies to both.[135]

134. Compensatory damages are intended to compensate the plaintiff for loss suffered as a result of the wrongful act of the defendant. Non-compensatory damages are intended to serve a different purpose, usually to punish the defendant for his wrongdoing, or to deter others from doing something similar. They are sometimes called "exemplary" or "punitive" damages. However, Article 10(1) is not limited to damages so called: it applies to all damages that are not compensatory.

135. **Non-compensatory damages.** The first sentence of Article 10(1) requires a court to recognise and enforce judgments for non-compensatory damages to the extent to which a court in the requested State could itself have awarded similar damages.[136] It does not expressly say that it is not obliged to recognise or enforce a judgment for noncompensatory damages if it could not itself have awarded similar or comparable damages, but this is what was intend-

---

[134] See p.111. In practice, at least, it will be applied only to compensatory damages, since non-compensatory damages are adequately dealt with by the first paragraph.

[135] During the First Part of the Diplomatic Conference in 2001, it was inquired whether statutory damages (where a statute has determined the amount to be awarded in case of breach), liquidated damages (where a contract has determined the amount to be paid in case of breach) and fixed interest on damages awards would fall within the scope of article 33 and, if so, whether their character would be compensatory or noncompensatory. The co-reporters indicated that article 33 would be applicable in such cases and that the classification of such damages as compensatory or punitive would be determined by the requested court. That court would take into account whether the statutory provision in question of the originating forum, or the contractual provision as interpreted according to its governing law, merely sought to estimate what was required to compensate the plaintiff or sought to impose a penalty (see footnote 176 to the 2001 Interim Text).

[136] It cannot, therefore, invoke the public policy exception in article 7(1)(e) as a ground for refusing to recognise an award solely because the damages are non-compensatory.

ed. If non-compensatory damages cannot be awarded in any circumstances in the State addressed, [137] the part of the foreign judgment awarding non-compensatory damages will never be recognised or enforced. [138]

136. A court in a Contracting State is required to recognise and enforce an award of non-compensatory damages if, and to the extent that, it could have awarded similar or comparable damages itself. The test is whether it could have done so if the action had originally been brought before it. "Similar" damages are damages of the same kind; "comparable" damages are non-compensatory damages of a different kind that nevertheless fulfil a comparable function.

137. The phrase "similar or comparable damages" refers not only to the circumstances in which non-compensatory damages may be awarded but also to the amount of the damages. Thus, if the court addressed could have awarded non-compensatory damages, but only for a small sum, it would not be obliged to recognise or enforce a judgment for a significantly greater sum. However, the word "comparable" makes clear that the award need not be for exactly the same amount. [139]

138. The position is, therefore, that a court is never obliged to recognise or enforce an award for non-compensatory damages if it cannot itself award non-compensatory damages. Moreover, if it can award them only in particular circumstances—for example, where the defendant deliberately commits a tort in the belief that the profit he or she will derive will outweigh any compensatory damages that could be awarded—it would not be obliged to recognise or enforce the judgment if those circumstances did not pertain. If it could have awarded non-compensatory damages in the circumstances of the case, but only for a much smaller amount, it is obliged to recognise and enforce the judgment only for that amount. In all cases, however, it is permitted to recognise and

---

[137] Generally speaking, this is the position in civil-law countries, where punishment is regarded as the business only of the criminal law.

[138] For judgments to this effect, see BGH 4 June 1992, BGHZ 118, 312 (Bundesgerichtshof, Germany); Supreme Court of Japan, judgment of 11 July 1997, Minshu, Vol. 51, No 6, p. 2578 (English translation in the Japanese Annual of International Law, No 41, p. 104). In both cases, the public policy exception was invoked to deny enforcement to the part of the award in an American judgment that represented punitive damages.

[139] On the question of severability, see paragraph 149.

enforce it to the full amount.

139. **Excessive damages.** Article 10(2) deals with excessive damages. Even if it also applies to non-compensatory damages, its main importance derives from its application to compensatory damages. The purpose of Article 10(2)(a) is to allow the court addressed to cut down an award of damages—even if they are purely compensatory—if it considers them to be grossly excessive. It may do this, however, only after proceedings have taken place in which the judgment-creditor has had the opportunity to be heard and only if the judgment-debtor satisfies the court—the onus is on him—that in all the circumstances, including those existing in the State of origin, the damages *are* grossly excessive. However, as is provided by Article 10(2)(b), the court must in no event recognise or enforce the judgment in an amount less than that which could have been awarded in the requested State in the same circumstances, including those existing in the State of origin. This is to prevent the abuse of Article 10(2)(a).

140. In applying Article 10(2), the court addressed must assess the appropriateness of the award on the basis of all the circumstances, including those in the State of origin. It cannot reduce the amount simply because things cost more in that State. The cost of medical treatment is much greater in some States than in others. To the extent that the award reflects this, it cannot be deemed excessive. The same is true with regard to salaries. If the award is based on lost earnings, it will naturally reflect what the victim would have earned if the tort had not occurred. By the standards of the requested State, this might seem a great deal of money; nevertheless, the award cannot normally be reduced for this reason.

141. Article 10(2) will apply most often with regard to damages for matters that cannot be objectively assessed—for example, pain and suffering; loss of an arm, a leg or an eye; loss of reputation; hurt feelings; or similar matters. Here the court of origin will normally make an award guided solely by the level of past awards. If this level is grossly excessive, the court addressed will reduce the award.

142. The Nygh/Pocar Report states that, as a general principle, "grossly excessive" is likely to mean "grossly excessive according to the standards usu-

ally applied by the courts of the State of origin"; [140] however, this view was strongly criticized by several delegations. If the court addressed had to apply the standards of the State of origin, Article 10(2) would be almost totally deprived of effect: if an award was "grossly excessive" by the standards of the State in which it was made, it would almost certainly be set aside on appeal, in which case the question of its enforcement would not arise.

143. It might be best not to use the word "standard", since it could suggest the application of rules, though if "standards" are to be applied, they must be those of the State addressed. This does not, however, mean that the court addressed can refuse to enforce an award simply because it would itself have made a smaller one, or even none at all. The test is not one of rules but of judgment. The court addressed must decide whether, in its judgment, the damages are grossly excessive.

144. The test under Article 10(2) is similar to that of public policy. The question of damages could have been left to the public policy exception in Article 7(1)(e), but it was decided to devote a special provision to it, partly to introduce greater certainty, and partly to reassure those States that might have been unwilling to sign the Convention if they had had to enforce awards they regarded as excessive. [141] Thus, though public policy is expressly mentioned only in Article 7(1)(e) as a ground for non-recognition of a judgment, the essential question that the court must ask when applying Article 10(2) is whether the award is so excessive that its recognition or enforcement would be contrary to public policy.

145. This test must be applied to the total award: it should not be applied separately to each head of damages. It may well be that the court of origin awarded very large damages under one head, but this might have been to compensate for the fact that it could not, or did not, award damages under another head. For example, take the case of a wrongful-death action brought by the widow of the victim. One legal system might compensate her on the basis of the financial support she lost as a result of her husband's death. Another might

---

[140] At p. 114.

[141] It was also intended to ensure that States would not use the public policy exception of the Convention to refuse to enforce an award of punitive damages if they could have awarded similar or comparable damages themselves.

compensate her for the emotional devastation she suffered. The final award might be much the same in both cases. It would be wrong, therefore, for the court addressed to apply the "grossly excessive" test individually to each item of compensation, since this might result in her receiving far less that she would have if the action had originally been brought before the court addressed.

146. The test is one of damages, not liability; therefore, the court addressed cannot refuse to enforce the judgment simply because it would not have regarded the defendant as liable, or because it could not have awarded damages for what he did. For example, in some legal systems defamation is a criminal offence but not a tort; in others, it is a tort but not a crime. If a court in a State where the latter system prevails grants an award of damages for libel, a court in a State that applies the former system cannot refuse to enforce it on the basis of Article 10(2)(a) simply because it could not have awarded damages in similar circumstances. However, if it feels that, in all the circumstances (including those in the State of origin), the sum awarded is out of all proportion to the wrong done, it will be entitled to reduce the award. [42]

147. The same would apply to actions in tort for inducing a breach of contract. Assume that A and B enter into a contract, and C induces B to break the contract. In these circumstances, most common law systems would consider that A can sue C in tort. In some other legal systems, this may not be possible. However, if a common law court were to award damages in such an action, another court ought not to refuse to enforce the judgment on the basis of Article 10(2)(a) simply because it would not have granted any damages if the action had originally been brought before it. However, it may cut the award down if it thinks that the amount of the award is out of all proportion to the harm inflicted on A.

148. **Legal costs and expenses**. The third paragraph of Article 10 applies to proceedings under both the first paragraph and the second paragraph. It provides that the court addressed must take into account whether, and to what extent, the award—whether stated to be compensatory or non-compensa-

---

[42] If the court addressed considers, on grounds other than the size of the award or the fact that it is noncompensatory, that it would be manifestly contrary to its public policy to recognise or enforce the judgment, it can invoke the public policy exception in article 7(1)(e). This might occur, for example, if it considered that a judgment for libel constituted an infringement of the right of free speech.

tory—is intended to cover costs and expenses relating to the proceedings. This provision was included because the rules regarding legal costs differ in different legal systems. In most countries, the successful plaintiff is entitled to "costs". This is a sum of money added to the damages to cover the costs and expenses of the legal proceedings. However, the rules for assessing costs can differ widely. In many countries, they cover lawyers' fees.⑭³ In the United States, they do not. To compensate for this, juries in the United States often grant higher damages, sometimes designated as punitive damages. The court addressed is obliged by Article 10(3) to take this into account in deciding whether the award is grossly excessive: it must take the amount of the judgment and compare it with the total amount it would have awarded, including costs. In doing this, it must also take into account the prevailing level of lawyers' fees in the State of origin.

Article 11   *Severability*

149. Article 11 provides for the recognition and enforcement of a severable part of a judgment where this is applied for, or where only part of the judgment is capable of being recognised or enforced under the Convention.⑭⁴ For example, if an award of punitive damages is not enforced by reason of Article 10(1), the remainder of the award must be enforced if it satisfies the requirements of Article 7.⑭⁵ In order to be severable, the part in question must be capable of standing alone, and it must be reasonable and appropriate to recognise or enforce it independently of the rest of the judgment.⑭⁶ In so far as this depends on a rule of law, the law of the court addressed must be applied.

Article 12   *Settlements*

150. Article 12 provides that settlements which, in the course of proceedings, are approved by, or concluded before, a court of a Contracting State des-

---

⑭³ There may, however, be considerable differences in the way in which these are assessed: they may cover more or less all that the successful party has had to pay his lawyer; or they may fall far short of this.

⑭⁴ The equivalent provision in the preliminary draft Convention 1999 is article 34. The commentary on this provision is at p. 115 of the Nygh/Pocar Report.

⑭⁵ See footnote 138 for cases in Germany and Japan where this occurred.

⑭⁶ This would normally depend on whether enforcing only one part of the judgment would significantly change the obligations of the parties: see the Nygh/Pocar Report, p. 115. If any questions of law arose, they would have to be decided by the law of the requested State: ibid.

ignated in an exclusive choice of court agreement, and which are enforceable in the same manner as a judgment in that State, must be enforced in other Contracting States in the same manner as a judgment.[147]

151. Such a settlement is sometimes called a "judicial settlement", a translation of the French "*transaction judiciaire*".[148] In the sense in which the term is used here, judicial settlements are unknown in the common-law world. In France and other civil law countries, they are contracts concluded before a judge by which the parties put an end to litigation, usually by making mutual concessions. A judicial settlement is different from a consent order in the common law sense (an order made by the court with the consent of both parties), since a consent order is a judgment and may be recognised and enforced as such under Article 7 of the Convention. On the other hand, a judicial settlement is different from an out-of-court settlement, since it is made before a judge and puts an end to the proceedings. For these reasons, a special provision is devoted to it in the Convention.

152. Article 12 does not provide for the recognition of judicial settlements, but only for their enforcement.[149] The significance of this is best explained by an example.

Assume that A and B conclude a contract with an exclusive choice of court clause in favour of the courts of State X. Subsequently, A sues B before a court in that State for 1000 Euros, a sum which he claims is due under the contract. The parties then enter into a judicial settlement under which B agrees to pay A 800 Euros, State X being a State where this may be done.

If B fails to pay, A may bring proceedings to enforce the settlement in State Y, another Contracting State. Such proceedings will be covered by Article 12 of the Convention. Assume, however, that B pays the money in compliance with the settlement without any need for enforcement proceedings. If A nevertheless

---

[147] The equivalent provision in the preliminary draft Convention 1999 is article 36. The commentary in the Nygh/Pocar Report is at pp. 118—119.

[148] On an analogous provision in the Brussels Regulation, see Hélène Gaudemet-Tallon, Compétence et exécution des jugements en Europe (3rd edn, 2002, LGDJ, Paris), Chapter 4 (pp. 387 et seq.).

[149] On the distinction between recognition and enforcement, see paragraph 120 supra.

brings a new action for the remaining 200 Euros before the courts of State Y, B cannot ask the court to *recognise* the settlement under the Convention as a defence to the claim. The Convention does not provide for this, mainly because the effects of settlements are so different in different legal systems. However, the Convention does not preclude a court from treating the settlement as a contractual defence to the claim, and this is what most courts would do.

Article 13   *No legalisation*

153. Article 13 provides that all documents forwarded or delivered under the Convention must be exempt from legalisation or any analogous formality.[149] The latter would include, for example, an *Apostille*.

Article 14   *Limitation of jurisdiction*

154. It was said above that it is the policy of the Convention to exclude wholly domestic situations from its scope. Effect is given to this policy by Articles 4(4), 5(f) and 15. Article 14 pursues the opposite policy: it permits a State to make a declaration that its courts will not apply Article 4 of the Convention to cases that are wholly *foreign*. It states that upon ratification, acceptance, approval or accession, a State may declare that its courts may refuse to determine disputes covered by an exclusive choice of court agreement if, except for the agreement, there is no connection between that State and the parties or the dispute.[150]

155. In practice, parties sometimes designate the courts of a State with which neither they nor the facts of the case have any connection. The reason is that neither party wants to go before the courts of the other party's State; so they agree to choose the courts of a neutral State. Some countries welcome this.[151] Others feel that it imposes an undue burden on their judicial systems. The purpose of Article 14 is to accommodate States in the latter category.

---

[149] This is equivalent to article 29(2) of the preliminary draft Convention 1999. The commentary on that provision in the Nygh/Pocar Report is at p.110, where it is stated that this is a practice that is well established in the context of the Hague Conventions.

[150] Since the Convention uses the words "may refuse", the courts of a State that made such a declaration would have a discretion whether or not to exercise jurisdiction.

[151] For example, English courts have for many years been willing to hear such cases, and in 1984 New York adopted special provisions to facilitate them: see New York Civil Practice Law and Rules, Rule 327(b) and New York General Obligations Law § 5—1402.

Article 15   Limitation of recognition and enforcement

156. Article 15 provides that upon ratification, acceptance, approval or accession, a State may declare that its courts may refuse to recognise or enforce a judgment of a court in another Contracting State if all parties are habitually resident [only] in the requested State, and the relationship of the parties and all other elements relevant to the dispute, other than the exclusive choice of court agreement, are connected with the requested State.[63] This provision pursues the policy, discussed above, of excluding wholly domestic situations from the scope of the Convention. It complements Article 5 f), the provision that permits a court other than that chosen to hear the case if the situation is wholly domestic to the State of that court. It applies where no proceedings are brought before that court. If, instead, the plaintiff brings proceedings before the chosen court, and that court gives judgment, the court that would have been entitled to invoke Article 5 f) could refuse to recognise or enforce the judgment on the basis of Article 15, if an appropriate declaration had been made.

Article 16   Limitation with respect to asbestos related matters

157. Article 16 provides that upon ratification, acceptance, approval or accession, a State may declare that it will not apply the provisions of the Convention to exclusive choice of court agreements in asbestos related matters. This is because personal-injury and wrongful-death claims for asbestosis have caused serious problems in certain countries, and some of these countries have limited or excluded choice of court agreements in such cases. This provision is intended to help those countries. It applies to actions concerning liability for injury or illness caused by exposure to asbestos, as well as actions (such as insurance claims) arising out of such liability.

Article 17   Uniform interpretation

158. Article 17 states that in the interpretation of the Convention regard must be had to its international character and to the need to promote uniformity in its application. This provision is addressed to courts applying the Conven-

---

[63] Since the Convention uses the words "may refuse", the courts of a State that made such a declaration would have discretion whether or not to recognise and enforce such judgments under the Convention.

tion. It requires them to interpret it in an international spirit so as to promote uniformity of application. Where reasonably possible, therefore, foreign decisions and writings should be taken into account. It should also be kept in mind that concepts and principles that are regarded as axiomatic in one legal system may be unknown or rejected in another. The objectives of the Convention can be attained only if all courts apply it in an open—minded way. [154]

Article 18   *Non-unified legal system*

159. Article 18 is concerned with the problems that result from the fact that some States are composed of two or more territorial units, each with its own judicial system. This occurs most often in the case of federations—for example, Canada or the United States—but can also occur in other States as well—for example, China or the United Kingdom. This can create a problem because one has to decide in any particular case whether the appropriate unit is the State as a whole ("State" in the international sense) or whether it is a particular territorial unit within that State.

160. Article 18(1) solves this problem by providing that, where different systems of law apply in the territorial units with regard to any matter dealt with in the Convention, the Convention is to be construed as applying to the "relevant territorial unit"—in other words, it applies either to the State in the international sense or to the relevant territorial unit, whichever is appropriate. This might seem unsatisfactory, but in fact it is usually obvious what the answer is.

161. The most important situation in which the question arises is in connection with the definition of an exclusive choice of court agreement in Article 2. The way in which Article 18 applies in this situation has already been discussed. [155] Another situation is the determination of the habitual residence of an individual or company. This is of importance under Articles 4(4), 5(f) and 15. It is considered further below in connection with Article 18(2). [156]

162. A reference in the Convention to the law of a State must be construed as referring to the law applicable in the circumstances of the case. Thus, the statement in Article 6 referring to interim measures under "the law

---

[154] The equivalent provision in the preliminary draft Convention 1999 is article 38(1). The commentary on this in the Nygh/Pocar Report is at pp. 118—119.

[155] Paragraph 51.

[156] See paragraphs 163 et seq.

of the State of the court" refers to the law applied by the court before which a request for interim measures has been made. If, as will normally be the case, interim measures are regarded as a matter of procedure, it will be the procedural law of that court. This will be either state law or federal law, depending on the system of the State in question. [157] The same applies to other provisions of the Convention which refer to procedural law. [158] It is not clear that any of the provisions of the Convention refer to the substantive law of a State, but if they do, the reference would be to the law that would be applied in the circumstances of the case. [159]

163. Article 18(2) gives further effect to the policy of not applying the Convention to wholly domestic situations. It states that a Contracting State with two or more territorial units in which different systems of law are applied is not bound to apply the Convention to situations involving solely such different territorial units.

164. There are three situations in which Article 18(2) could be relevant. The first concerns the requirement in Article 4 that the chosen court must hear the case. This requirement is subject to the qualification in Article 4(4) that it does not apply in wholly domestic situations as defined in that provision. [**The precise details of the definition have yet to be settled.**] The effect of Article 18(2) is that, when Article 4(4) is applied, "State" must be construed to mean "State" in the international sense. Thus, for example, if the chosen court is in England and the situation is entirely internal to the United Kingdom on the basis of the test laid down in Article 4(4), that provision is not rendered inapplicable by virtue of the fact that one of the parties is habitually resident in Scotland. The same would apply if the chosen court was a state court in New Jersey: "State" in Article 4(4) would nevertheless refer to the United States as a whole, so that if one party was habitually resident in the state of

---

[157] In the United States, state courts apply state procedural law and federal courts apply federal procedural law.

[158] See, for example, articles 7(3), 7(4) and 9.

[159] For example, article 10(1) states that a court must recognise an award of punitive damages to the extent that it could itself have granted similar damages in the circumstances of the case. This is a reference to the law that the court would have applied if the proceedings had originally been brought before it. In some States, it would probably be regarded as governed by the law of procedure.

New York, Article 4(4) would not thereby be rendered inapplicable.[159] The case would still be purely internal to the U.S.

165. The second situation in which Article 18(2) would apply is with regard to the obligation imposed by Article 5 on courts other than that chosen not to hear the case. Under Article 5 f), that obligation does not apply where, except for the location of the chosen court, the situation is wholly domestic to the State of the court seised. The effect of Article 18(2) is again to require "State" to be construed in the international sense. Consequently, if the parties choose the courts of England, but otherwise the case is wholly domestic to the United States, Article 5 f) will not be rendered inapplicable simply because the parties are habitually resident in different states of the United States.[160]

166. The third situation in which Article 18(2) would apply is where a court is asked to recognise or enforce a judgment under the Convention. Chapter III of the Convention contains no provision relating to wholly domestic situations; however, Article 15 allows a State to make a declaration that it will not recognise or enforce a judgment of a court in another Contracting State if, except for the location of the chosen court, the situation is wholly domestic to the requested State. The effect of Article 18(2) with regard to this question is two-fold. First of all, if the requested State has made a declaration under Article 15, the phrase "requested State" in that article must be construed to mean "State" in the international sense. Thus, for example, if the United Kingdom were to make such a declaration, it would not be obliged to recognise a judgment given by the court (outside the United Kingdom) that was designated by the parties, simply because one party is domiciled in England and the other in Scotland. Secondly, even if no declaration is made under Article 15, a court in England would never be obliged to apply the Convention with regard to the recognition of a judgment given by a Scottish court.

167. Article 18(3) provides that a court in a territorial unit of a Contracting State is not bound to recognise or enforce a judgment from another Con-

---

[159] The same result would follow if, on the basis of article 18(1)(b), one construed the word "State" in article 3(2) to refer to "State" in the international sense. An American company would then be habitually resident in the United States as a whole, rather than in any particular state of the United States.

[160] See previous footnote.

tracting State solely because the judgment has been recognised or enforced under the Convention by a court in another territorial unit of the first Contracting State. This means, for example, that a court in New York is not bound to recognise a judgment from Japan solely because a court in New Jersey has done so.

Article 21   Non-unified legal system[162]

168. Article 21 is also concerned with States that consist of two or more territorial units. It permits such a State to declare that the Convention will extend to only some of its territorial units. Such a declaration may be modified at any time. This provision is particularly important for States in which the legislation necessary to give effect to the Convention would have to be passed by the legislatures of the units (for example, by provincial legislatures in Canada), though it could also be of use to other States. Thus, the United Kingdom could ratify for England only, and China for Hong Kong only.

---

[162]   [**Since this title has already been used for article 18, it might be better to choose another title.**]

ANNEX

HAGUE CONFERENCE ON PRIVATE INTERNATIONAL LAW

WORK. DOC. No 49 E
Revised *

Commission spéciale sur la compétence,
la reconnaissance et l'exécution des jugements
étrangers en matière civile et commerciale
(du 1er au 9 décembre 2003)
Special Commission on Jurisdiction,
Recognition and Enforcement of Foreign Judgments
in Civil and Commercial Matters
(1 to 9 December 2003)

Distribution: By mail

Proposal by the Drafting Committee
DRAFT ON EXCLUSIVE CHOICE OF COURT AGREEMENTS

The States signatory to the present Convention,

Desiring to promote international trade and investment through enhanced judicial cooperation,

Believing that such enhanced cooperation requires a secure international legal regime that ensures the effectiveness of exclusive choice of court agreements by parties to commercial transactions and that governs the recognition and enforcement of judgments resulting from proceedings based on such agreements,

Have resolved to conclude the following *Convention on Exclusive Choice of Court Agreements* and have agreed upon the following provisions—

---

* Upon request of the Special Commission, the Permanent Bureau has aligned the English and French versions of this Document with the terminology traditionally used in Hague Conventions. Changes were made in agreement with the Chairman of the Drafting Committee.

CHAPTER I SCOPE AND DEFINITIONS

Article 1 *Scope*

1. The present Convention shall apply to exclusive choice of court agreements concluded in civil or commercial matters.

2. The Convention shall not apply to exclusive choice of court agreements—

a) between a natural person acting primarily for personal, family or household purposes (the consumer) and another party acting for the purposes of its trade or profession, or between consumers; or

b) relating to individual or collective contracts of employment.

3. The Convention shall not apply to proceedings that have as their object any of the following matters—

a) the status and legal capacity of natural persons;

b) maintenance obligations;

c) other family law matters, including matrimonial property regimes and other rights or obligations arising out of marriage or similar relationships;

d) wills and succession;

e) insolvency, composition and analogous matters;

f) contracts for the carriage of goods by sea [and other admiralty or maritime matters];

g) anti-trust/competition matters;

h) nuclear liability;

i) rights *in rem* in immovable property;

j) the validity, nullity, or dissolution of legal persons, and the validity of decisions of their organs;

k) the validity of patents, trademarks, protected industrial designs, and layout-designs of integrated circuits;

l) [the validity of other intellectual property rights the validity of which depends on, or arises from, their registration, except copyright]; or

m) the validity of entries in public registers.

4. Proceedings are not excluded from the scope of the Convention if a matter referred to in paragraph 3 arises merely as an incidental question.

5. The Convention shall not apply to arbitration and proceedings related thereto, nor shall it require a Contracting State to recognise and enforce a judgment if the exercise of jurisdiction by the court of origin was contrary to the terms of an arbitration agreement.

6. Proceedings are not excluded from the scope of the Convention by the mere fact that a government, a governmental agency or any person acting for a State is a party thereto.

7. Nothing in this Convention affects the privileges and immunities of sovereign States or of entities of sovereign States, or of international organisations.

Article 2 Exclusive choice of court agreements

1. In this Convention, "exclusive choice of court agreement" means an agreement concluded by two or more parties that meets the requirements of paragraph 3 and designates, for the purpose of deciding disputes which have arisen or may arise in connection with a particular legal relationship, the courts of one State or one specific court to the exclusion of the jurisdiction of any other courts.

2. A choice of court agreement which designates the courts of one State or one specific court shall be deemed to be exclusive unless the parties have expressly provided otherwise.

3. An exclusive choice of court agreement must be entered into or evidenced—

a) in writing; or

b) by any other means of communication which renders information accessible so as to be usable for subsequent reference.

4. An exclusive choice of court agreement that forms part of a contract shall be treated as an agreement independent of the other terms of the contract. The validity of the exclusive choice of court agreement cannot be contested solely on the ground that the contract is not valid.

Article 3 Other definitions

1. In this Convention "judgment" means any decision on the merits given by a court, whatever it may be called, including a decree or order, and a determination of costs or expenses by the court (including an officer of the court), provided that such determination relates to a judgment which may be

recognised or enforced under this Convention.

2. For the purposes of this Convention, an entity or person other than a natural person shall be considered to be habitually resident in the State—

a) where it has its statutory seat;

b) under whose law it was incorporated or formed;

c) where it has its central administration; or

d) where it has its principal place of business.

CHAPTER II JURISDICTION

Article 4   Jurisdiction of the chosen court

1. The court or courts of a Contracting State designated in an exclusive choice of court agreement shall have jurisdiction to decide a dispute to which the agreement applies, unless the agreement is null and void under the law of that State.

2. A court that has jurisdiction under paragraph 1 shall not decline to exercise jurisdiction on the ground that the dispute should be decided in a court of another State.

3. The preceding paragraphs shall not affect rules on jurisdiction related to subject matter or to the value of the claim, or the internal allocation of jurisdiction among the courts of a Contracting State [unless the parties designated a specific court].

4. The preceding paragraphs shall not apply if all the parties to the agreement are habitually resident [only] in the State of the chosen court [and the relationship of the parties and all elements relevant to the dispute are connected with that State]. ①

Article 5   Obligations of a court not chosen

If the parties have entered into an exclusive choice of court agreement, a court in a Contracting State other than the State of the chosen court shall suspend or dismiss the proceedings unless—

a) the agreement is null and void under the law of the State of the chosen court;

---

① The relevant time for the purposes of this test (e.g. the time of the agreement and/or the time of commencement of the proceedings) remains to be discussed.

b) a party lacked the capacity to enter into the agreement under the law of the State of the court seised;

c) giving effect to the agreement would lead to a very serious injustice or would② be manifestly contrary to fundamental principles of public policy;

d) for exceptional reasons the agreement cannot reasonably be performed;

e) the chosen court has decided not to hear the case; or

f) the parties are habitually resident [only] in the State of the court seised, and the relationship of the parties and all other elements relevant to the dispute, other than the agreement, are connected with that State. ③

Article 6   Interim measures of protection

Nothing in this Convention shall prevent a party from requesting an interim measure of protection from any court or prevent a court from granting such a measure under the law of the State of the court.

CHAPTER III   RECOGNITION AND ENFORCEMENT

*Article 7   Recognition and enforcement*④

1. A judgment given by a court of a Contracting State designated in an exclusive choice of court agreement shall be recognised and enforced in other Contracting States in accordance with this Chapter. Recognition or enforcement may be refused only on the following grounds⑤—

a) the agreement was null and void under the law of the State of the chosen court, unless the chosen court has determined that the agreement is valid;

b) a party lacked the capacity to enter into the agreement under the law of the requested State;

c) the document which instituted the proceedings or an equivalent document, including the essential elements of the claim, was not notified to the de-

---

② One delegation suggested the inclusion of the word "otherwise" at this point.

③ The relevant time for the purposes of this test (e.g. the time of the agreement and/or the time of commencement of the proceedings) remains to be discussed.

④ Recognition and enforcement of judgments where a matter referred to in article 1(3) or article 16 has arisen as an incidental question remains to be discussed. Further reflection may also have to be given to the question of irreconcilable judgments.

⑤ Further consideration is required as to whether the matters covered by article 5(c) and (d) are adequately reflected in this paragraph.

fendant in sufficient time and in such a way as to enable him to arrange for his defence [or was not notified in accordance with the law of the State where such notification took place], [unless the defendant entered an appearance and presented his case without contesting notification in the court of origin, provided that the law of the State of origin permitted notification to be contested];

  d) the judgment was obtained by fraud in connection with a matter of procedure; or

  e) cognition or enforcement would be manifestly incompatible with the public policy of the requested State, in particular if the specific proceedings leading to the judgment were incompatible with fundamental principles of procedural fairness of that State. [6]

Page 4 of 11

  2. hout prejudice to such review as is necessary for the application of the provisions of this Chapter, there shall be no review of the merits of the judgment rendered by the court of origin. The court addressed shall be bound by the findings of fact on which the court of origin based its jurisdiction, unless the judgment was given by default.

  3. Judgment shall be recognised only if it has effect in the State of origin, and shall be enforced only if it is enforceable in the State of origin.

  4. Recognition or enforcement may be postponed or refused if the judgment is the subject of review in the State of origin or if the time limit for seeking ordinary review has not expired. A refusal does not prevent a subsequent application for recognition or enforcement of the judgment.

Article 8 *Documents to be produced*

  1. The party seeking recognition or applying for enforcement shall produce—

  a) a complete and certified copy of the judgment;

  b) if the judgment was rendered by default, the original or a certified copy of a document establishing that the document which instituted the pro-

---

  [6] The Drafting Committee was not able to accommodate the concerns of one member with respect to this paragraph, and considers there is an issue to be resolved. An alternative text was suggested:

  (e) recognition or enforcement would be manifestly incompatible with the public policy of the requested State, including where the specific proceedings leading to the judgment were seriously unjust with respect to procedural fairness.

ceedings or an equivalent document was notified to the defaulting party;

c) all documents necessary to establish that the judgment has effect or, where applicable, is enforceable in the State of origin.

2. If the terms of the judgment do not permit the court addressed to verify whether the conditions of this Chapter have been complied with, that court may require evidence of the exclusive choice of court agreement, and any other necessary documents.

3. An application for recognition or enforcement may be accompanied by a form recommended and published by the Hague Conference on Private International Law.

4. The court addressed may require a translation of any document referred to in this Article.

Article 9 *Procedure*

The procedure for recognition, declaration of enforceability or registration for enforcement, and the enforcement of the judgment, are governed by the law of the requested State unless this Convention provides otherwise. The court addressed shall act expeditiously.

Article 10 *Damages*

1. A judgment which awards non-compensatory damages, including exemplary or punitive damages, shall be recognised and enforced to the extent that a court in the requested State could have awarded similar or comparable damages. Nothing in this paragraph shall preclude the court addressed from recognising and enforcing the judgment under its law for an amount up to the full amount of the damages awarded by the court of origin.

2. a) Where the debtor, after proceedings in which the creditor has the opportunity to be heard, satisfies the court addressed that in the circumstances, including those existing in the State of origin, grossly excessive damages have been awarded, recognition and enforcement may be limited to a lesser amount.

b) In no event shall the court addressed recognise or enforce the judgment in an amount less than that which could have been awarded in the requested State in the same circumstances, including those existing in the State of origin.

3. In applying the preceding paragraphs, the court addressed shall take into account whether and to what extent the damages awarded by the court of origin serve to cover costs and expenses relating to the proceedings.

Article 11　*Severability*

Recognition or enforcement of a severable part of a judgment shall be granted where recognition or enforcement of that part is applied for, or only part of the judgment is capable of being recognised or enforced under this Convention.

Article 12　*Settlements*

Settlements which a court of a Contracting State designated in an exclusive choice of court agreement has approved, or which have been concluded before that court in the course of proceedings, and which are enforceable in the same manner as a judgment in the State of origin, shall be enforced under this Convention in the same manner as a judgment.

CHAPTER IV　GENERAL CLAUSES

Article 13　*No legalisation*

All documents forwarded or delivered under this Convention shall be exempt from legalisation or any analogous formality.

Article 14　*Limitation of jurisdiction*

Upon ratification, acceptance, approval or accession, a State may declare that its courts may refuse to determine disputes covered by an exclusive choice of court agreement if, except for the agreement, there is no connection between that State and the parties or the dispute. ⑦

Article 15　*Limitation of recognition and enforcement*

Upon ratification, acceptance, approval or accession, a State may declare that its courts may refuse to recognise or enforce a judgment of a court in another Contracting State if all parties are habitually resident [only] in the requested State, and the relationship of the parties and all other elements relevant to the dispute, other than the exclusive choice of court agreement, are

---

⑦　The relevant time for the purposes of this test (*e. g.* the time of the agreement and/or the time of commencement of the proceedings) remains to be discussed.

connected with the requested State. ⑧

Article 16 Limitation with respect to asbestos related matters

Upon ratification, acceptance, approval or accession, a State may declare that it will not apply the provisions of the Convention to exclusive choice of court agreements in asbestos related matters.

Article 17 Uniform interpretation

In the interpretation of this Convention, regard shall be had to its international character and to the need to promote uniformity in its application.

*Article 18 Non-unified legal system*⑨

1. In relation to a Contracting State in which two or more systems of law apply in different territorial units with regard to any matter dealt with in this Convention—

a) any reference to the law or procedure of a State shall be construed as referring to the law or procedure in force in the relevant territorial unit;

b) any reference to habitual residence in a State shall be construed as referring to habitual residence in the relevant territorial unit;

c) any reference to the court or courts of a State shall be construed as referring to the court or courts in the relevant territorial unit; and

d) any reference to the connection with a State shall be construed as referring to the connection with the relevant territorial unit.

2. Notwithstanding the preceding paragraphs, a Contracting State with two or more territorial units in which different systems of law are applied shall not be bound to apply this Convention to situations involving solely such different territorial units.

3. The court in a territorial unit of a Contracting State with two or more territorial units in which different systems of law are applied shall not be bound to recognise or enforce a judgment from another Contracting State solely because the judgment has been recognised or enforced by the court in another territorial unit of the same Contracting State under this Convention.

---

⑧ The relevant time for the purposes of this test (e.g. the time of the agreement and/or the time of commencement of the proceedings) remains to be discussed. The time of enforcement should not be relevant.

⑨ The matters dealt with in this article will require further study and discussion.

Article 19 Relationship with other international instruments
This matter has not yet been discussed.

CHAPTER V FINAL CLAUSES

Article 20 Signature, ratification, acceptance, approval or accession
Article 21 Non-unified legal system

1. If a State has two or more territorial units in which different systems of law apply in relation to matters dealt with in this Convention, it may at the time of signature, ratification, acceptance, approval or accession declare that the Convention shall extend to all its territorial units or only to one or more of them and may modify this declaration by submitting another declaration at any time.

2. Any such declaration shall be notified to the depositary and shall state expressly the territorial units to which the Convention applies.

3. If a State makes no declaration under this Article, the Convention is to extend to all territorial units of that State.

Article 22 Regional Economic Integration Organisations
Article 23 Entry into force
Article 24 Reservations
Article 25 Declarations
Article 26 Denunciation
Article 27 Notifications by the Depositary

RECOMMENDED FORM

(Sample form confirming the issuance and content of a judgment by the Court of Origin for the purposes of recognition and enforcement under the Convention on Exclusive Choice of Court Agreements (the "Convention"))

(THE COURT OF ORIGIN) ···
(ADDRESS OF THE COURT OF ORIGIN) ·····························

(CONTACT PERSON AT THE COURT OF ORIGIN) …………
(TEL./FAX/EMAIL OF THE COURT OF ORIGIN) ……………
CASE/DOCKET NUMBER: ……………………………………………

_____ (PLAINTIFF)
v. _____ (DEFENDANT)

(THE COURT OF ORIGIN) hereby confirms that it rendered a judgment in the above captioned matter on (DATE) in (CITY, STATE), which is a Contracting State to the Convention. Attached to this form is a complete and certified copy of the judgment rendered by (THE COURT OF ORIGIN).

1. This Court based its jurisdiction on an exclusive choice of court agreement:

YES _____   NO _____

If so, the agreement was found in or evidenced by the following document(s):

2. This Court awarded the following payment of money (*Please indicate any relevant categories of damages included*):

3. This Court awarded interest as follows (*Please specify the rate of interest, the portion(s) of the award to which interest applies, and the date from which interest is computed*):

4. This Court included within the judgment the following court costs and expenses (including lawyers' fees) related to the proceedings (*Please specify the amounts of any such awards, including where applicable, any amount(s) within a monetary award intended to cover costs and expenses relating to the proceedings*):

5. This Court awarded, in whole or in part, the following non-monetary

remedy (*Please describe the nature of the remedy*):

6. This judgment was rendered by default:
YES _____ NO _____
(*If this judgment was rendered by default, please attach the original or a certified copy of the document verifying notice to the defendant of the proceedings.*)

7. This judgment (or a part thereof) is currently the subject of review in (STATE OF THE COURT OF ORIGIN):
YES _____ NO _____

8. This judgment (or a part thereof) is enforceable in (STATE OF THE COURT OF ORIGIN):
YES _____ NO _____

List of documents annexed:
Dated this _____ day of _____, 20 _____.
Signature and/or stamp by an officer of the Court